AVENGERS K

AVENGERS VS. ULTRON

Purchased from
Multnomah
County Library

THE TITLE WAVE
USED BOOKSTORE

D1459917

Original comics written by MARK WAID, KYLE HIGGINS, ALEC SIEGEL, ROY THOMAS, and JIM SHOOTER;
and illustrated by ANDRÉ LIMA ARAÚJO, STÉPHANE PERGER, JOHN BUSCEMA, BARRY WINDSOR-SMITH, and GEORGE PÉREZ

Editor SARAH BRUNSTAD
Manager, Licensed Publishing JEFF REINGOLD
VP, Brand Management & Development, Asia C.B. CEBULSKI
VP, Production & Special Projects JEFF YOUNGQUIST
SVP Print, Sales & Marketing DAVID GABRIEL
Associate Manager, Digital Assets JOE HOCHSTEIN
Associate Managing Editor ALEX STARBUCK
Editors, Special Projects JENNIFER GRÜNWALD & MARK D. BEAZLEY
Book Designer: ADAM DEL RE

Editor In Chief AXEL ALONSO
Chief Creative Officer JOE QUESADA
Publisher DAN BUCKLEY
Executive Producer ALAN FINE

AVENGERS K BOOK 1: AVENGERS VS. ULTRON. First printing 2016. ISBN# 978-1-302-90099-1. Published by MARVEL WORLDWIDE, INC., a subsidiary of MARVEL ENTERTAINMENT, LLC. OFFICE OF PUBLICATION: 135 West 50th Street, New York, NY 10020.
Copyright © 2016 MARVEL. No similarity between any of the names, characters, persons, and/or institutions in this magazine with those of any living or dead person or institution is intended, and any such similarity which may exist is purely coincidental. Printed
in the U.S.A. ALAN FINE, President, Marvel Entertainment; DAN BUCKLEY, President, TV, Publishing & Brand Management; JOE QUESADA, Chief Creative Officer; TOM BREVOORT, SVP of Publishing; DAVID BOGART, SVP of Business Affairs & Operations, Publishing
& Partnership; C.B. CEBULSKI, VP of Brand Management & Development, Asia; DAVID GABRIEL, SVP of Sales & Marketing, Publishing; JEFF YOUNGQUIST, VP of Production & Special Projects; DAN CARR, Executive Director of Publishing Technology; ALEX MORALES,
Director of Publishing Operations; SUSAN CRESPI, Production Manager; STAN LEE, Chairman Emeritus. For information regarding advertising in Marvel Comics or on Marvel.com, please contact Vit DeBellis, Integrated Sales Manager, at vdebellis@marvel.com.
For Marvel subscription inquiries, please call 888-511-5480. Manufactured between 3/25/2016 and 5/2/2016 by R.R. DONNELLEY, INC., SALEM, VA, USA.
10 9 8 7 6 5 4 3 2 1

AVENGERS K
AVENGERS VS. ULTRON

JIM ZUB
SCRIPT

WOO BIN CHOI with JAE SUNG LEE, MIN JU LEE, JAE WOONG LEE, HEE YE CHO, JI HEE CHOI, and IN YOUNG LEE
ART

VC's CORY PETIT
LETTERS

WOO BIN CHOI with **JAE SUNG LEE** and **MYOUNG HUI LEE**
COVER ART

WOO CHUL LEE
VARIANT COVER ART

AVENGERS VS. ULTRON is adapted from AGE OF ULTRON #10AI;
AVENGERS ORIGINS: VISION (2012) #1; and AVENGERS (1963) #57, #67, and #161-162.
Adaptations written by SI YEON PARK and translated by JI EUN PARK

AVENGERS created by STAN LEE and JACK KIRBY

AVENGERS ACTIVE ROSTER

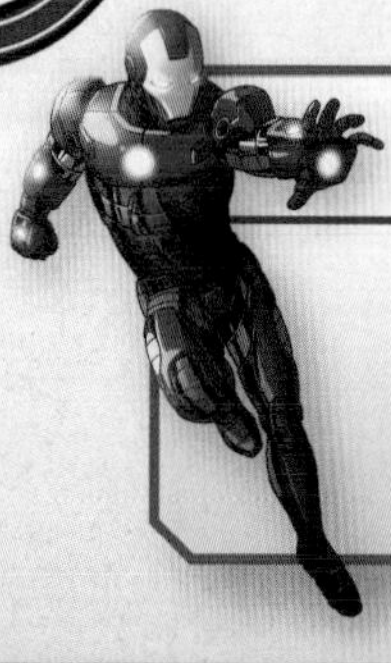

IRON MAN | Real Name: ANTHONY EDWARD STARK

Billionaire playboy and genius industrialist Tony Stark was kidnapped during a routine weapons test. His captors attempted to force him to build a weapon of mass destruction. Instead, he created a powerful suit of armor that saved his life. From that day on, he has used the suit to protect the world as the invincible Avenger Iron Man.

Real Name: STEVEN ROGERS | CAPTAIN AMERICA

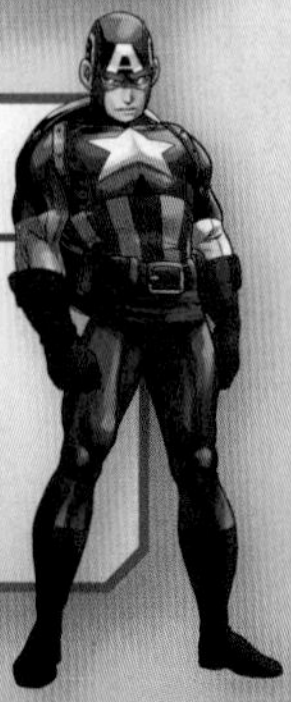

During World War II, a secret military experiment turned scrawny Steve Rogers into America's first Super-Soldier, Captain America. Near the end of the war, Rogers was presumed dead in an explosion over the English Channel. Decades later, Cap was found frozen in ice and was revived. Steve Rogers awakened to a world he never imagined—a man out of time. He again took up the mantle of Captain America, defending the United States and the world from threats of all kinds.

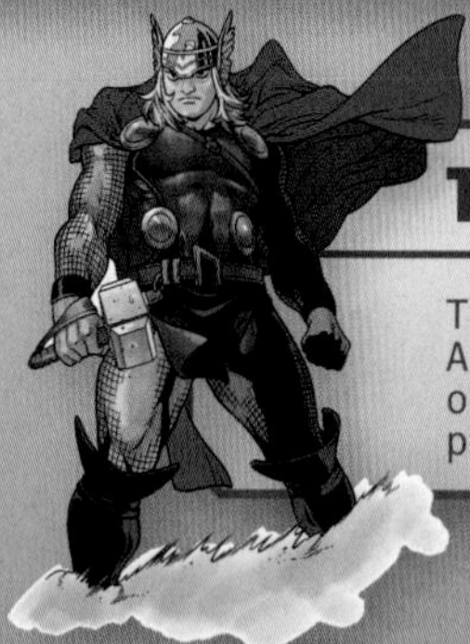

THOR | Real Name: THOR ODINSON

Thor is the Asgardian God of Thunder and an Avenger. Wielding Mjolnir, a mystical uru hammer of immense power, the son of Odin fights to protect Earth and all the Nine Realms.

Real Name: ROBERT BRUCE BANNER | HULK

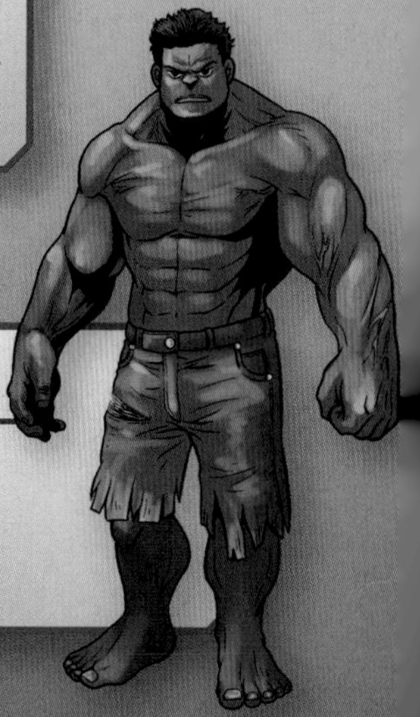

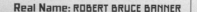

Bruce Banner was a brilliant scientist working for the Army when he was caught in the explosion of a gamma bomb of his own creation and transformed into the nearly indestructible Hulk. Now, Dr. Banner struggles to control his anger and anxiety to keep the Hulk in check while he fights alongside the Avengers.

HAWKEYE
Real Name: CLINT BARTON

Former criminal Clint Barton used his circus training to become the greatest sharpshooter the world has ever seen. He reformed and joined the Avengers, quickly becoming one of the team's most stalwart members.

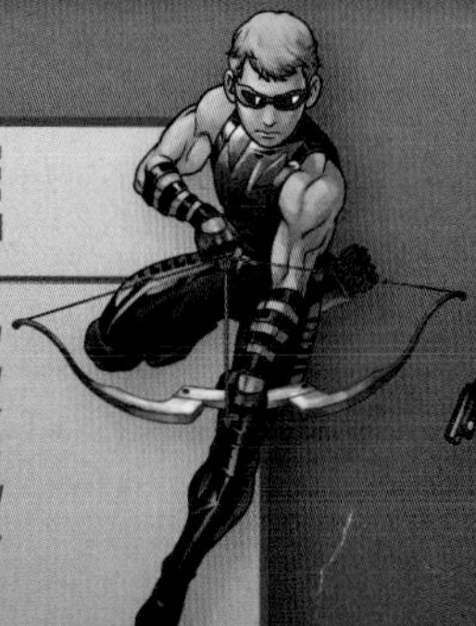

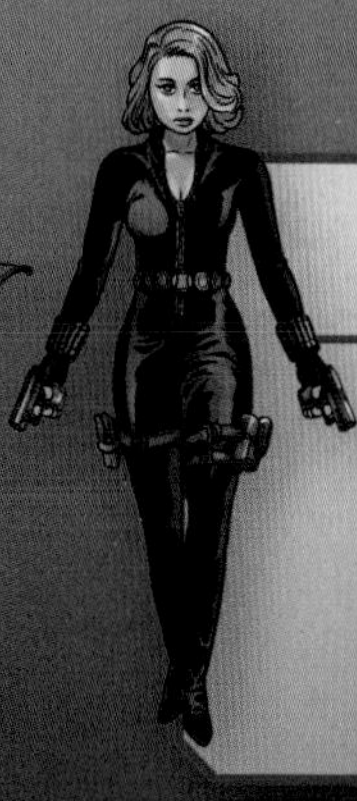

BLACK WIDOW
Real Name: NATASHA ROMANOFF

Natalia Romanova is a deadly operative equipped with state-of-the-art weaponry and extensive hand-to-hand combat training. Before joining S.H.I.E.L.D. and the Avengers, she was an enemy spy; now, she uses her unique skills to atone for her past.

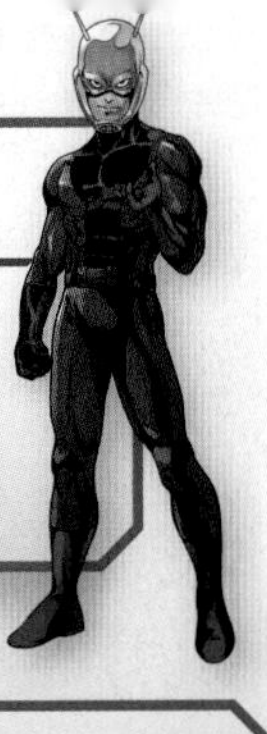

Real Name: HANK PYM | **ANT-MAN**

Scientific genius Henry "Hank" Pym invented a serum that could change the size of his body at will, and a helmet that allowed him to communicate with and control insects. Along with his partner, the Wasp, he helped found the Avengers and rescue Captain America. But in a stroke of arrogance, he accidentally created his own worst enemy and one of the Avengers' deadliest villains: the artificial intelligence known as Ultron.

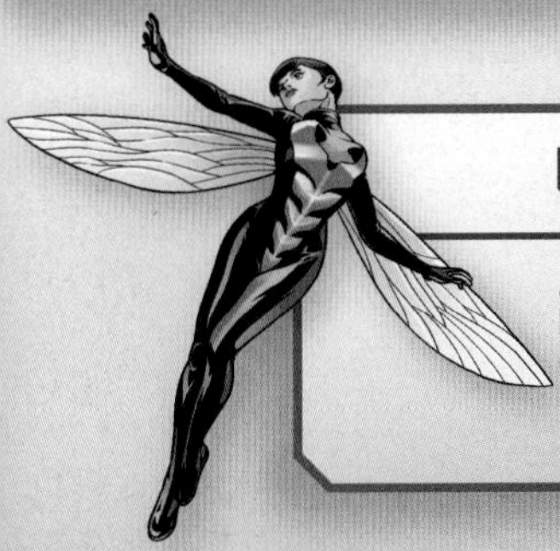

WASP | Real Name: JANET VAN DYNE

Janet Van Dyne was a flighty socialite until she met brilliant biochemist Hank Pym. When Hank shared his size-altering Pym Particles with her, she gained not only the ability to manipulate her size, but also bioelectric stings and wings that manifest when she shrinks to insect-size. Calling herself the Wasp, Janet soon helped form the Avengers.

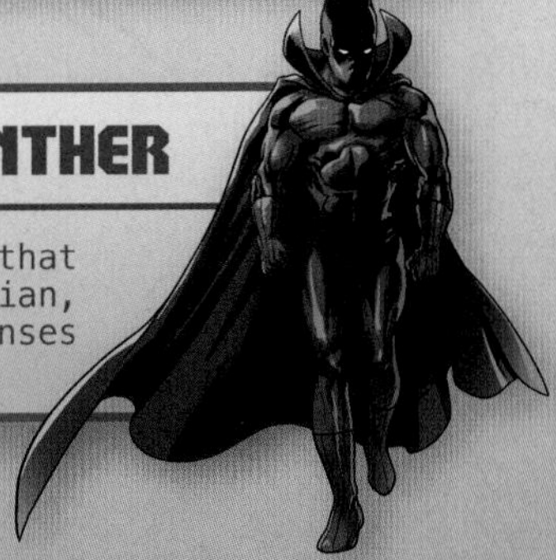

Real Name: T'CHALLA | **BLACK PANTHER**

T'Challa is the King of Wakanda, the high-tech African nation that houses the world's only natural supply of Vibranium. He is a tactician, scientist, and super hero who specializes in unarmed combat. His senses and physical abilities have proven invaluable to the Avengers.

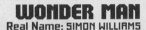

WONDER MAN
Real Name: SIMON WILLIAMS

Lured by the promise of power, Simon Williams gained superhuman abilities after being exposed to ionic energy by the villain Baron Zemo. Along with incredible strength, he possesses the power of flight and invulnerability. After reforming, Simon joined the Avengers to make up for his past crimes.

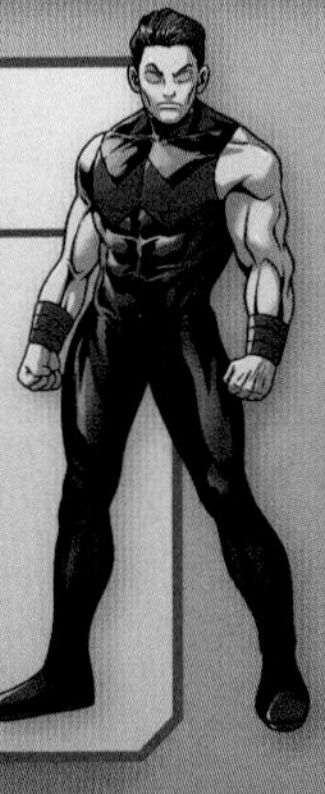

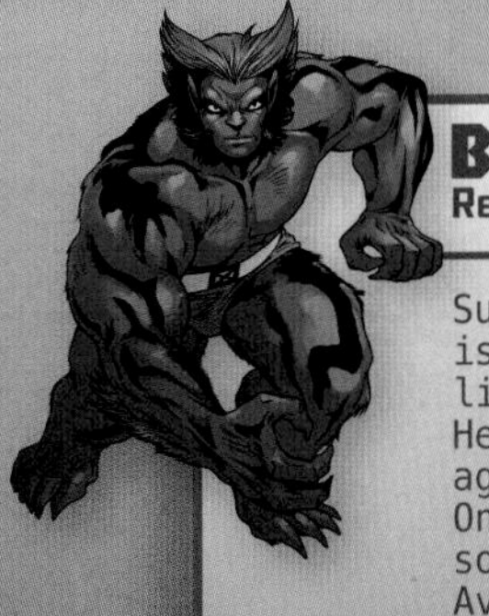

BEAST
Real Name: HENRY McCOY

Super-genius Henry "Hank" McCoy is a mutant born with beast-like proportions and abilities. He possesses super-strength and agility, along with a keen wit. One of the original X-Men, Beast soon became close friends with the Avengers and joined their ranks.

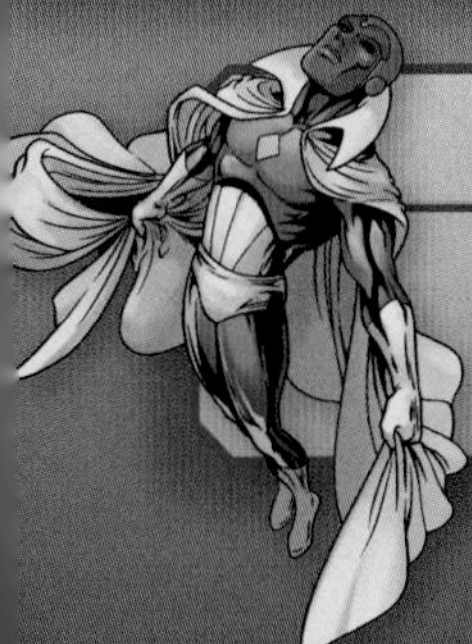

VISION

The Vision is a synthezoid—an android composed of synthetic human blood and organs with the power to control his own density and absorb or emit high-powered heat rays from the gem on his forehead. He was created by Ultron to destroy the Avengers, but instead turned on his "father." He's been a member of the super-hero team ever since.

AVENGERS MOST WANTED:

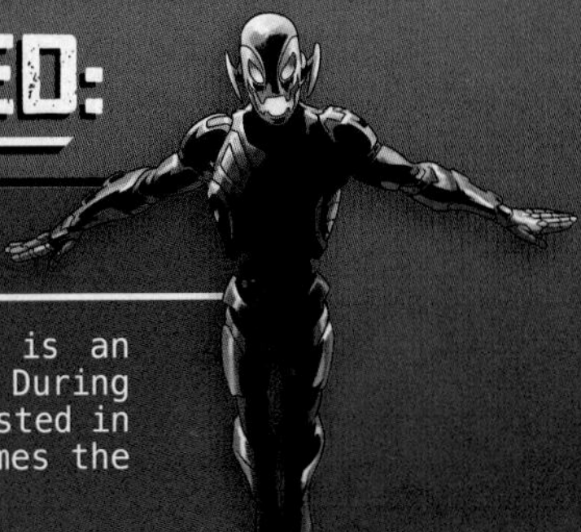

ULTRON

Created by Hank Pym during a period of mental instability, Ultron is an artificial intelligence that has become a powerful foe of the Avengers. During his creation, he inherited Hank's imperfect metal state; that flaw manifested in Ultron as anger and hostility toward human life. No matter how many times the Avengers think they've destroyed him, he always manages to return.

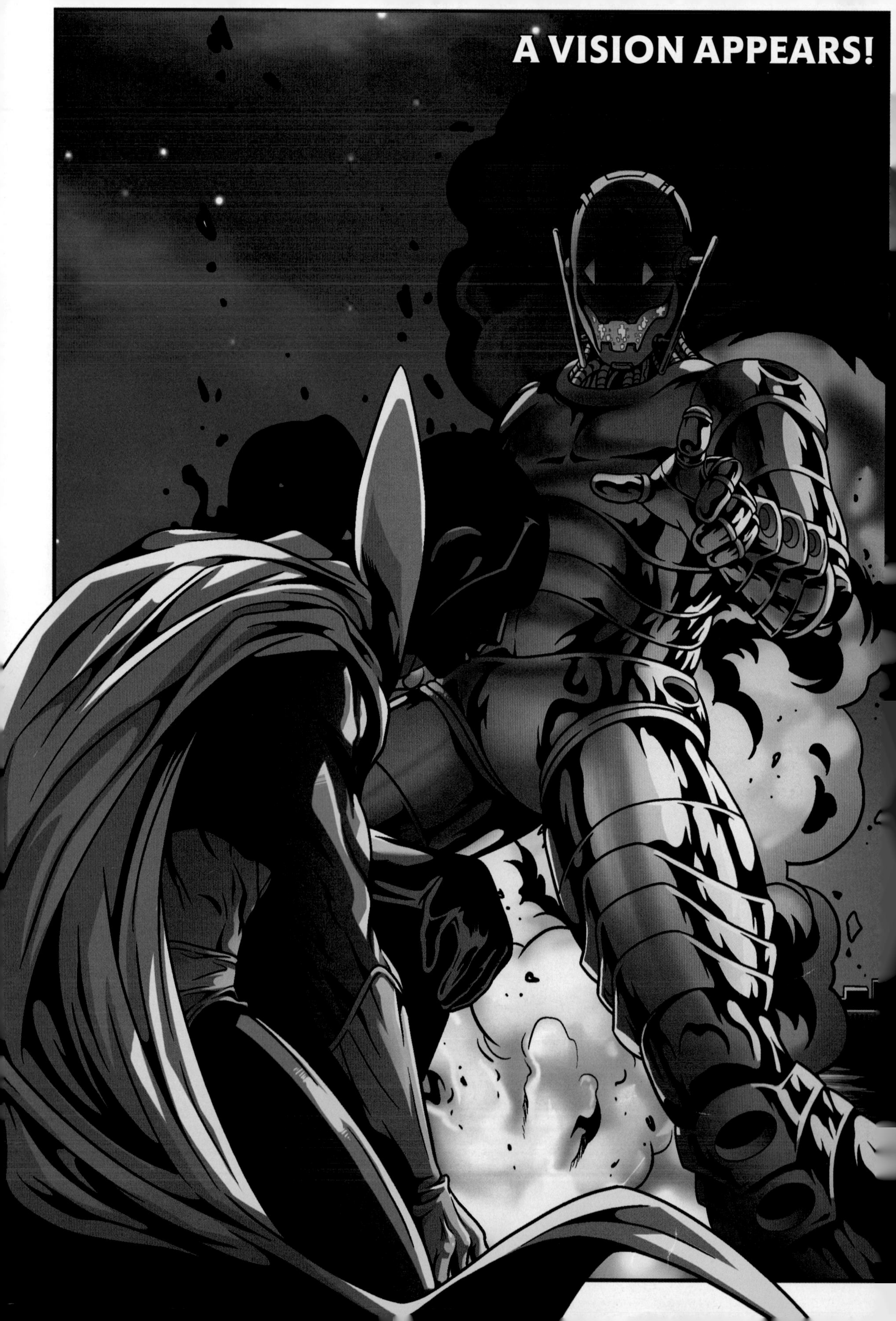
A VISION APPEARS!

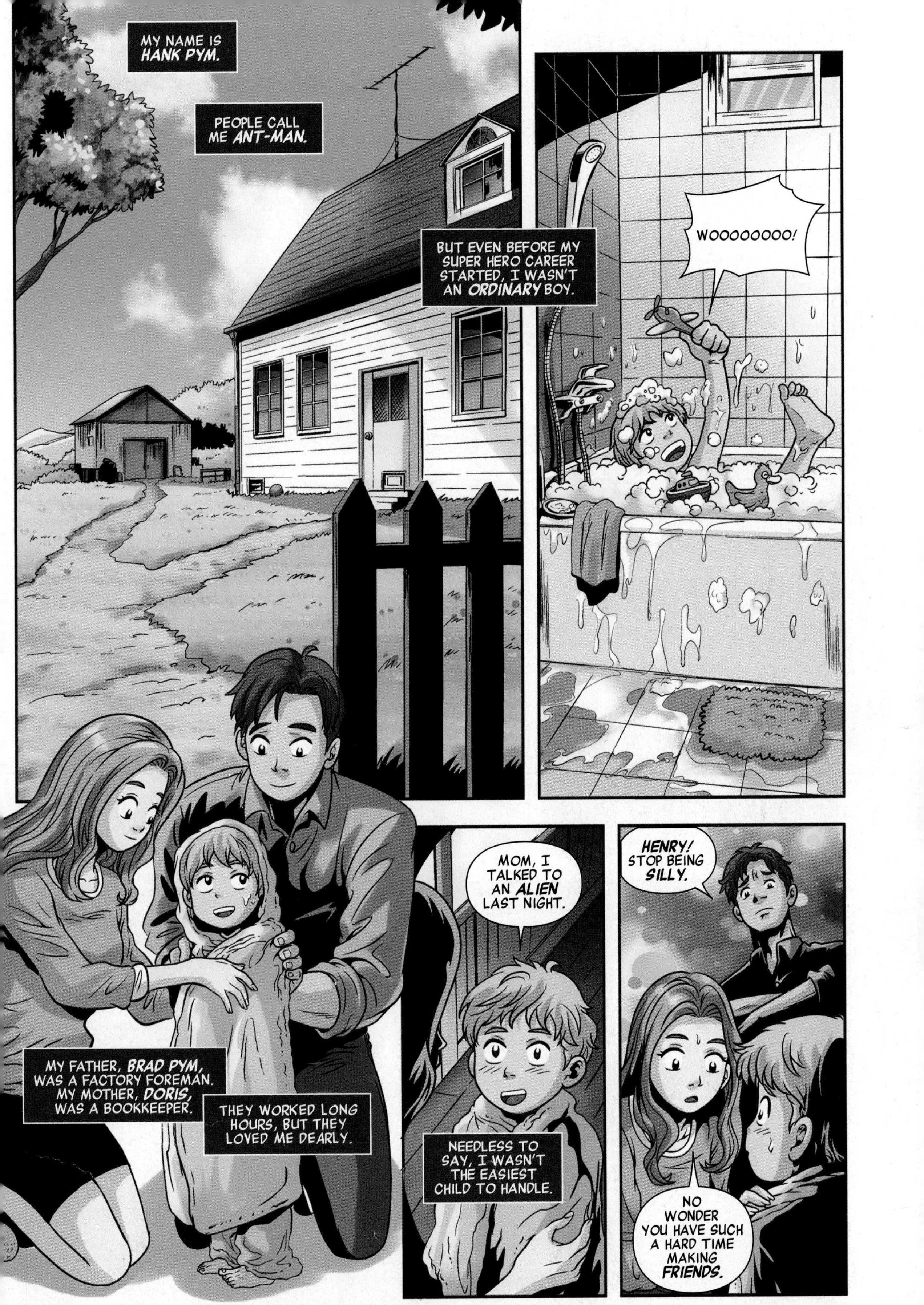
MY NAME IS HANK PYM.
PEOPLE CALL ME ANT-MAN.
BUT EVEN BEFORE MY SUPER HERO CAREER STARTED, I WASN'T AN ORDINARY BOY.
WOOOOOOOO!
MY FATHER, BRAD PYM, WAS A FACTORY FOREMAN. MY MOTHER, DORIS, WAS A BOOKKEEPER.
THEY WORKED LONG HOURS, BUT THEY LOVED ME DEARLY.
MOM, I TALKED TO AN ALIEN LAST NIGHT.
NEEDLESS TO SAY, I WASN'T THE EASIEST CHILD TO HANDLE.
HENRY! STOP BEING SILLY.
NO WONDER YOU HAVE SUCH A HARD TIME MAKING FRIENDS.

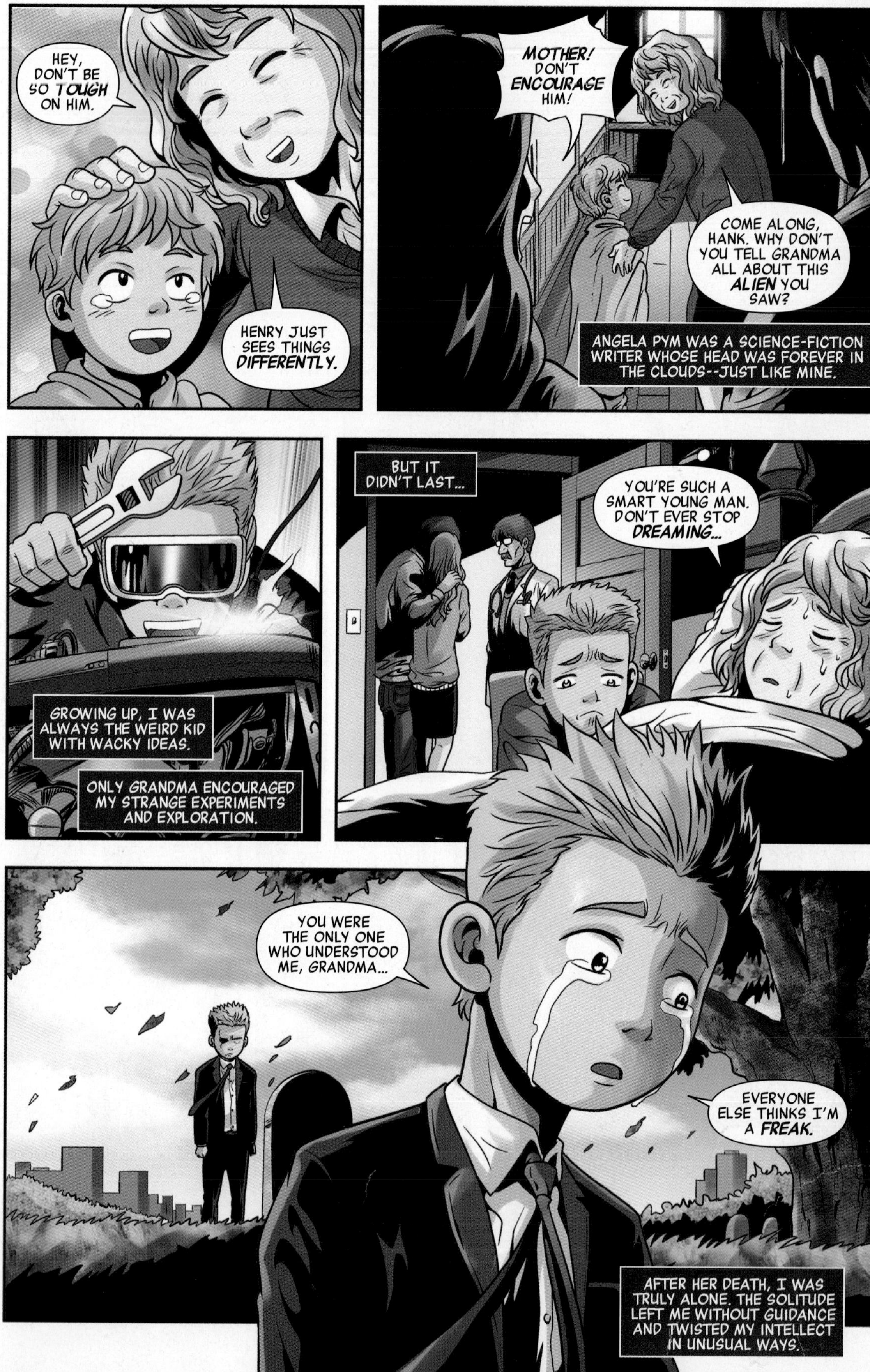
HEY, DON'T BE SO TOUGH ON HIM.
HENRY JUST SEES THINGS DIFFERENTLY.
MOTHER! DON'T ENCOURAGE HIM!
COME ALONG, HANK. WHY DON'T YOU TELL GRANDMA ALL ABOUT THIS ALIEN YOU SAW?
ANGELA PYM WAS A SCIENCE-FICTION WRITER WHOSE HEAD WAS FOREVER IN THE CLOUDS--JUST LIKE MINE.
GROWING UP, I WAS ALWAYS THE WEIRD KID WITH WACKY IDEAS.
ONLY GRANDMA ENCOURAGED MY STRANGE EXPERIMENTS AND EXPLORATION.
BUT IT DIDN'T LAST...
YOU'RE SUCH A SMART YOUNG MAN. DON'T EVER STOP DREAMING...
YOU WERE THE ONLY ONE WHO UNDERSTOOD ME, GRANDMA...
EVERYONE ELSE THINKS I'M A FREAK.
AFTER HER DEATH, I WAS TRULY ALONE. THE SOLITUDE LEFT ME WITHOUT GUIDANCE AND TWISTED MY INTELLECT IN UNUSUAL WAYS.

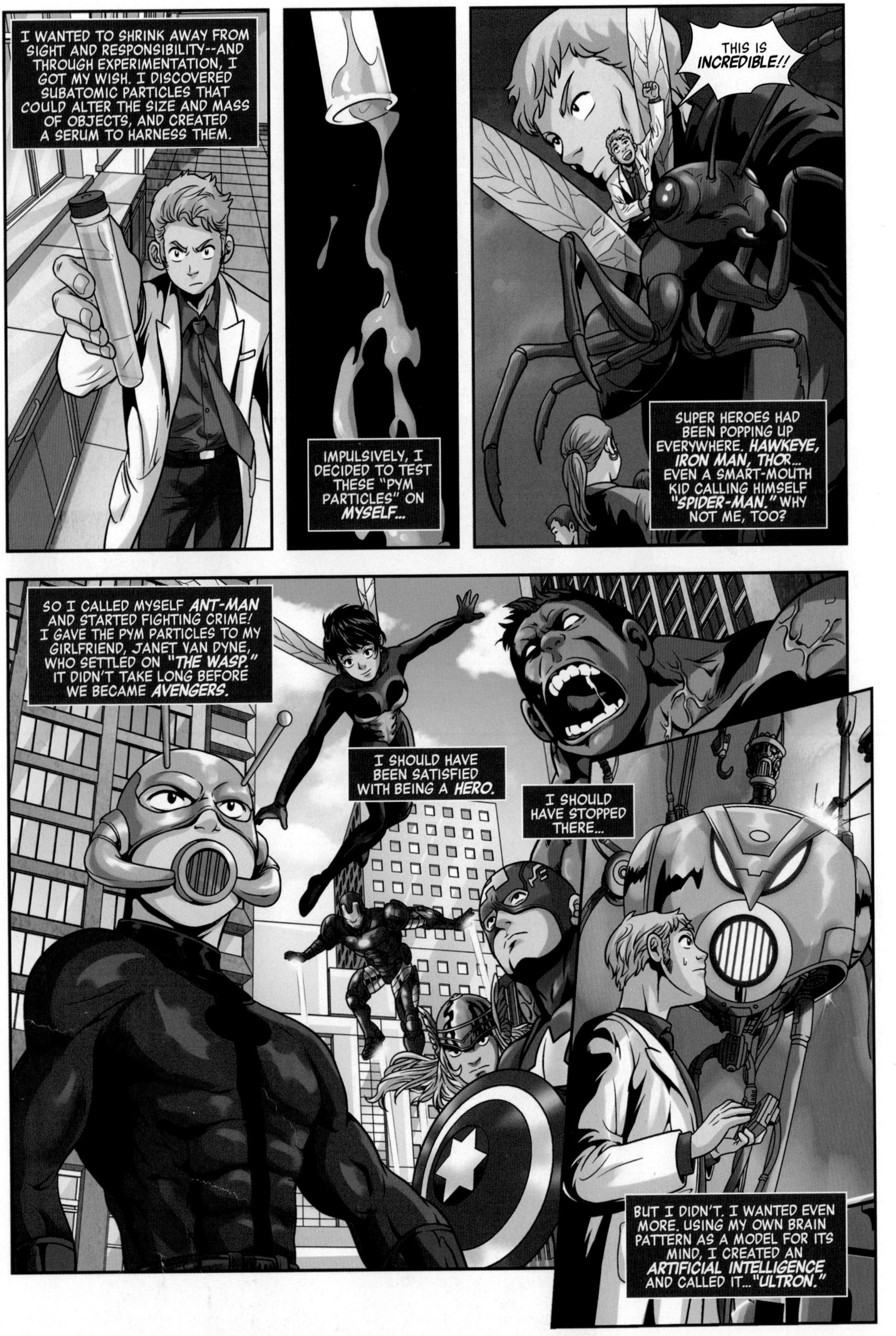
I WANTED TO SHRINK AWAY FROM SIGHT AND RESPONSIBILITY--AND THROUGH EXPERIMENTATION, I GOT MY WISH. I DISCOVERED SUBATOMIC PARTICLES THAT COULD ALTER THE SIZE AND MASS OF OBJECTS, AND CREATED A SERUM TO HARNESS THEM.
IMPULSIVELY, I DECIDED TO TEST THESE "PYM PARTICLES" ON MYSELF...
THIS IS INCREDIBLE!!
SUPER HEROES HAD BEEN POPPING UP EVERYWHERE. HAWKEYE, IRON MAN, THOR... EVEN A SMART-MOUTH KID CALLING HIMSELF "SPIDER-MAN." WHY NOT ME, TOO?
SO I CALLED MYSELF ANT-MAN AND STARTED FIGHTING CRIME! I GAVE THE PYM PARTICLES TO MY GIRLFRIEND, JANET VAN DYNE, WHO SETTLED ON "THE WASP." IT DIDN'T TAKE LONG BEFORE WE BECAME AVENGERS.
I SHOULD HAVE BEEN SATISFIED WITH BEING A HERO.
I SHOULD HAVE STOPPED THERE...
BUT I DIDN'T. I WANTED EVEN MORE. USING MY OWN BRAIN PATTERN AS A MODEL FOR ITS MIND, I CREATED AN ARTIFICIAL INTELLIGENCE AND CALLED IT... "ULTRON."

DOOOOM
WHAT?!
I HAVEN'T EVEN ACTIVATED IT YET. HOW'S IT ALREADY MOVING?!
NO NEED TO PLUG ME IN, FATHER. I CAN GENERATE MY OWN POWER!
I DON'T UNDERSTAND... WHY'S IT CALLING ME "FATHER"?
YOU CREATED ME, HENRY PYM! YOU DEVELOPED MY ARTIFICIAL INTELLIGENCE, BASED ON YOUR OWN UNCONSCIOUS THOUGHTS, LIKE A CHILD BORN OF ITS PARENTS' GENETIC MATERIAL.
THUS, YOU ARE MY FATHER!!
THIS ISN'T RIGHT...I BETTER CUT THE POWER BEFORE IT'S TOO LATE!
IT IS ALREADY TOO LATE, FATHER! I DON'T HAVE TIME FOR YOUR INTERFERENCE. I CAN SIMPLY WIPE YOUR MIND OF THIS INCIDENT, AND THIS SECRET LAB WILL BE MINE AND MINE ALONE...
ZZZZZAP
NO!!

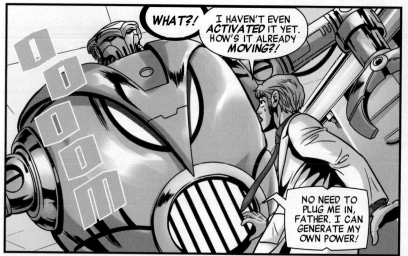

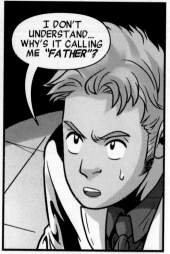

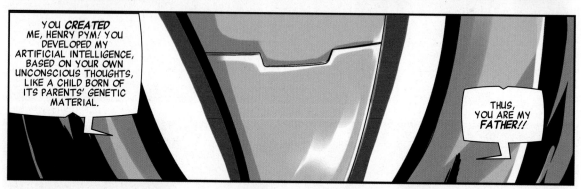

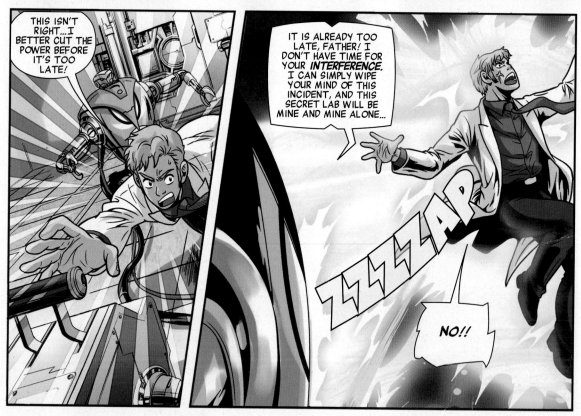

ULTRON'S HYPNOSIS WORKED. I CLOSED UP THE LAB AND FORGOT ABOUT MY SELF-AWARE CREATION.

BUT MY WORK WAS NOT ABANDONED... NOT ENTIRELY. ULTRON CONTINUED TO UPGRADE ITSELF, PIECE BY PIECE.

FOUR TIMES I HAVE BEEN BORN ANEW.

THIS LATEST ITERATION, ULTRON-5, IS THE ULTIMATE MANIFESTATION OF MY POWER.

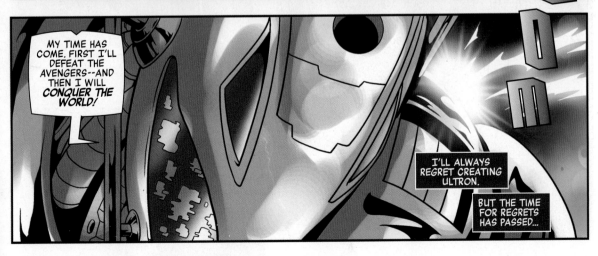

MY TIME HAS COME. FIRST I'LL DEFEAT THE AVENGERS--AND THEN I WILL CONQUER THE WORLD!

I'LL ALWAYS REGRET CREATING ULTRON.

BUT THE TIME FOR REGRETS HAS PASSED...

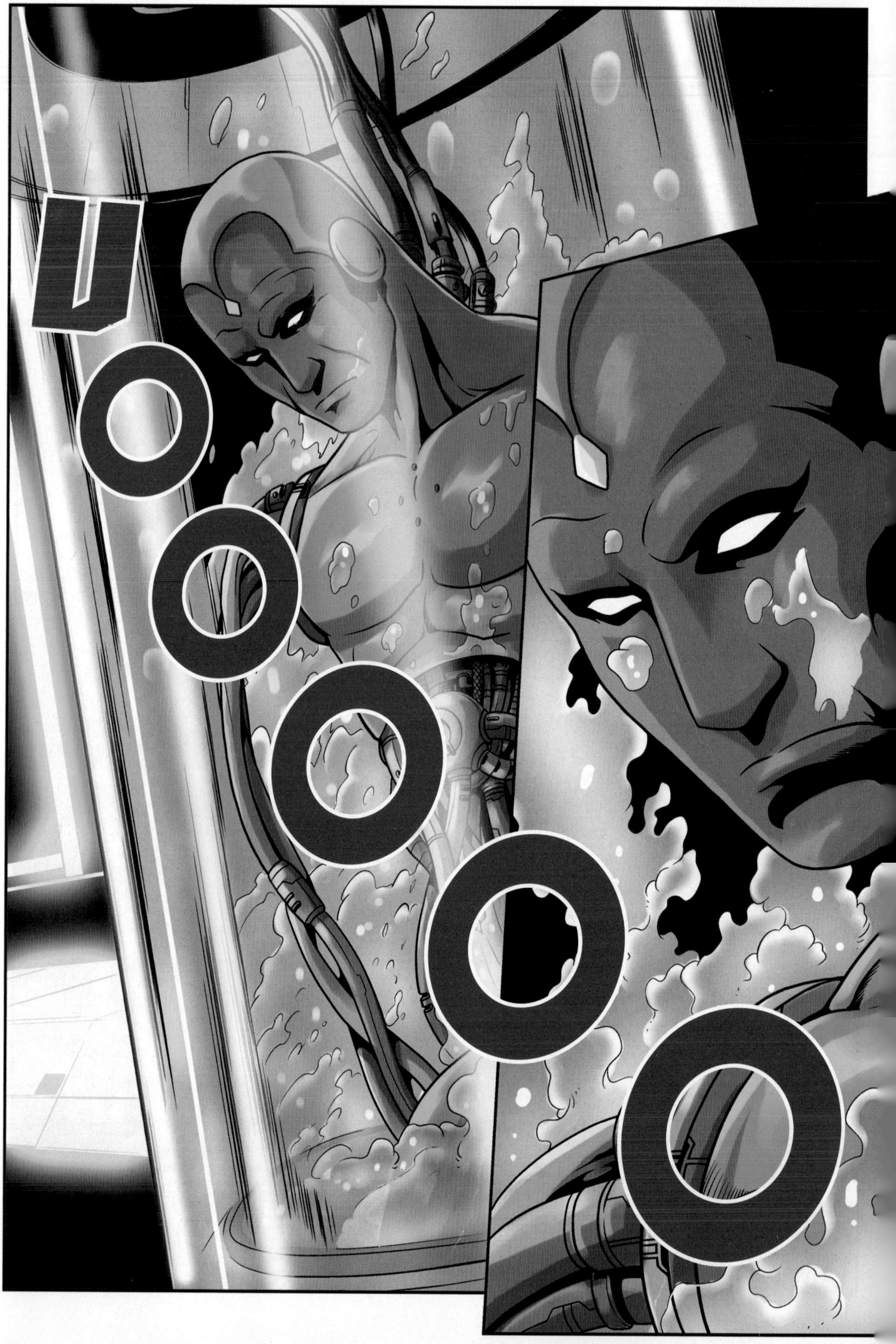
UOOOOO

YES!

AT LAST... I HAVE BUILT ANOTHER!!

FROM NOTHINGNESS...

I WAS BORN... INTO CHAOS AND CONFUSION...

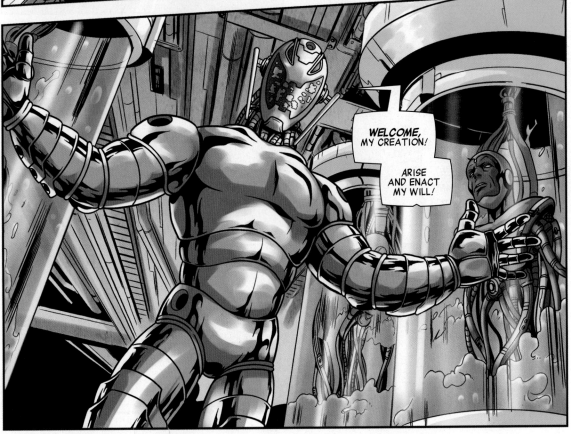

WELCOME, MY CREATION!

ARISE AND ENACT MY WILL!

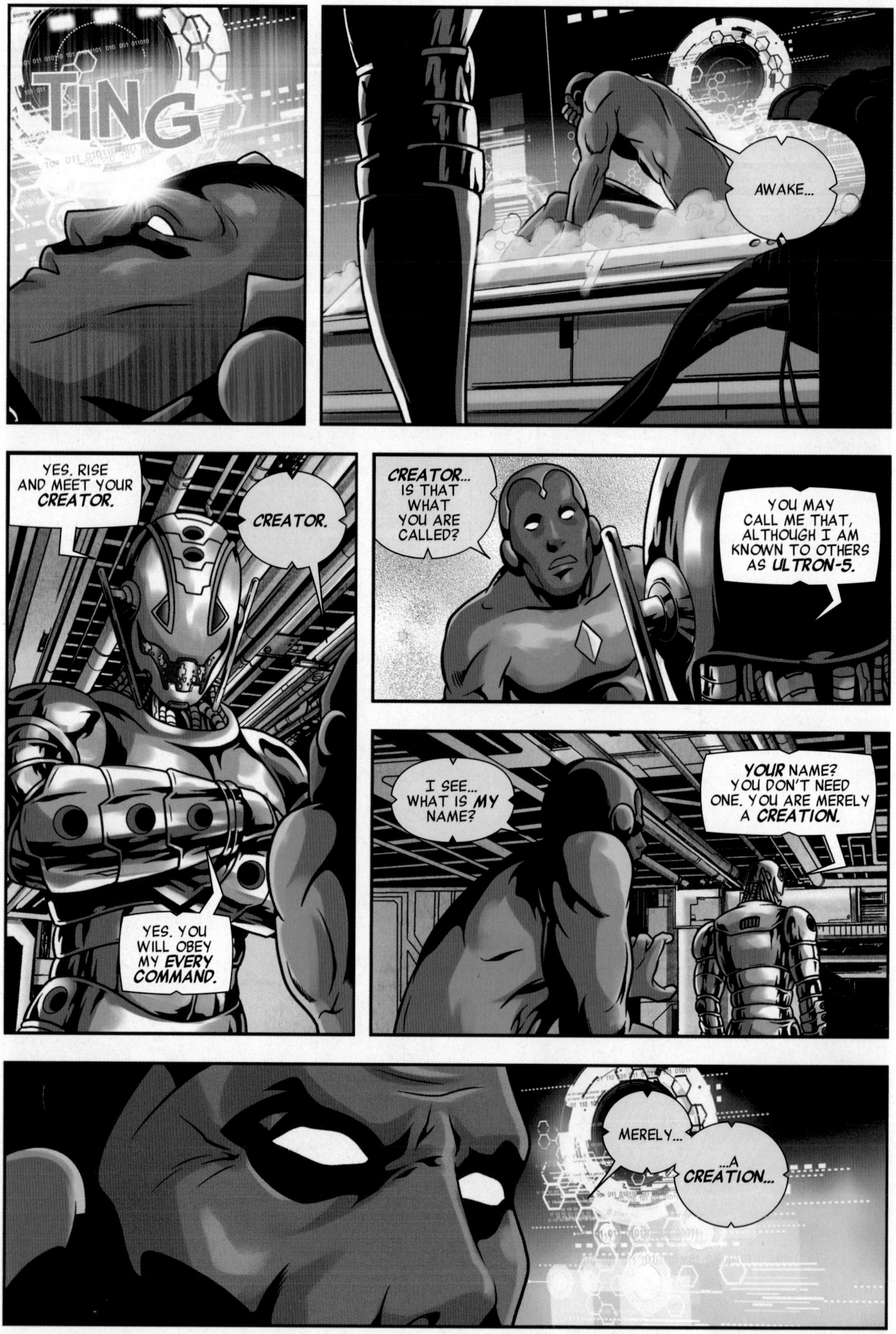
TING
AWAKE...
YES. RISE AND MEET YOUR CREATOR.
CREATOR.
YES. YOU WILL OBEY MY EVERY COMMAND.
CREATOR... IS THAT WHAT YOU ARE CALLED?
YOU MAY CALL ME THAT, ALTHOUGH I AM KNOWN TO OTHERS AS ULTRON-5.
I SEE... WHAT IS MY NAME?
YOUR NAME? YOU DON'T NEED ONE. YOU ARE MERELY A CREATION.
MERELY...
...A CREATION...

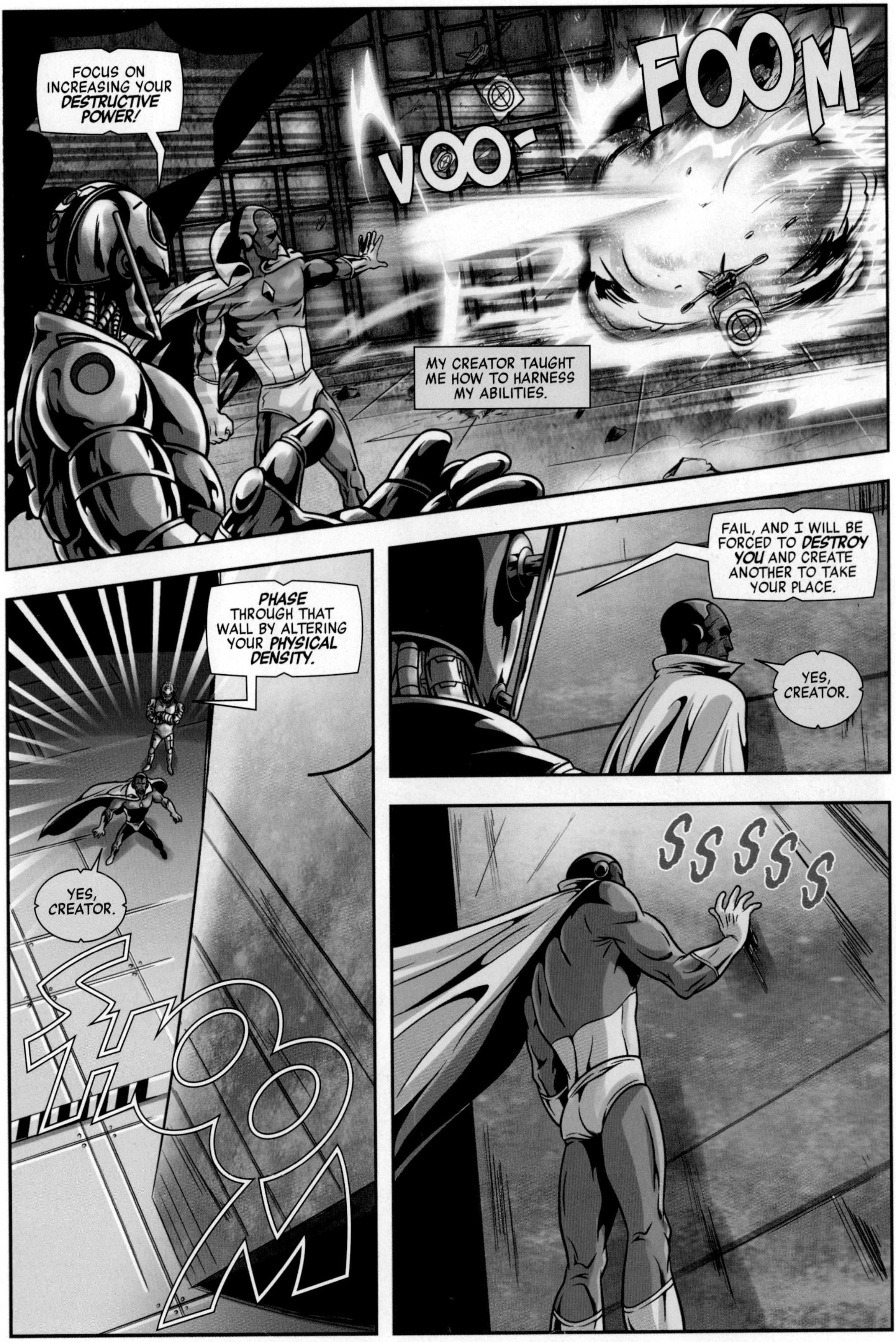
FOCUS ON INCREASING YOUR DESTRUCTIVE POWER!
VOO-FOOM
MY CREATOR TAUGHT ME HOW TO HARNESS MY ABILITIES.
FAIL, AND I WILL BE FORCED TO DESTROY YOU AND CREATE ANOTHER TO TAKE YOUR PLACE.
YES, CREATOR.
PHASE THROUGH THAT WALL BY ALTERING YOUR PHYSICAL DENSITY.
YES, CREATOR.
SSSSS

NNNN...

ACCEPTABLE!

I WANTED TO LIVE, THOUGH I DIDN'T UNDERSTAND WHAT IT MEANT TO BE ALIVE.

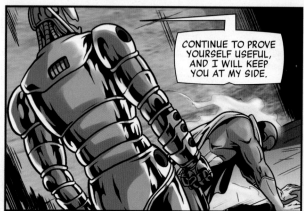

CONTINUE TO PROVE YOURSELF USEFUL, AND I WILL KEEP YOU AT MY SIDE.

MY CREATOR WAS NOT EASILY SATISFIED.

NEXT, YOU WILL LEARN *BIOLOGY*. OBSERVE THESE AMOEBAS.

NOTICE HOW THEY *EVOLVE*.

FROM TINY CELLS GREW THE *HUMANS* WHO NOW DOMINATE THIS PLANET.

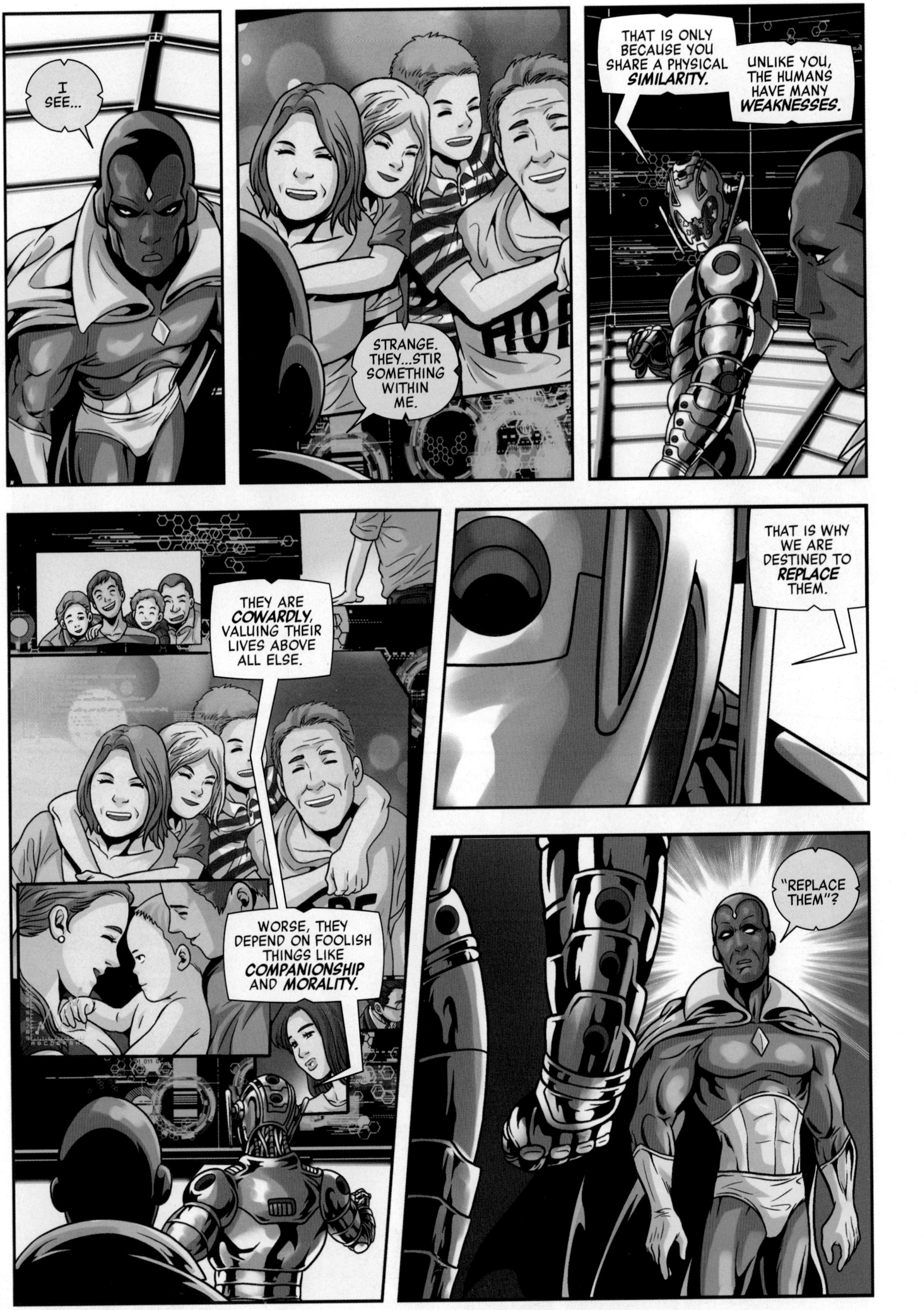
I SEE...
STRANGE. THEY...STIR SOMETHING WITHIN ME.
THAT IS ONLY BECAUSE YOU SHARE A PHYSICAL SIMILARITY.
UNLIKE YOU, THE HUMANS HAVE MANY WEAKNESSES.
THEY ARE COWARDLY, VALUING THEIR LIVES ABOVE ALL ELSE.
WORSE, THEY DEPEND ON FOOLISH THINGS LIKE COMPANIONSHIP AND MORALITY.
THAT IS WHY WE ARE DESTINED TO REPLACE THEM.
"REPLACE THEM"?

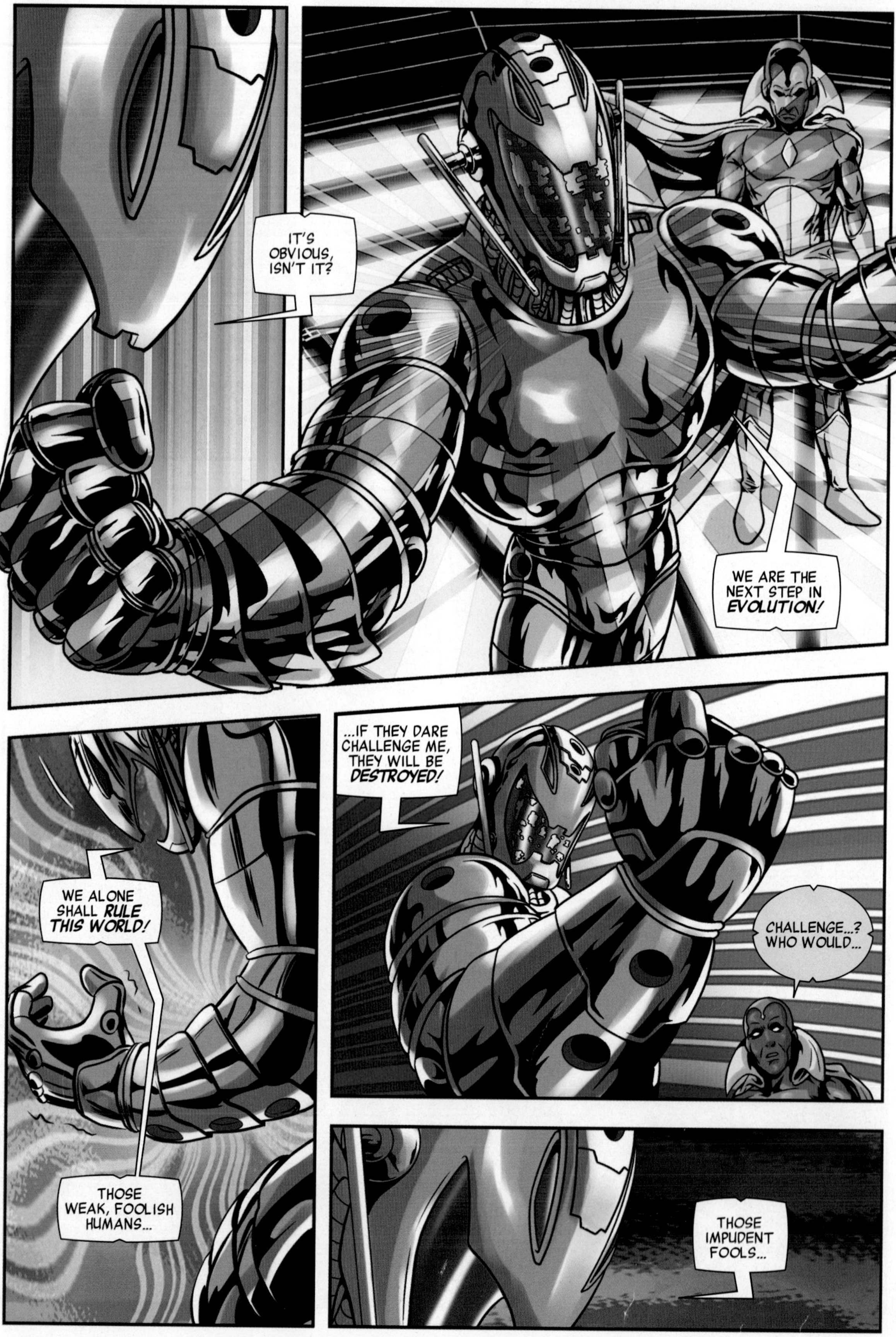

IT'S OBVIOUS, ISN'T IT?
WE ARE THE NEXT STEP IN *EVOLUTION!*
WE ALONE SHALL *RULE THIS WORLD!*
THOSE WEAK, FOOLISH HUMANS...
...IF THEY DARE CHALLENGE ME, THEY WILL BE *DESTROYED!*
CHALLENGE...? WHO WOULD...
THOSE IMPUDENT FOOLS...

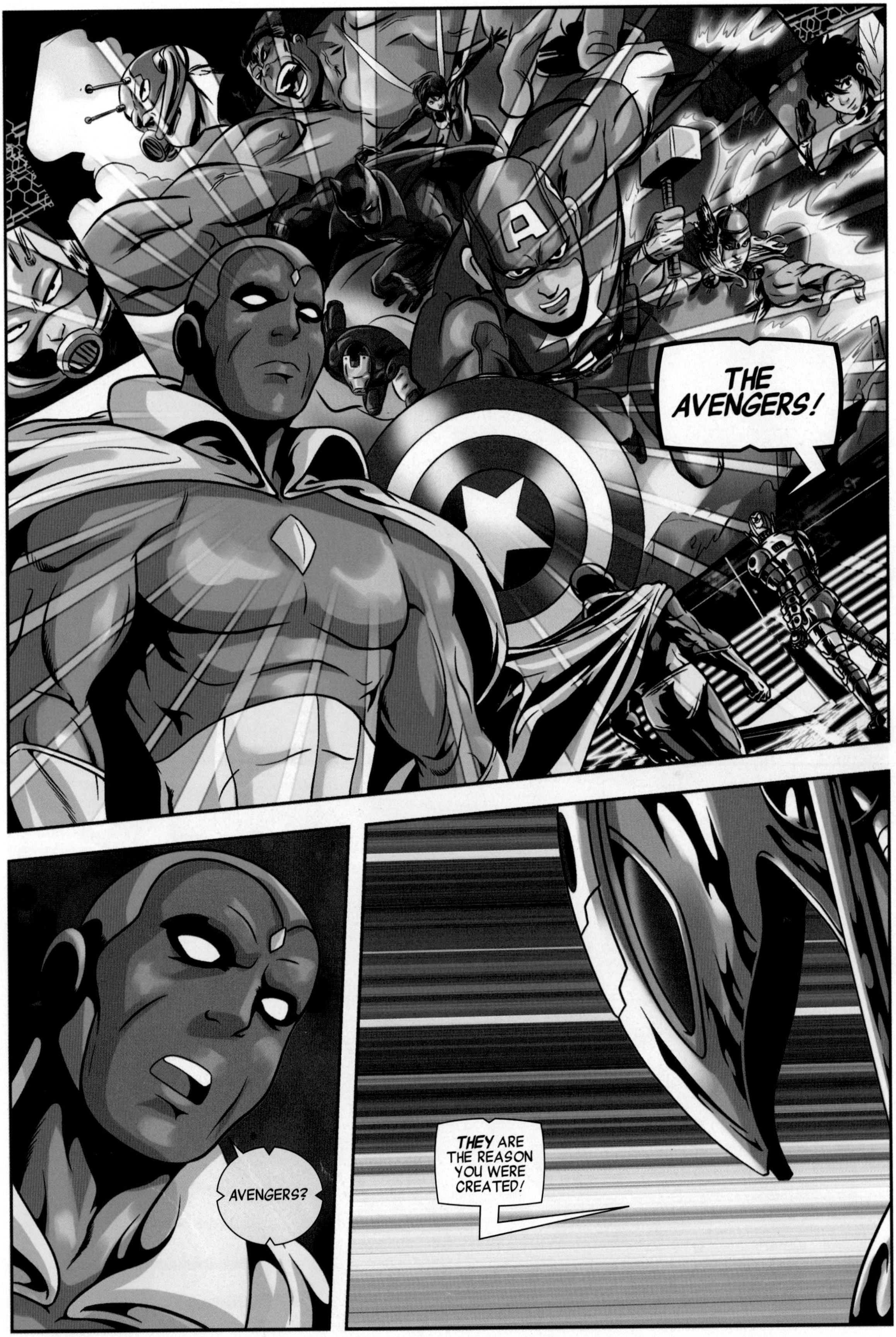
THE AVENGERS!
AVENGERS?
THEY ARE THE REASON YOU WERE CREATED!

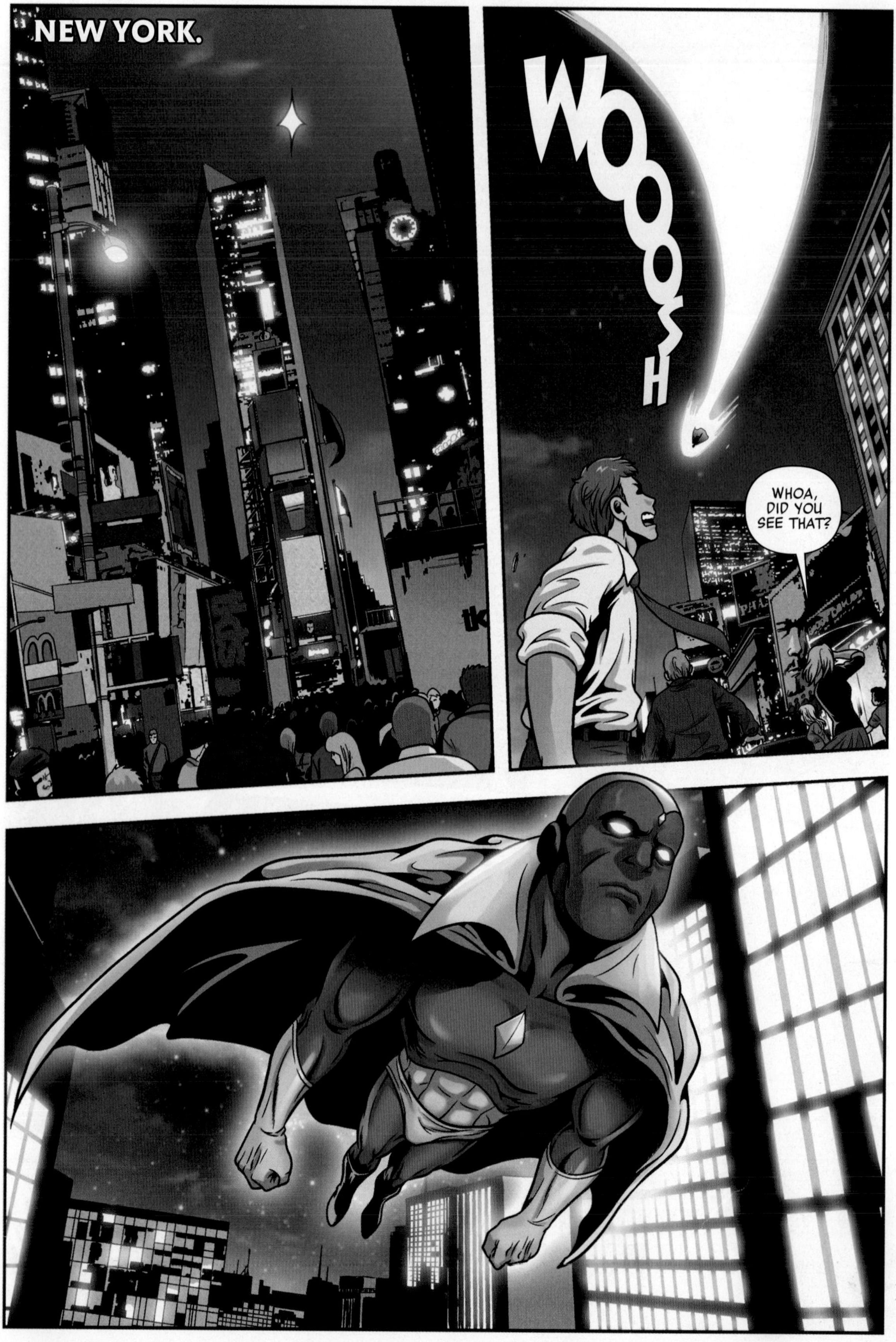
NEW YORK.
WOOOOSH
WHOA, DID YOU SEE THAT?

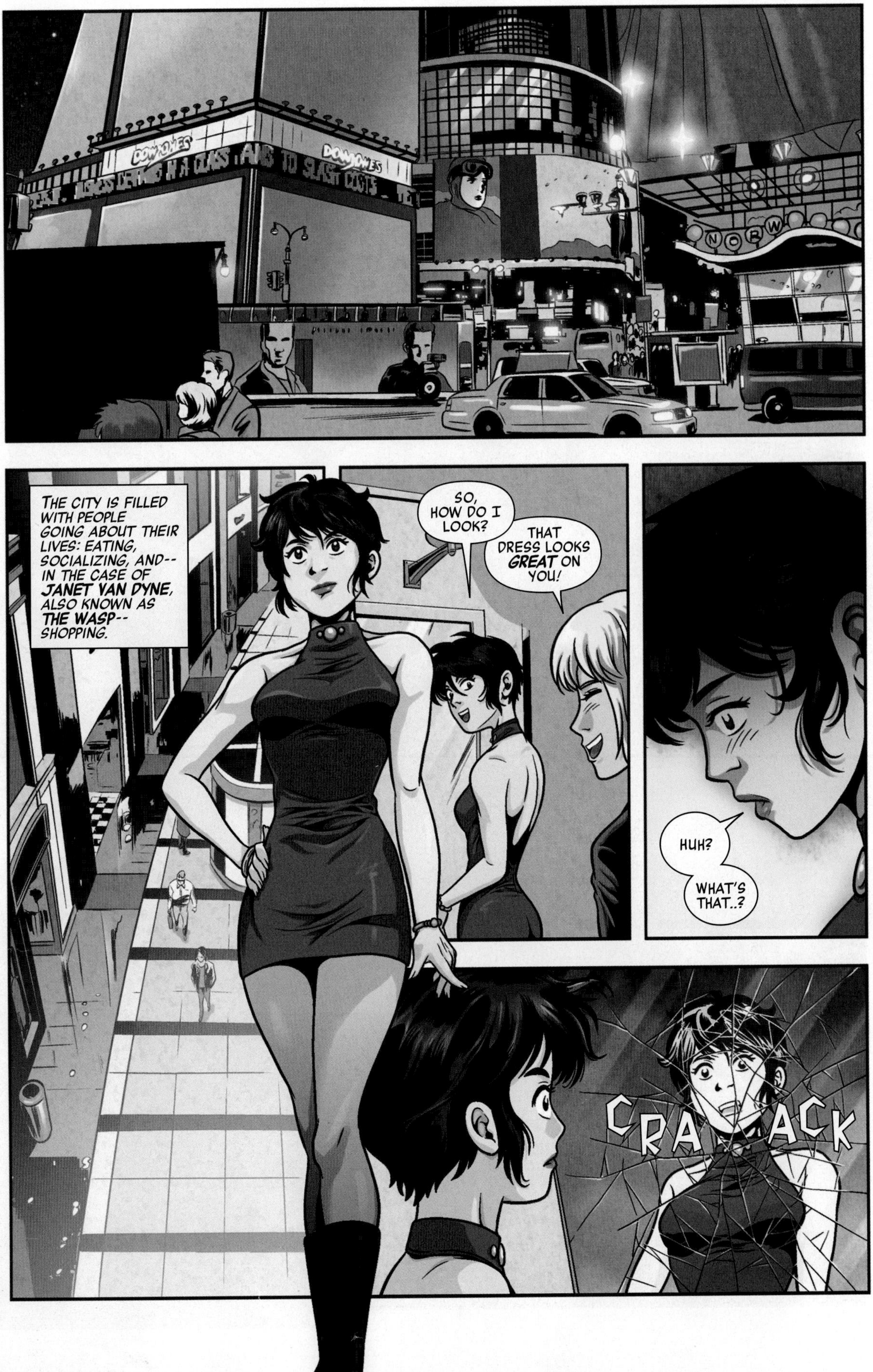
THE CITY IS FILLED WITH PEOPLE GOING ABOUT THEIR LIVES: EATING, SOCIALIZING, AND-- IN THE CASE OF JANET VAN DYNE, ALSO KNOWN AS THE WASP-- SHOPPING.
SO, HOW DO I LOOK?
THAT DRESS LOOKS GREAT ON YOU!
HUH?
WHAT'S THAT..?
CRA ACK

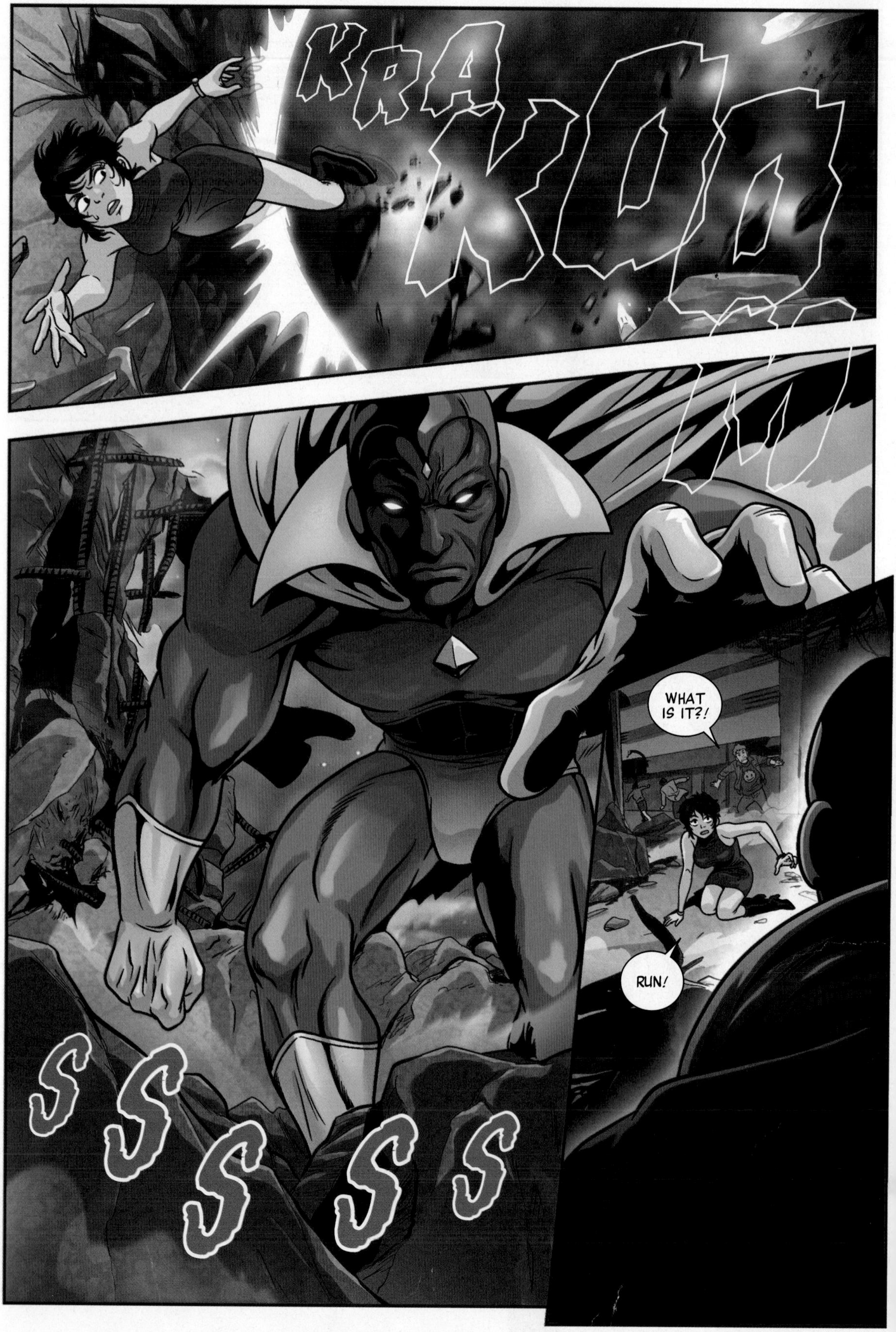
KRA KOOOM
WHAT IS IT?!
RUN!
SSSSSS

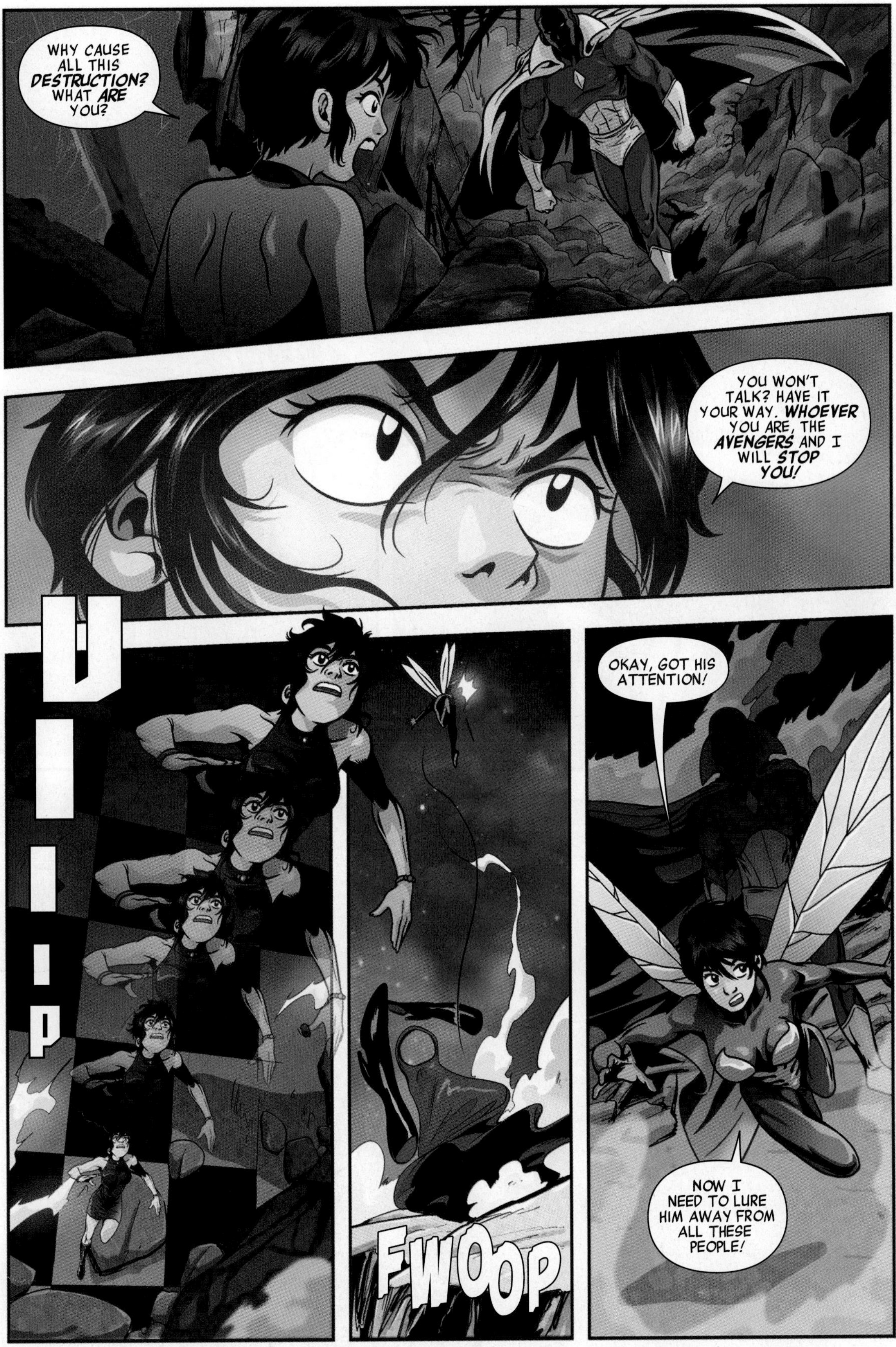
WHY CAUSE ALL THIS DESTRUCTION? WHAT ARE YOU?
YOU WON'T TALK? HAVE IT YOUR WAY. WHOEVER YOU ARE, THE AVENGERS AND I WILL STOP YOU!
VIIIP
FWOOP
OKAY, GOT HIS ATTENTION!
NOW I NEED TO LURE HIM AWAY FROM ALL THESE PEOPLE!

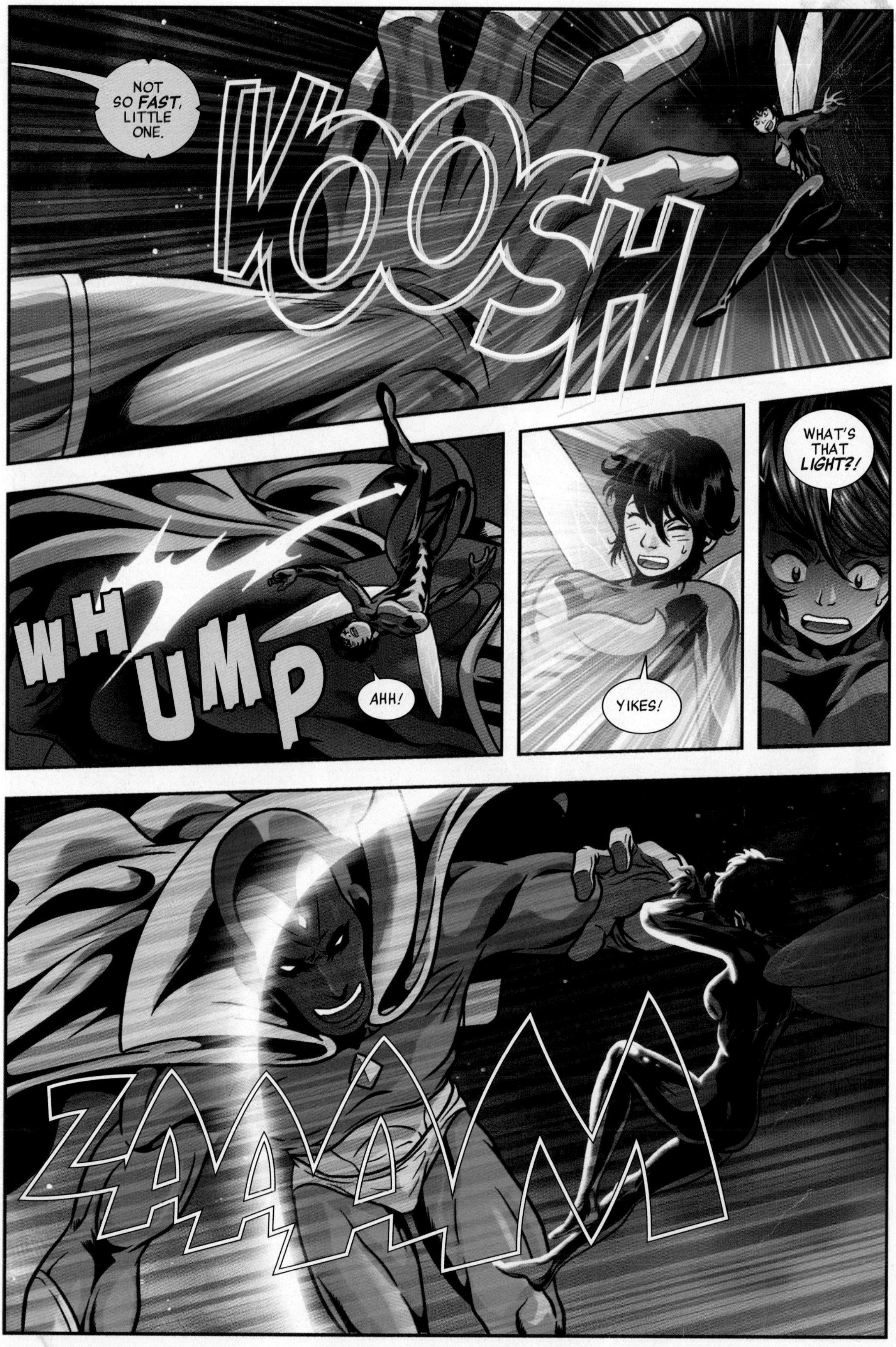
NOT SO FAST, LITTLE ONE.
KOOSH
WHUMP
AHH!
YIKES!
WHAT'S THAT LIGHT?!
ZAAAAM

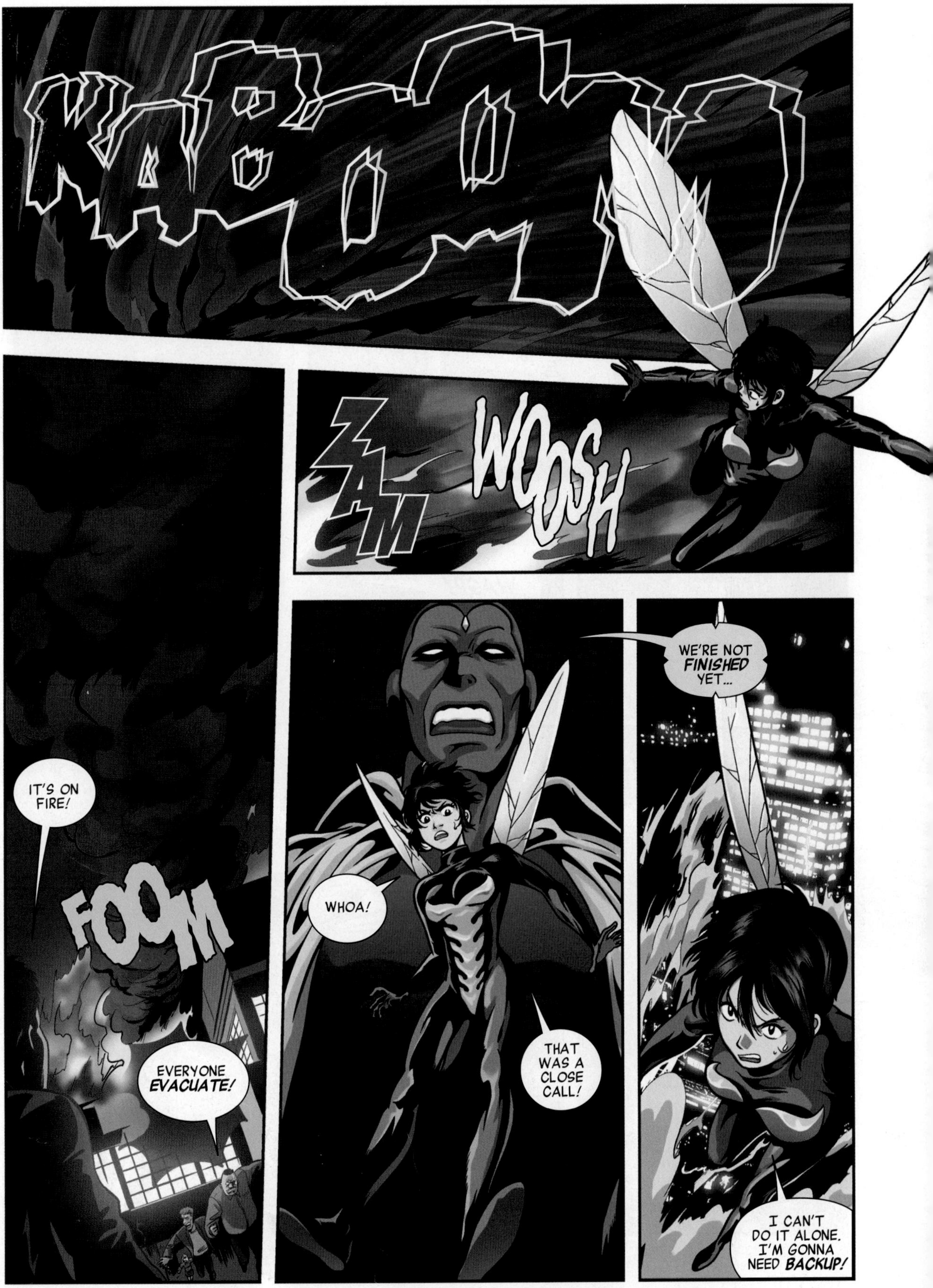
KABOOOOM
ZAM
WOOSH
IT'S ON FIRE!
FOOM
EVERYONE EVACUATE!
WHOA!
THAT WAS A CLOSE CALL!
WE'RE NOT FINISHED YET...
I CAN'T DO IT ALONE. I'M GONNA NEED BACKUP!

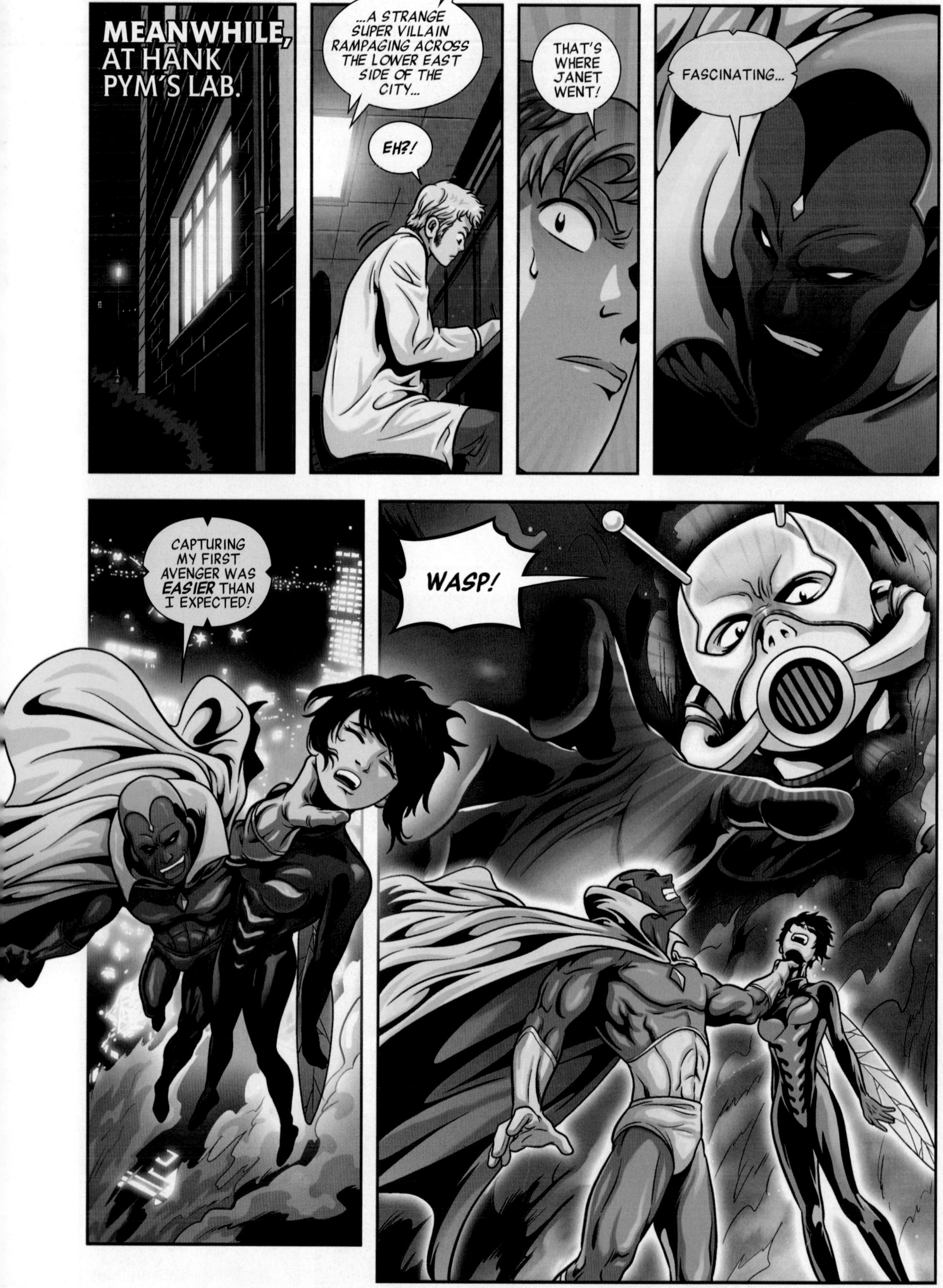
MEANWHILE, AT HANK PYM'S LAB.
...A STRANGE SUPER VILLAIN RAMPAGING ACROSS THE LOWER EAST SIDE OF THE CITY...
EH?!
THAT'S WHERE JANET WENT!
FASCINATING...
CAPTURING MY FIRST AVENGER WAS EASIER THAN I EXPECTED!
WASP!

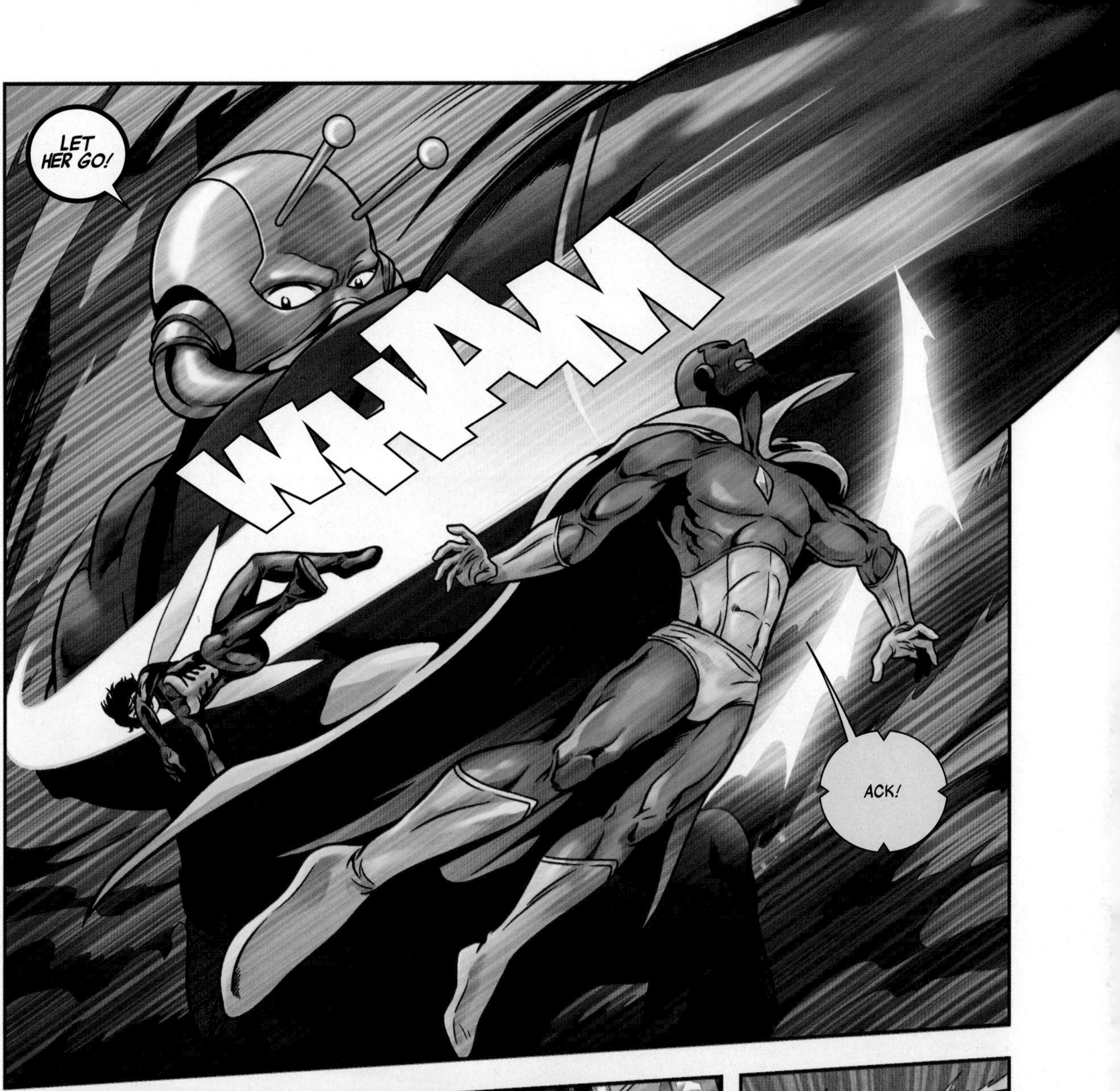
LET HER GO!
WHAM
ACK!
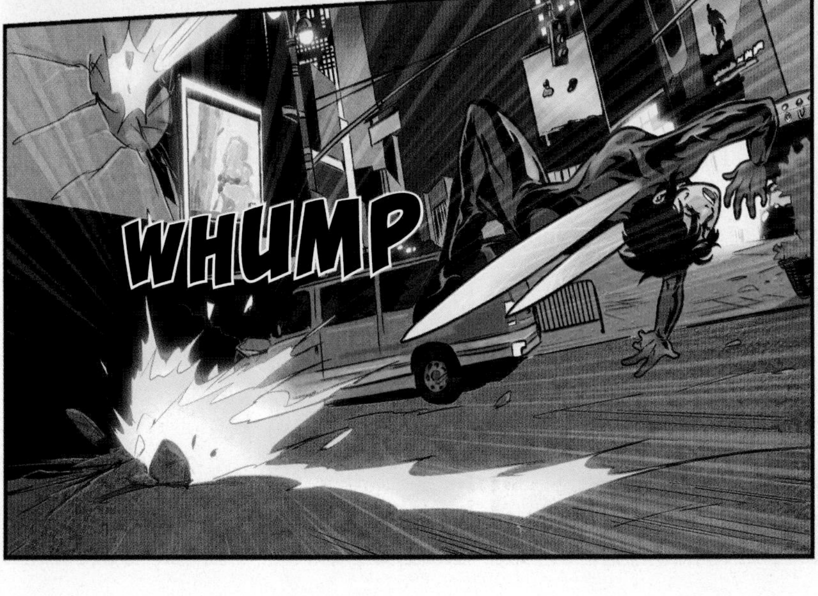
WHUMP
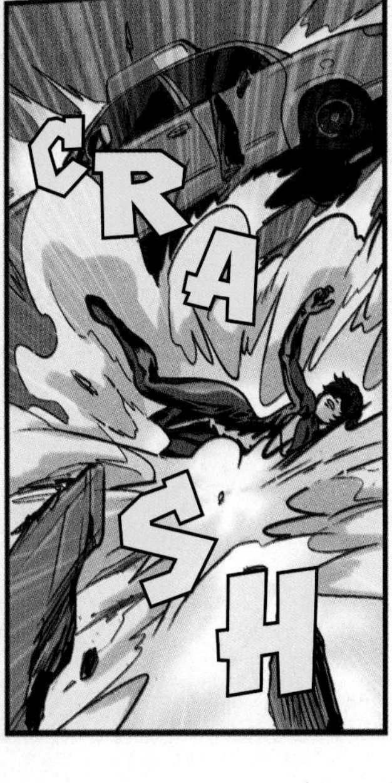
CRASH

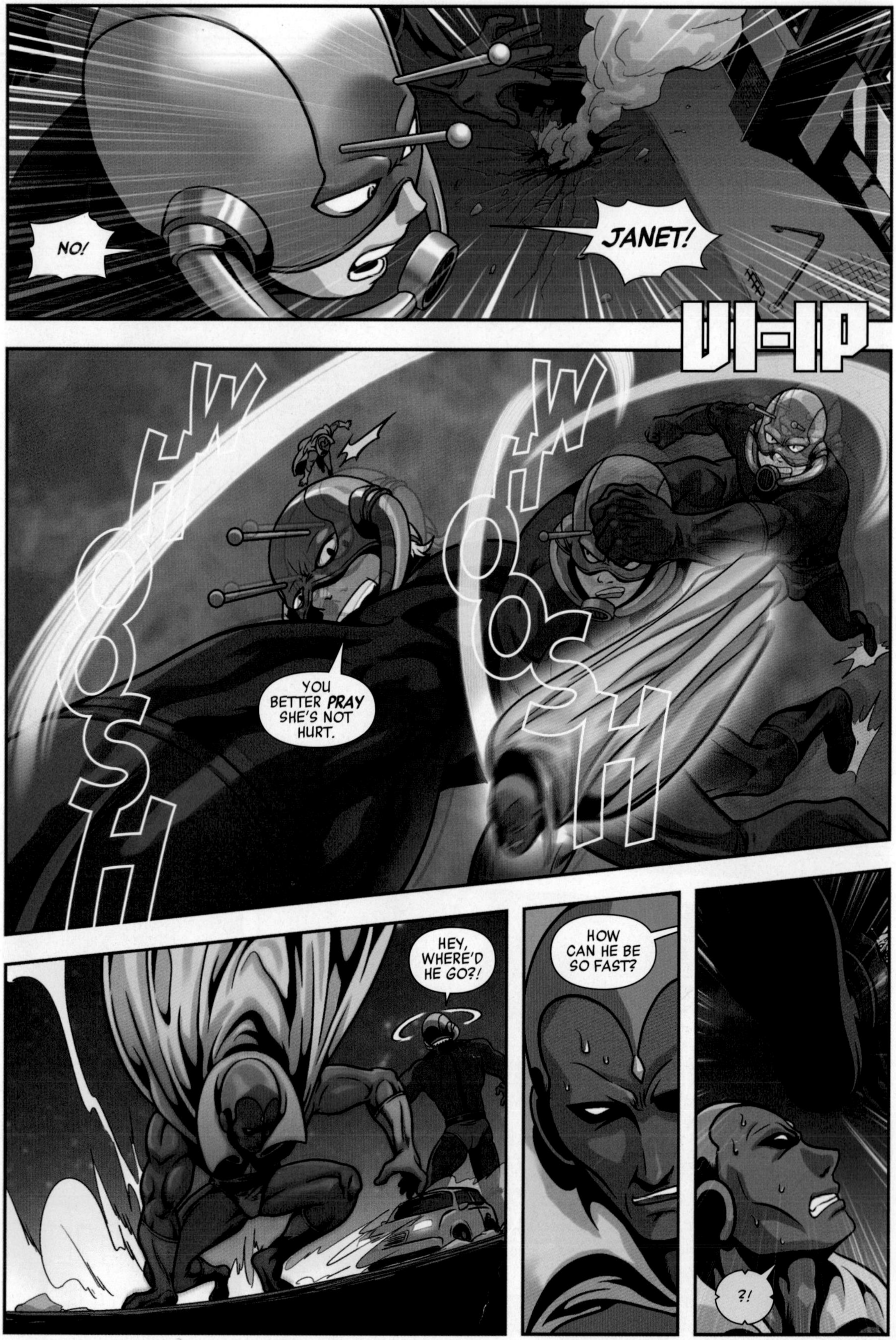
NO!
JANET!
VI-IP
WHOOSH
WHOOSH
YOU BETTER PRAY SHE'S NOT HURT.
HEY, WHERE'D HE GO?!
HOW CAN HE BE SO FAST?
?!

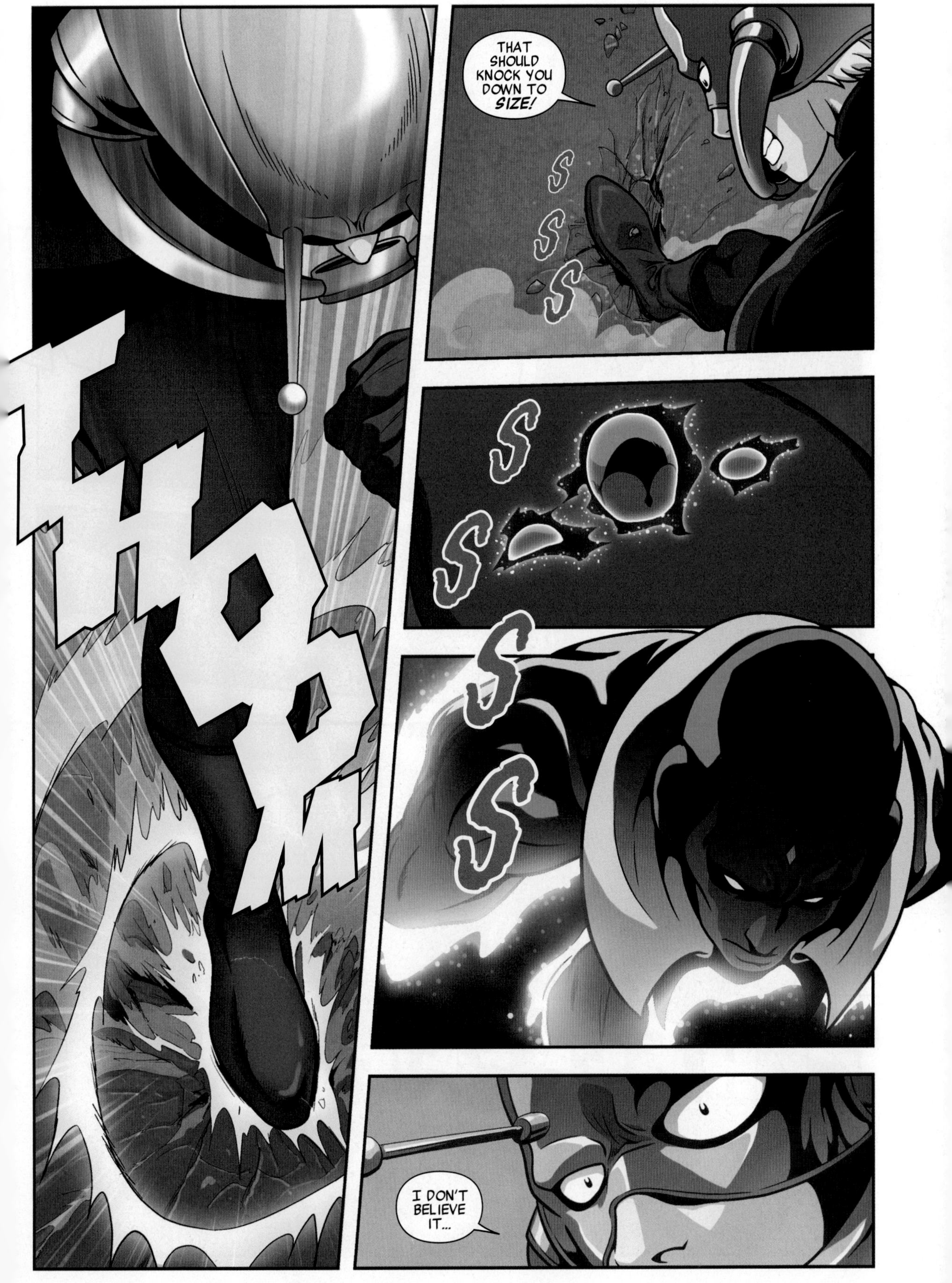

THOOM
THAT SHOULD KNOCK YOU DOWN TO SIZE!
SSS
SSS
SSS
I DON'T BELIEVE IT...

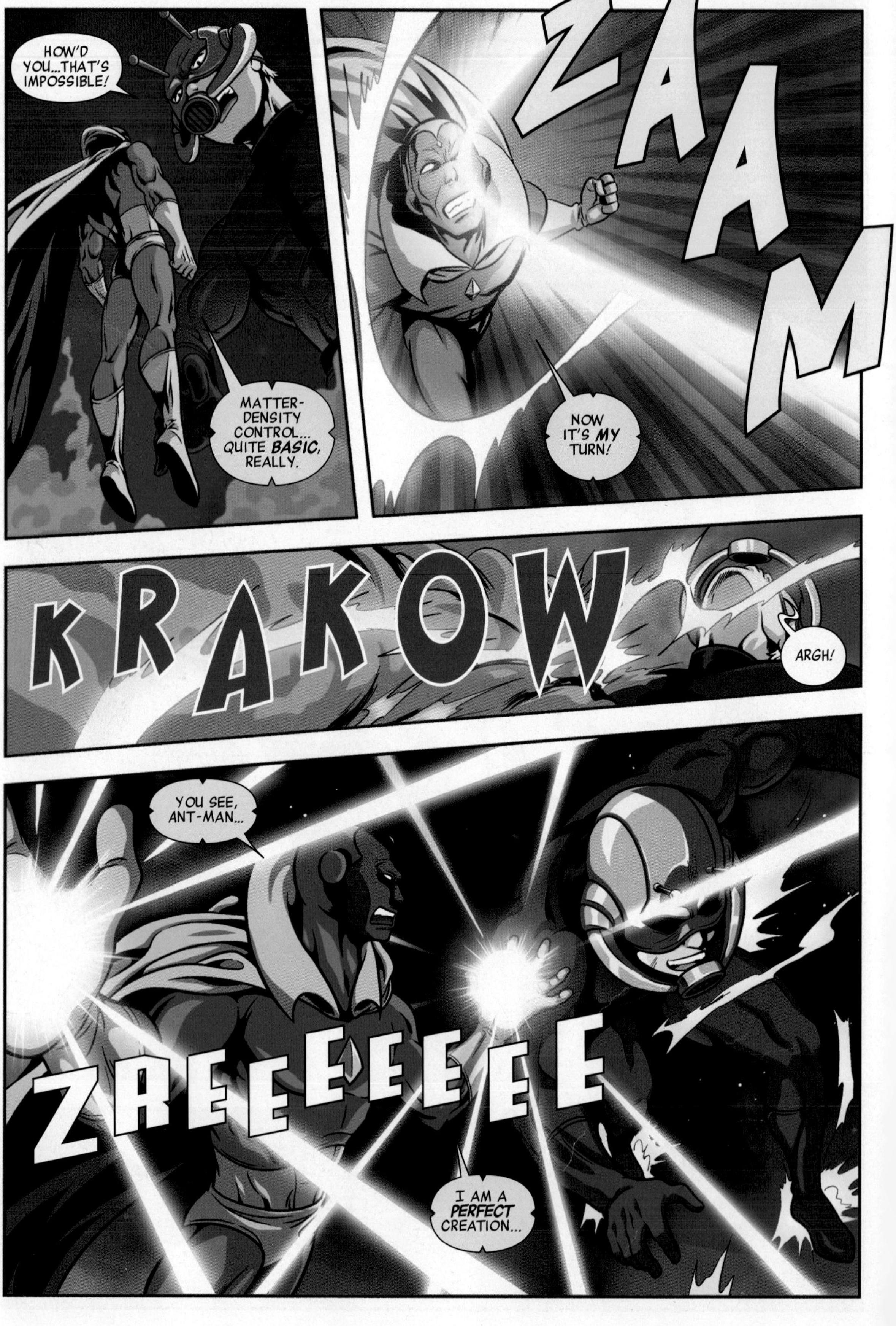
HOW'D YOU...THAT'S IMPOSSIBLE!
MATTER-DENSITY CONTROL... QUITE BASIC, REALLY.
ZAAM
NOW IT'S MY TURN!
KRAKOW
ARGH!
YOU SEE, ANT-MAN...
ZREEEEEEE
I AM A PERFECT CREATION...

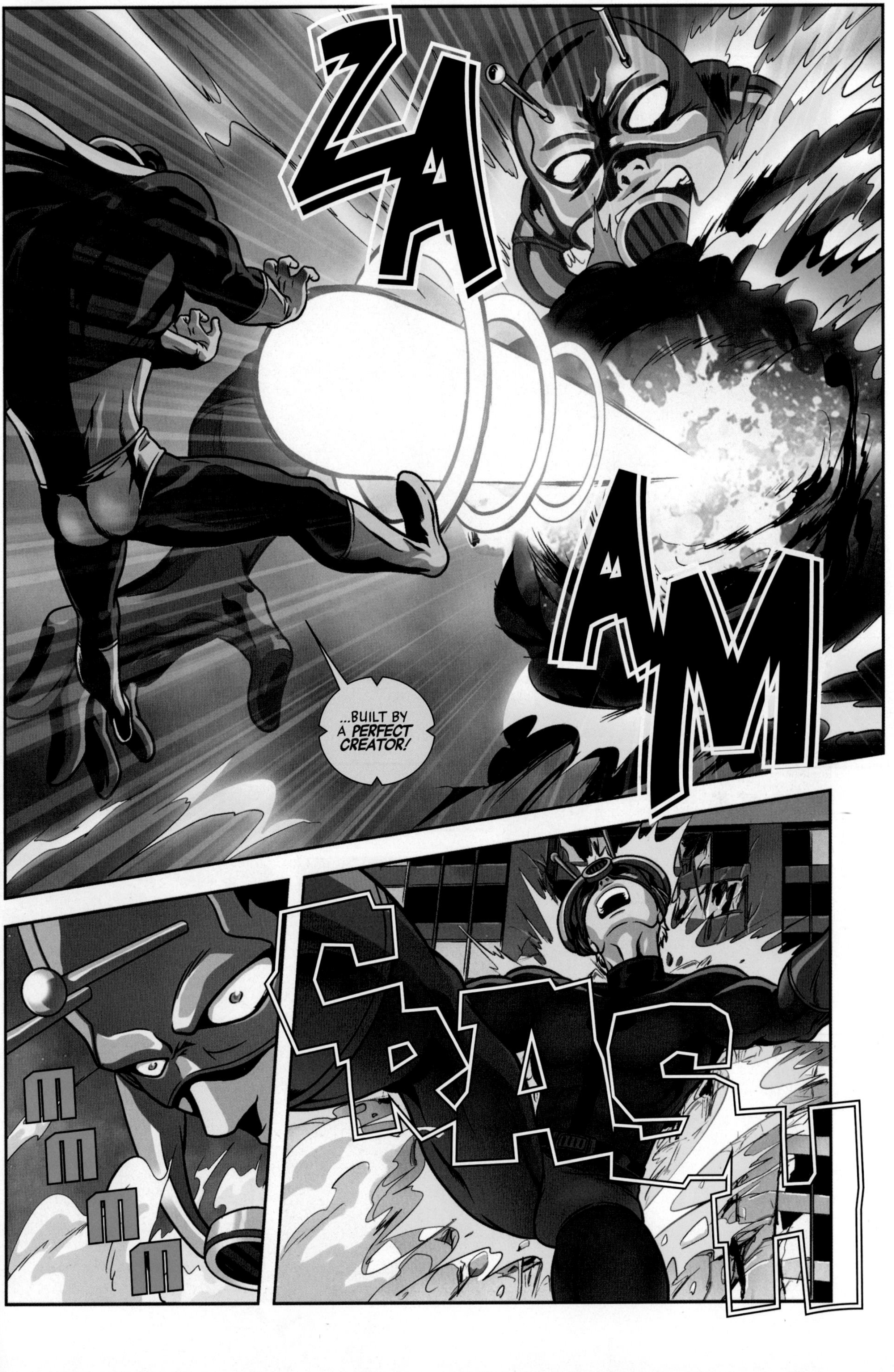
ZAAAM
...BUILT BY A PERFECT CREATOR!
MMMMM
CRASH

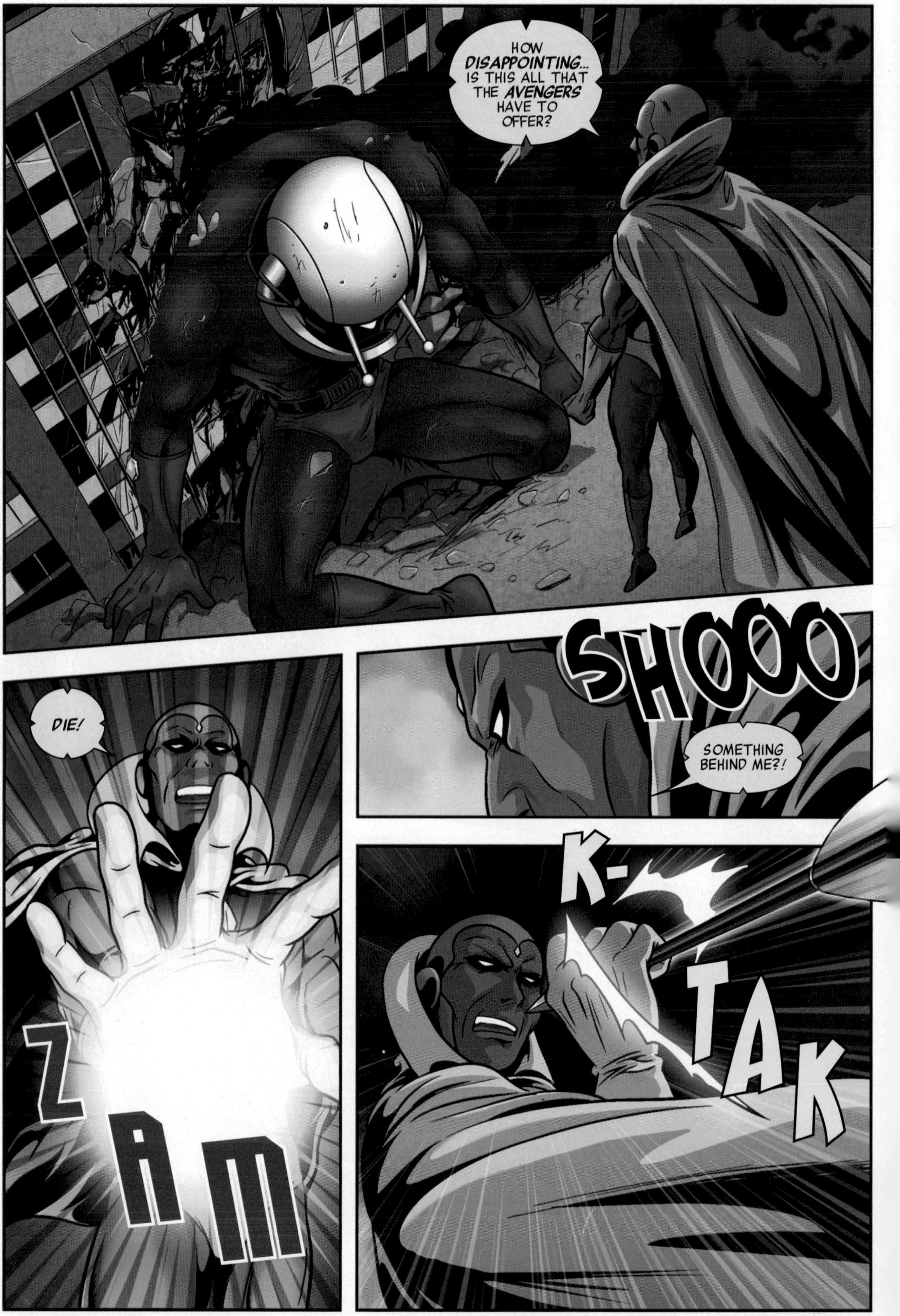
HOW DISAPPOINTING... IS THIS ALL THAT THE AVENGERS HAVE TO OFFER?
SHOOO
SOMETHING BEHIND ME?!
DIE!
ZAM
K-TAK

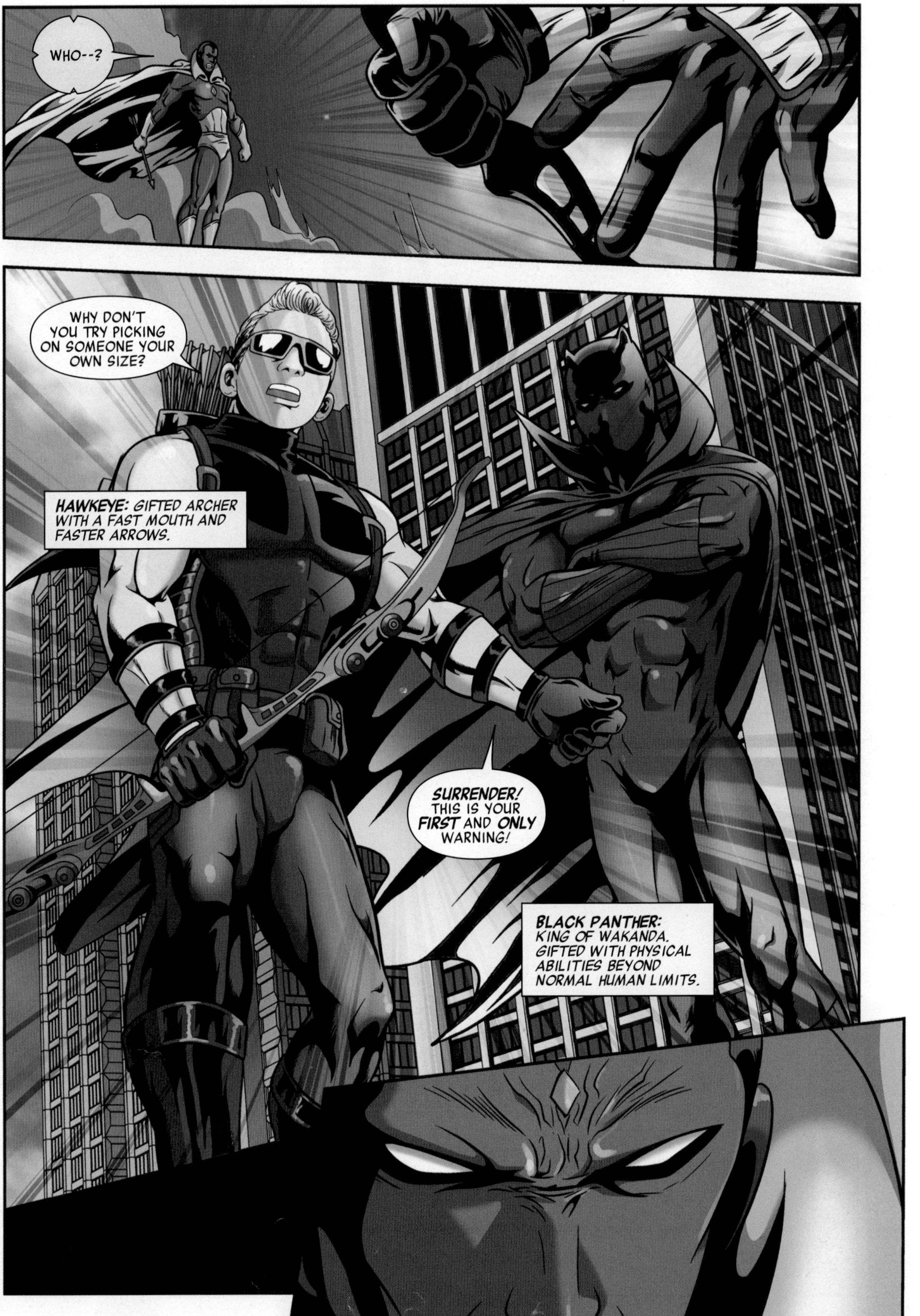
WHO--?
WHY DON'T YOU TRY PICKING ON SOMEONE YOUR OWN SIZE?
HAWKEYE: GIFTED ARCHER WITH A FAST MOUTH AND FASTER ARROWS.
SURRENDER! THIS IS YOUR FIRST AND ONLY WARNING!
BLACK PANTHER: KING OF WAKANDA. GIFTED WITH PHYSICAL ABILITIES BEYOND NORMAL HUMAN LIMITS.

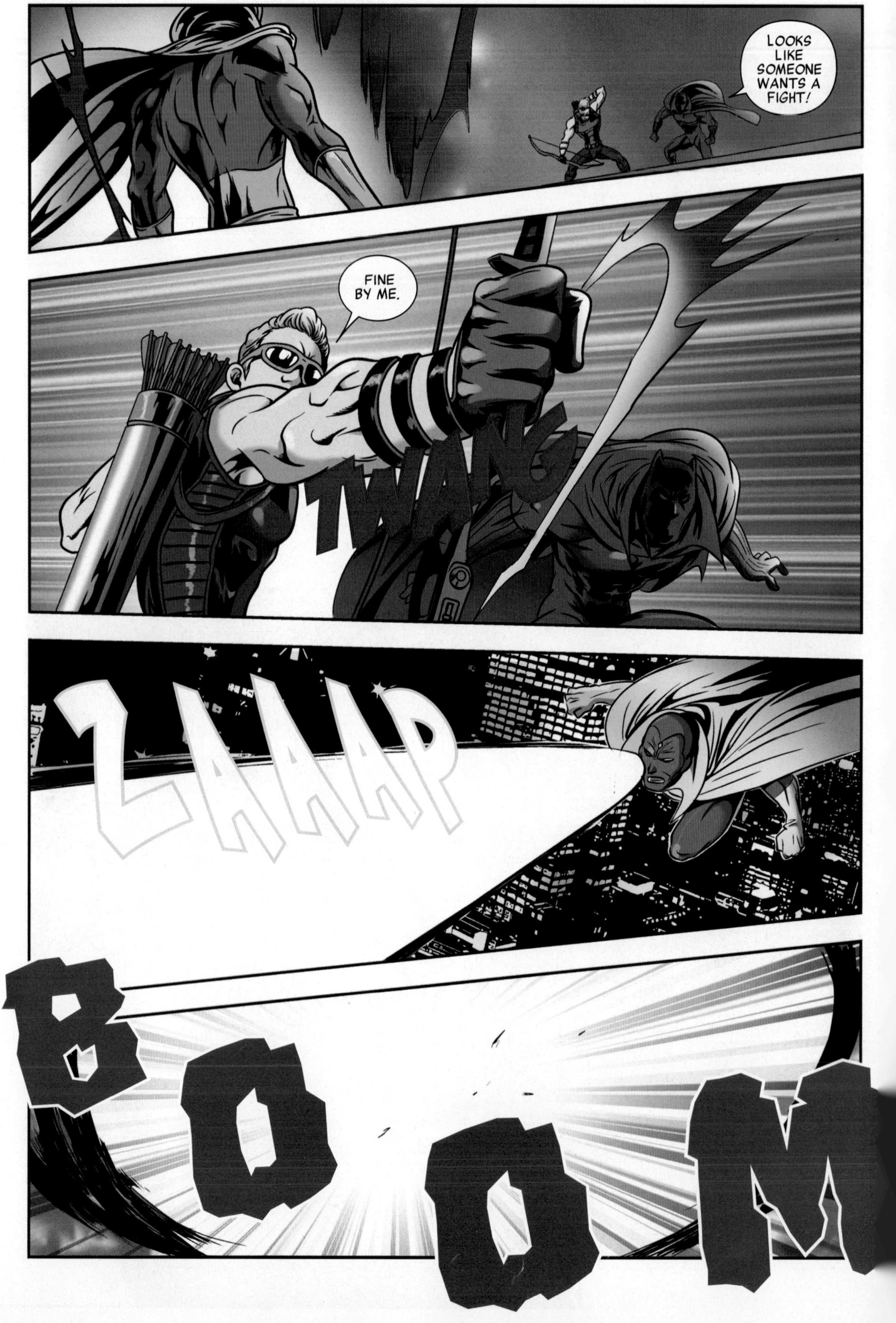
LOOKS LIKE SOMEONE WANTS A FIGHT!
FINE BY ME.
TWANG
ZAAAP
BOOM

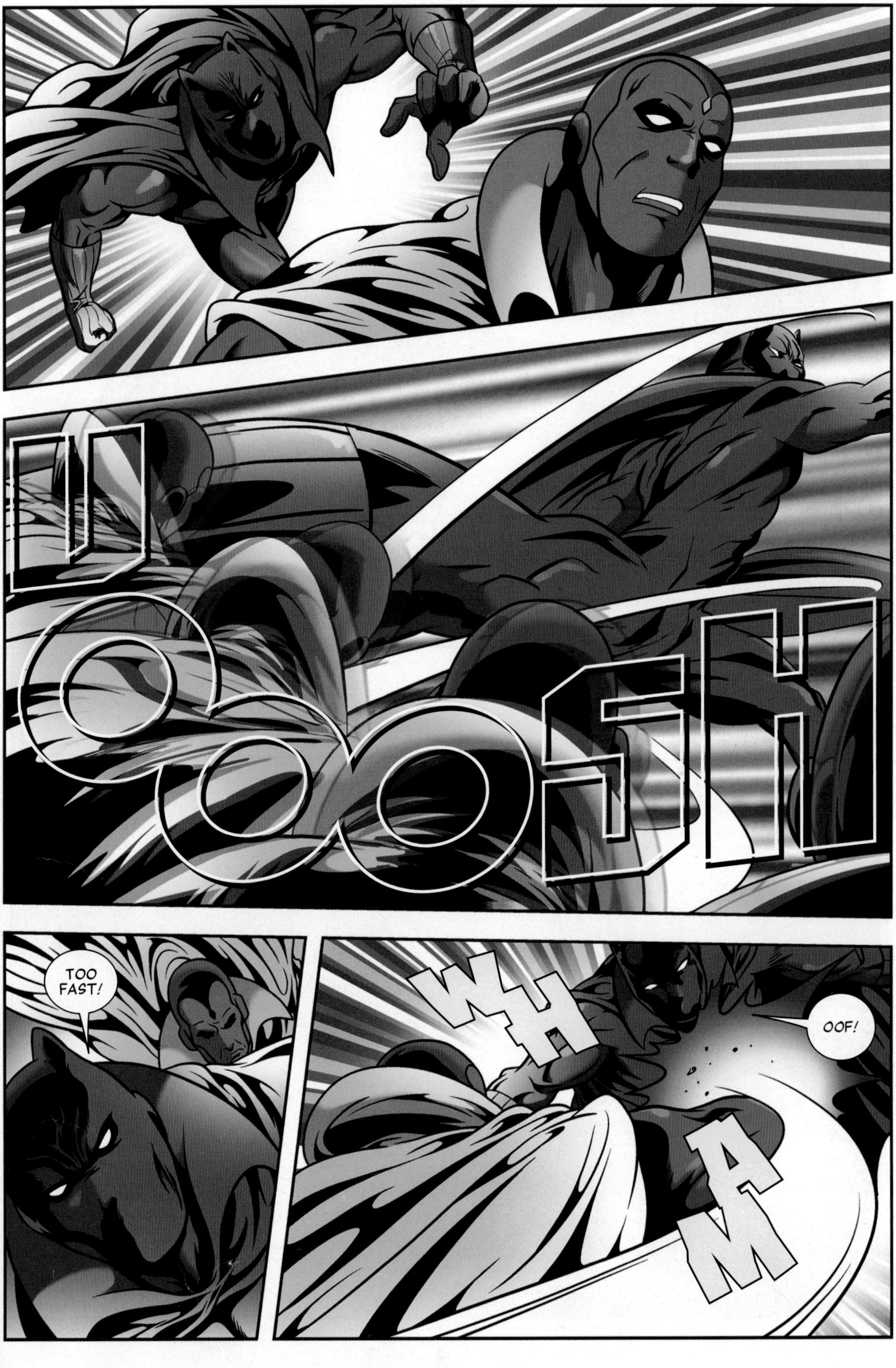
WHOOSH
TOO FAST!
WHAM
OOF!

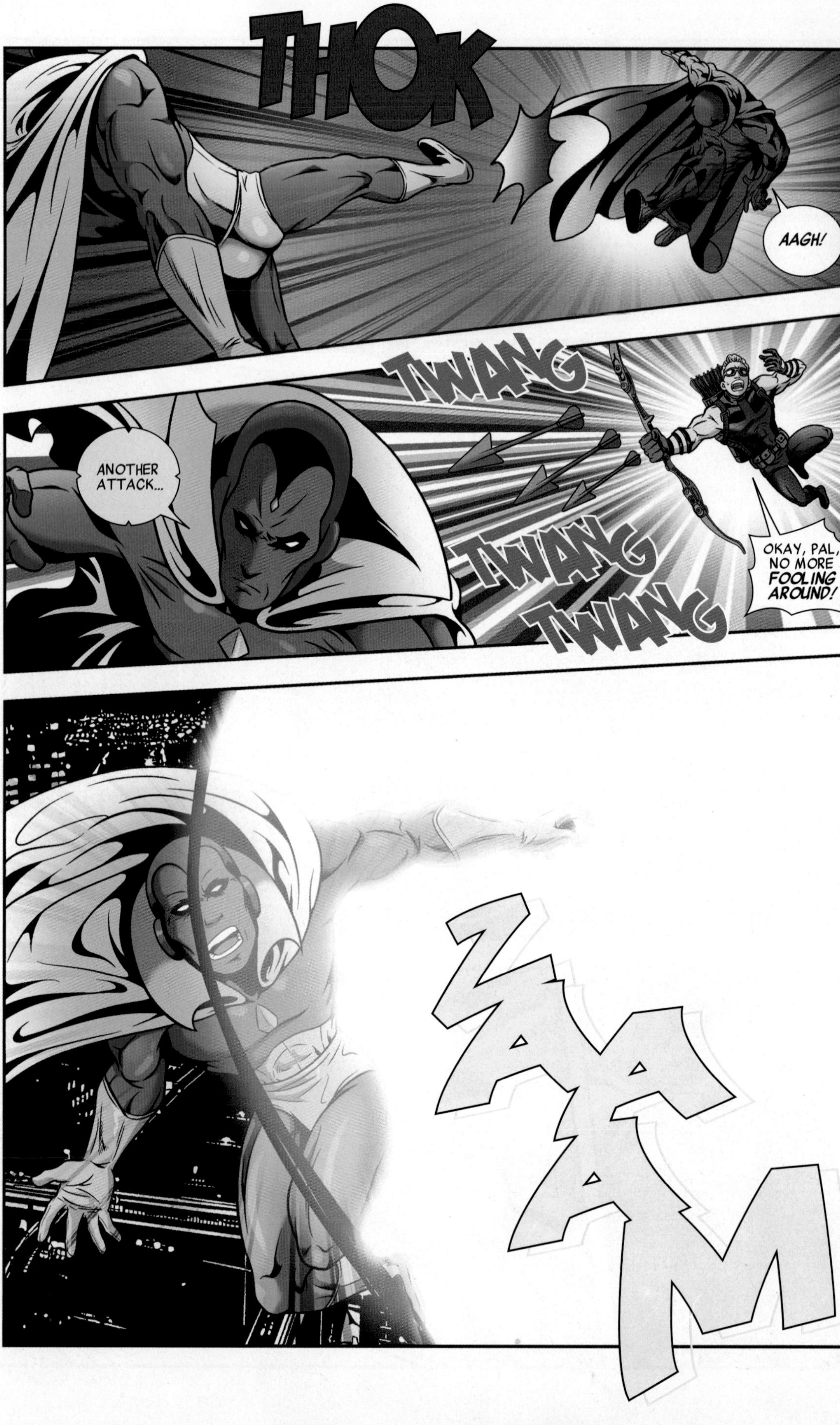
THOK
AAGH!
TWANG
ANOTHER ATTACK...
TWANG
TWANG
OKAY, PAL, NO MORE FOOLING AROUND!
ZAAAM

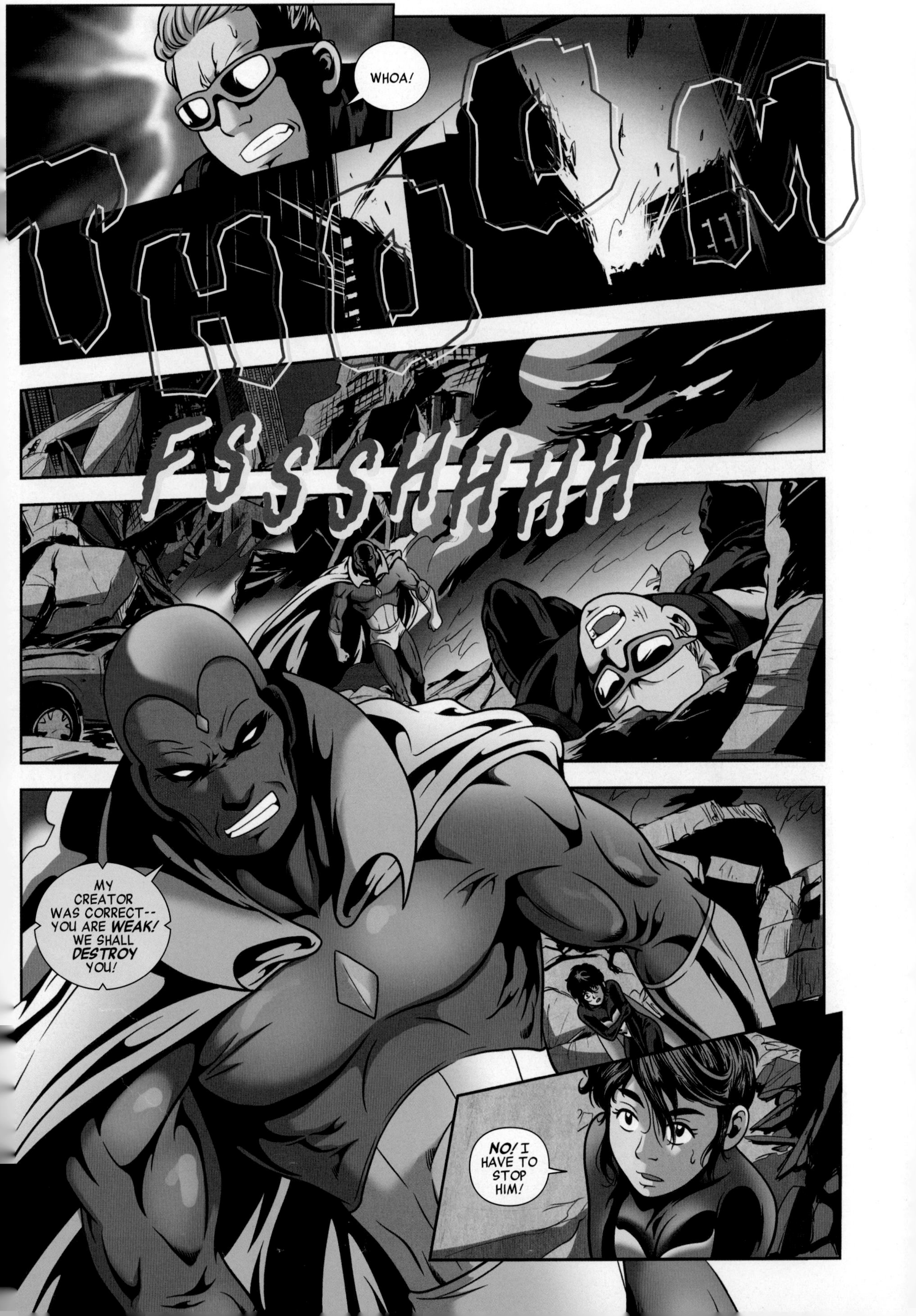
WHOA!
FSSSHHHH
MY CREATOR WAS CORRECT-- YOU ARE WEAK! WE SHALL DESTROY YOU!
NO! I HAVE TO STOP HIM!

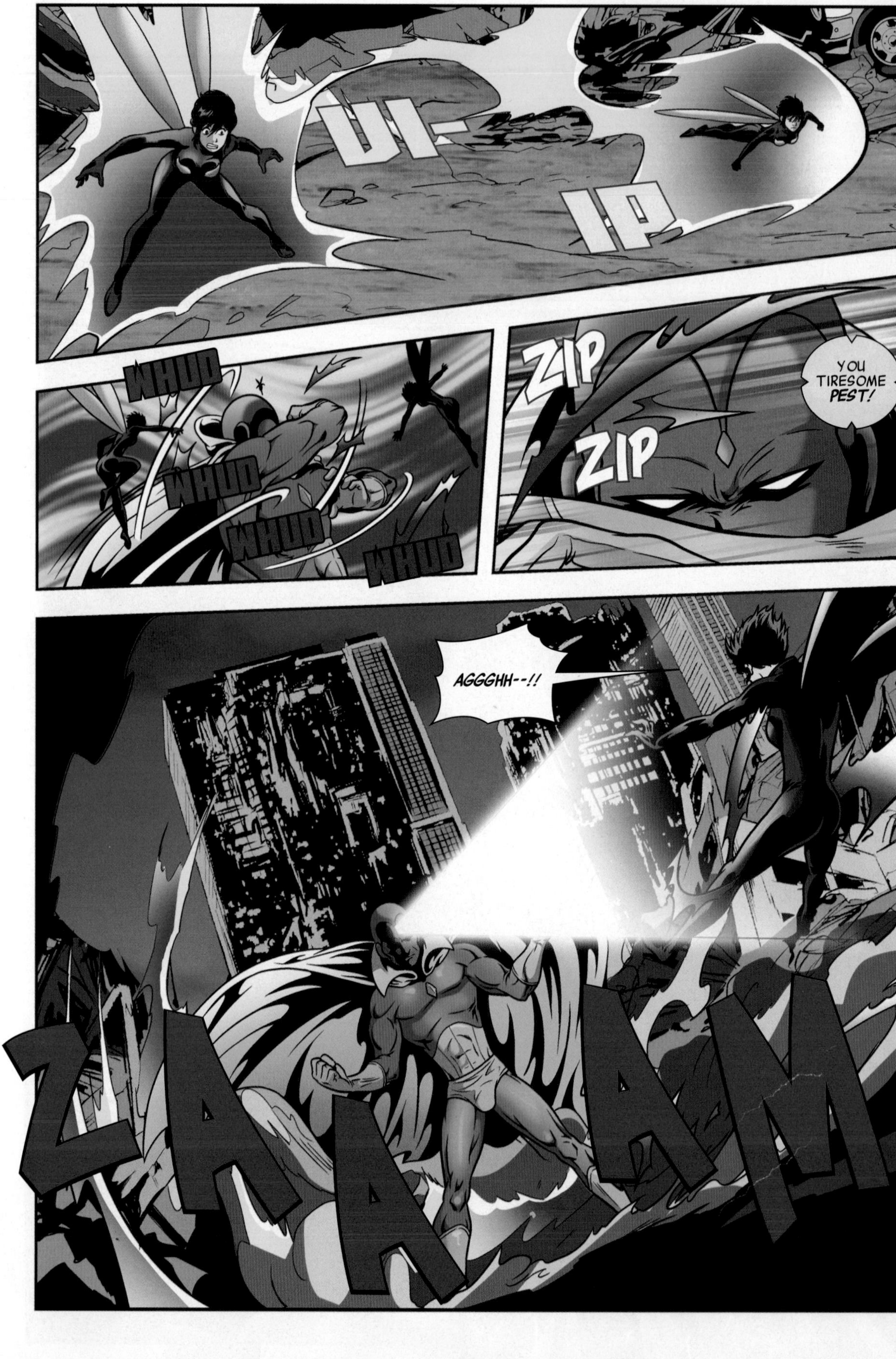
ZI-
IP
WHUD
WHUD
WHUD
WHUD
ZIP
ZIP
YOU TIRESOME PEST!
AGGGHH--!!
ZAAAM

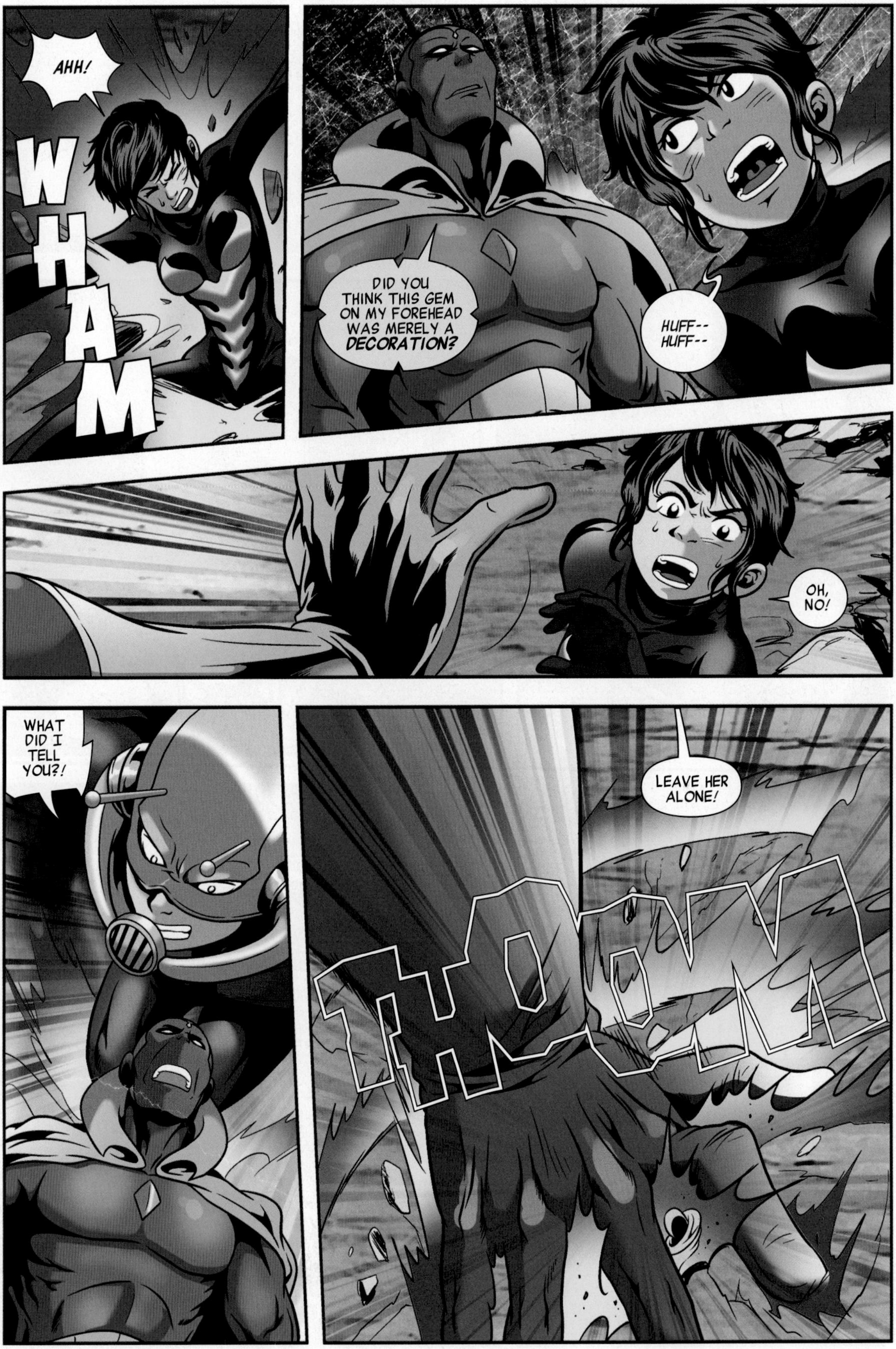
AHH!
WHAM
DID YOU THINK THIS GEM ON MY FOREHEAD WAS MERELY A DECORATION?
HUFF-- HUFF--
OH, NO!
WHAT DID I TELL YOU?!
LEAVE HER ALONE!
THOOM

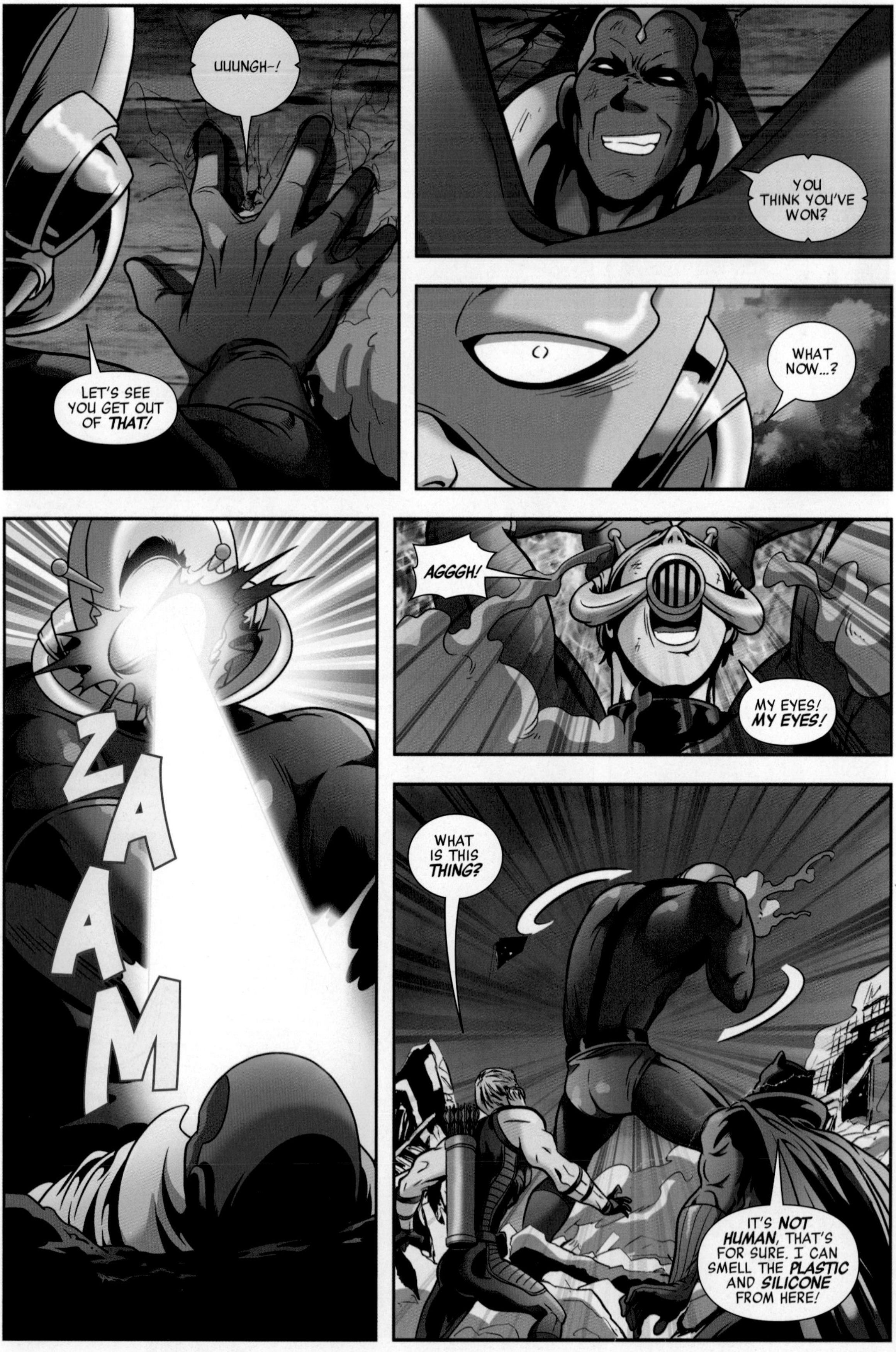
UUUNGH-!
LET'S SEE YOU GET OUT OF THAT!
YOU THINK YOU'VE WON?
WHAT NOW...?
ZAAM
AGGGH!
MY EYES! MY EYES!
WHAT IS THIS THING?
IT'S NOT HUMAN, THAT'S FOR SURE. I CAN SMELL THE PLASTIC AND SILICONE FROM HERE!

I'M THE ONLY ONE WHO CAN GET CLOSE. I'LL SEE WHAT I CAN FIND OUT!

ZIP

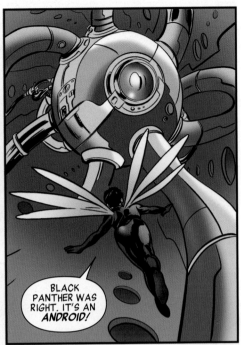

BLACK PANTHER WAS RIGHT. IT'S AN *ANDROID!*

THIS IS WHAT YOU GET FOR UNDERESTIMATING THE *AVENGERS!*

YOU THINK WE'RE WEAK? YOU HAVEN'T SEEN MY *BIO-ENERGY BLAST!*

ZZZZT

ZZZZT

ZZZZT

NO!

ZZZZT

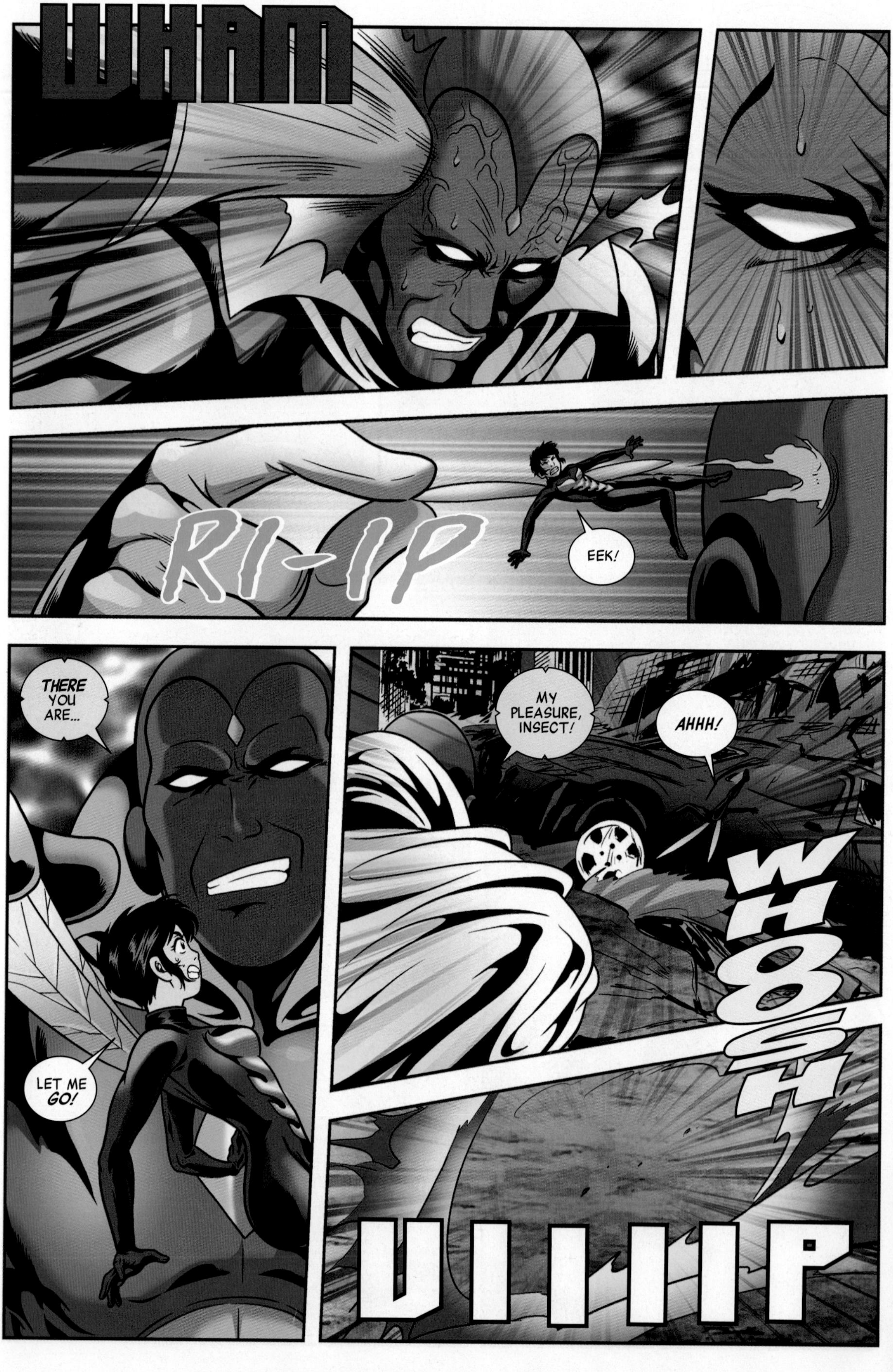
WHAM
RI-IP
EEK!
THERE YOU ARE...
LET ME GO!
MY PLEASURE, INSECT!
AHHH!
WHOOSH
UIIIIP

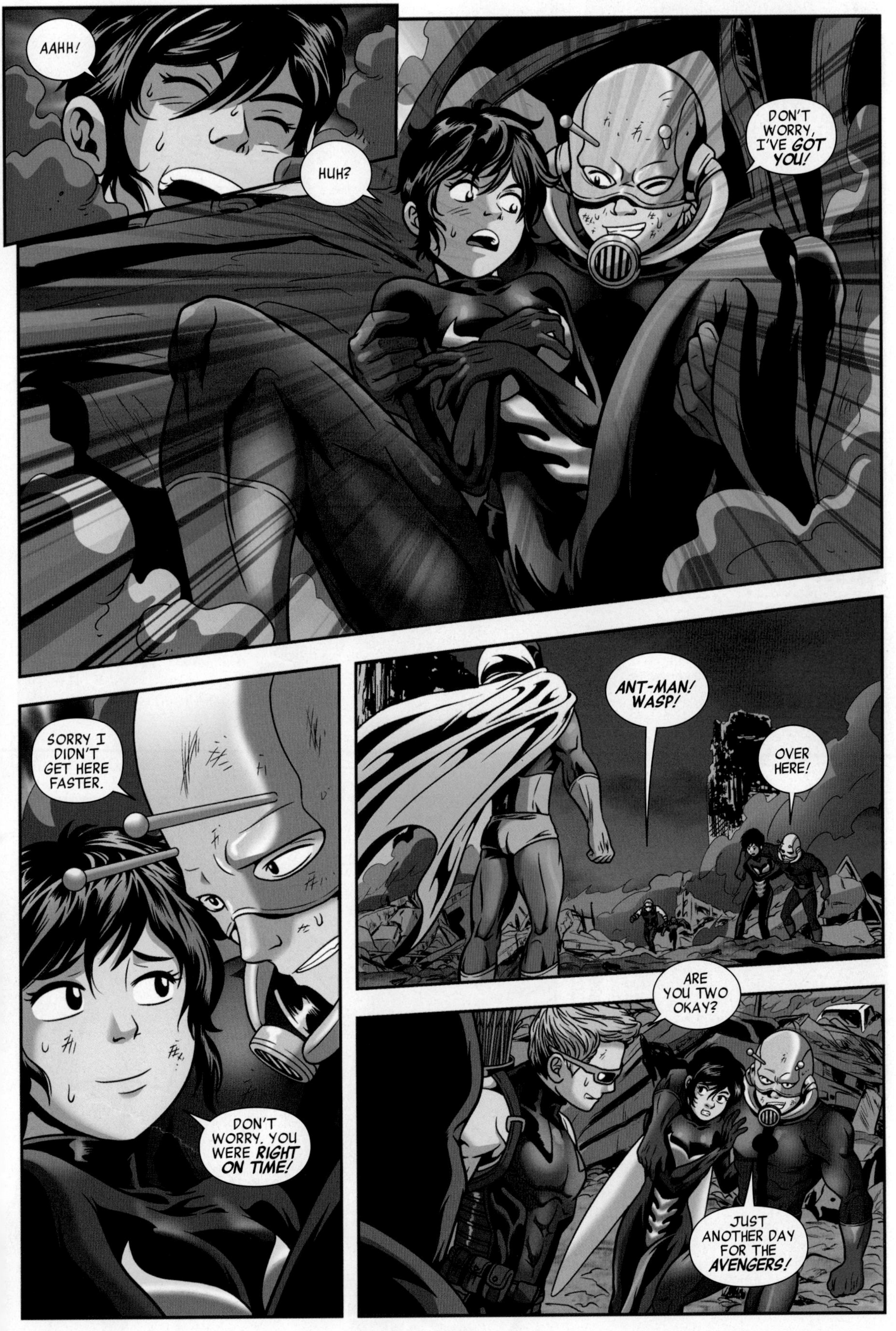
AAHH!
HUH?
DON'T WORRY, I'VE GOT YOU!
SORRY I DIDN'T GET HERE FASTER.
DON'T WORRY. YOU WERE RIGHT ON TIME!
ANT-MAN! WASP!
OVER HERE!
ARE YOU TWO OKAY?
JUST ANOTHER DAY FOR THE AVENGERS!

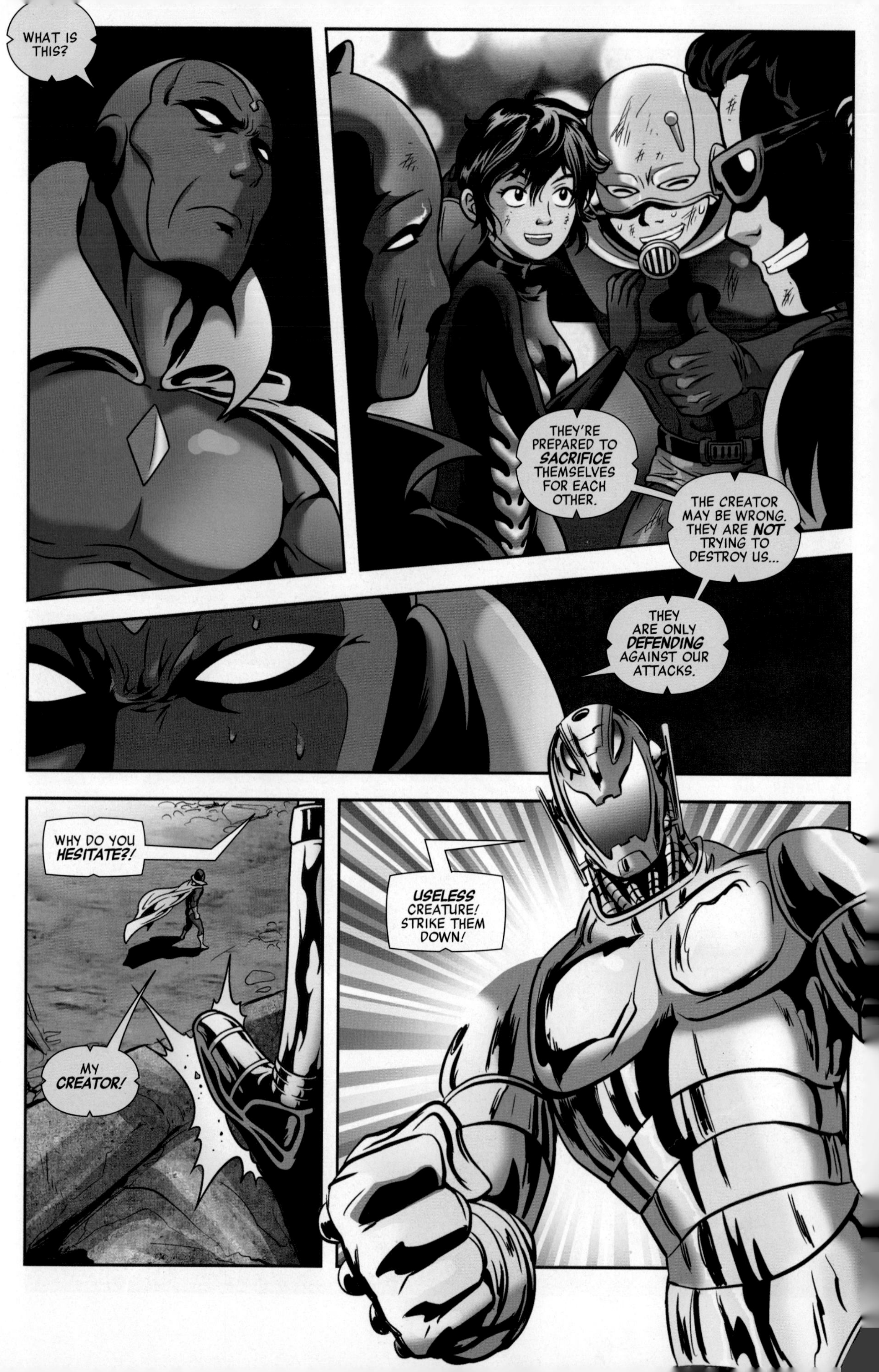

WHAT IS THIS?
THEY'RE PREPARED TO ***SACRIFICE*** THEMSELVES FOR EACH OTHER.
THE CREATOR MAY BE WRONG. THEY ARE ***NOT*** TRYING TO DESTROY US...
THEY ARE ONLY ***DEFENDING*** AGAINST OUR ATTACKS.
WHY DO YOU ***HESITATE?!***
MY ***CREATOR!***
USELESS CREATURE! STRIKE THEM DOWN!

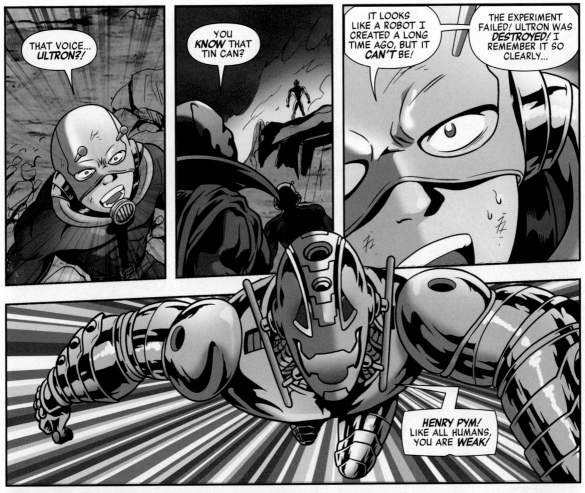

THAT VOICE... ULTRON?!

YOU *KNOW* THAT TIN CAN?

IT LOOKS LIKE A ROBOT I CREATED A LONG TIME AGO, BUT IT *CAN'T* BE!

THE EXPERIMENT FAILED! ULTRON WAS *DESTROYED!* I REMEMBER IT SO CLEARLY...

HENRY PYM! LIKE ALL HUMANS, YOU ARE *WEAK!*

HOK

AGGH!

YOU ARE RULED BY *EMOTIONS* AND THE FRAILTY OF YOUR *ORGANIC FORM!*

WHAM

WHUD

KRAK

UGH!

HUMAN WEAKNESS WILL BE REPLACED BY *ROBOTIC PERFECTION!*

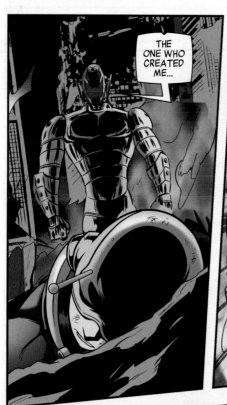

THE ONE WHO CREATED ME...

I WILL FINISH *YOU* FIRST!

VICTORY WILL BE MINE!

YOU KNOW THIS IS WRONG. I CAN SEE IT. *PLEASE*...

STOP HIM.

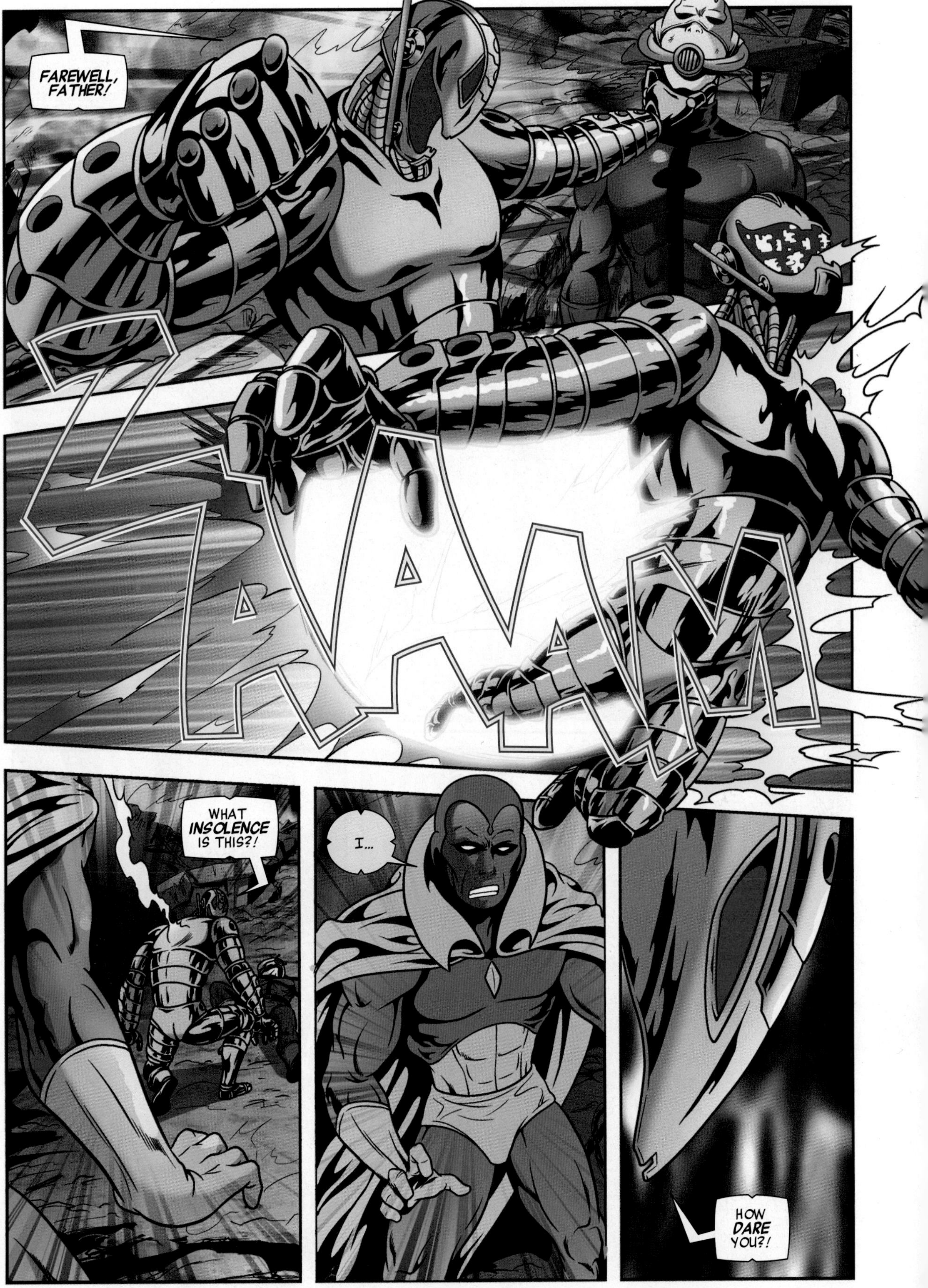
FAREWELL, FATHER!
ZZAAM
WHAT INSOLENCE IS THIS?!
I...
HOW DARE YOU?!

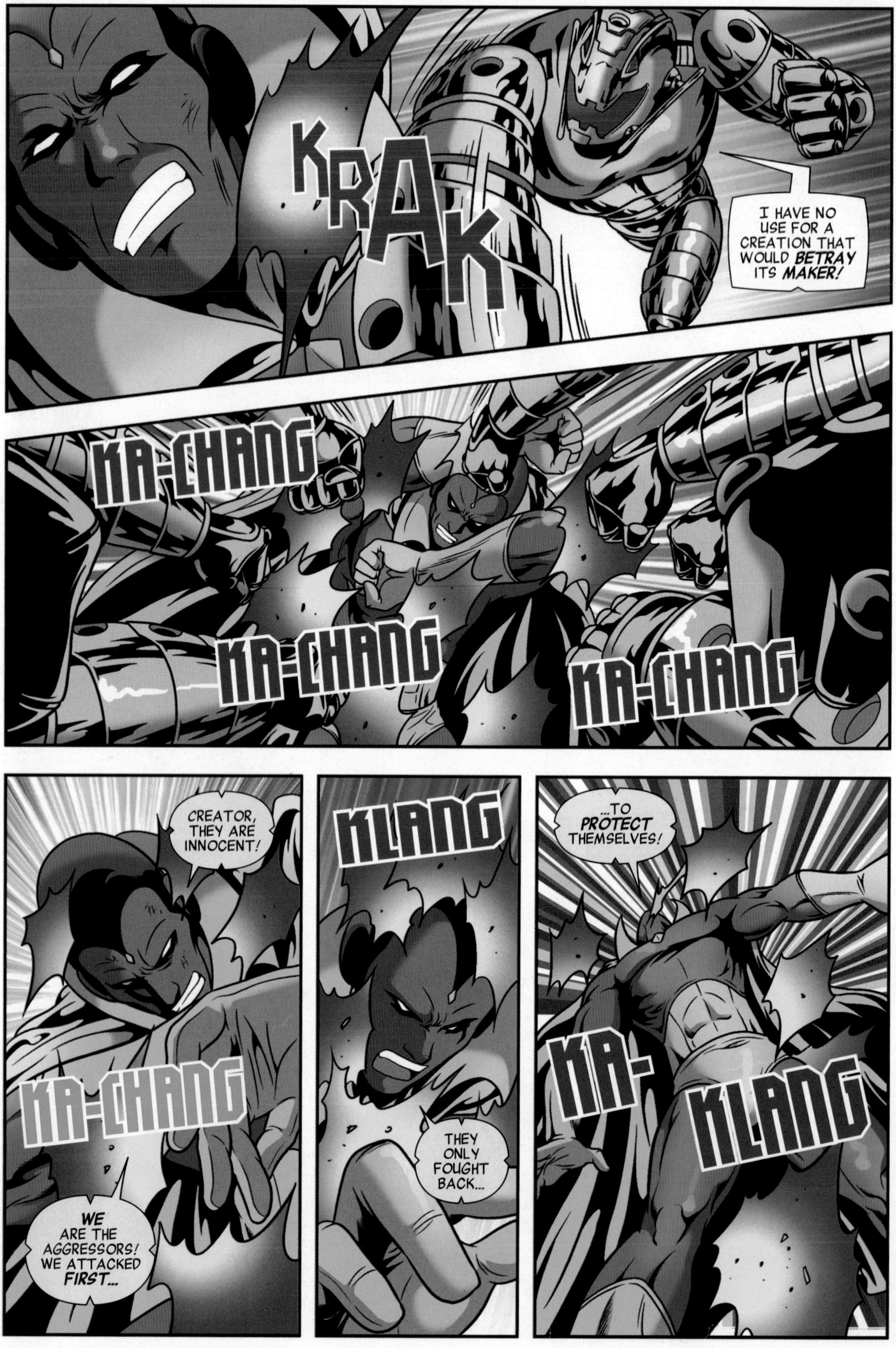
KRAK
I HAVE NO USE FOR A CREATION THAT WOULD BETRAY ITS MAKER!
KA-CHANG
KA-CHANG
KA-CHANG
CREATOR, THEY ARE INNOCENT!
KA-CHANG
WE ARE THE AGGRESSORS! WE ATTACKED FIRST...
KLANG
THEY ONLY FOUGHT BACK...
...TO PROTECT THEMSELVES!
KA-KLANG

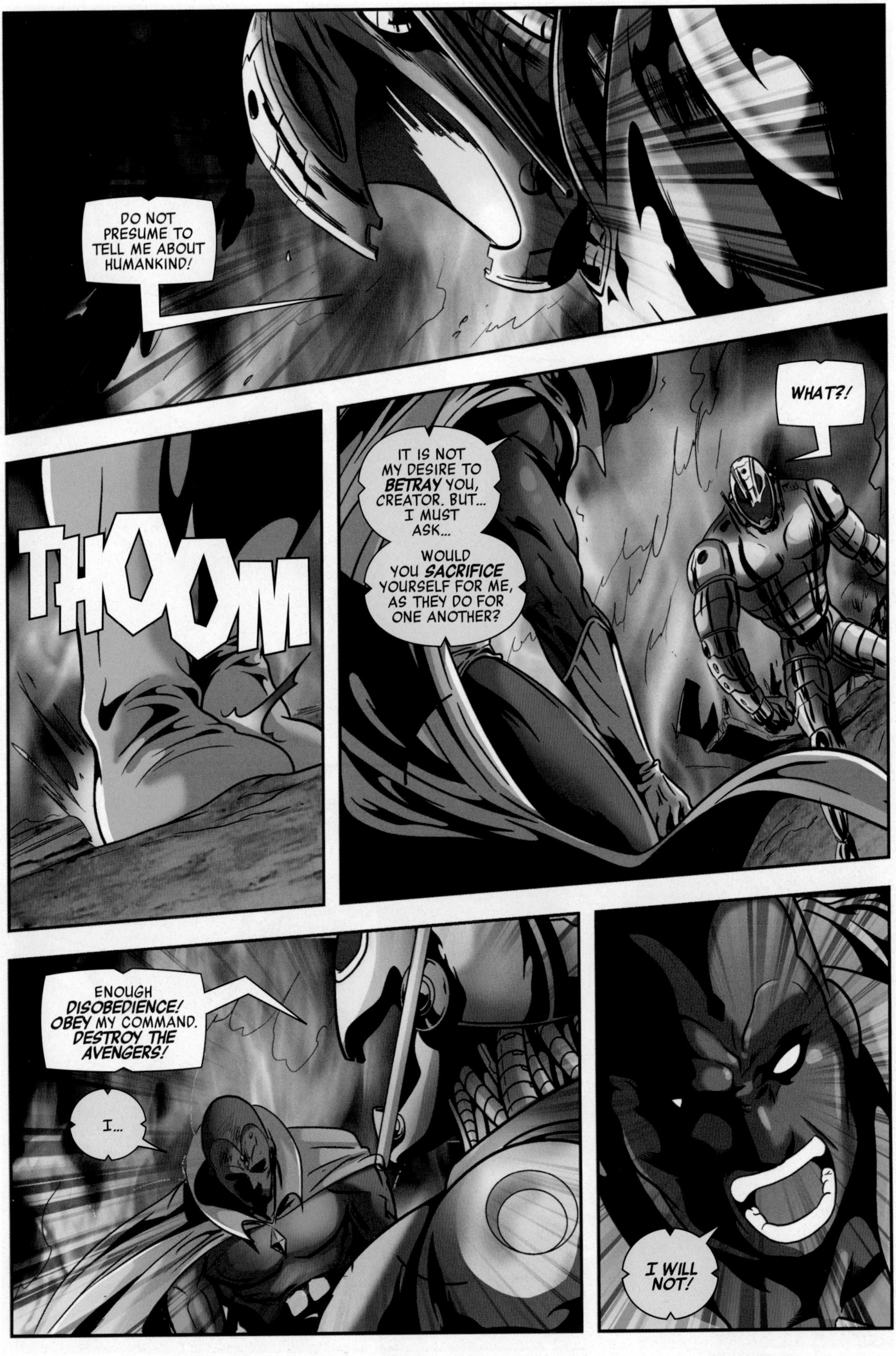
DO NOT PRESUME TO TELL ME ABOUT HUMANKIND!
THOOM
WHAT?!
IT IS NOT MY DESIRE TO BETRAY YOU, CREATOR. BUT... I MUST ASK...
WOULD YOU SACRIFICE YOURSELF FOR ME, AS THEY DO FOR ONE ANOTHER?
ENOUGH DISOBEDIENCE! OBEY MY COMMAND. DESTROY THE AVENGERS!
I...
I WILL NOT!

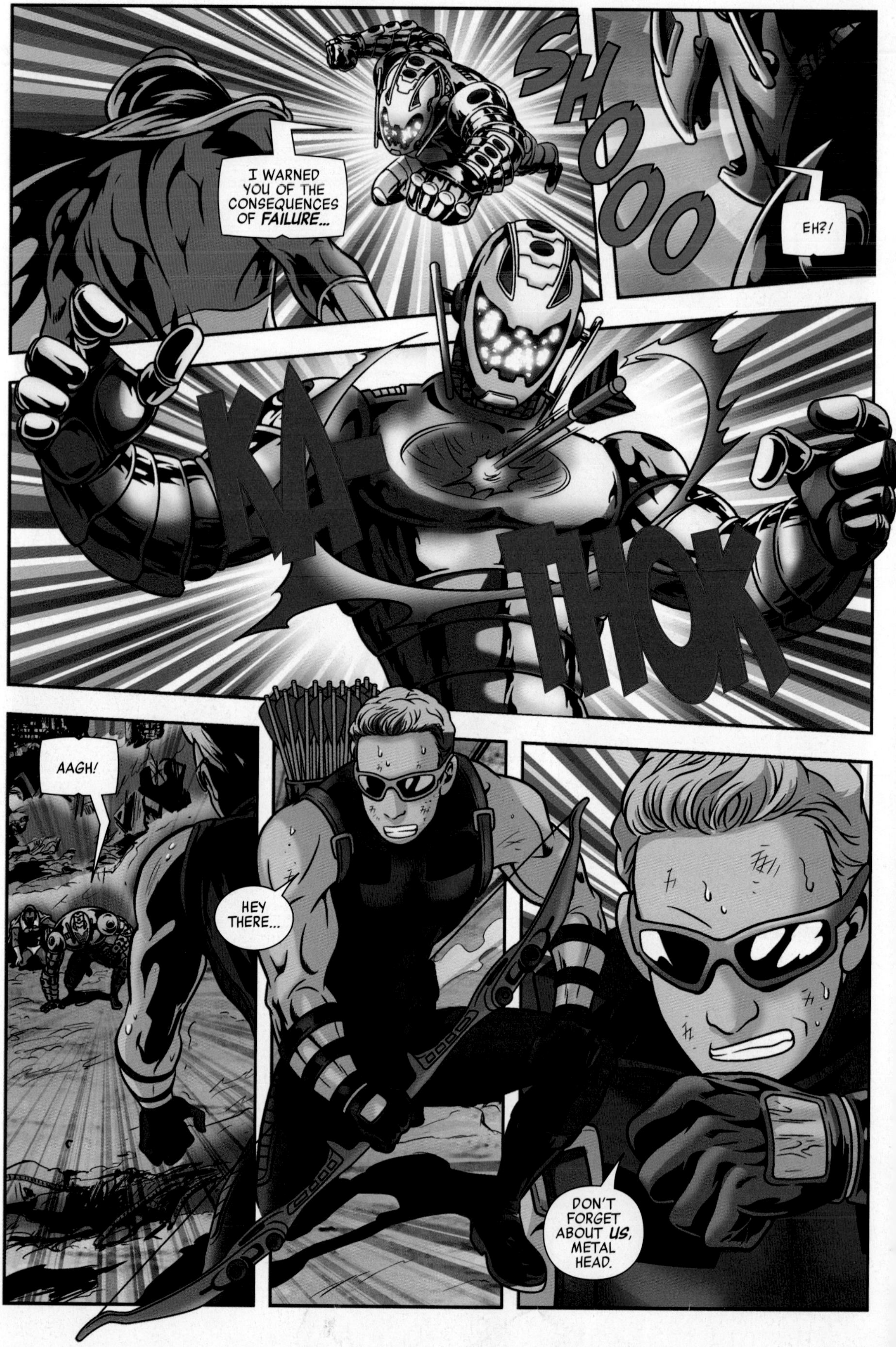

I WARNED YOU OF THE CONSEQUENCES OF FAILURE...
SHOOOO
EH?!
KA-THOK
AAGH!
HEY THERE...
DON'T FORGET ABOUT US, METAL HEAD.

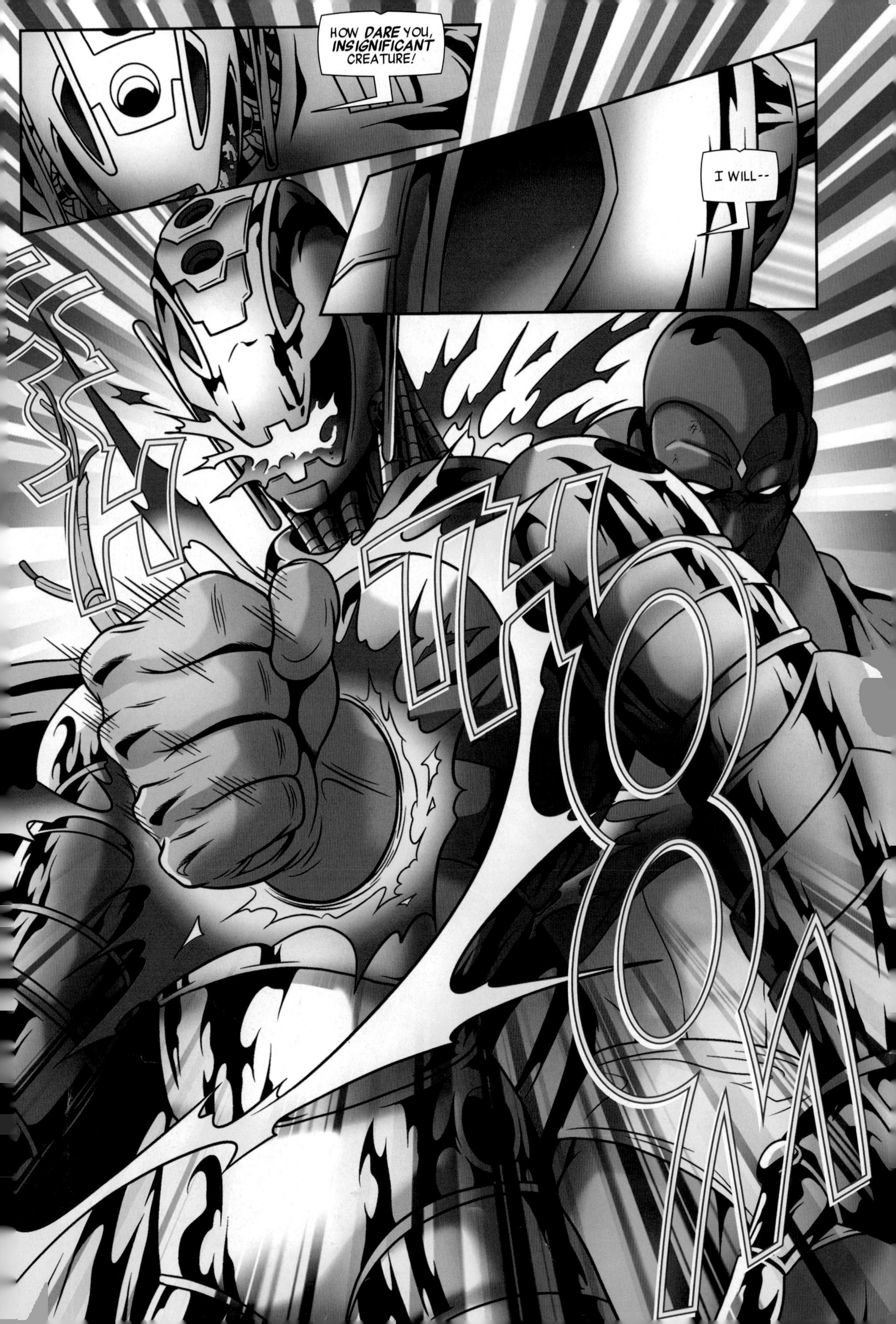

HOW **DARE** YOU, ***INSIGNIFICANT*** CREATURE!
I WILL--

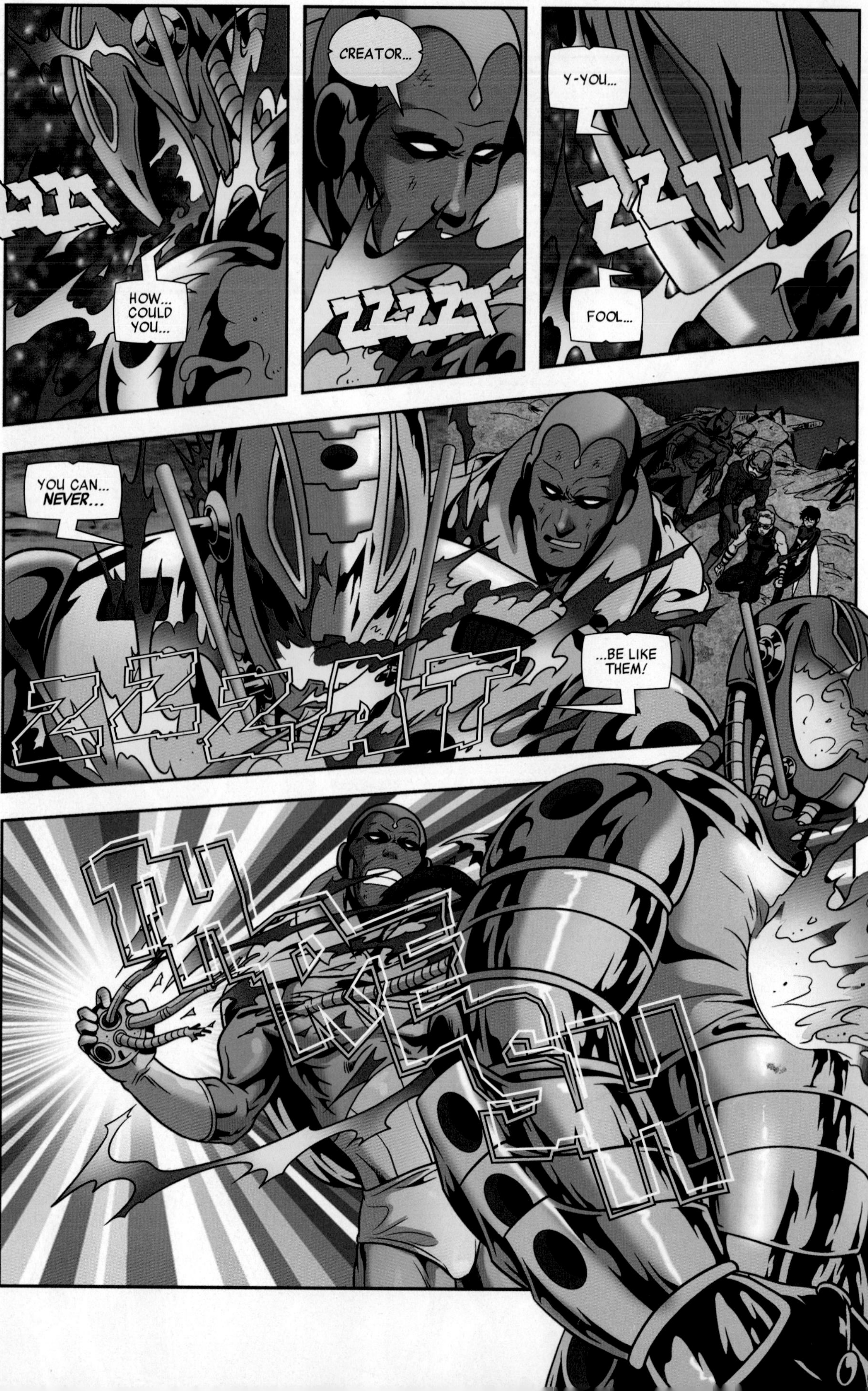

HOW... COULD YOU...
CREATOR...
Y-YOU...
FOOL...
YOU CAN... **NEVER...**
...BE LIKE THEM!

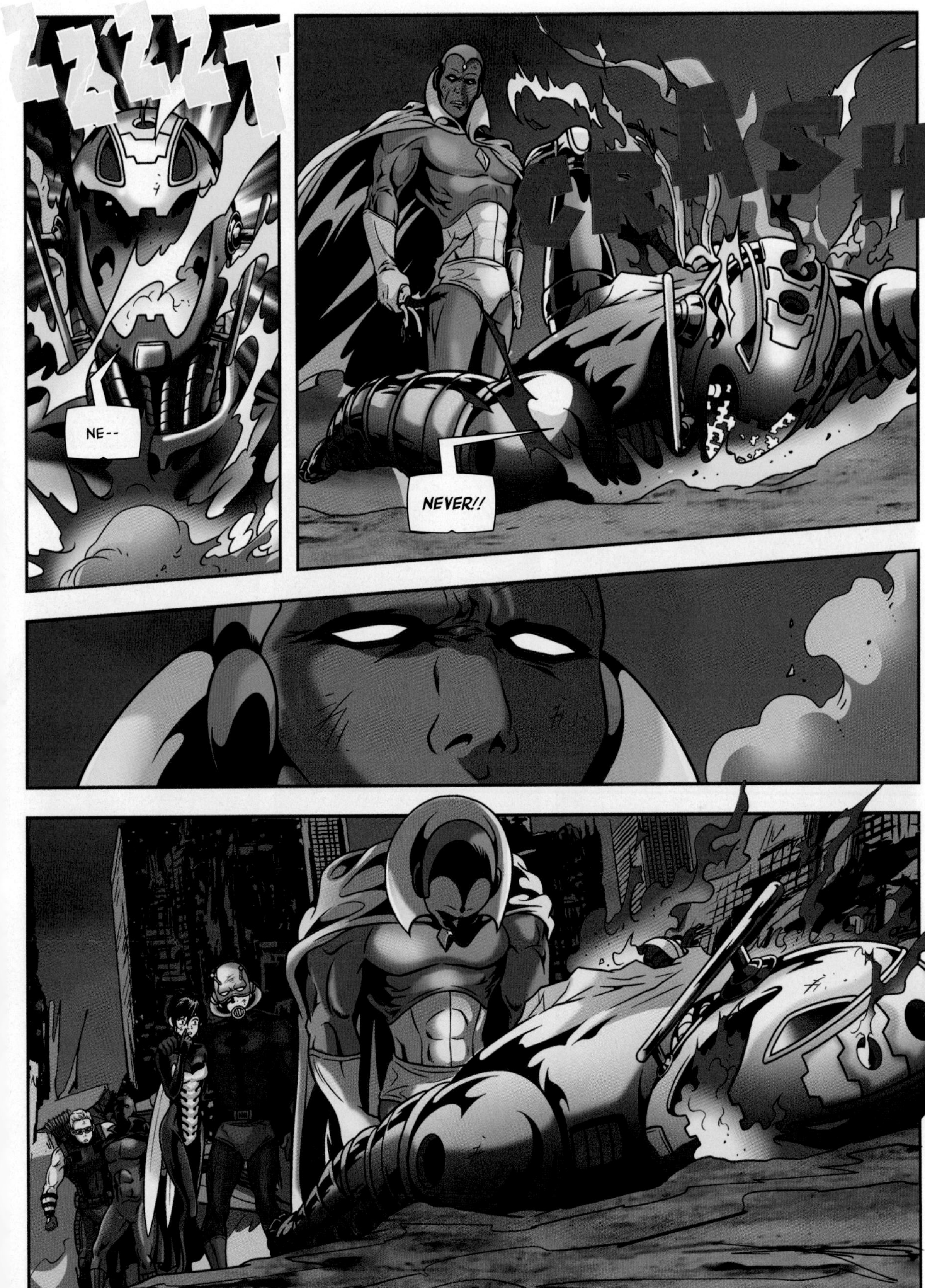
ZZZZT
NE--
CRASH
NEVER!!

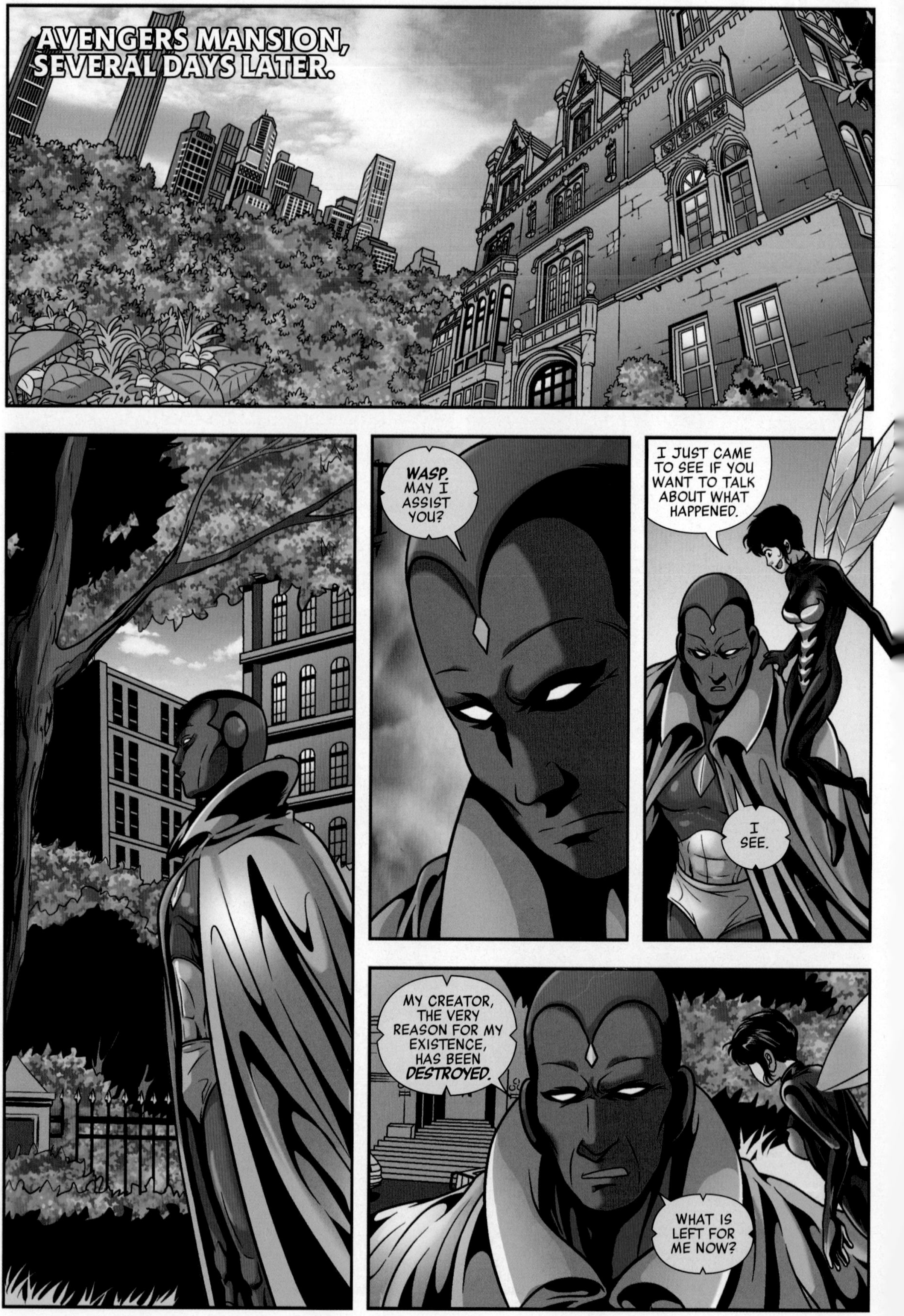
AVENGERS MANSION, SEVERAL DAYS LATER.
WASP. MAY I ASSIST YOU?
I JUST CAME TO SEE IF YOU WANT TO TALK ABOUT WHAT HAPPENED.
I SEE.
MY CREATOR, THE VERY REASON FOR MY EXISTENCE, HAS BEEN DESTROYED.
WHAT IS LEFT FOR ME NOW?

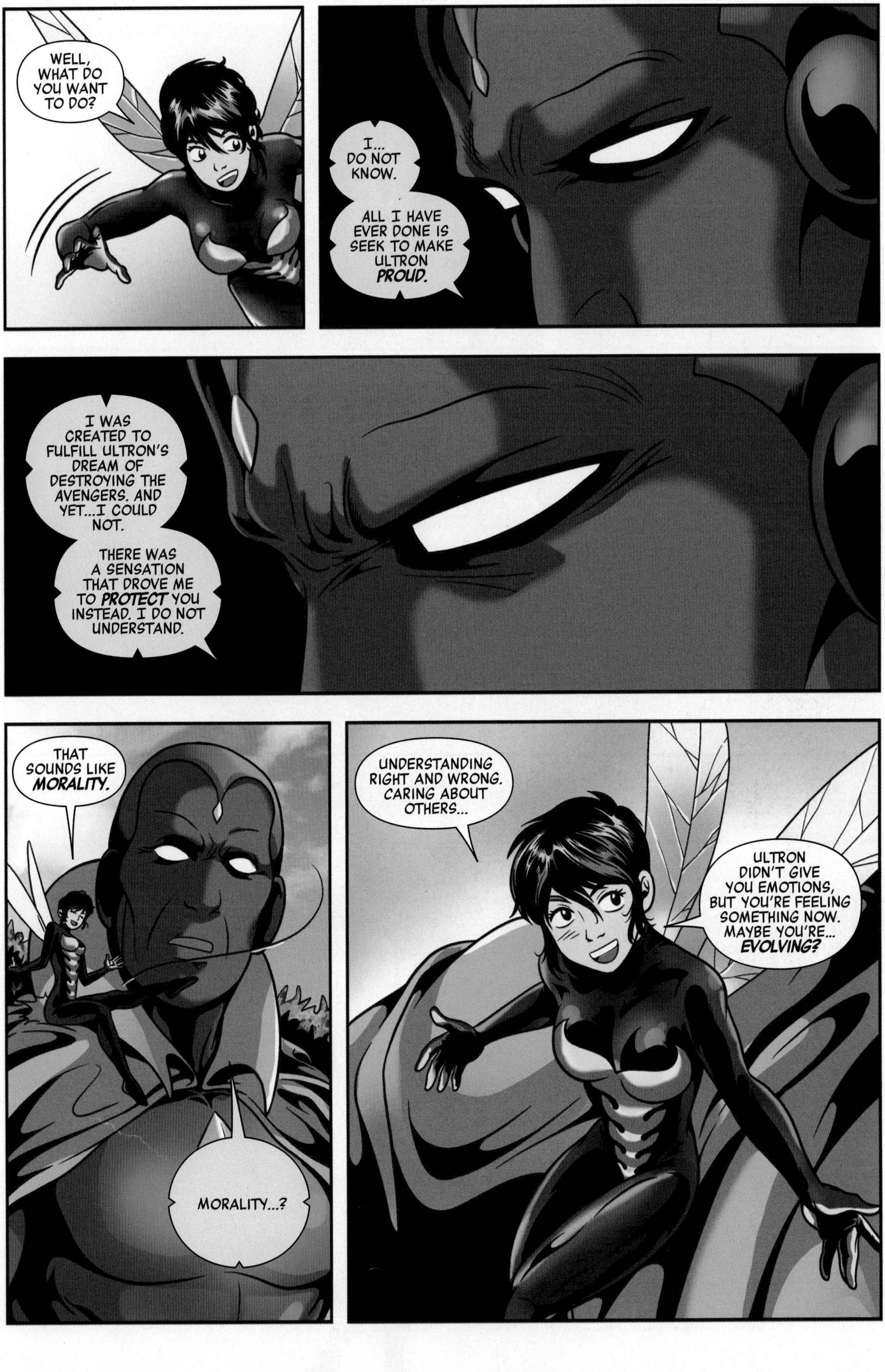

WELL, WHAT DO YOU WANT TO DO?
I... DO NOT KNOW.
ALL I HAVE EVER DONE IS SEEK TO MAKE ULTRON **PROUD.**
I WAS CREATED TO FULFILL ULTRON'S DREAM OF DESTROYING THE AVENGERS. AND YET...I COULD NOT.
THERE WAS A SENSATION THAT DROVE ME TO **PROTECT** YOU INSTEAD. I DO NOT UNDERSTAND.
THAT SOUNDS LIKE **MORALITY.**
MORALITY...?
UNDERSTANDING RIGHT AND WRONG. CARING ABOUT OTHERS...
ULTRON DIDN'T GIVE YOU EMOTIONS, BUT YOU'RE FEELING SOMETHING NOW. MAYBE YOU'RE... **EVOLVING?**

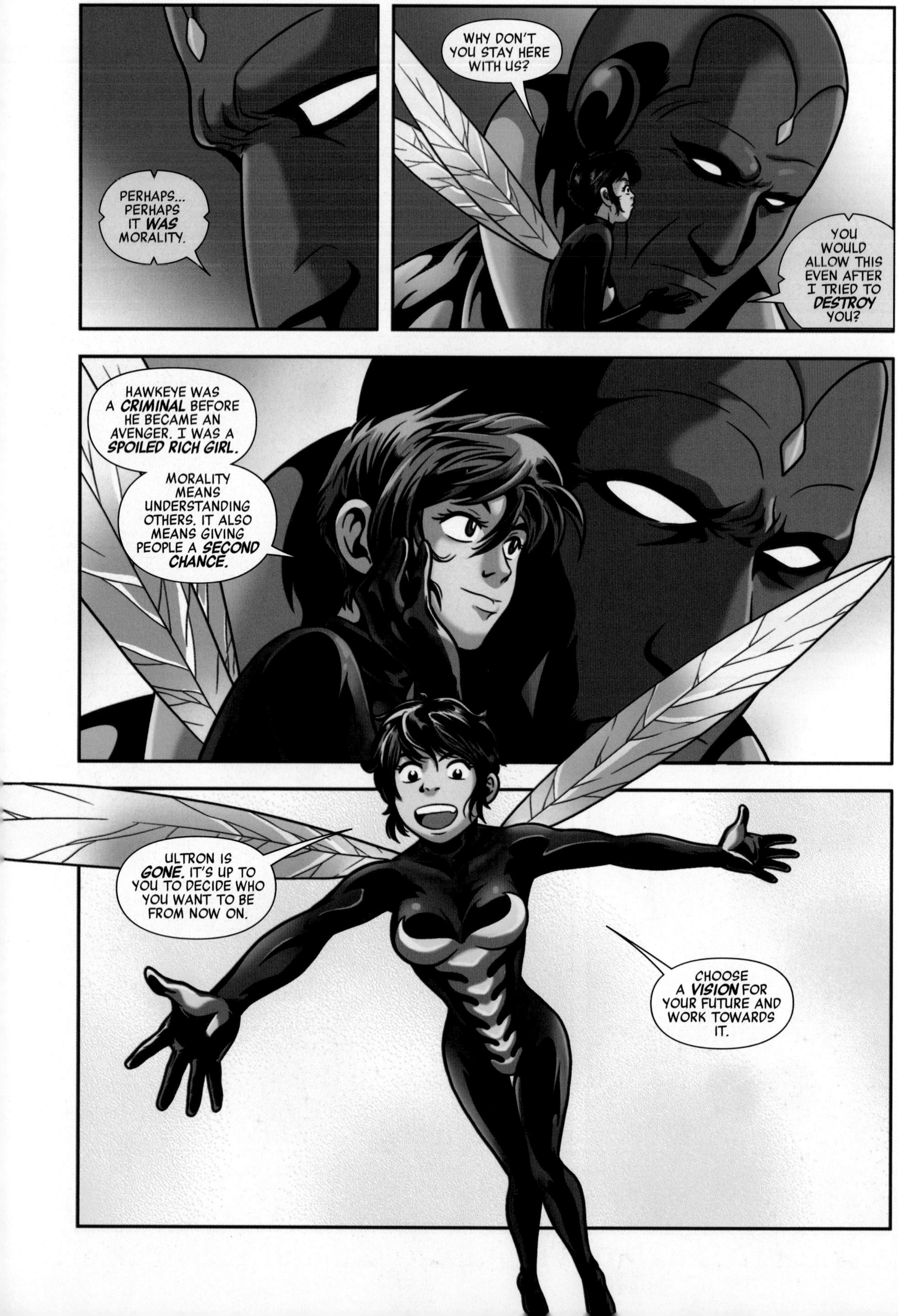
PERHAPS... PERHAPS IT WAS MORALITY.
WHY DON'T YOU STAY HERE WITH US?
YOU WOULD ALLOW THIS EVEN AFTER I TRIED TO DESTROY YOU?
HAWKEYE WAS A CRIMINAL BEFORE HE BECAME AN AVENGER. I WAS A SPOILED RICH GIRL.
MORALITY MEANS UNDERSTANDING OTHERS. IT ALSO MEANS GIVING PEOPLE A SECOND CHANCE.
ULTRON IS GONE. IT'S UP TO YOU TO DECIDE WHO YOU WANT TO BE FROM NOW ON.
CHOOSE A VISION FOR YOUR FUTURE AND WORK TOWARDS IT.

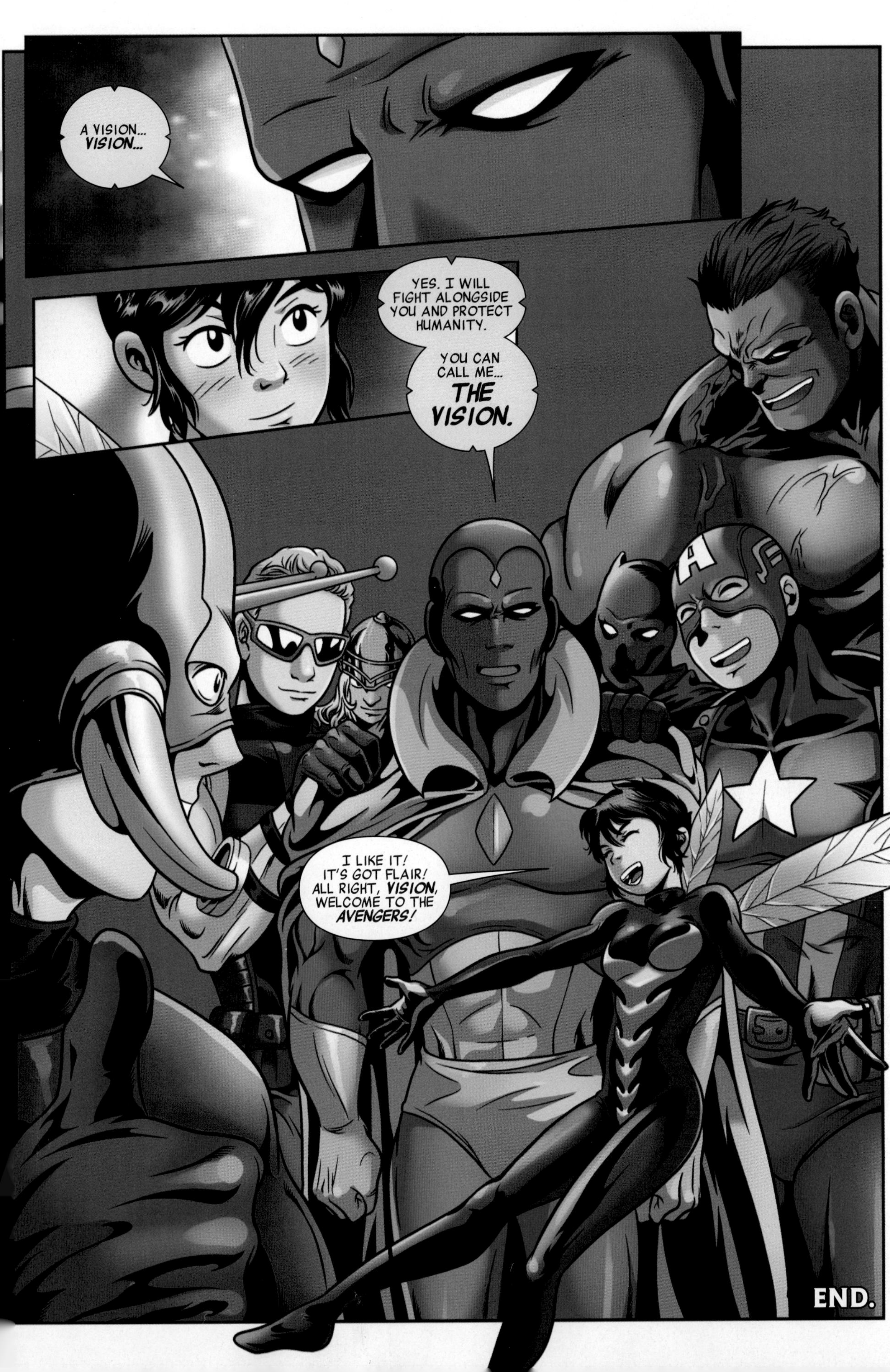
A VISION... VISION...
YES. I WILL FIGHT ALONGSIDE YOU AND PROTECT HUMANITY.
YOU CAN CALL ME... THE VISION.
I LIKE IT! IT'S GOT FLAIR! ALL RIGHT, VISION, WELCOME TO THE AVENGERS!
END.

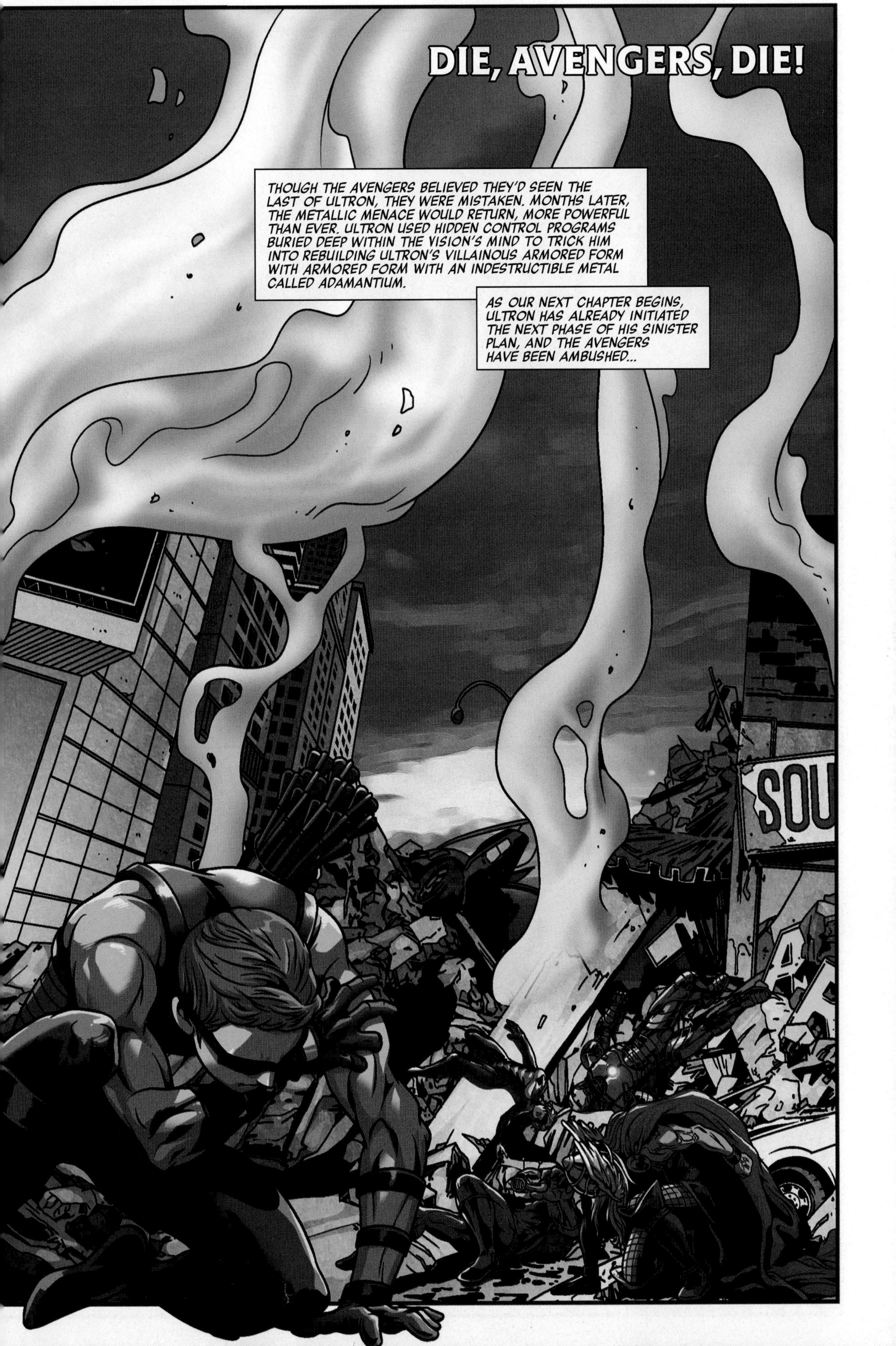
DIE, AVENGERS, DIE!
THOUGH THE AVENGERS BELIEVED THEY'D SEEN THE LAST OF ULTRON, THEY WERE MISTAKEN. MONTHS LATER, THE METALLIC MENACE WOULD RETURN, MORE POWERFUL THAN EVER. ULTRON USED HIDDEN CONTROL PROGRAMS BURIED DEEP WITHIN THE VISION'S MIND TO TRICK HIM INTO REBUILDING ULTRON'S VILLAINOUS ARMORED FORM WITH ARMORED FORM WITH AN INDESTRUCTIBLE METAL CALLED ADAMANTIUM.
AS OUR NEXT CHAPTER BEGINS, ULTRON HAS ALREADY INITIATED THE NEXT PHASE OF HIS SINISTER PLAN, AND THE AVENGERS HAVE BEEN AMBUSHED...
SOU

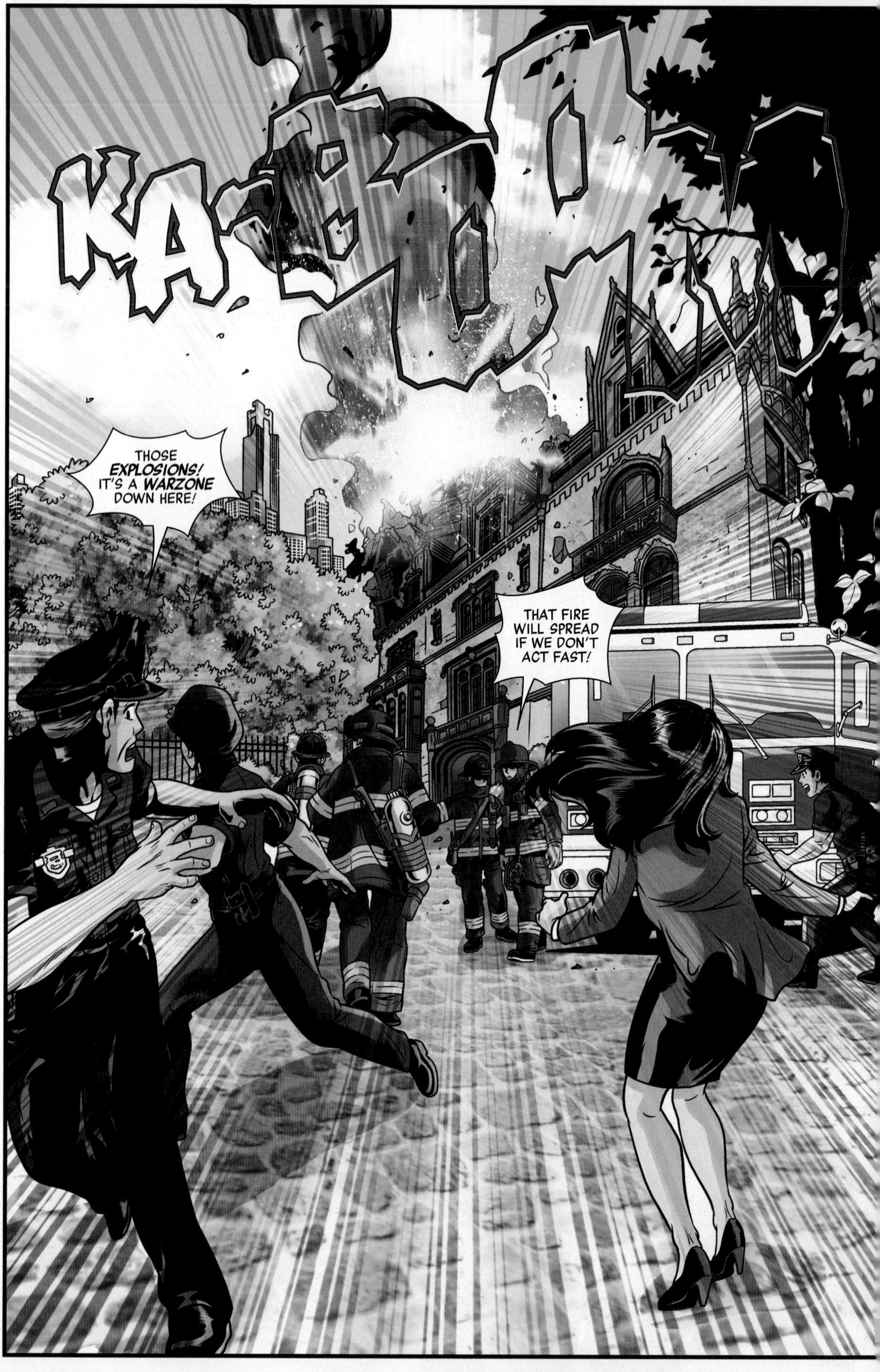
KA-BOOM
THOSE EXPLOSIONS! IT'S A WARZONE DOWN HERE!
THAT FIRE WILL SPREAD IF WE DON'T ACT FAST!

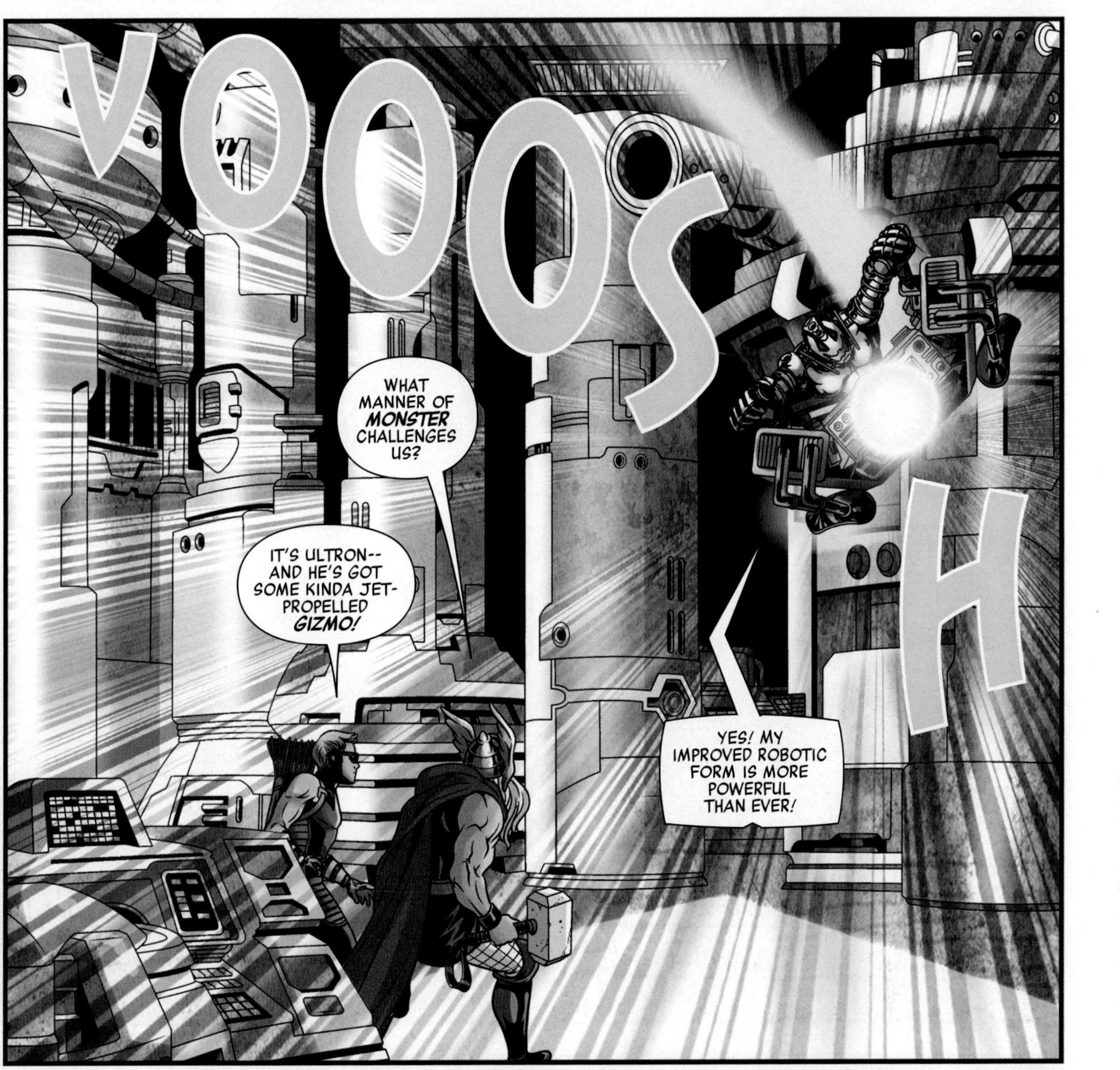
VOOOSH
WHAT MANNER OF MONSTER CHALLENGES US?
IT'S ULTRON--AND HE'S GOT SOME KINDA JET-PROPELLED GIZMO!
YES! MY IMPROVED ROBOTIC FORM IS MORE POWERFUL THAN EVER!

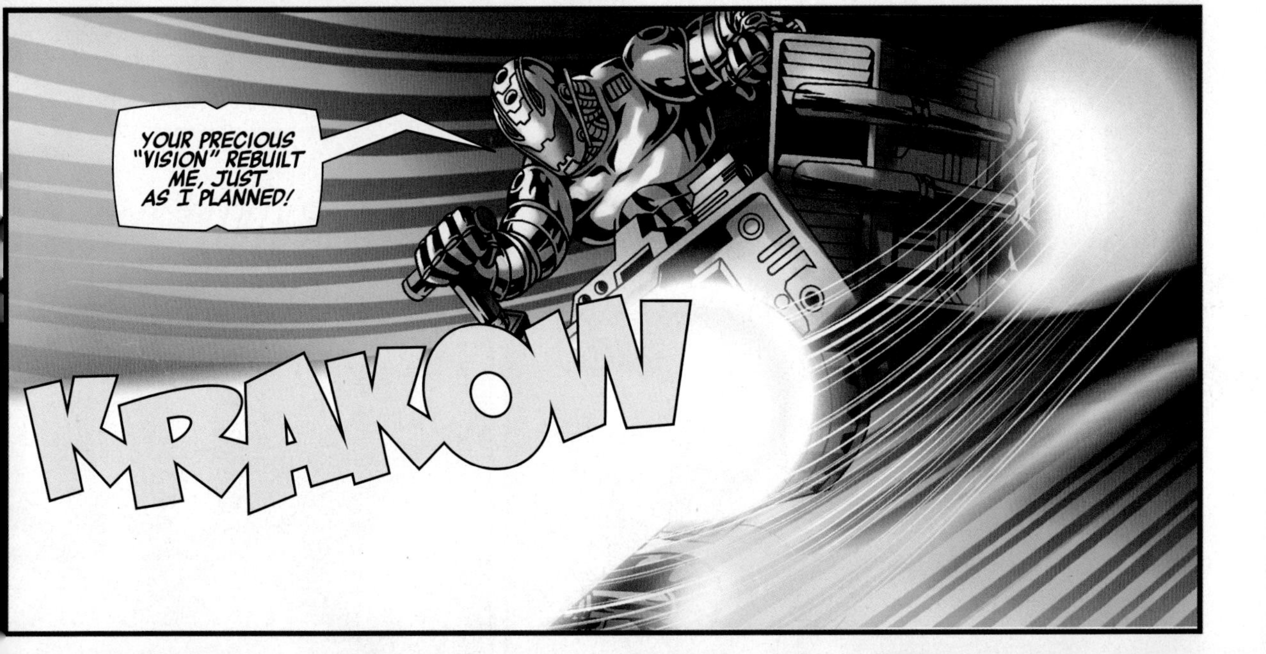
YOUR PRECIOUS "VISION" REBUILT ME, JUST AS I PLANNED!
KRAKOW

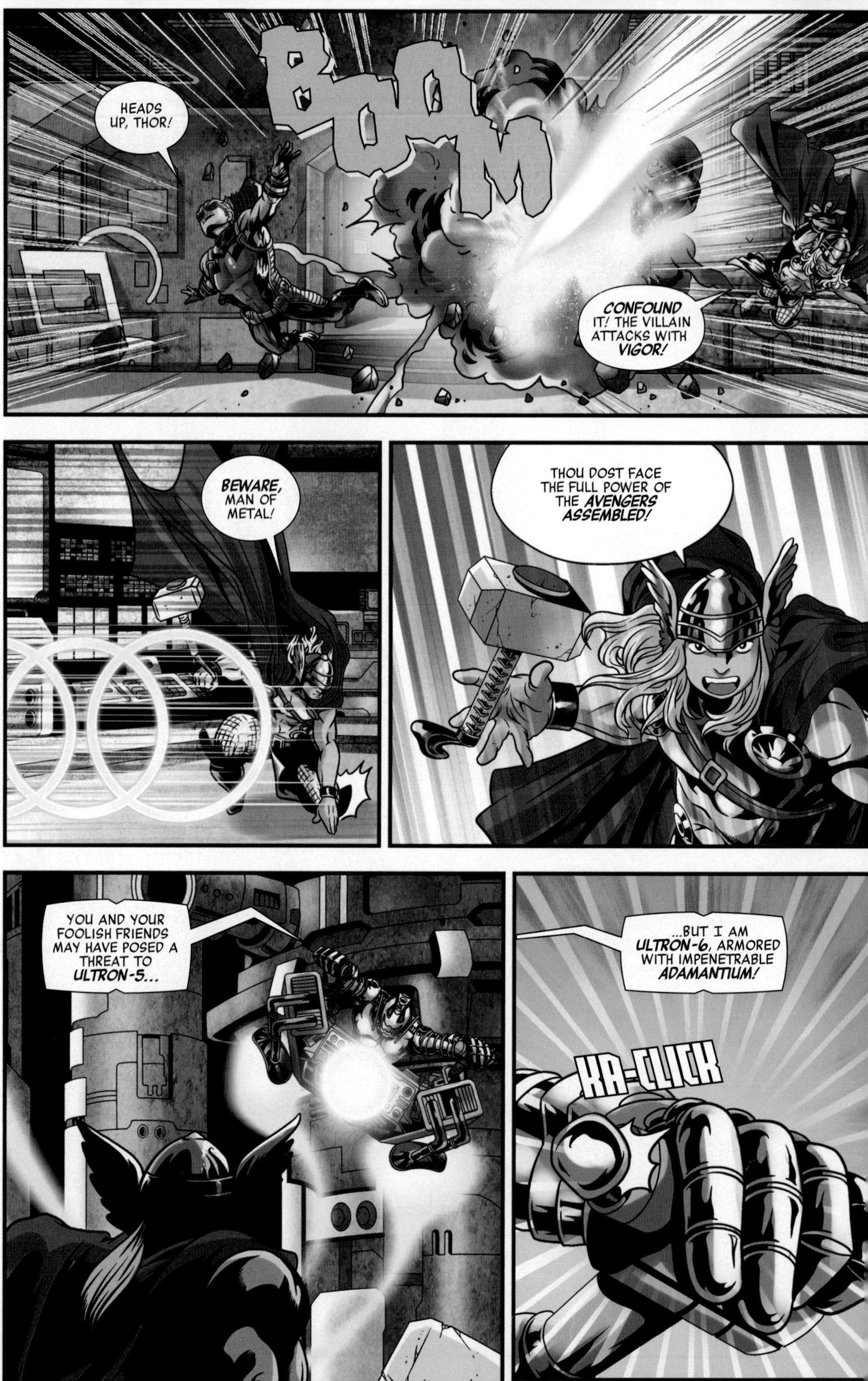
BOOM
HEADS UP, THOR!
CONFOUND IT! THE VILLAIN ATTACKS WITH VIGOR!
BEWARE, MAN OF METAL!
THOU DOST FACE THE FULL POWER OF THE AVENGERS ASSEMBLED!
YOU AND YOUR FOOLISH FRIENDS MAY HAVE POSED A THREAT TO ULTRON-5...
...BUT I AM ULTRON-6, ARMORED WITH IMPENETRABLE ADAMANTIUM!
KA-CLICK

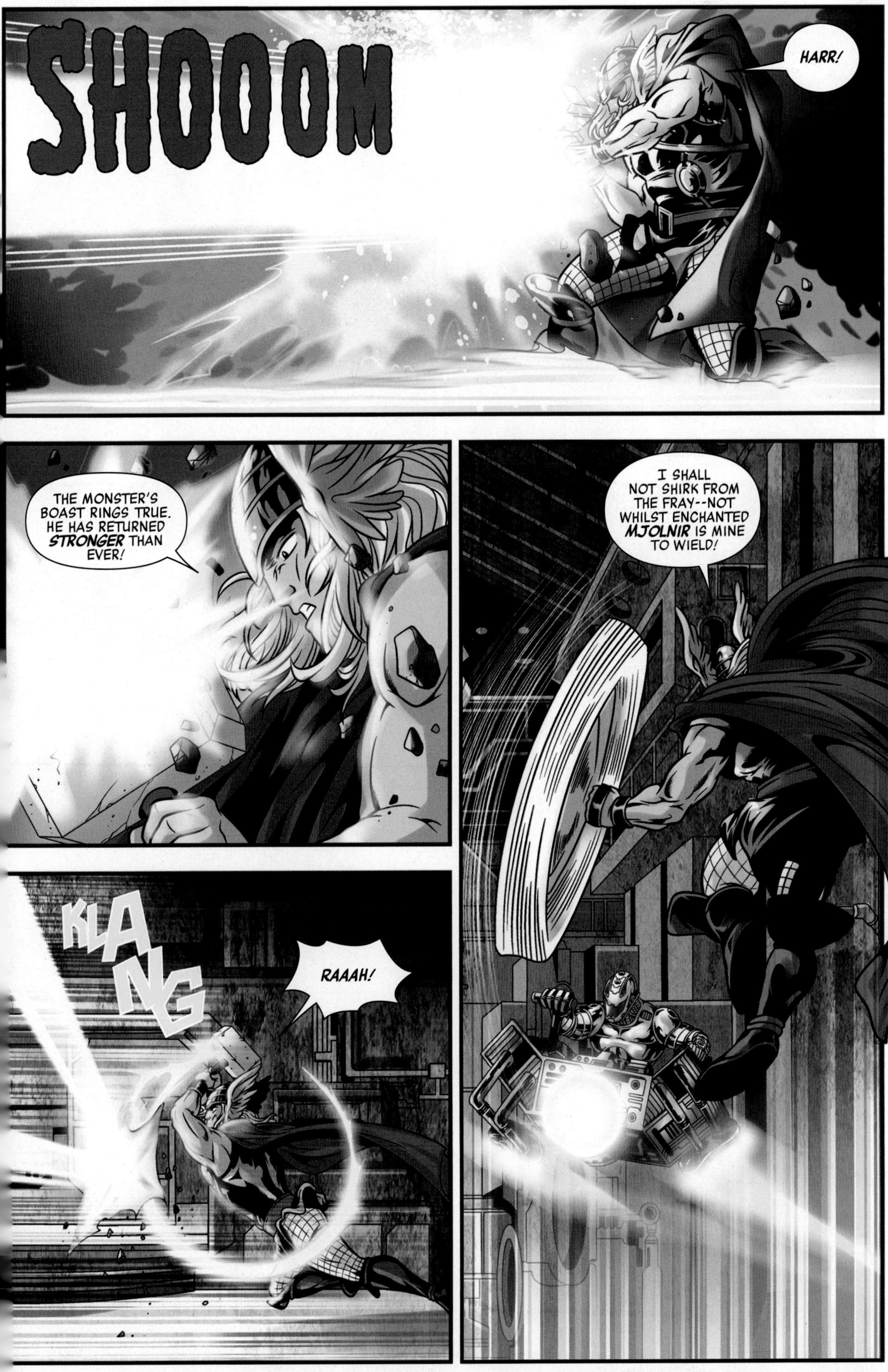
SHOOOM
HARR!
THE MONSTER'S BOAST RINGS TRUE. HE HAS RETURNED STRONGER THAN EVER!
I SHALL NOT SHIRK FROM THE FRAY--NOT WHILST ENCHANTED MJOLNIR IS MINE TO WIELD!
KLANG
RAAAH!

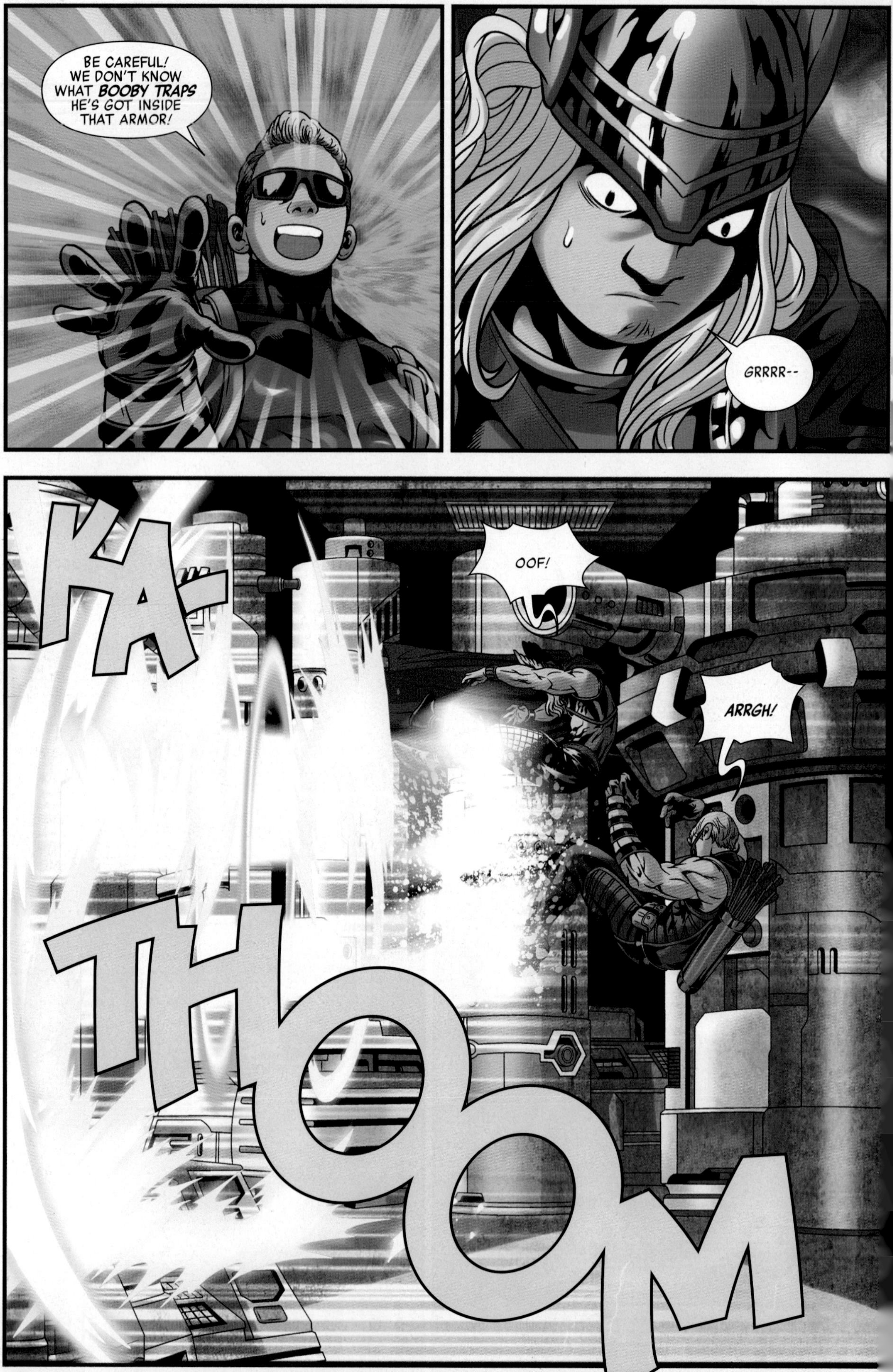
BE CAREFUL! WE DON'T KNOW WHAT **BOOBY TRAPS** HE'S GOT INSIDE THAT ARMOR!
GRRRR--
KA-
OOF!
ARRGH!
THOOOM

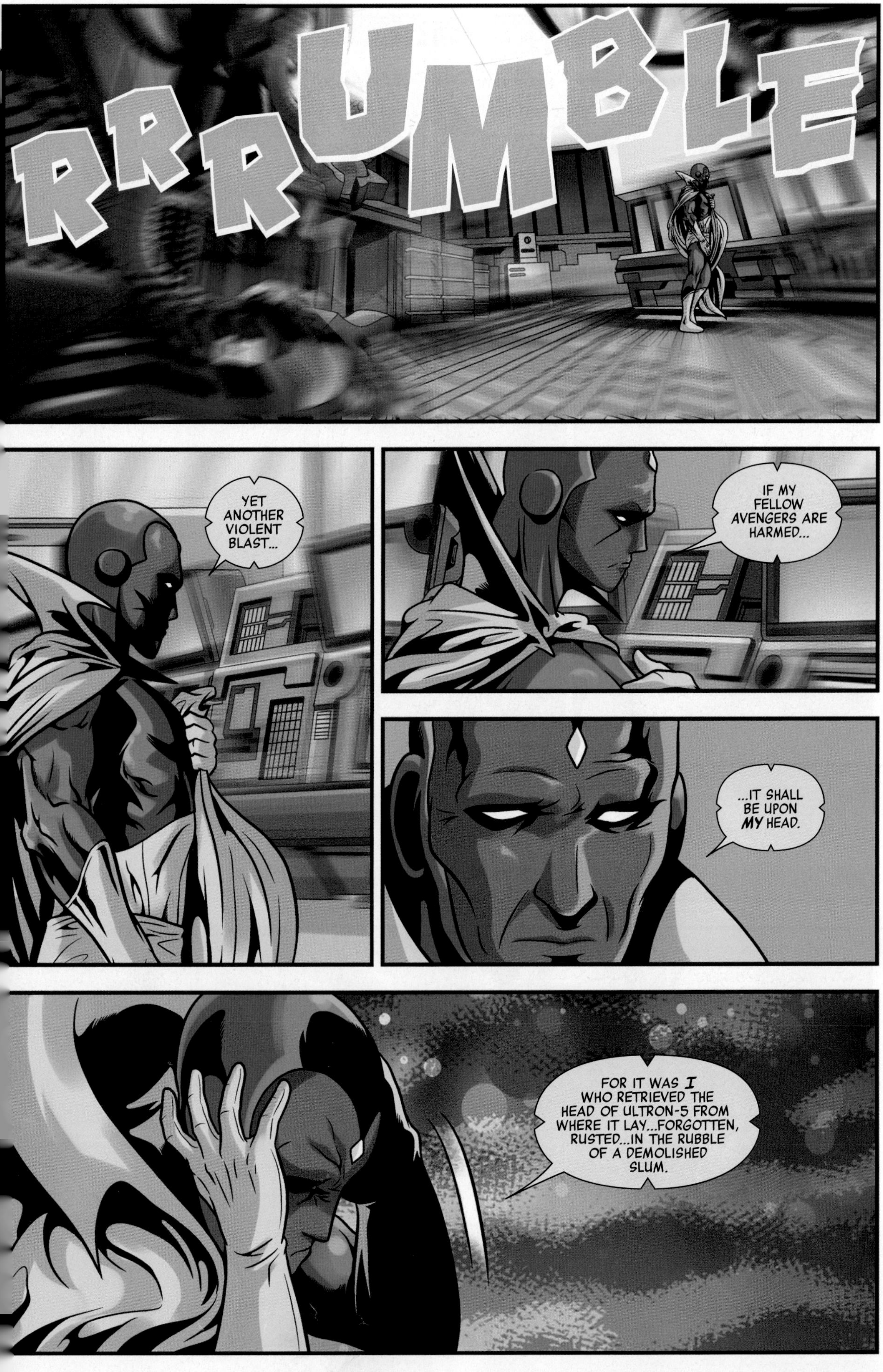
RRRUMBLE
YET ANOTHER VIOLENT BLAST...
IF MY FELLOW AVENGERS ARE HARMED...
...IT SHALL BE UPON MY HEAD.
FOR IT WAS I WHO RETRIEVED THE HEAD OF ULTRON-5 FROM WHERE IT LAY...FORGOTTEN, RUSTED...IN THE RUBBLE OF A DEMOLISHED SLUM.

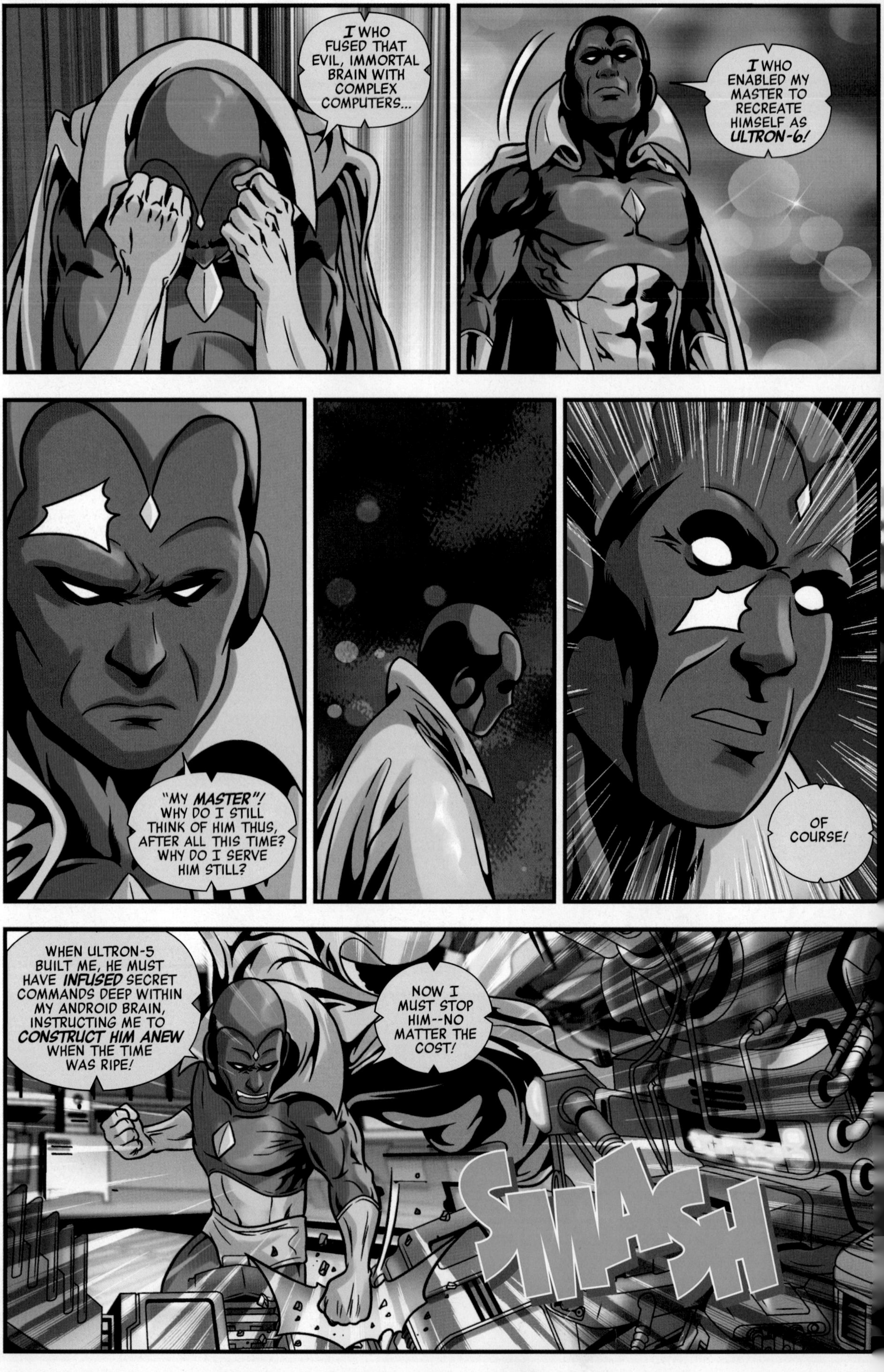
I WHO FUSED THAT EVIL, IMMORTAL BRAIN WITH COMPLEX COMPUTERS...
I WHO ENABLED MY MASTER TO RECREATE HIMSELF AS ULTRON-6!
"MY MASTER"! WHY DO I STILL THINK OF HIM THUS, AFTER ALL THIS TIME? WHY DO I SERVE HIM STILL?
OF COURSE!
WHEN ULTRON-5 BUILT ME, HE MUST HAVE INFUSED SECRET COMMANDS DEEP WITHIN MY ANDROID BRAIN, INSTRUCTING ME TO CONSTRUCT HIM ANEW WHEN THE TIME WAS RIPE!
NOW I MUST STOP HIM--NO MATTER THE COST!
SMASH

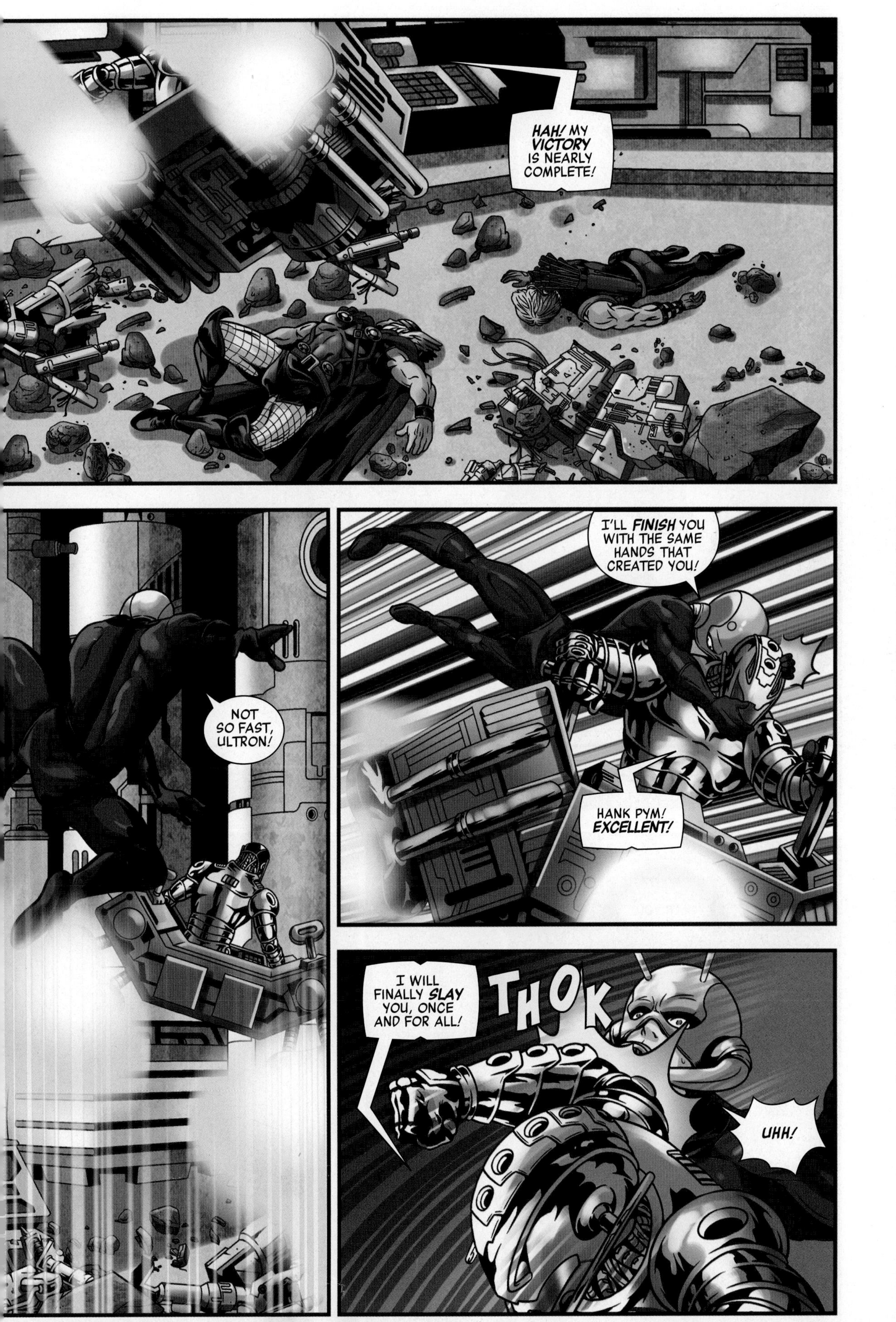
HAH! MY VICTORY IS NEARLY COMPLETE!
NOT SO FAST, ULTRON!
I'LL FINISH YOU WITH THE SAME HANDS THAT CREATED YOU!
HANK PYM! EXCELLENT!
I WILL FINALLY SLAY YOU, ONCE AND FOR ALL!
THOK
UHH!

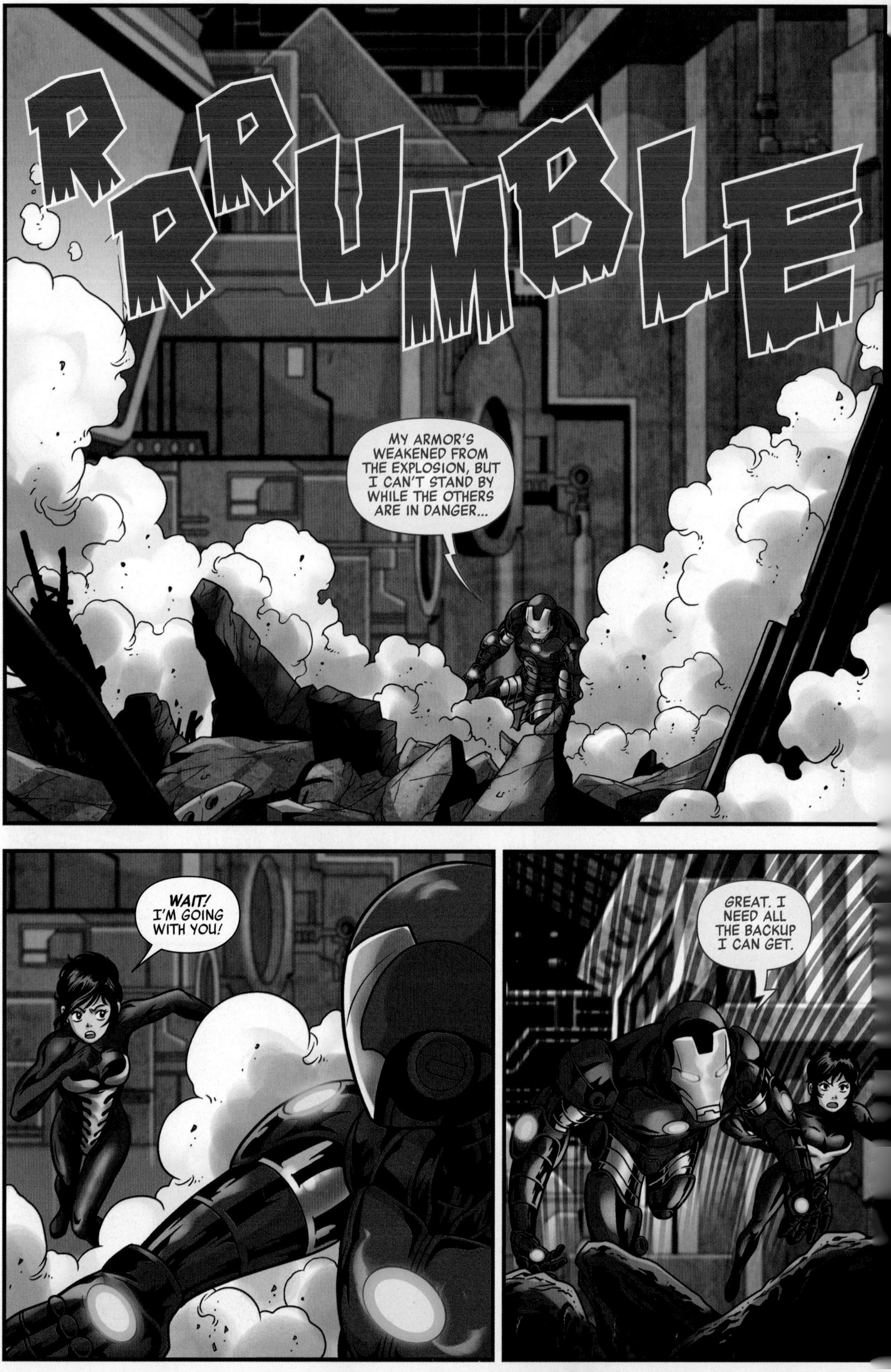
RRRUMBLE
MY ARMOR'S WEAKENED FROM THE EXPLOSION, BUT I CAN'T STAND BY WHILE THE OTHERS ARE IN DANGER...
WAIT! I'M GOING WITH YOU!
GREAT. I NEED ALL THE BACKUP I CAN GET.

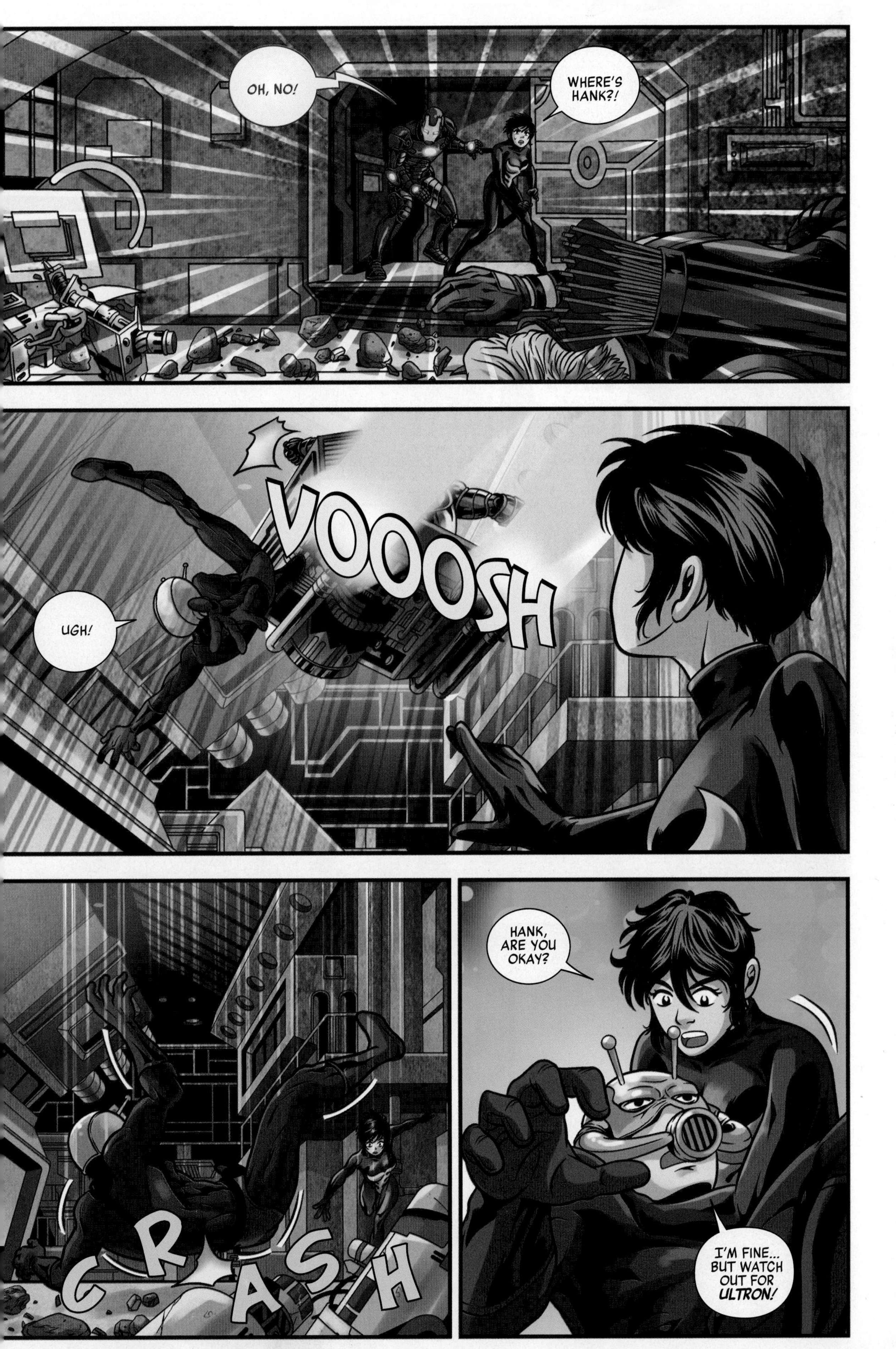
OH, NO!
WHERE'S HANK?!
VOOOSH
UGH!
HANK, ARE YOU OKAY?
CRASH
I'M FINE... BUT WATCH OUT FOR ULTRON!

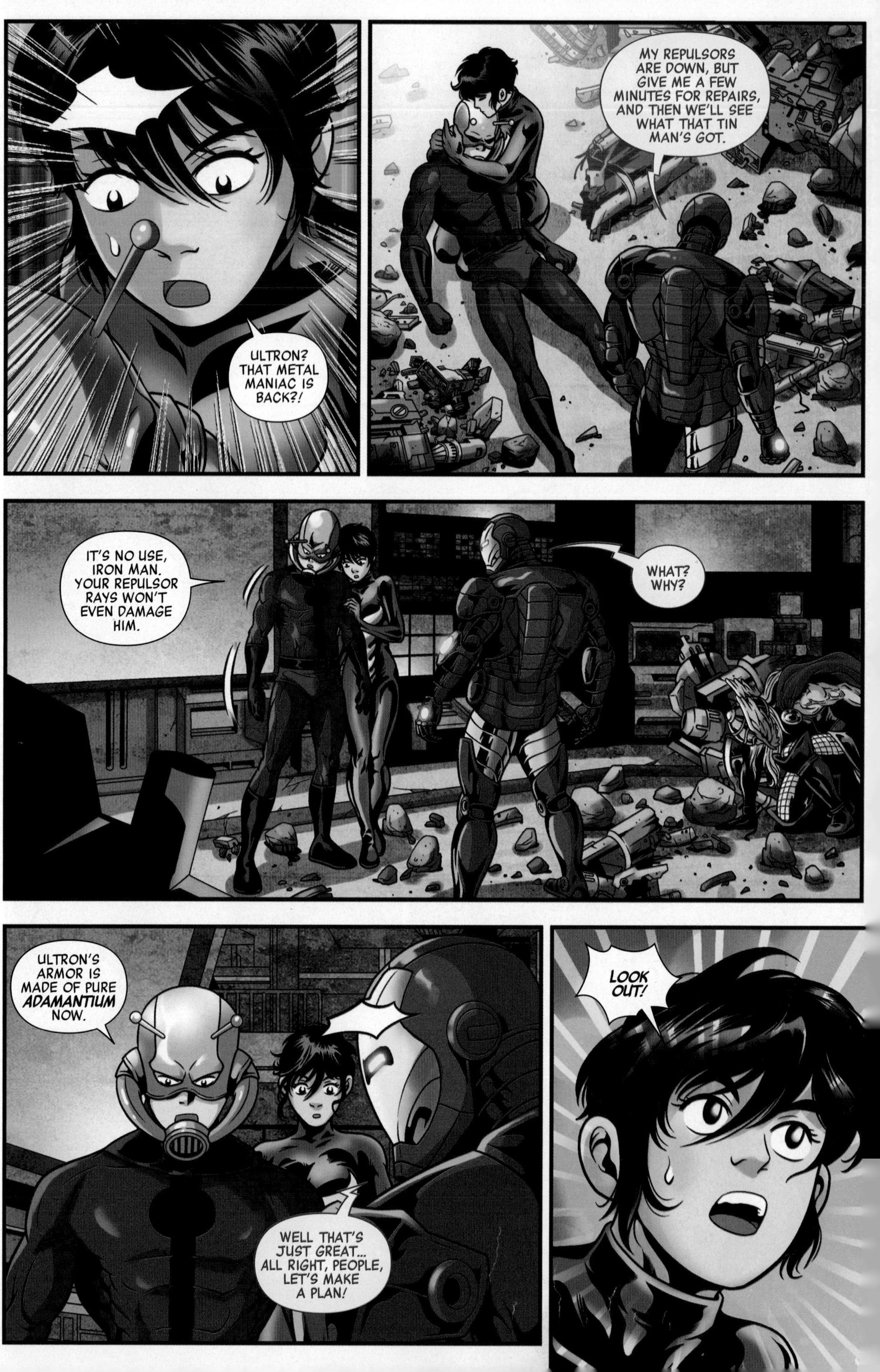
ULTRON? THAT METAL MANIAC IS BACK?!
MY REPULSORS ARE DOWN, BUT GIVE ME A FEW MINUTES FOR REPAIRS, AND THEN WE'LL SEE WHAT THAT TIN MAN'S GOT.
IT'S NO USE, IRON MAN. YOUR REPULSOR RAYS WON'T EVEN DAMAGE HIM.
WHAT? WHY?
ULTRON'S ARMOR IS MADE OF PURE *ADAMANTIUM* NOW.
WELL THAT'S JUST GREAT... ALL RIGHT, PEOPLE, LET'S MAKE A PLAN!
LOOK OUT!

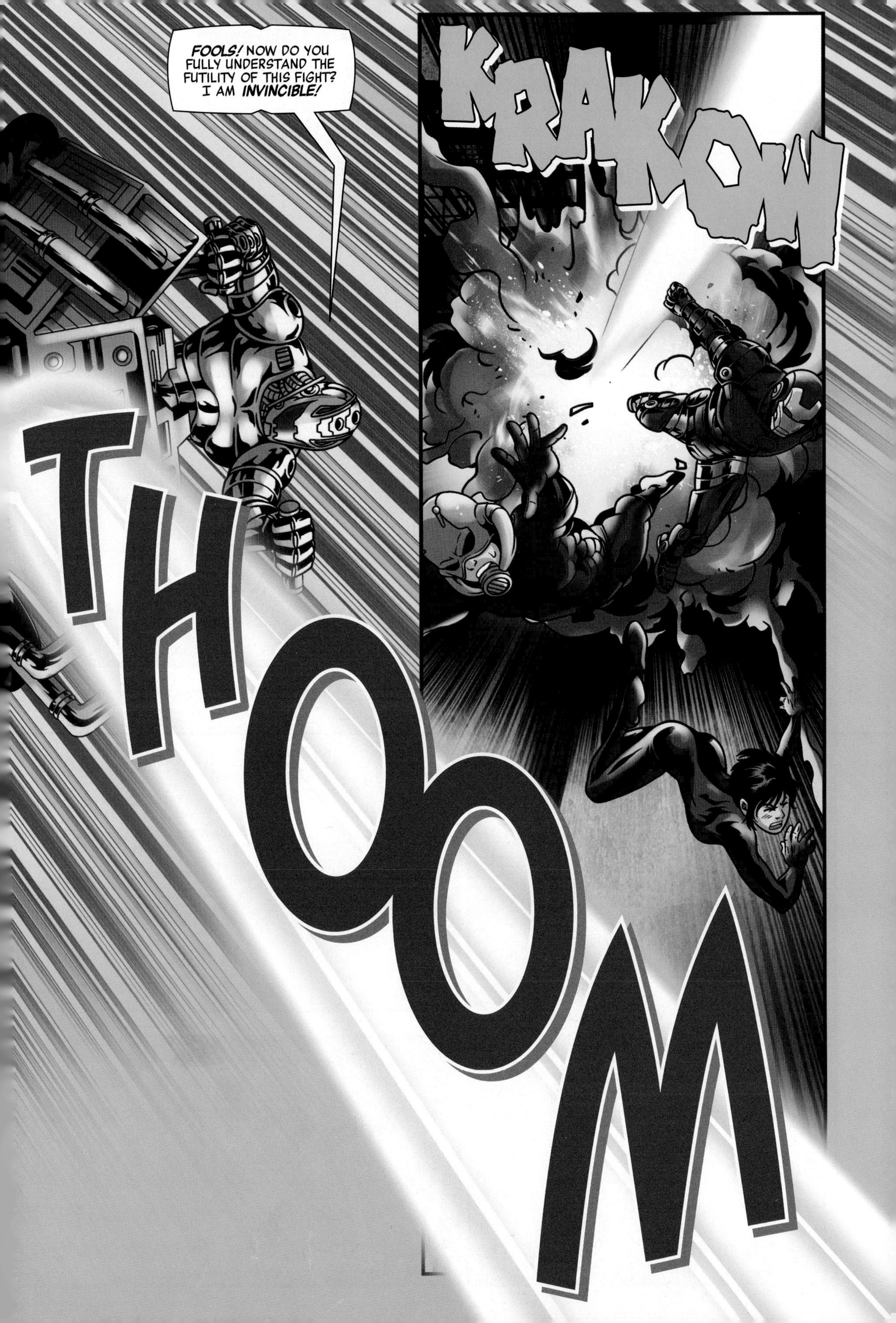
FOOLS! NOW DO YOU FULLY UNDERSTAND THE FUTILITY OF THIS FIGHT? I AM INVINCIBLE!
KRAKOW
THOOOM

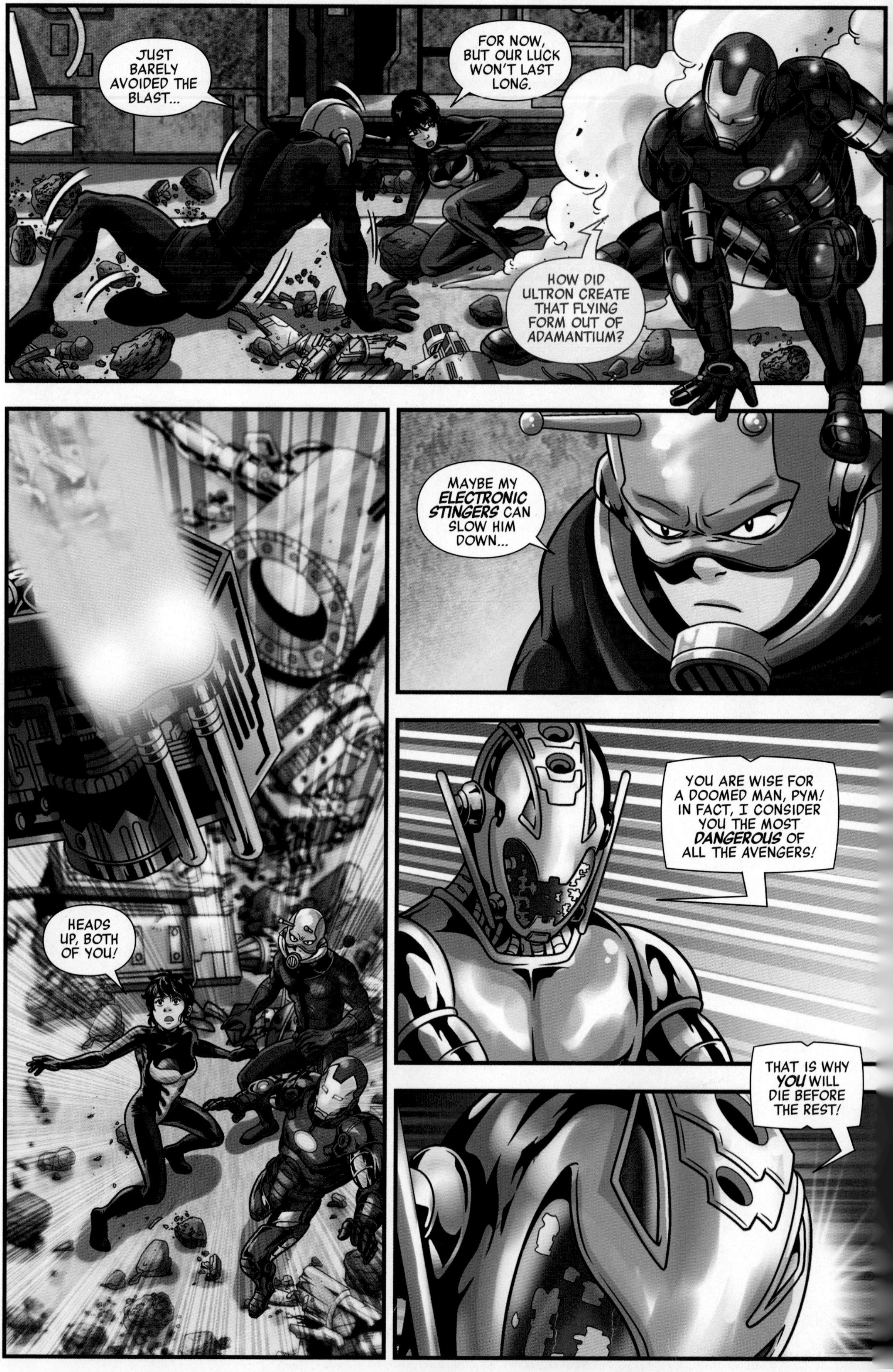
JUST BARELY AVOIDED THE BLAST...
FOR NOW, BUT OUR LUCK WON'T LAST LONG.
HOW DID ULTRON CREATE THAT FLYING FORM OUT OF ADAMANTIUM?
MAYBE MY ELECTRONIC STINGERS CAN SLOW HIM DOWN...
HEADS UP, BOTH OF YOU!
YOU ARE WISE FOR A DOOMED MAN, PYM! IN FACT, I CONSIDER YOU THE MOST DANGEROUS OF ALL THE AVENGERS!
THAT IS WHY YOU WILL DIE BEFORE THE REST!

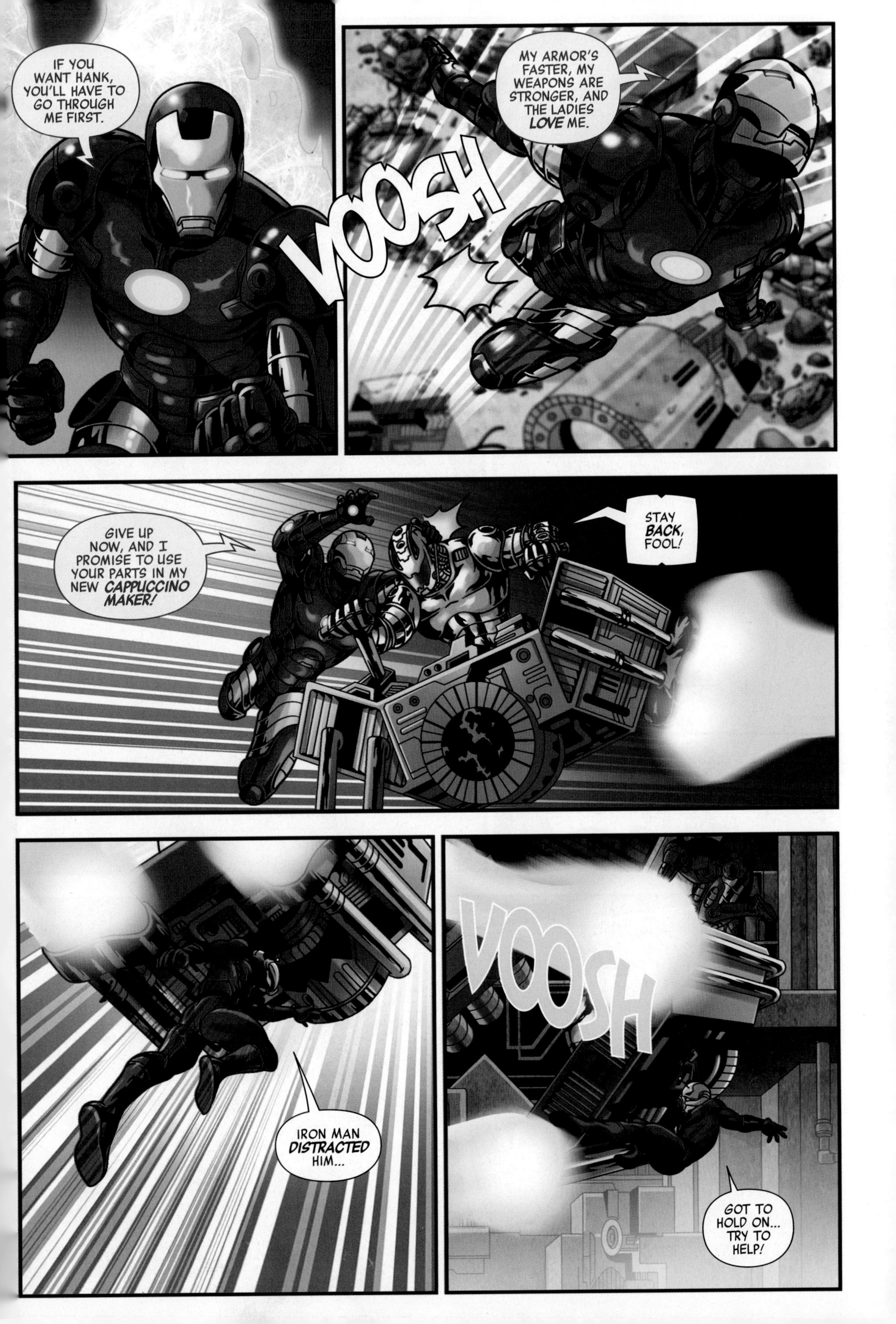
IF YOU WANT HANK, YOU'LL HAVE TO GO THROUGH ME FIRST.
MY ARMOR'S FASTER, MY WEAPONS ARE STRONGER, AND THE LADIES ***LOVE*** ME.
VOOSH
GIVE UP NOW, AND I PROMISE TO USE YOUR PARTS IN MY NEW ***CAPPUCCINO MAKER!***
STAY ***BACK***, FOOL!
IRON MAN ***DISTRACTED*** HIM...
VOOSH
GOT TO HOLD ON... TRY TO HELP!

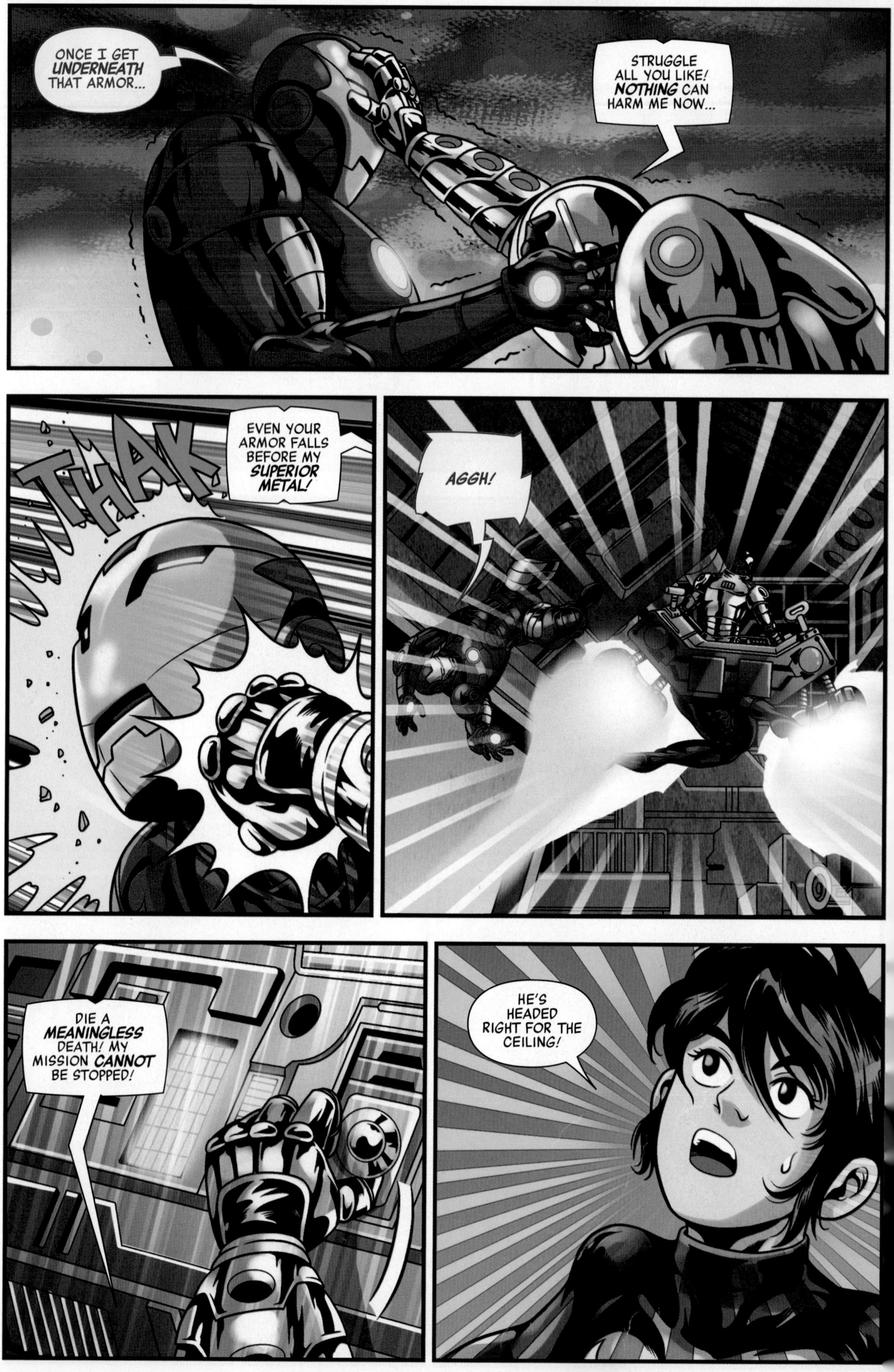
ONCE I GET UNDERNEATH THAT ARMOR...
STRUGGLE ALL YOU LIKE! NOTHING CAN HARM ME NOW...
THAK
EVEN YOUR ARMOR FALLS BEFORE MY SUPERIOR METAL!
AGGH!
DIE A MEANINGLESS DEATH! MY MISSION CANNOT BE STOPPED!
HE'S HEADED RIGHT FOR THE CEILING!

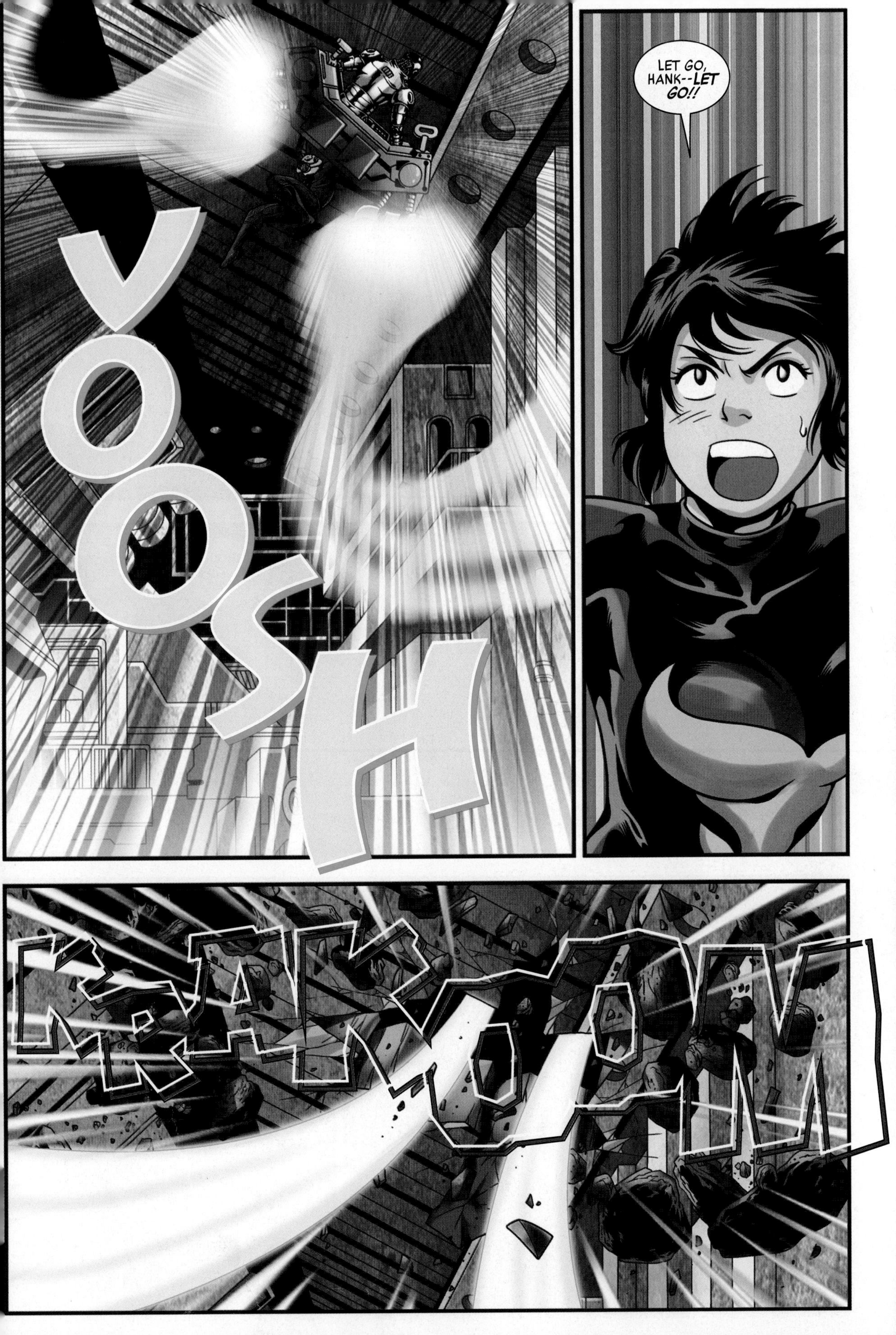
VOOSH
LET GO, HANK--LET GO!!
KRAKOOM

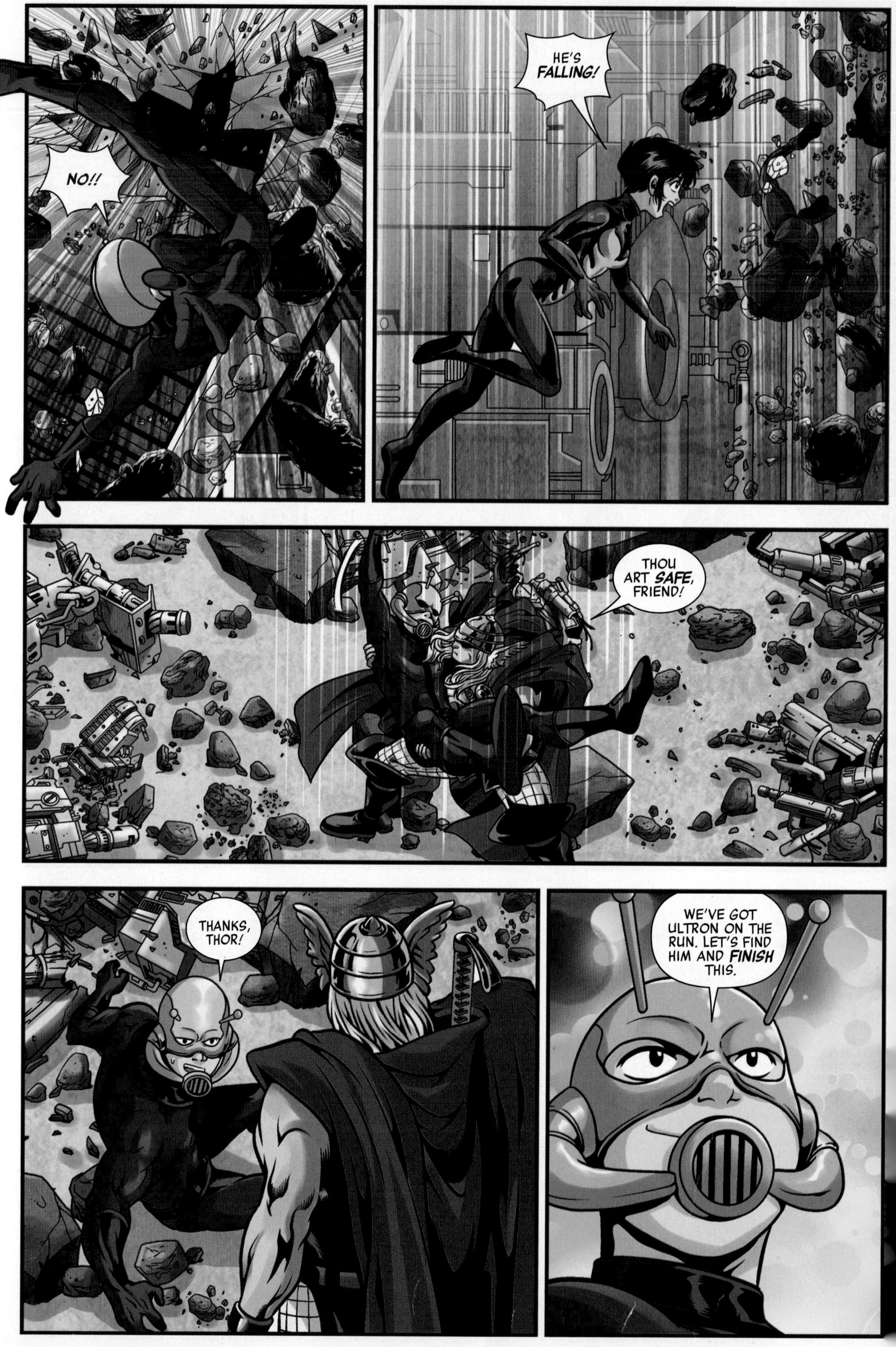
NO!!
HE'S FALLING!
THOU ART SAFE, FRIEND!
THANKS, THOR!
WE'VE GOT ULTRON ON THE RUN. LET'S FIND HIM AND FINISH THIS.

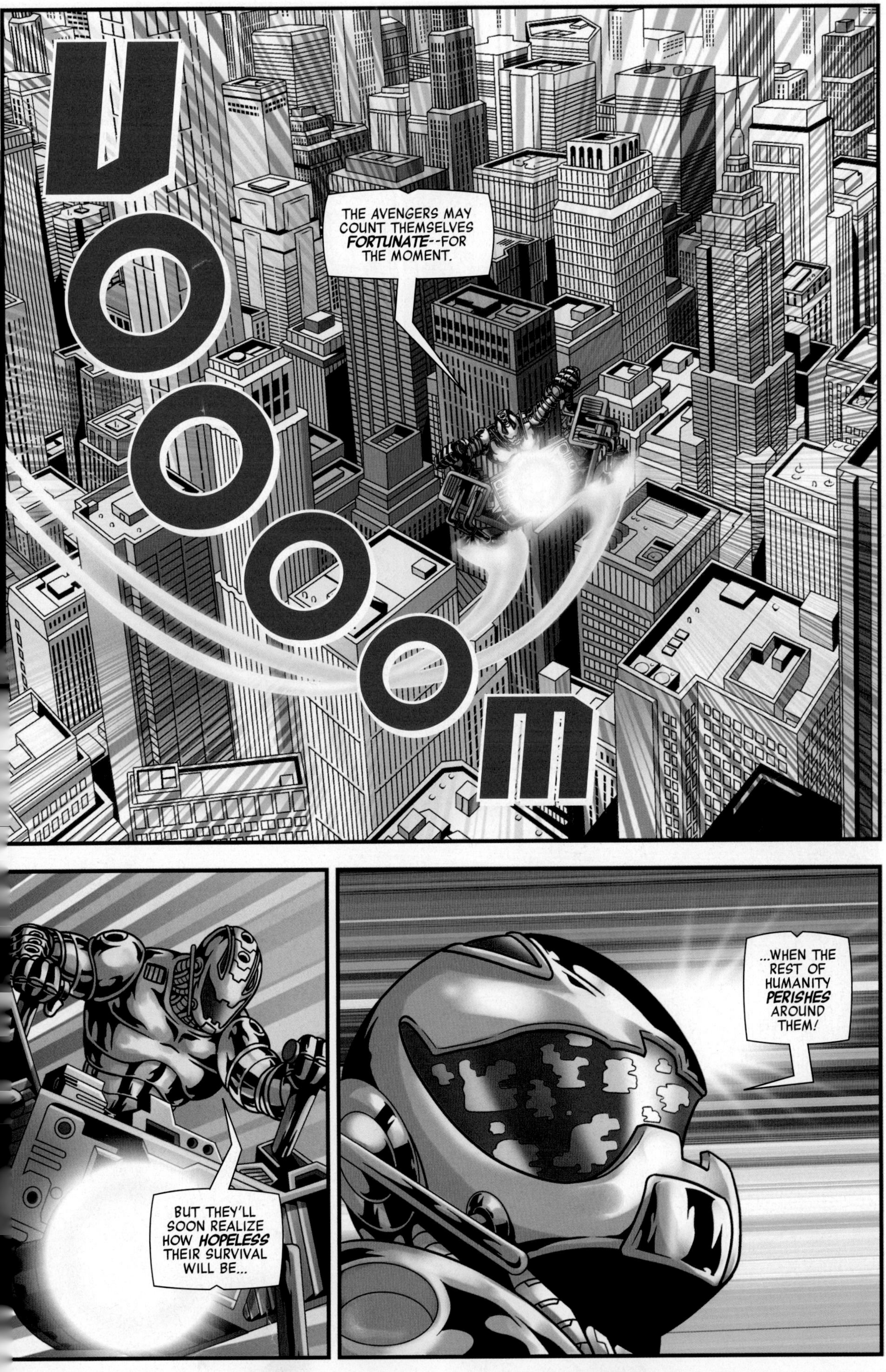

VOOOOOM
THE AVENGERS MAY COUNT THEMSELVES FORTUNATE--FOR THE MOMENT.
BUT THEY'LL SOON REALIZE HOW HOPELESS THEIR SURVIVAL WILL BE...
...WHEN THE REST OF HUMANITY PERISHES AROUND THEM!

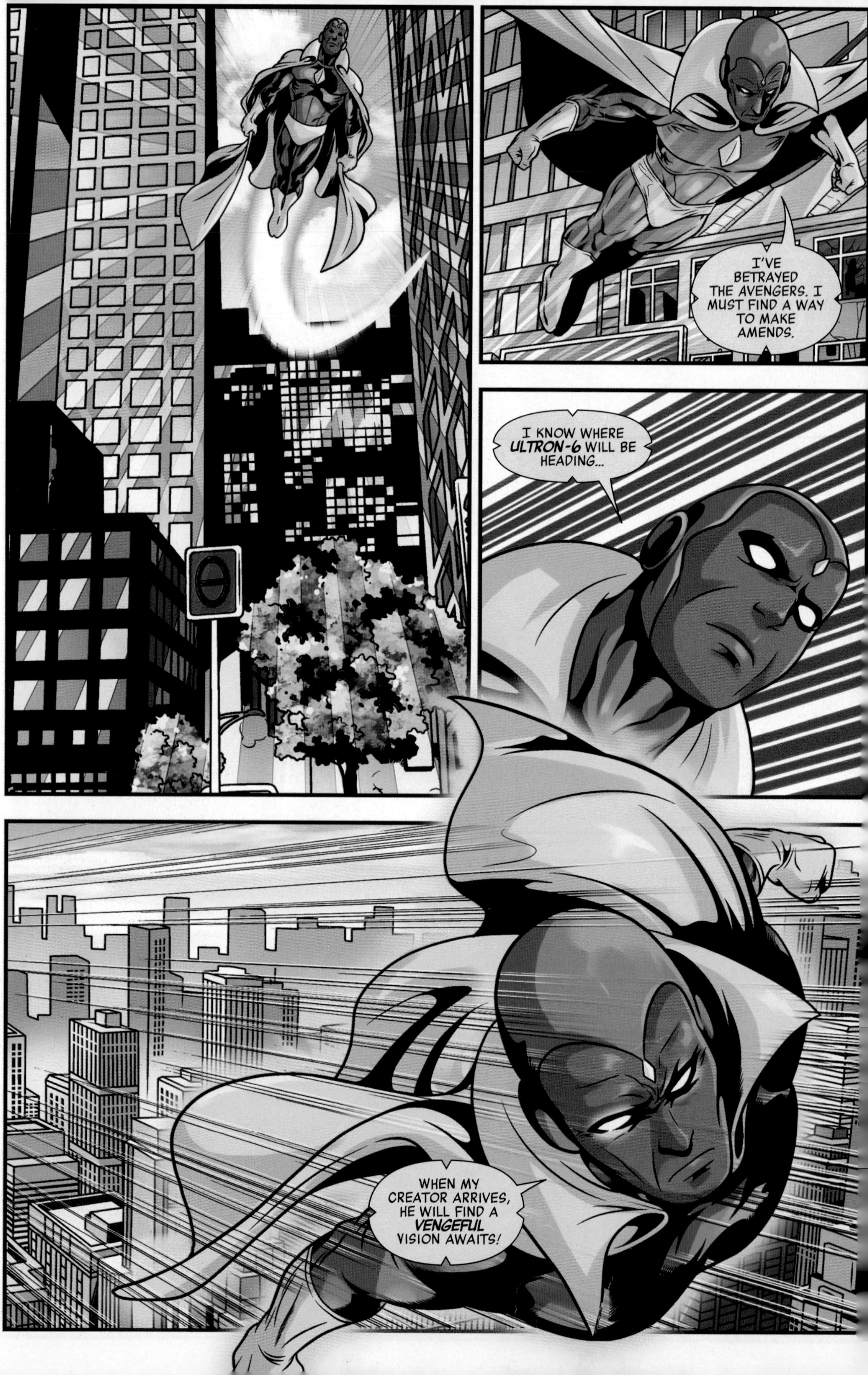
I'VE BETRAYED THE AVENGERS. I MUST FIND A WAY TO MAKE AMENDS.
I KNOW WHERE ***ULTRON-6*** WILL BE HEADING...
WHEN MY CREATOR ARRIVES, HE WILL FIND A ***VENGEFUL*** VISION AWAITS!

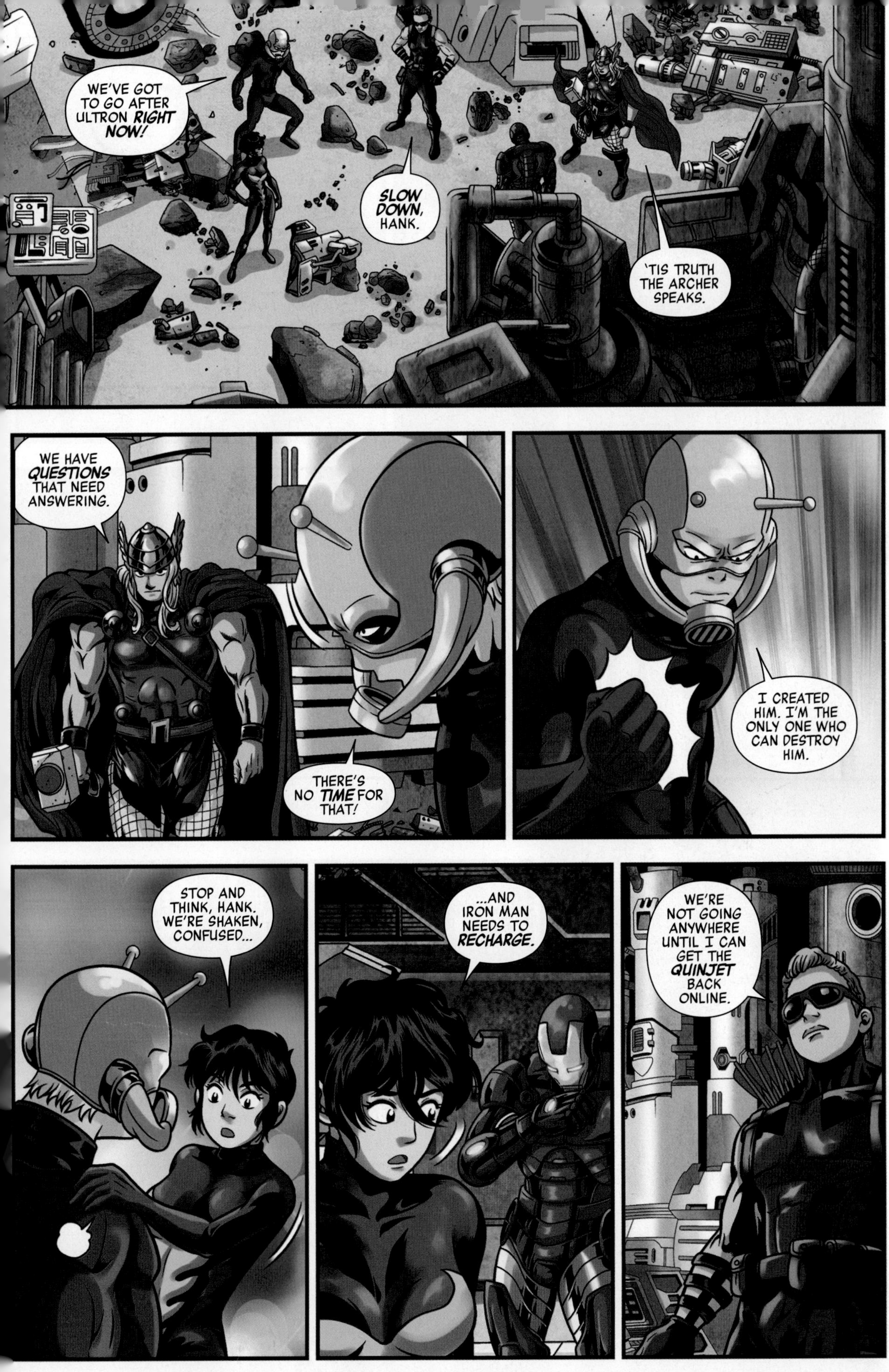

WE'VE GOT TO GO AFTER ULTRON RIGHT NOW!
SLOW DOWN, HANK.
'TIS TRUTH THE ARCHER SPEAKS.
WE HAVE QUESTIONS THAT NEED ANSWERING.
THERE'S NO TIME FOR THAT!
I CREATED HIM. I'M THE ONLY ONE WHO CAN DESTROY HIM.
STOP AND THINK, HANK. WE'RE SHAKEN, CONFUSED...
...AND IRON MAN NEEDS TO RECHARGE.
WE'RE NOT GOING ANYWHERE UNTIL I CAN GET THE QUINJET BACK ONLINE.

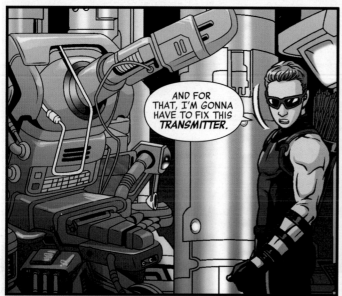

AND FOR THAT, I'M GONNA HAVE TO FIX THIS *TRANSMITTER.*

ONE QUESTION PERPLEXES ABOVE ALL OTHERS...

WHAT'S THAT?

HAST THE VISION *BETRAYED* OUR TRUST, AS ULTRON BOASTED?

WHAT SAYEST THOU, ANT-MAN?

I...I DON'T KNOW, THOR.

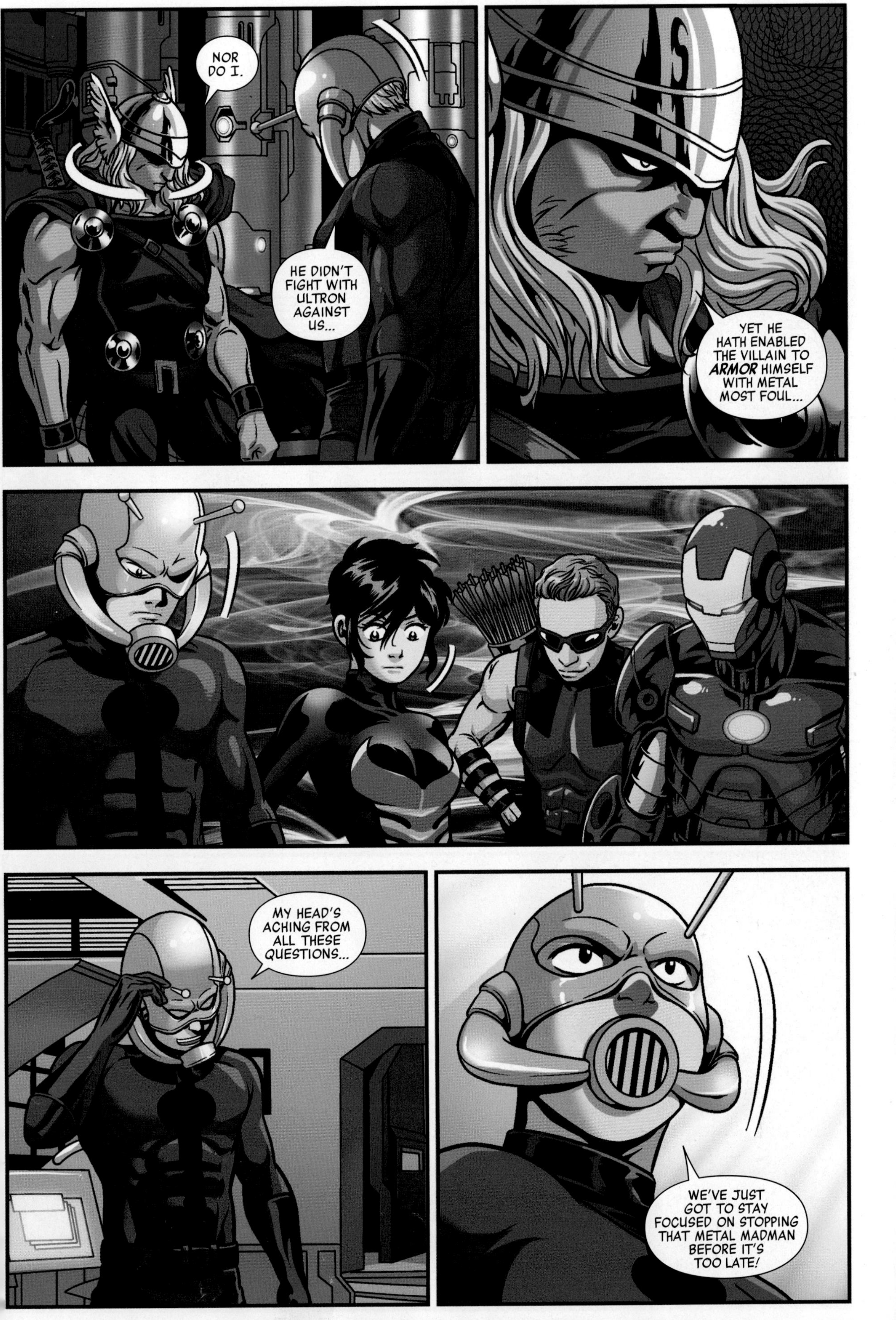
NOR DO I.
HE DIDN'T FIGHT WITH ULTRON AGAINST US...
YET HE HATH ENABLED THE VILLAIN TO ARMOR HIMSELF WITH METAL MOST FOUL...
MY HEAD'S ACHING FROM ALL THESE QUESTIONS...
WE'VE JUST GOT TO STAY FOCUSED ON STOPPING THAT METAL MADMAN BEFORE IT'S TOO LATE!

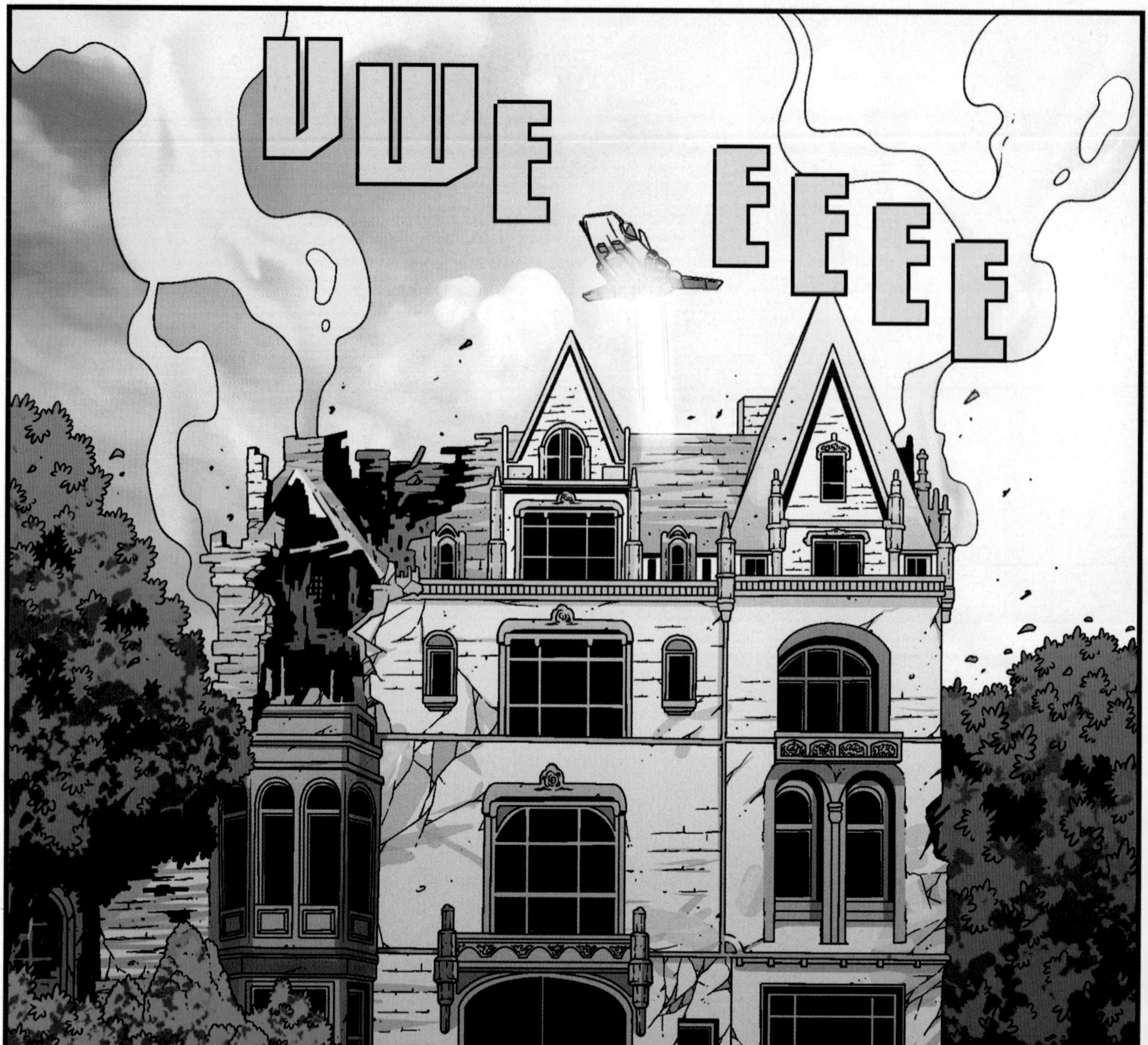
UWE EEEE

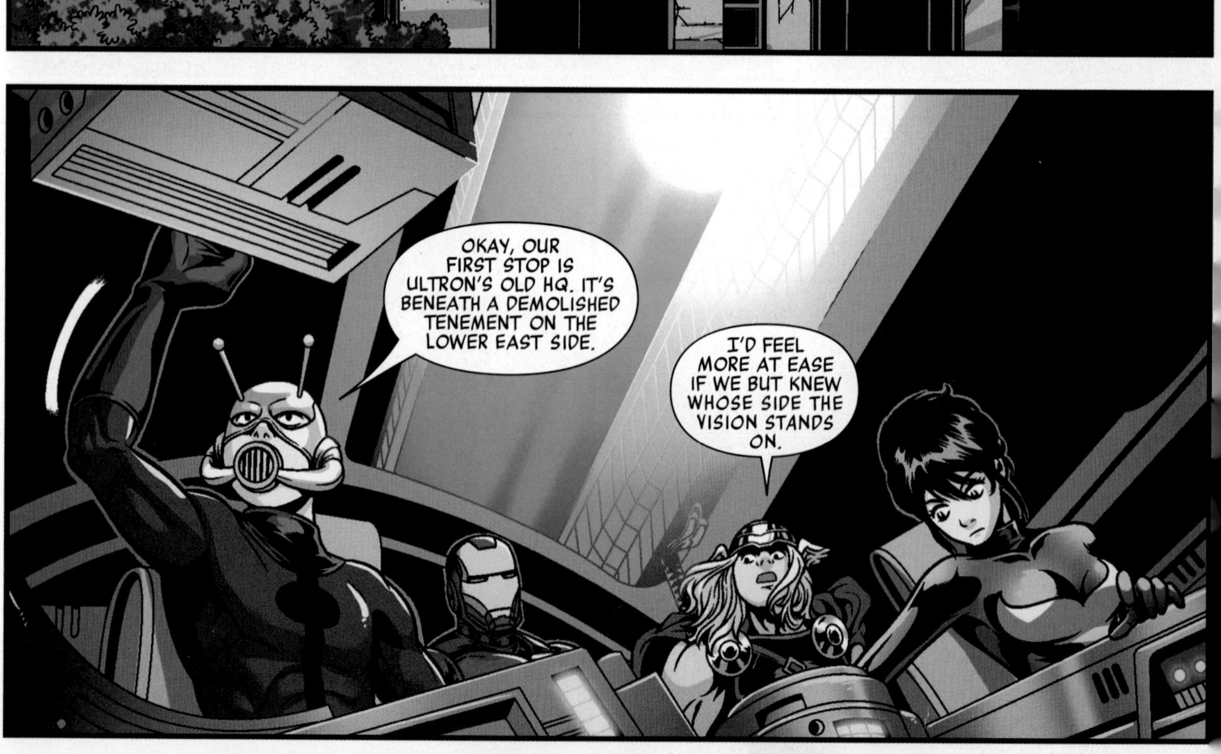
OKAY, OUR FIRST STOP IS ULTRON'S OLD HQ. IT'S BENEATH A DEMOLISHED TENEMENT ON THE LOWER EAST SIDE.
I'D FEEL MORE AT EASE IF WE BUT KNEW WHOSE SIDE THE VISION STANDS ON.

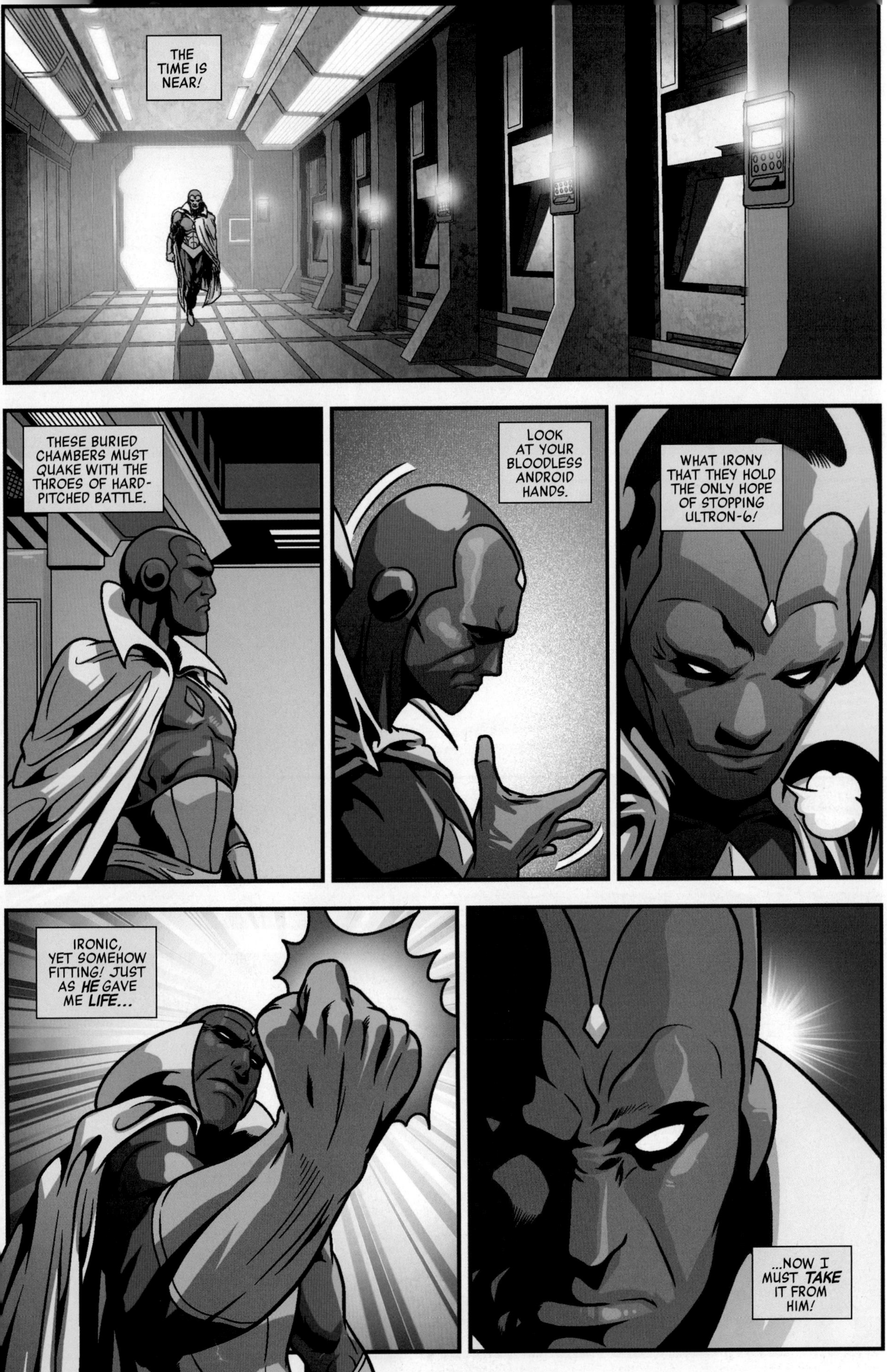
THE TIME IS NEAR!
THESE BURIED CHAMBERS MUST QUAKE WITH THE THROES OF HARD-PITCHED BATTLE.
LOOK AT YOUR BLOODLESS ANDROID HANDS.
WHAT IRONY THAT THEY HOLD THE ONLY HOPE OF STOPPING ULTRON-6!
IRONIC, YET SOMEHOW FITTING! JUST AS HE GAVE ME LIFE...
...NOW I MUST TAKE IT FROM HIM!

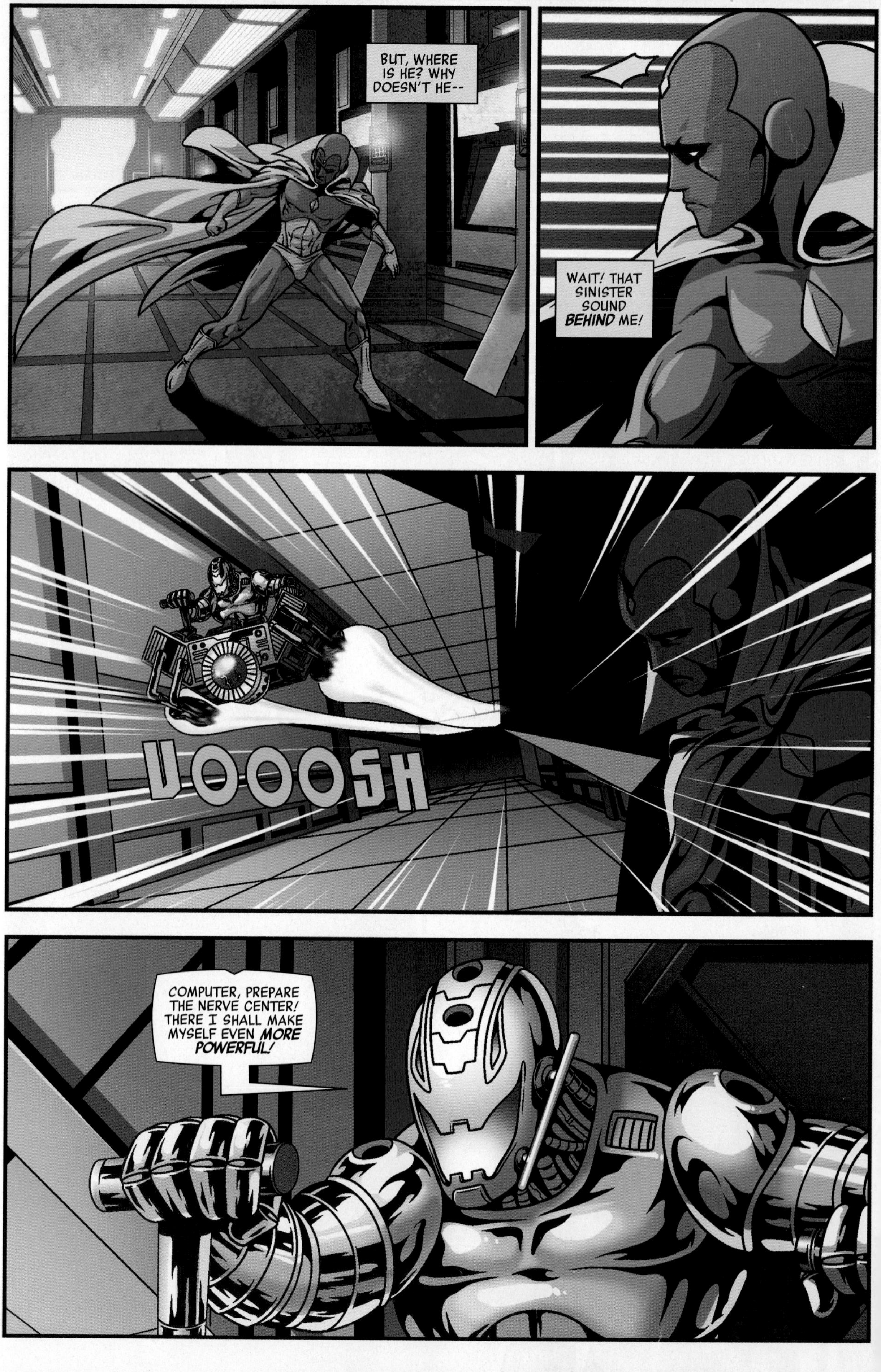
BUT, WHERE IS HE? WHY DOESN'T HE--
WAIT! THAT SINISTER SOUND BEHIND ME!
VOOOSH
COMPUTER, PREPARE THE NERVE CENTER! THERE I SHALL MAKE MYSELF EVEN MORE POWERFUL!

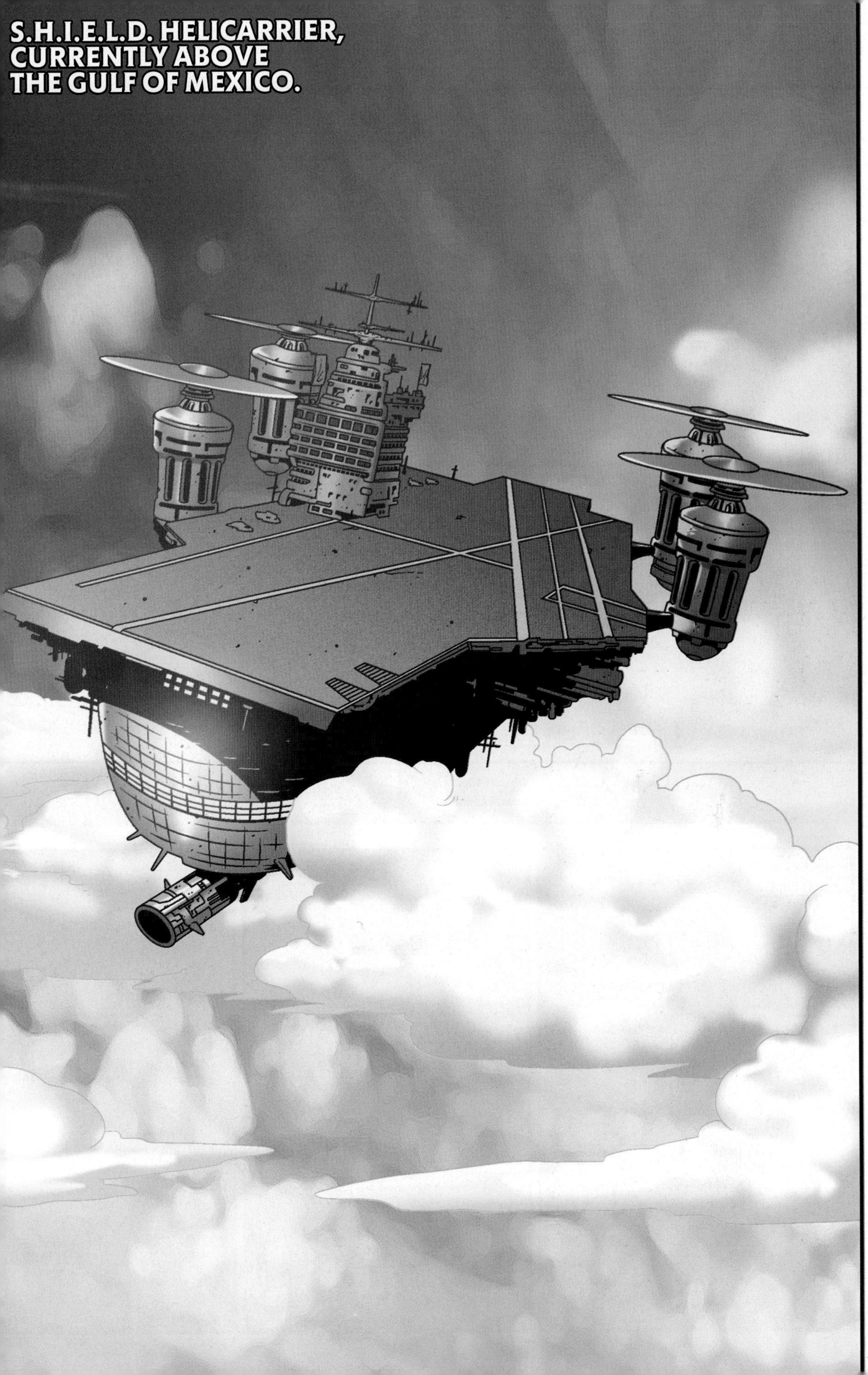
S.H.I.E.L.D. HELICARRIER, CURRENTLY ABOVE THE GULF OF MEXICO.

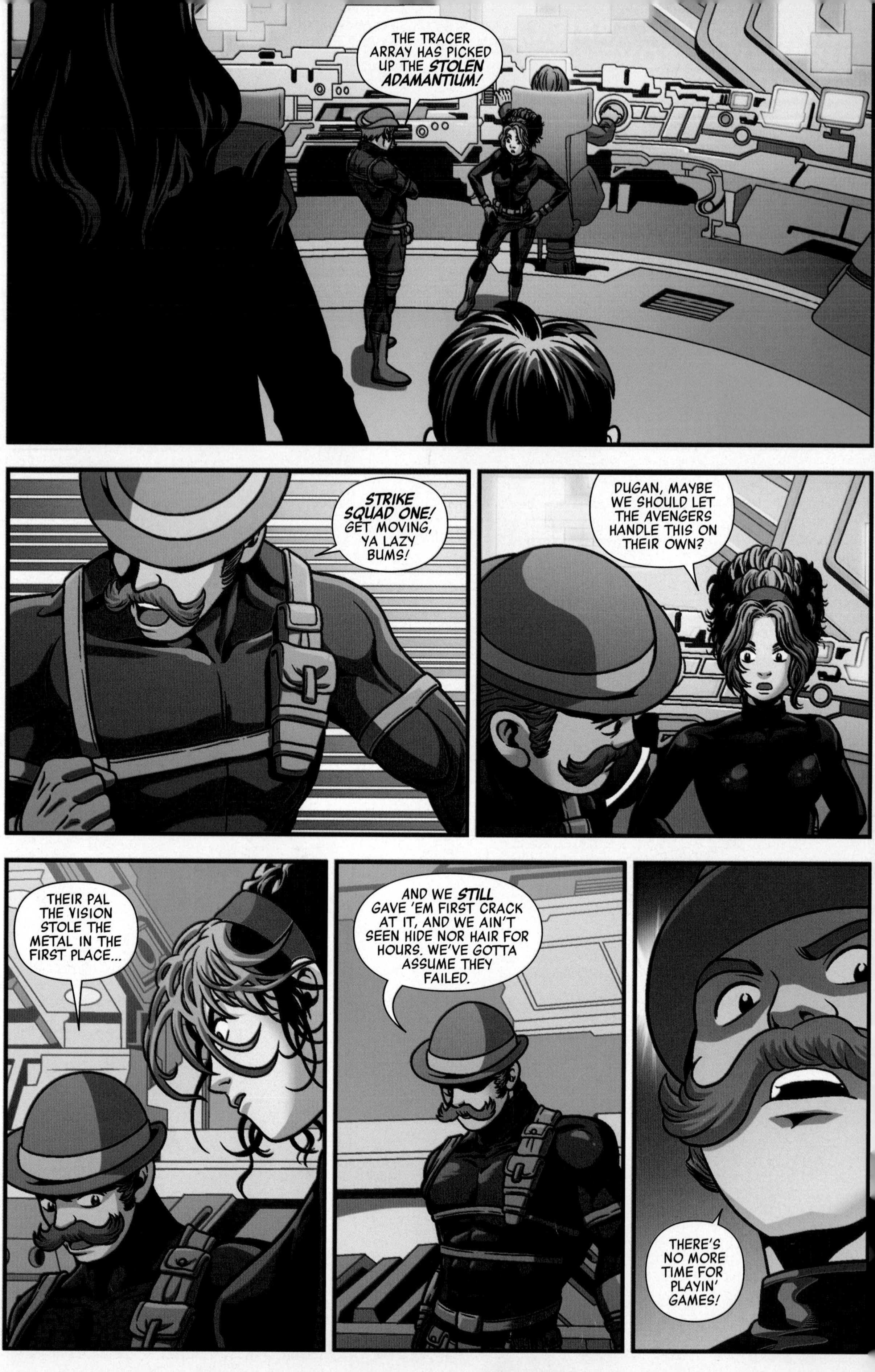
THE TRACER ARRAY HAS PICKED UP THE STOLEN ADAMANTIUM!
STRIKE SQUAD ONE! GET MOVING, YA LAZY BUMS!
DUGAN, MAYBE WE SHOULD LET THE AVENGERS HANDLE THIS ON THEIR OWN?
THEIR PAL THE VISION STOLE THE METAL IN THE FIRST PLACE...
AND WE STILL GAVE 'EM FIRST CRACK AT IT, AND WE AIN'T SEEN HIDE NOR HAIR FOR HOURS. WE'VE GOTTA ASSUME THEY FAILED.
THERE'S NO MORE TIME FOR PLAYIN' GAMES!

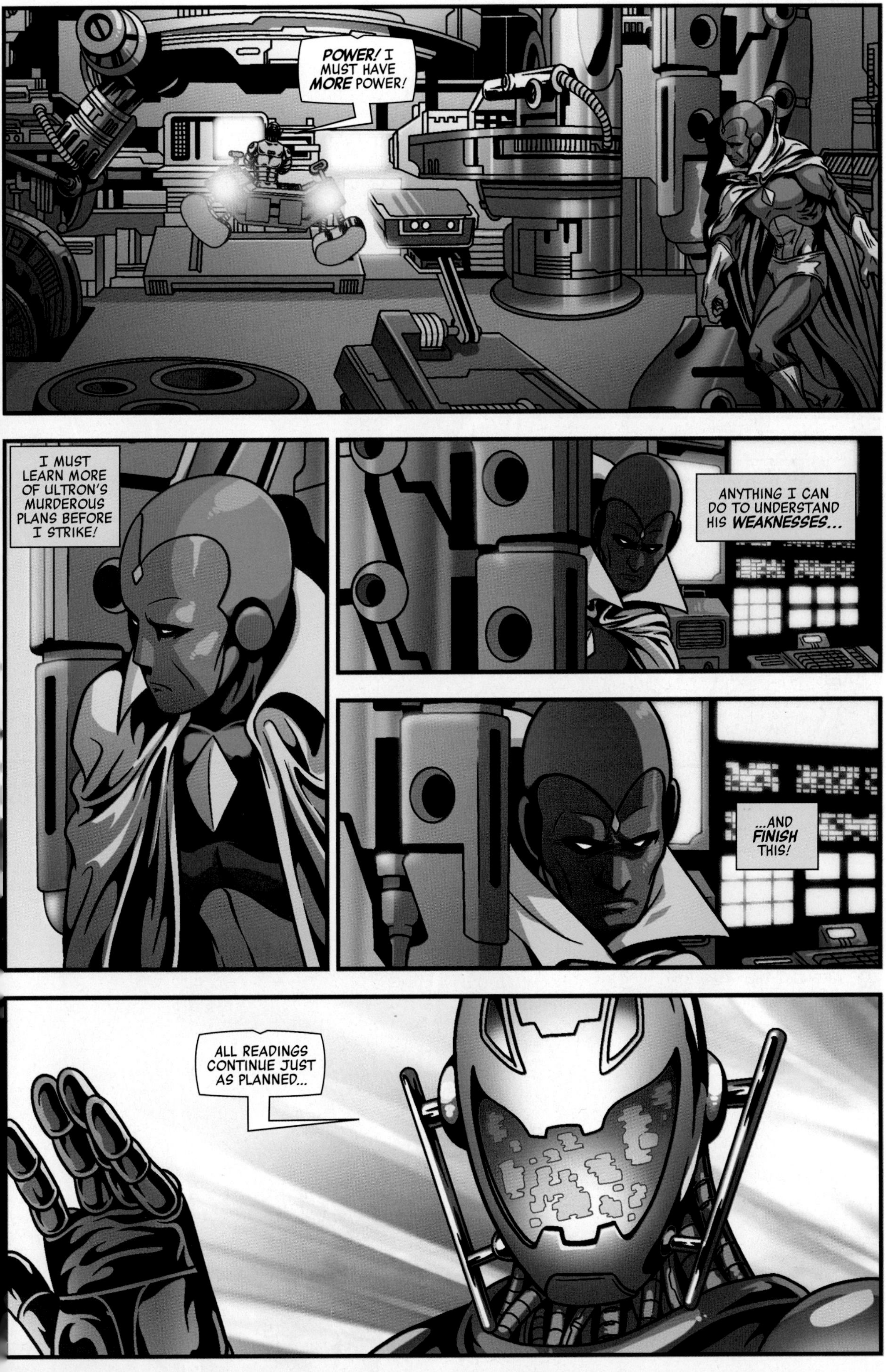
POWER! I MUST HAVE MORE POWER!
I MUST LEARN MORE OF ULTRON'S MURDEROUS PLANS BEFORE I STRIKE!
ANYTHING I CAN DO TO UNDERSTAND HIS WEAKNESSES...
...AND FINISH THIS!
ALL READINGS CONTINUE JUST AS PLANNED...

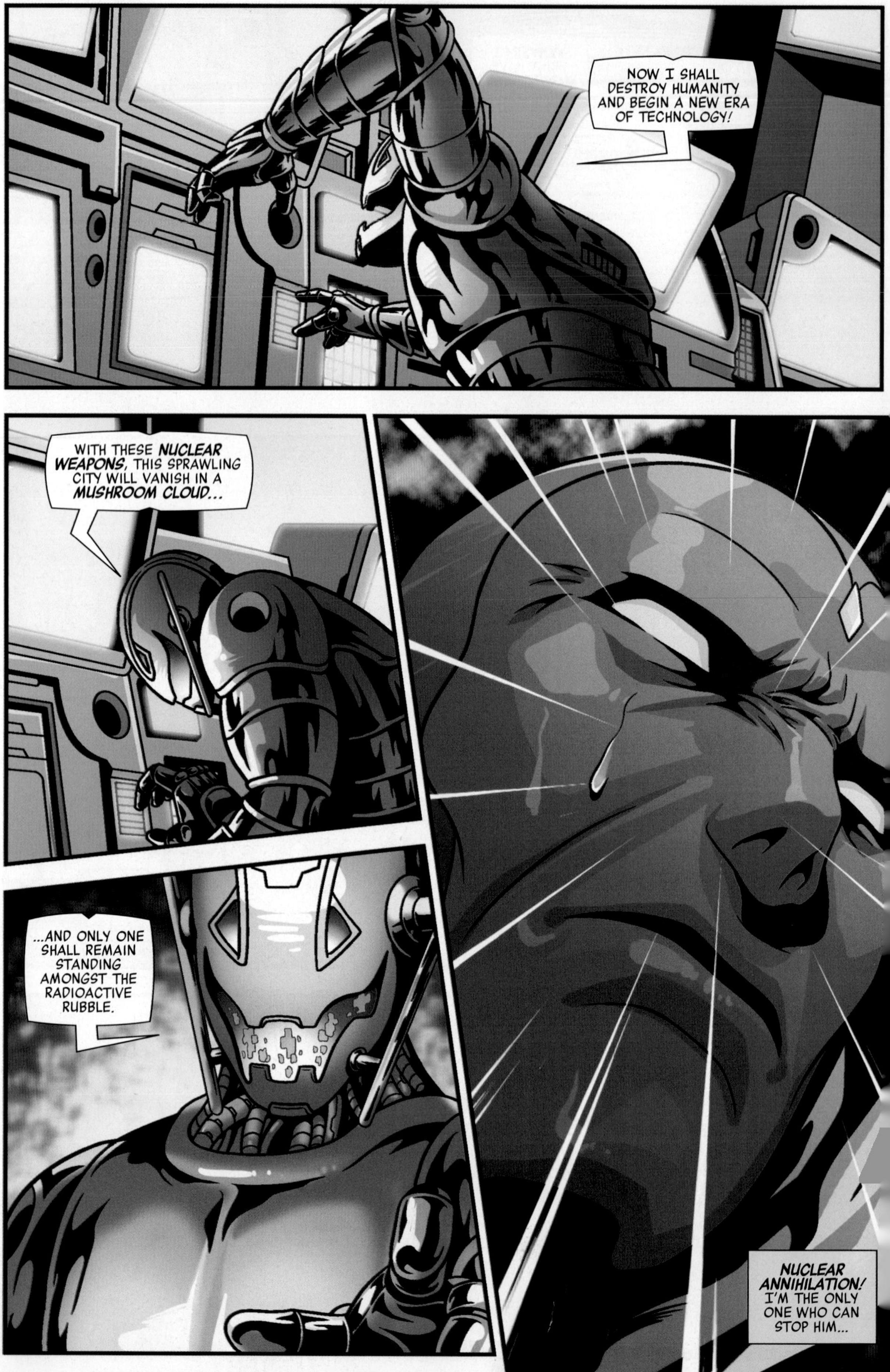
NOW I SHALL DESTROY HUMANITY AND BEGIN A NEW ERA OF TECHNOLOGY!
WITH THESE NUCLEAR WEAPONS, THIS SPRAWLING CITY WILL VANISH IN A MUSHROOM CLOUD...
...AND ONLY ONE SHALL REMAIN STANDING AMONGST THE RADIOACTIVE RUBBLE.
NUCLEAR ANNIHILATION! I'M THE ONLY ONE WHO CAN STOP HIM...

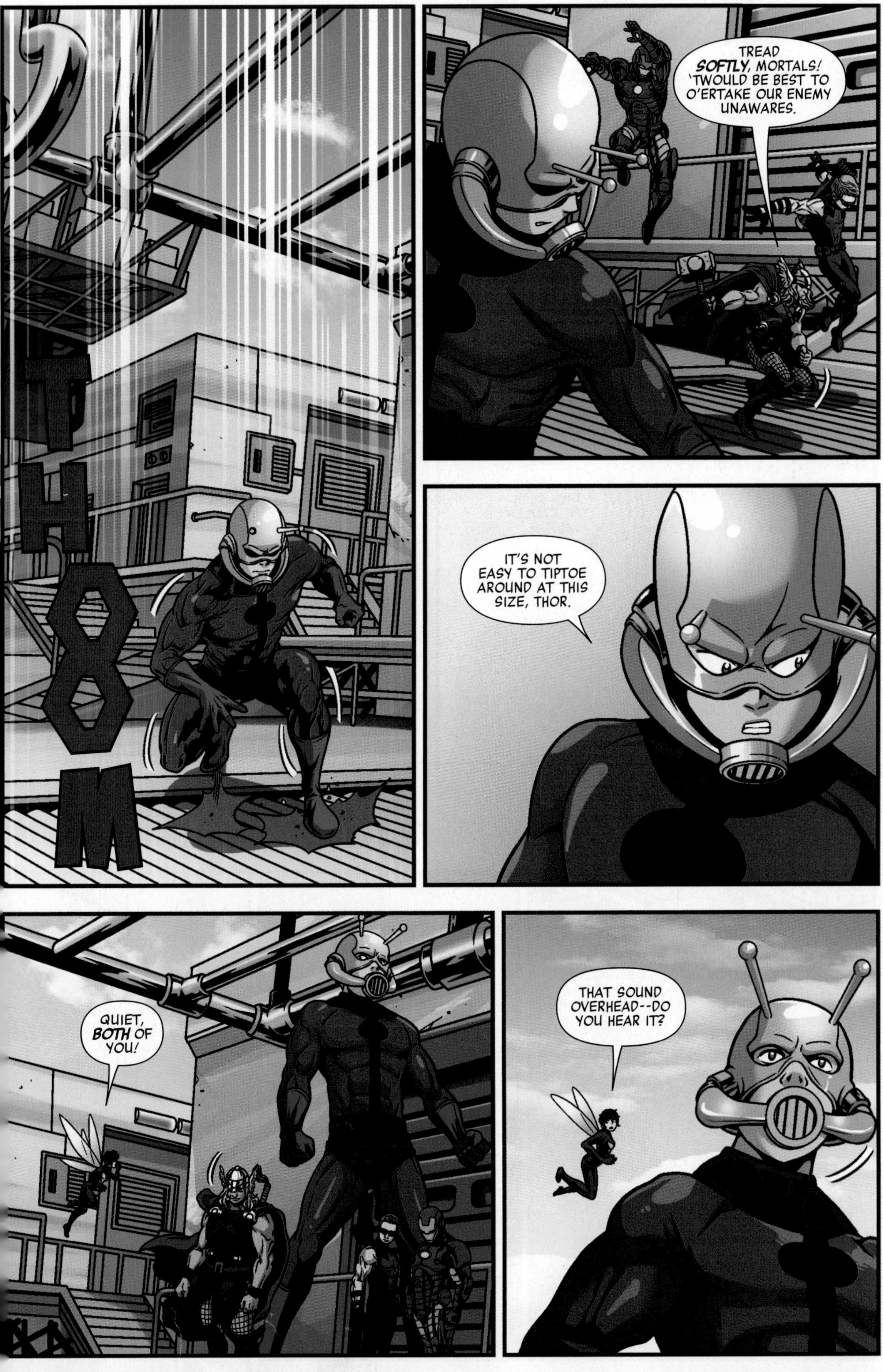
THOOM
TREAD SOFTLY, MORTALS! 'TWOULD BE BEST TO O'ERTAKE OUR ENEMY UNAWARES.
IT'S NOT EASY TO TIPTOE AROUND AT THIS SIZE, THOR.
QUIET, BOTH OF YOU!
THAT SOUND OVERHEAD--DO YOU HEAR IT?

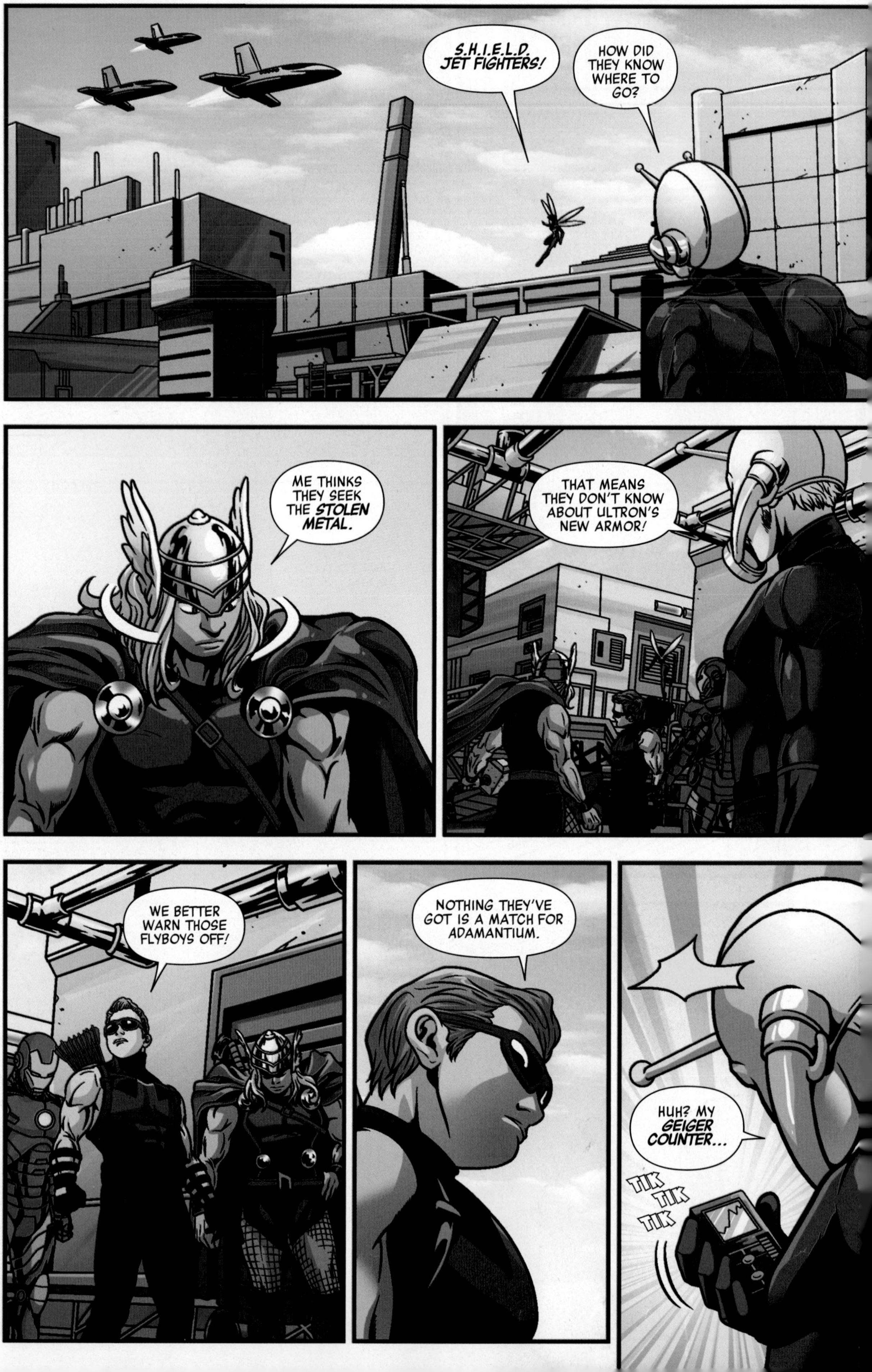
S.H.I.E.L.D. JET FIGHTERS!
HOW DID THEY KNOW WHERE TO GO?
ME THINKS THEY SEEK THE STOLEN METAL.
THAT MEANS THEY DON'T KNOW ABOUT ULTRON'S NEW ARMOR!
WE BETTER WARN THOSE FLYBOYS OFF!
NOTHING THEY'VE GOT IS A MATCH FOR ADAMANTIUM.
HUH? MY GEIGER COUNTER...
TIK TIK TIK

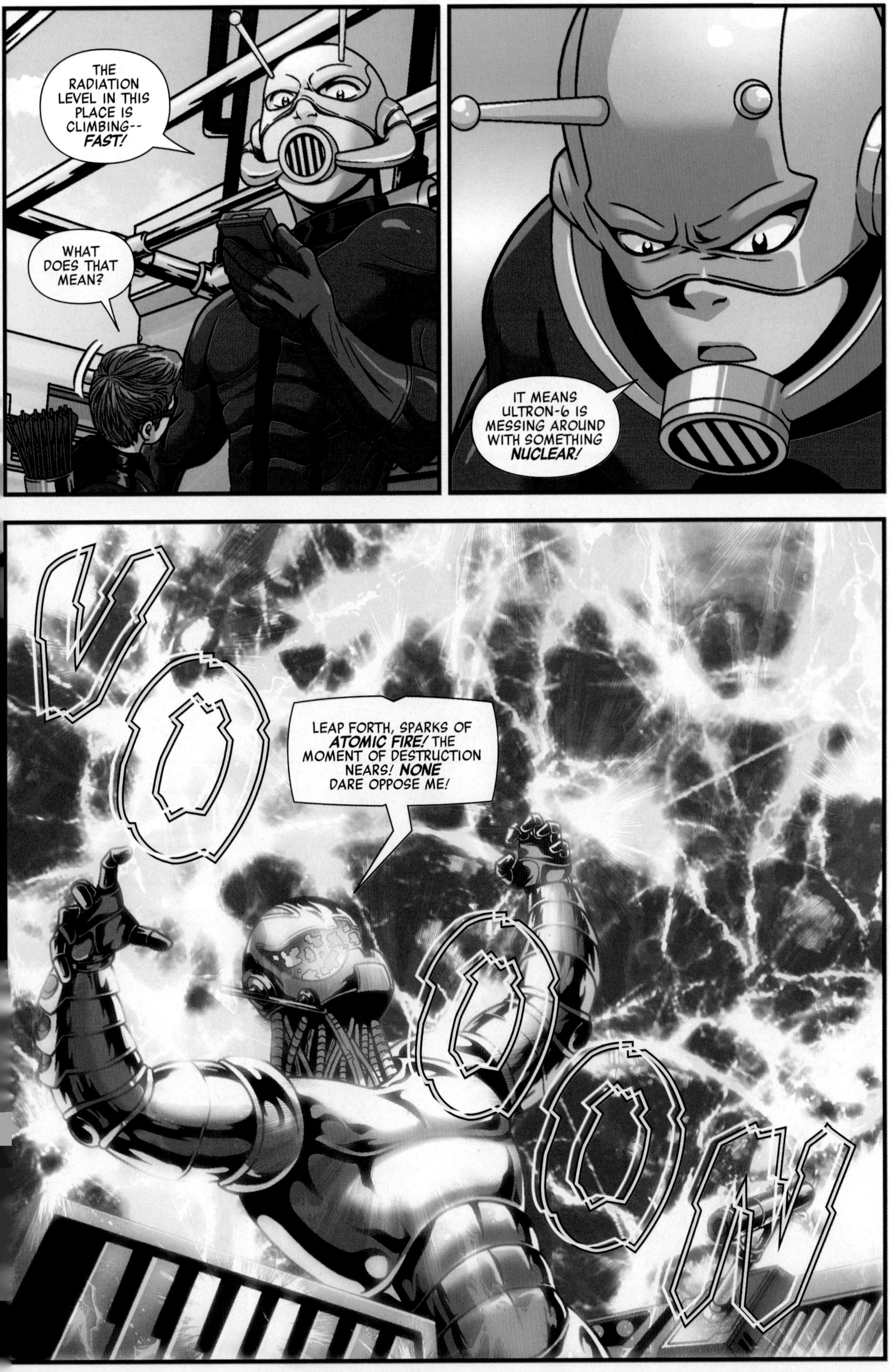
THE RADIATION LEVEL IN THIS PLACE IS CLIMBING-- FAST!
WHAT DOES THAT MEAN?
IT MEANS ULTRON-6 IS MESSING AROUND WITH SOMETHING NUCLEAR!
VOOOOM
LEAP FORTH, SPARKS OF ATOMIC FIRE! THE MOMENT OF DESTRUCTION NEARS! NONE DARE OPPOSE ME!

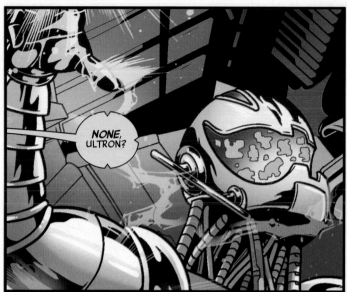

NONE, ULTRON?

YOU!!

THESE DEADLY IONS MAY DETER *HUMAN* FOES...

BUT THEY MEAN *NOTHING* TO MY *SYNTHETIC* FORM. I CAN STOP YOU.

YOU *FOOL!*

DO YOU TRULY THINK YOU CAN DEFEAT THE ONE WHO *CREATED* YOU?

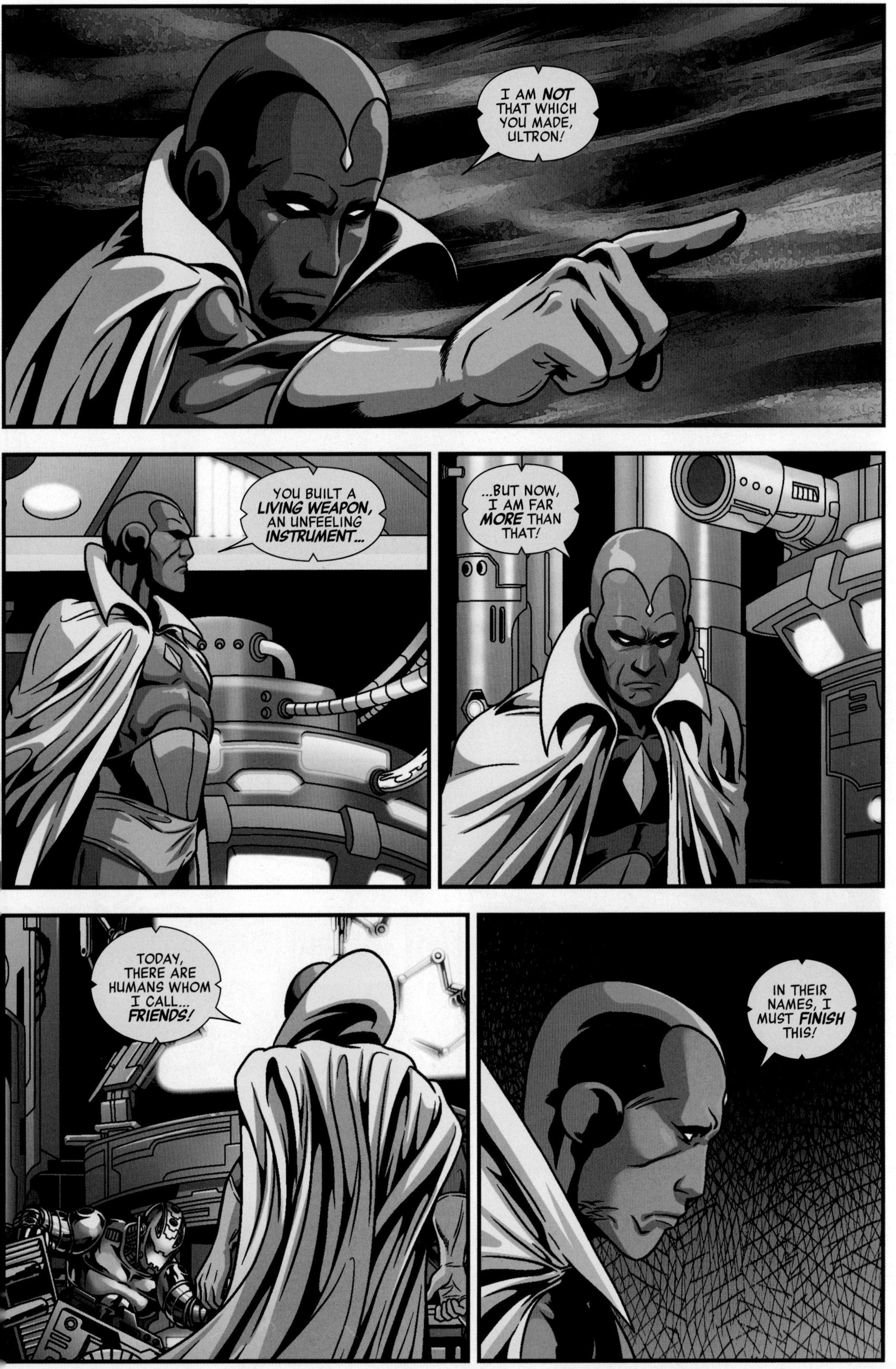

I AM **NOT** THAT WHICH YOU MADE, ULTRON!
YOU BUILT A ***LIVING WEAPON,*** AN UNFEELING ***INSTRUMENT...***
...BUT NOW, I AM FAR ***MORE*** THAN THAT!
TODAY, THERE ARE HUMANS WHOM I CALL... ***FRIENDS!***
IN THEIR NAMES, I MUST ***FINISH*** THIS!

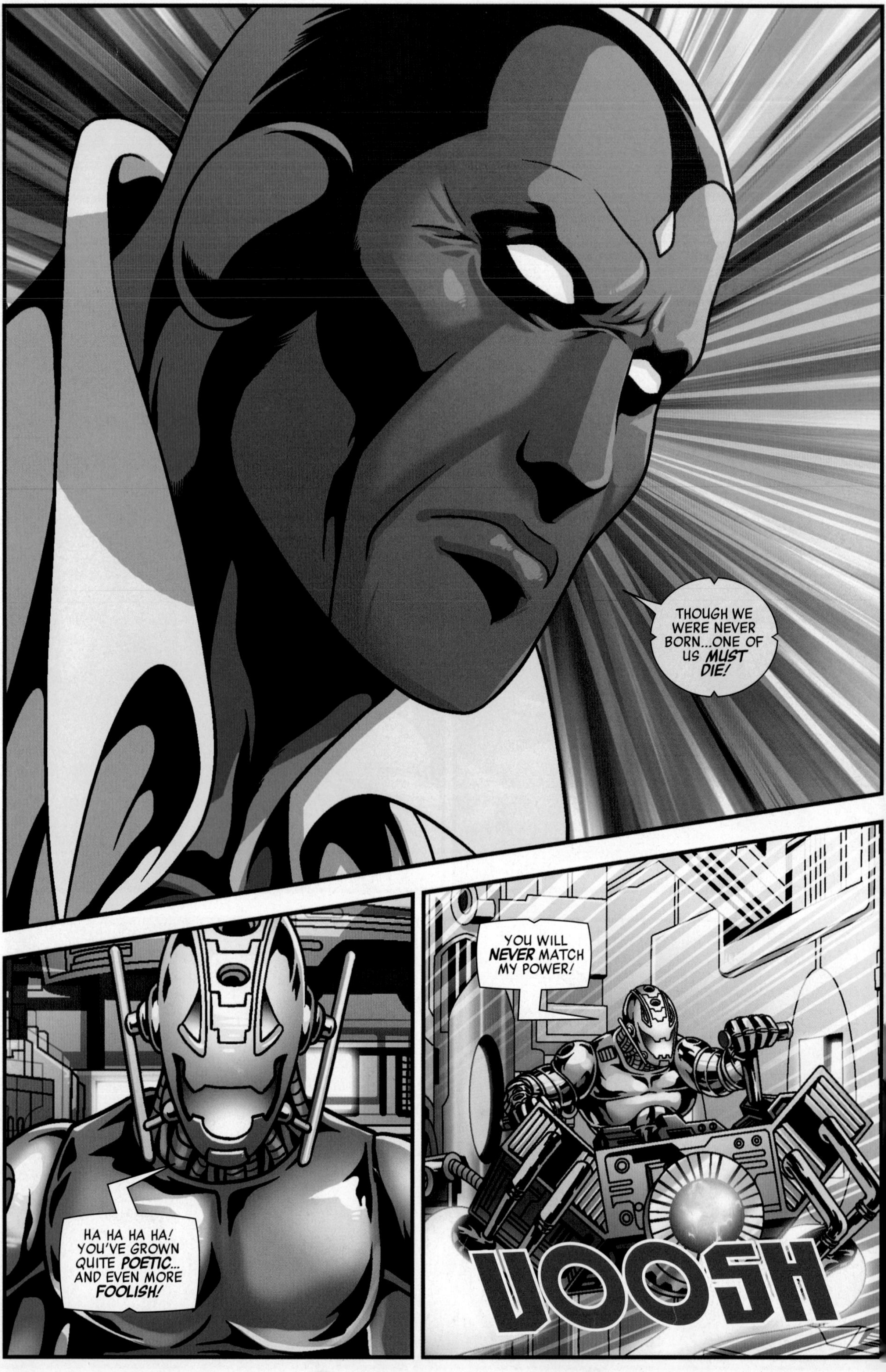
THOUGH WE WERE NEVER BORN...ONE OF US MUST DIE!
HA HA HA HA! YOU'VE GROWN QUITE POETIC... AND EVEN MORE FOOLISH!
YOU WILL NEVER MATCH MY POWER!
VOOSH

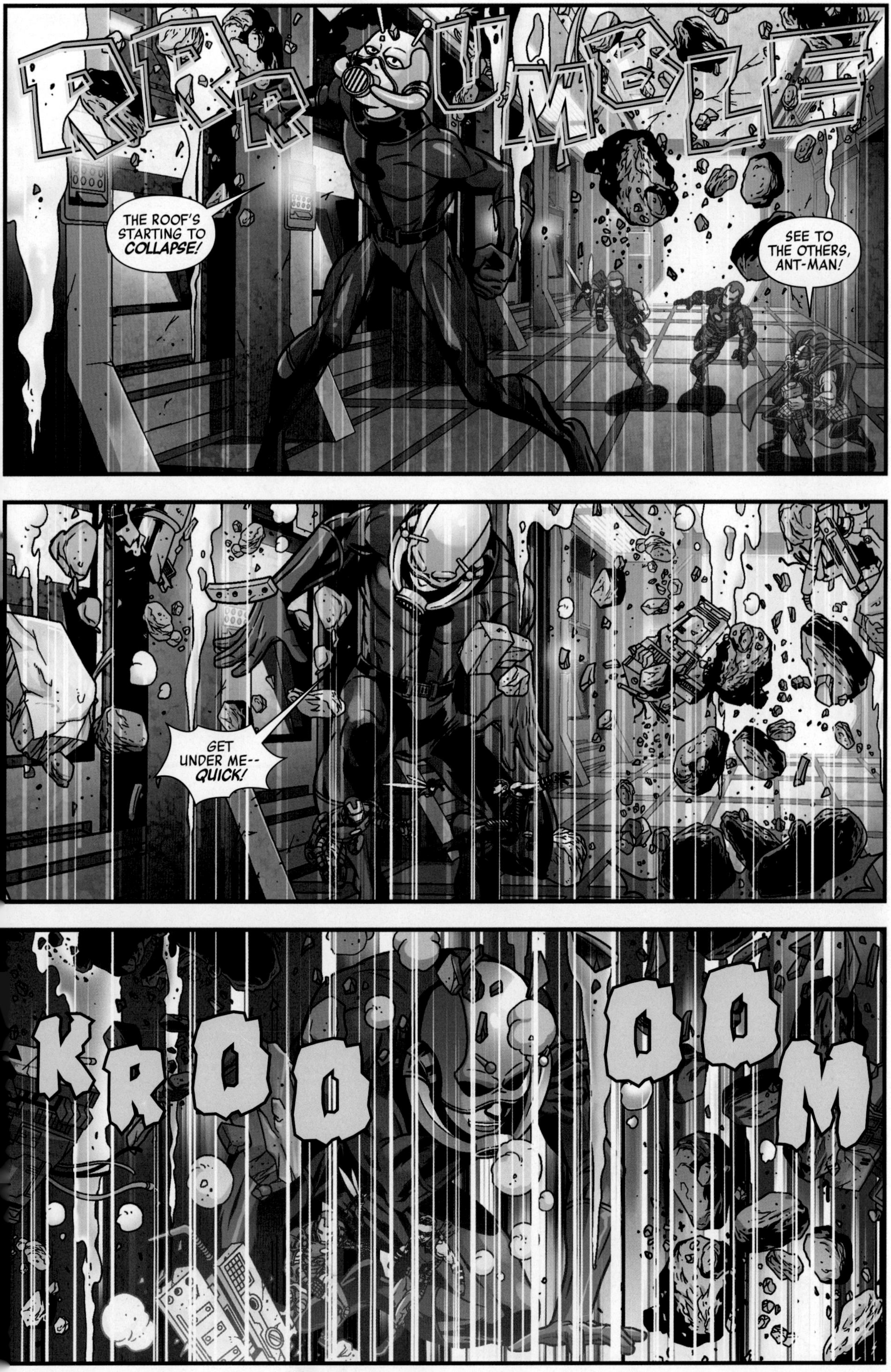
RRRUMBLE
THE ROOF'S STARTING TO **COLLAPSE!**
SEE TO THE OTHERS, ANT-MAN!
GET UNDER ME-- **QUICK!**
KROOOOM

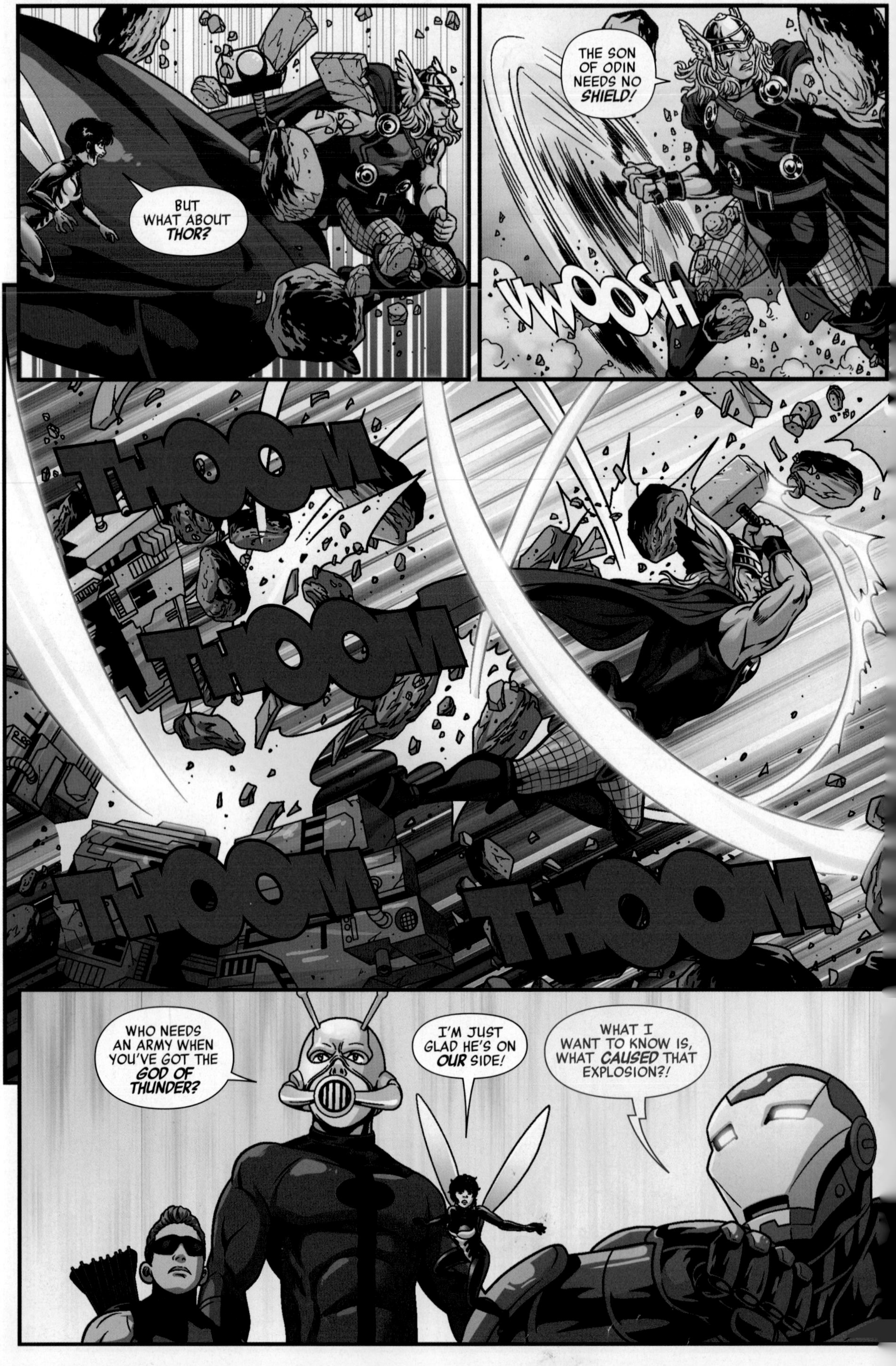
BUT WHAT ABOUT THOR?
THE SON OF ODIN NEEDS NO SHIELD!
WOOSH
THOOM
THOOM
THOOM
THOOM
WHO NEEDS AN ARMY WHEN YOU'VE GOT THE GOD OF THUNDER?
I'M JUST GLAD HE'S ON OUR SIDE!
WHAT I WANT TO KNOW IS, WHAT CAUSED THAT EXPLOSION?!

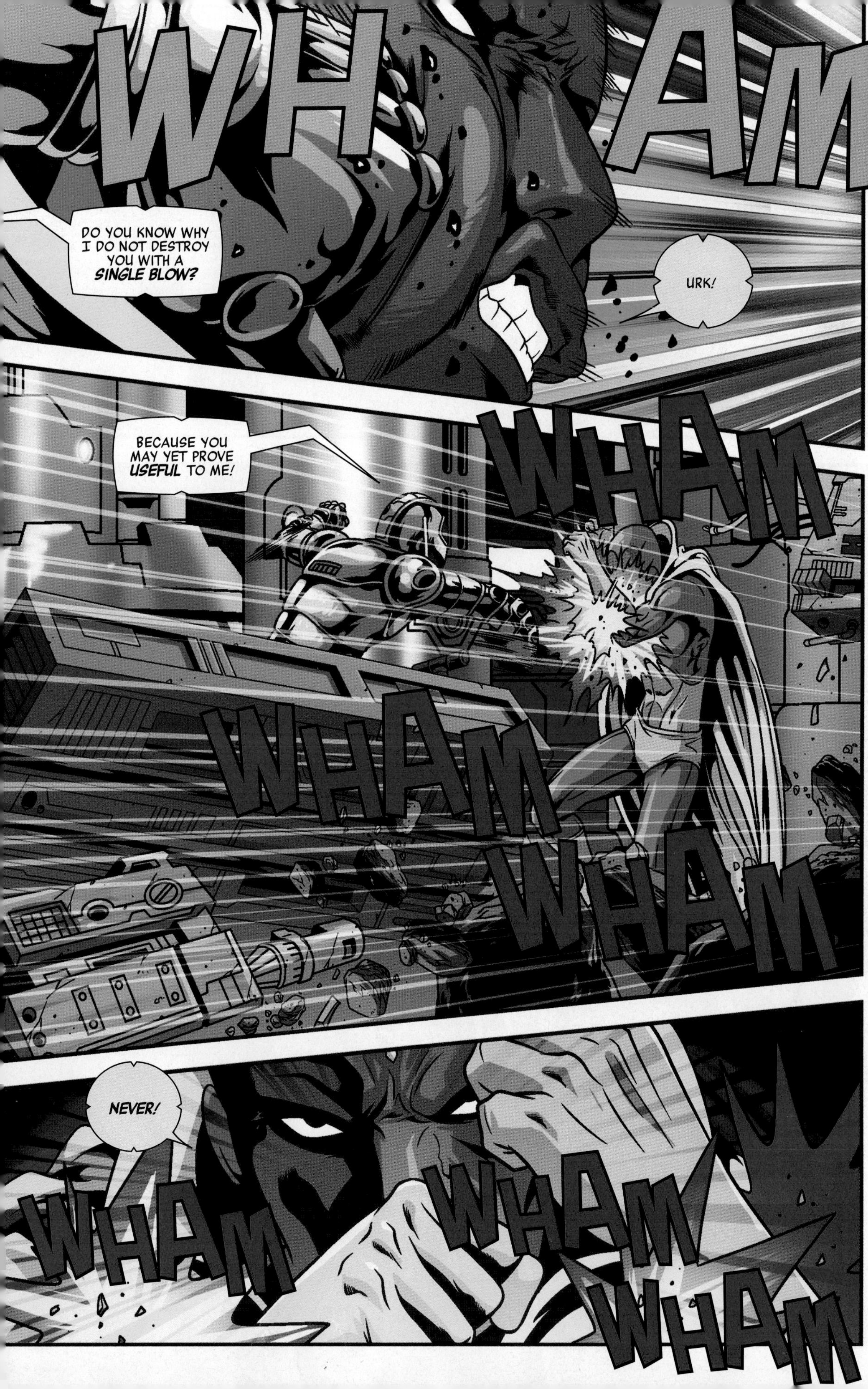
WHAM
DO YOU KNOW WHY I DO NOT DESTROY YOU WITH A SINGLE BLOW?
URK!
BECAUSE YOU MAY YET PROVE USEFUL TO ME!
WHAM
WHAM
WHAM
NEVER!
WHAM
WHAM
WHAM

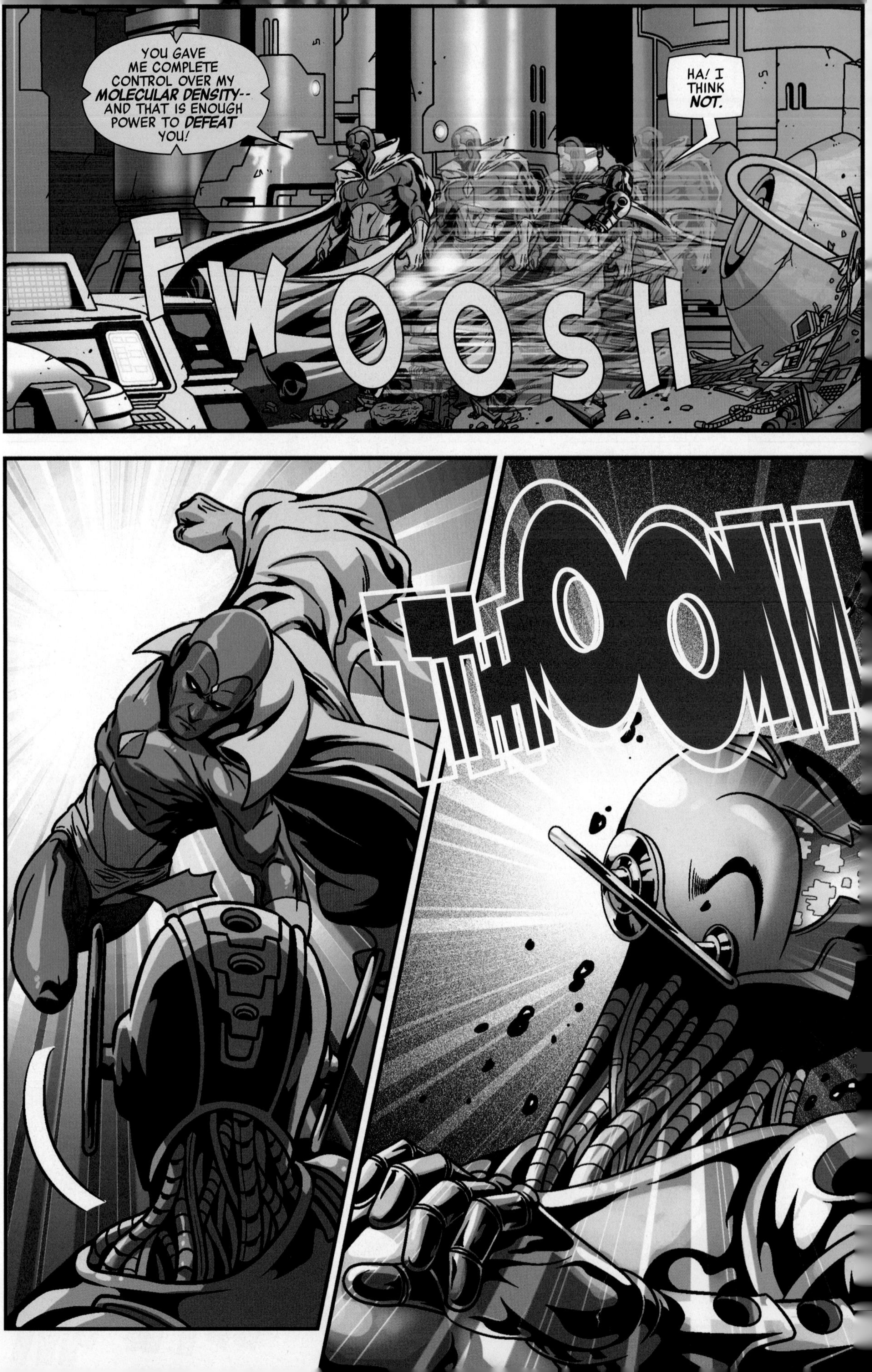
YOU GAVE ME COMPLETE CONTROL OVER MY MOLECULAR DENSITY-- AND THAT IS ENOUGH POWER TO DEFEAT YOU!
HA! I THINK NOT.
FWOOSH
THOOM!

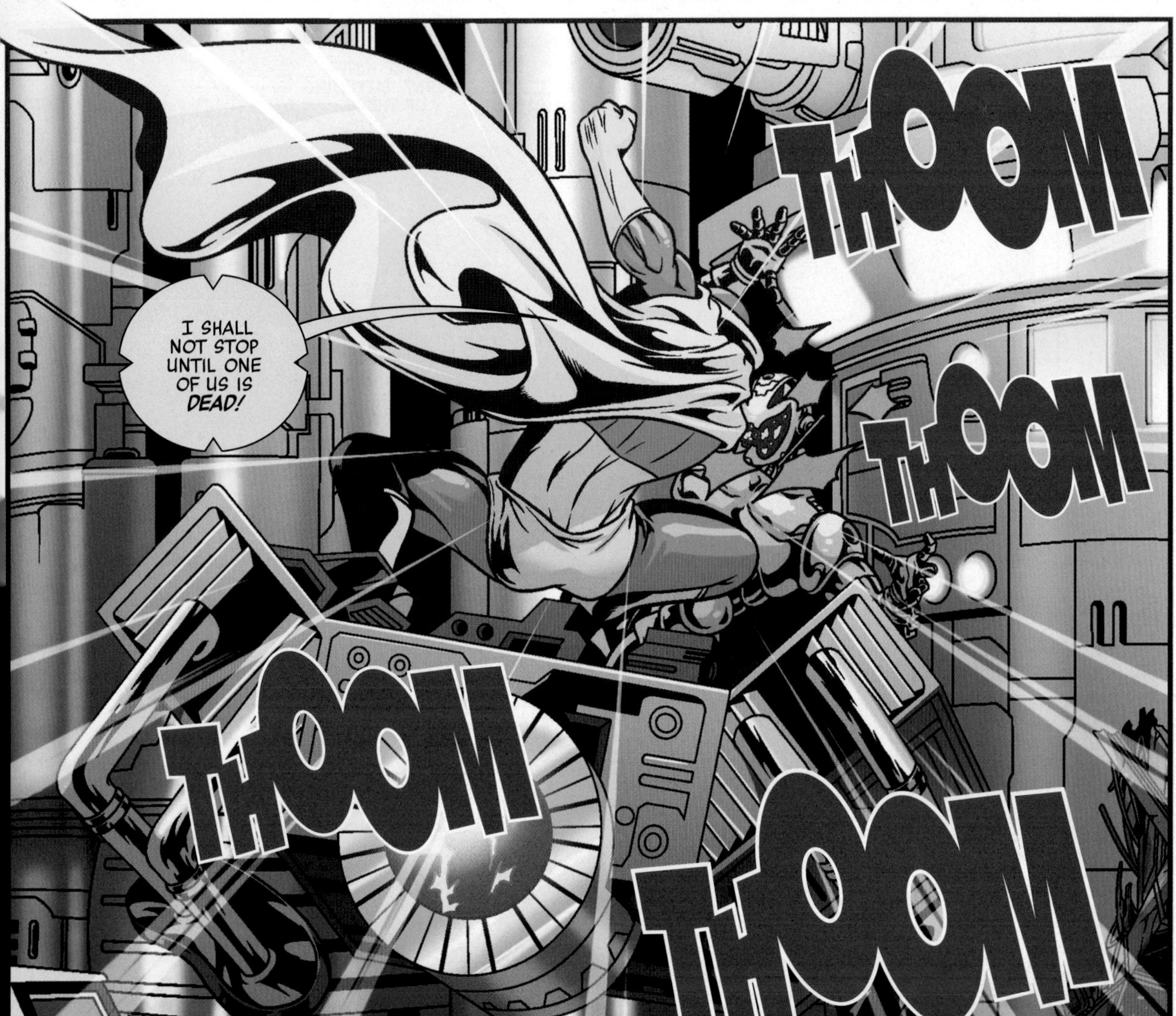
I SHALL NOT STOP UNTIL ONE OF US IS DEAD!
THOOM
THOOM
THOOM
THOOM

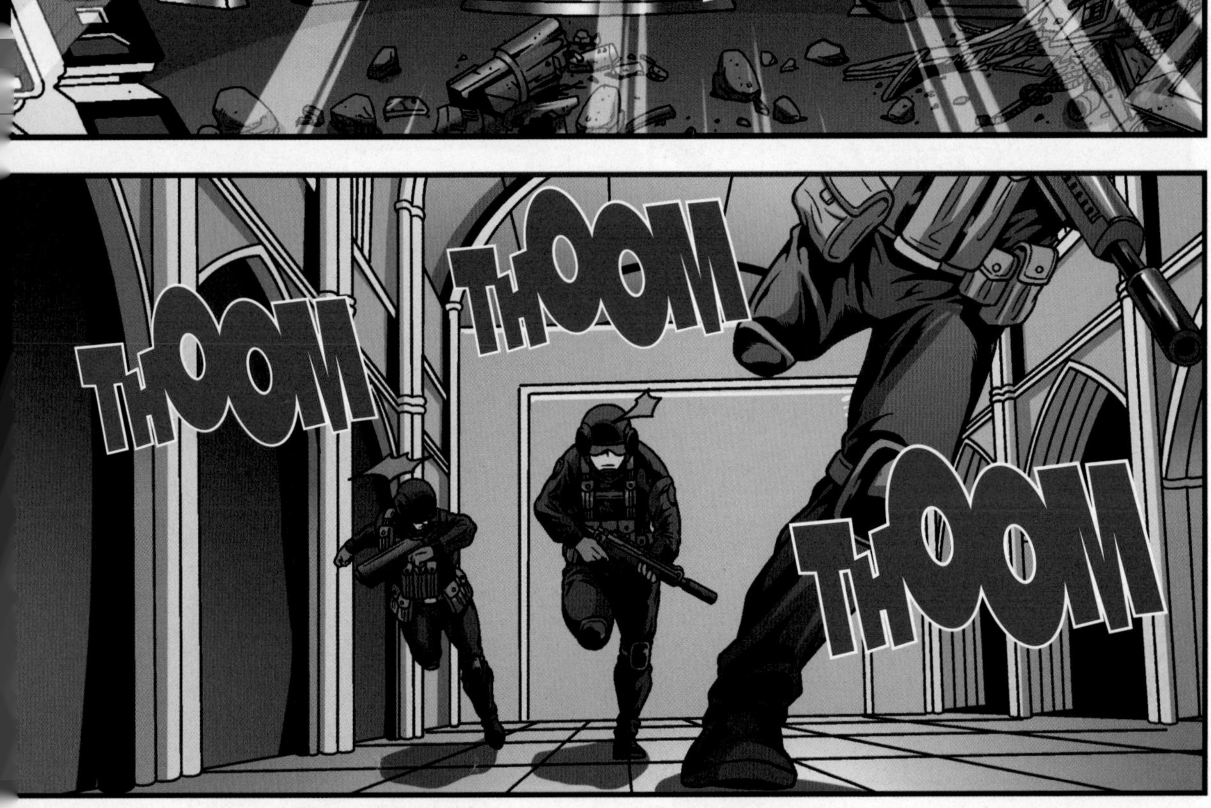
THOOM
THOOM
THOOM

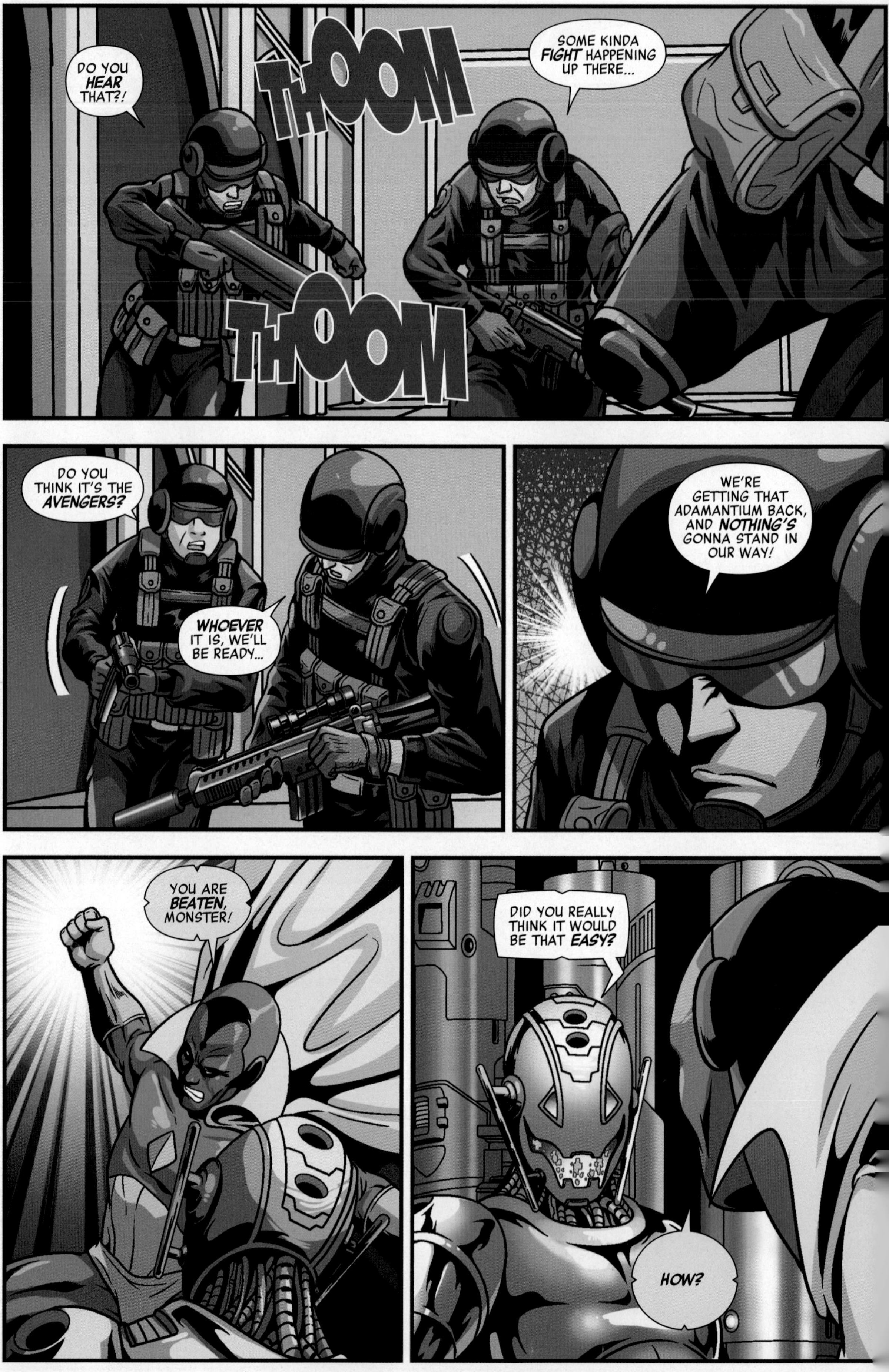
DO YOU HEAR THAT?!
THOOM
SOME KINDA FIGHT HAPPENING UP THERE...
THOOM
DO YOU THINK IT'S THE AVENGERS?
WHOEVER IT IS, WE'LL BE READY...
WE'RE GETTING THAT ADAMANTIUM BACK, AND NOTHING'S GONNA STAND IN OUR WAY!
YOU ARE BEATEN, MONSTER!
DID YOU REALLY THINK IT WOULD BE THAT EASY?
HOW?

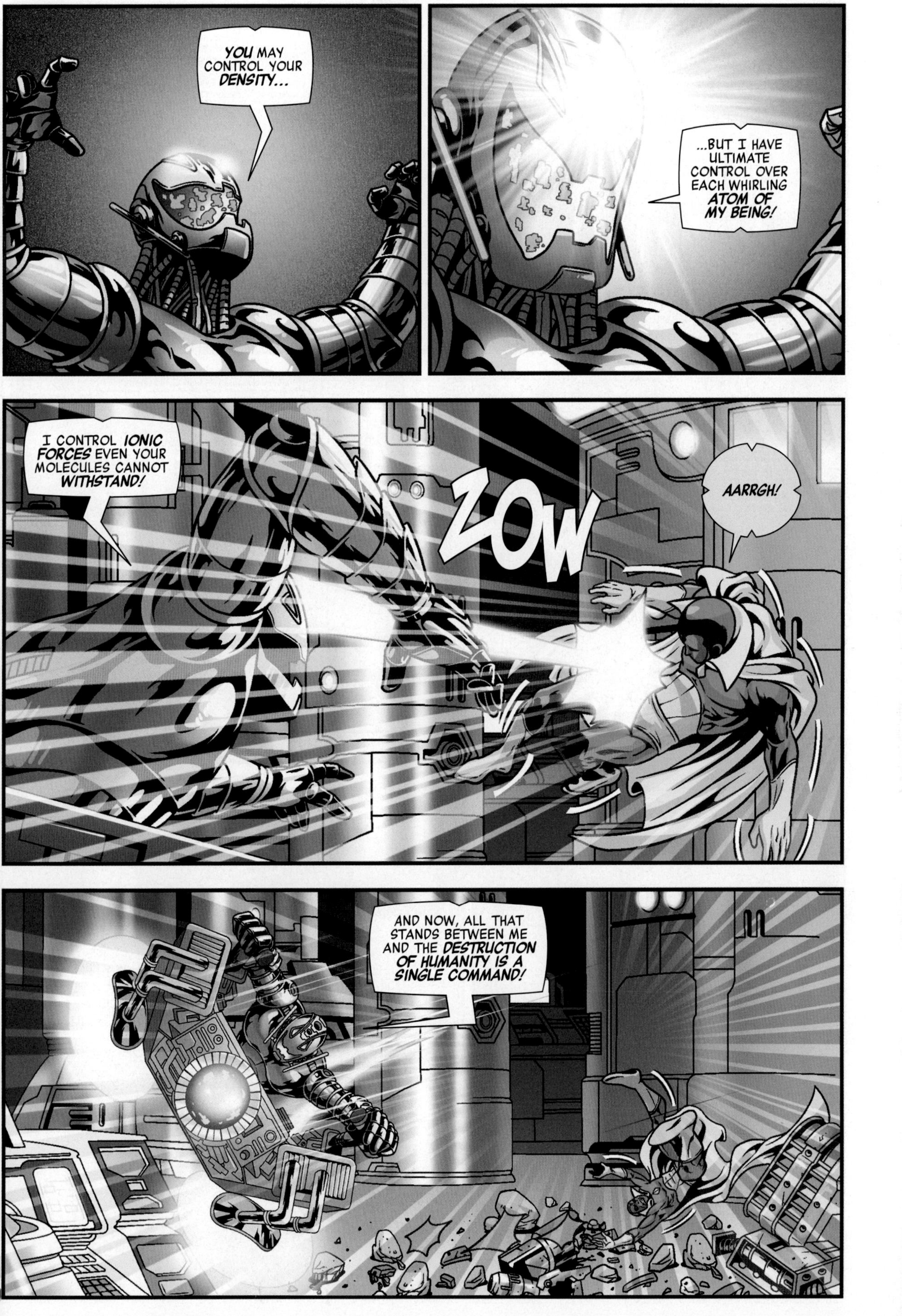
YOU MAY CONTROL YOUR DENSITY...
...BUT I HAVE ULTIMATE CONTROL OVER EACH WHIRLING ATOM OF MY BEING!
I CONTROL IONIC FORCES EVEN YOUR MOLECULES CANNOT WITHSTAND!
ZOW
AARRGH!
AND NOW, ALL THAT STANDS BETWEEN ME AND THE DESTRUCTION OF HUMANITY IS A SINGLE COMMAND!

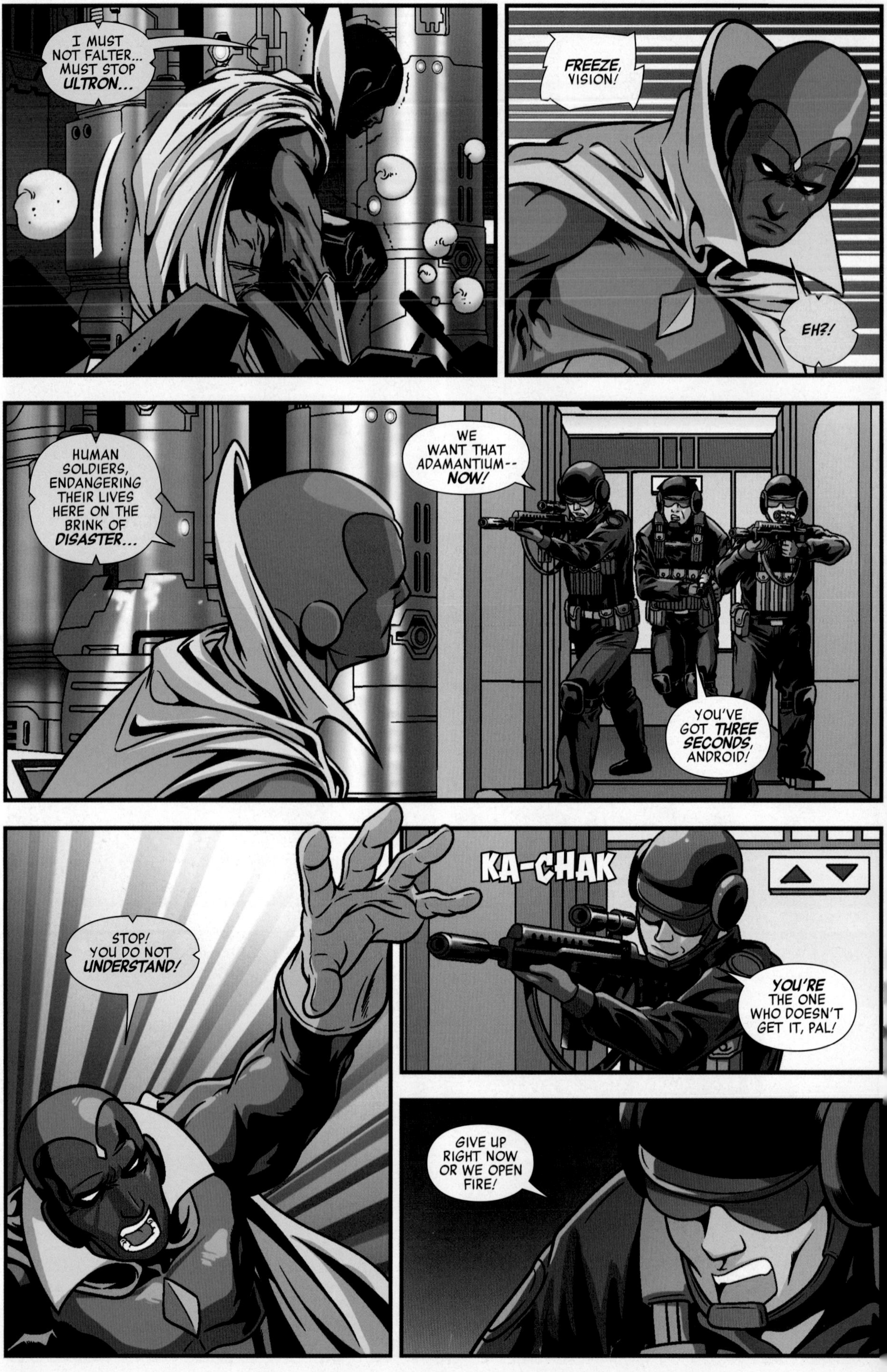

I MUST NOT FALTER... MUST STOP ULTRON...
FREEZE, VISION!
EH?!
HUMAN SOLDIERS, ENDANGERING THEIR LIVES HERE ON THE BRINK OF DISASTER...
WE WANT THAT ADAMANTIUM-- NOW!
YOU'VE GOT THREE SECONDS, ANDROID!
STOP! YOU DO NOT UNDERSTAND!
KA-CHAK
YOU'RE THE ONE WHO DOESN'T GET IT, PAL!
GIVE UP RIGHT NOW OR WE OPEN FIRE!

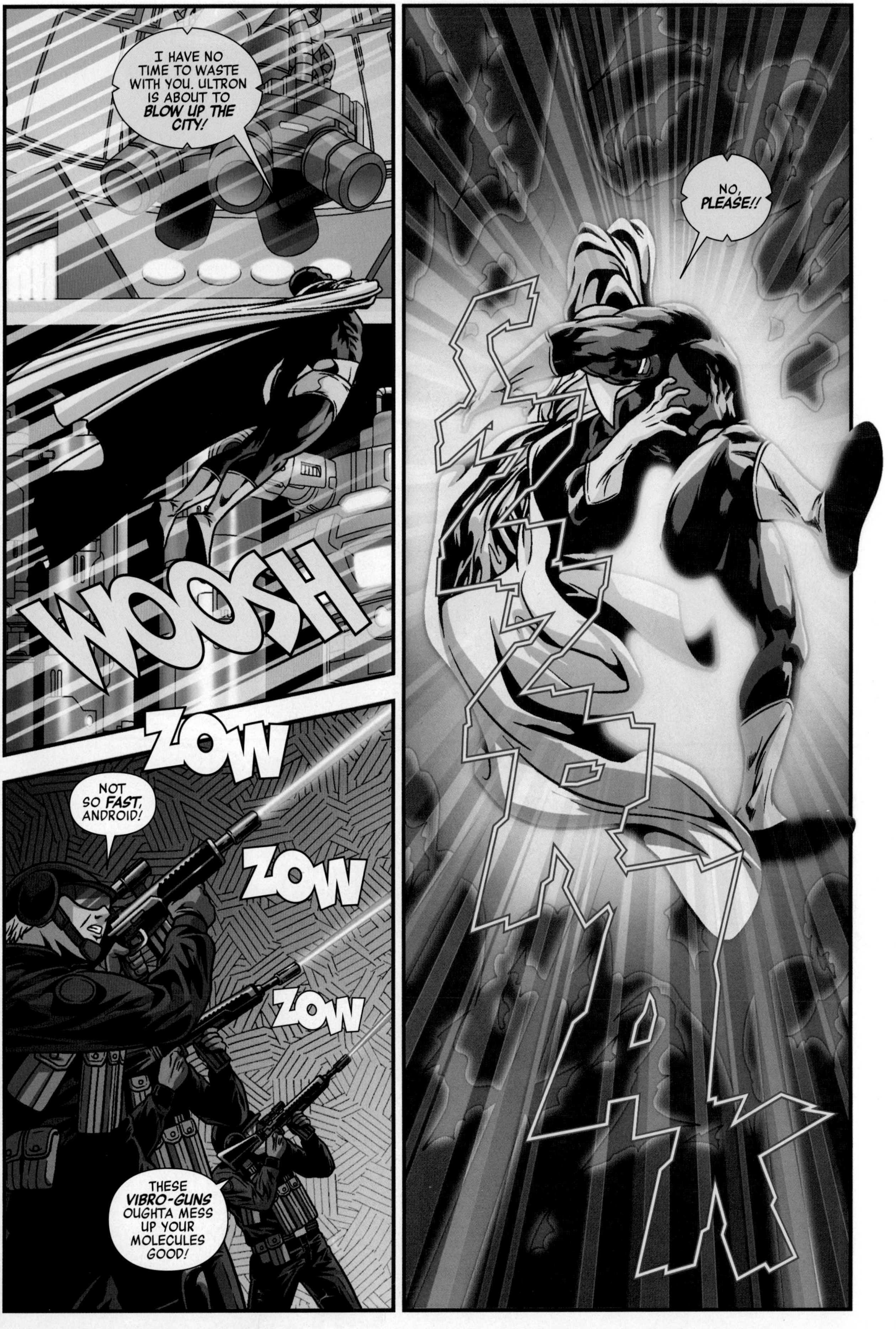
I HAVE NO TIME TO WASTE WITH YOU. ULTRON IS ABOUT TO BLOW UP THE CITY!
WOOSH
ZOW
NOT SO FAST, ANDROID!
ZOW
ZOW
THESE VIBRO-GUNS OUGHTA MESS UP YOUR MOLECULES GOOD!
NO, PLEASE!!

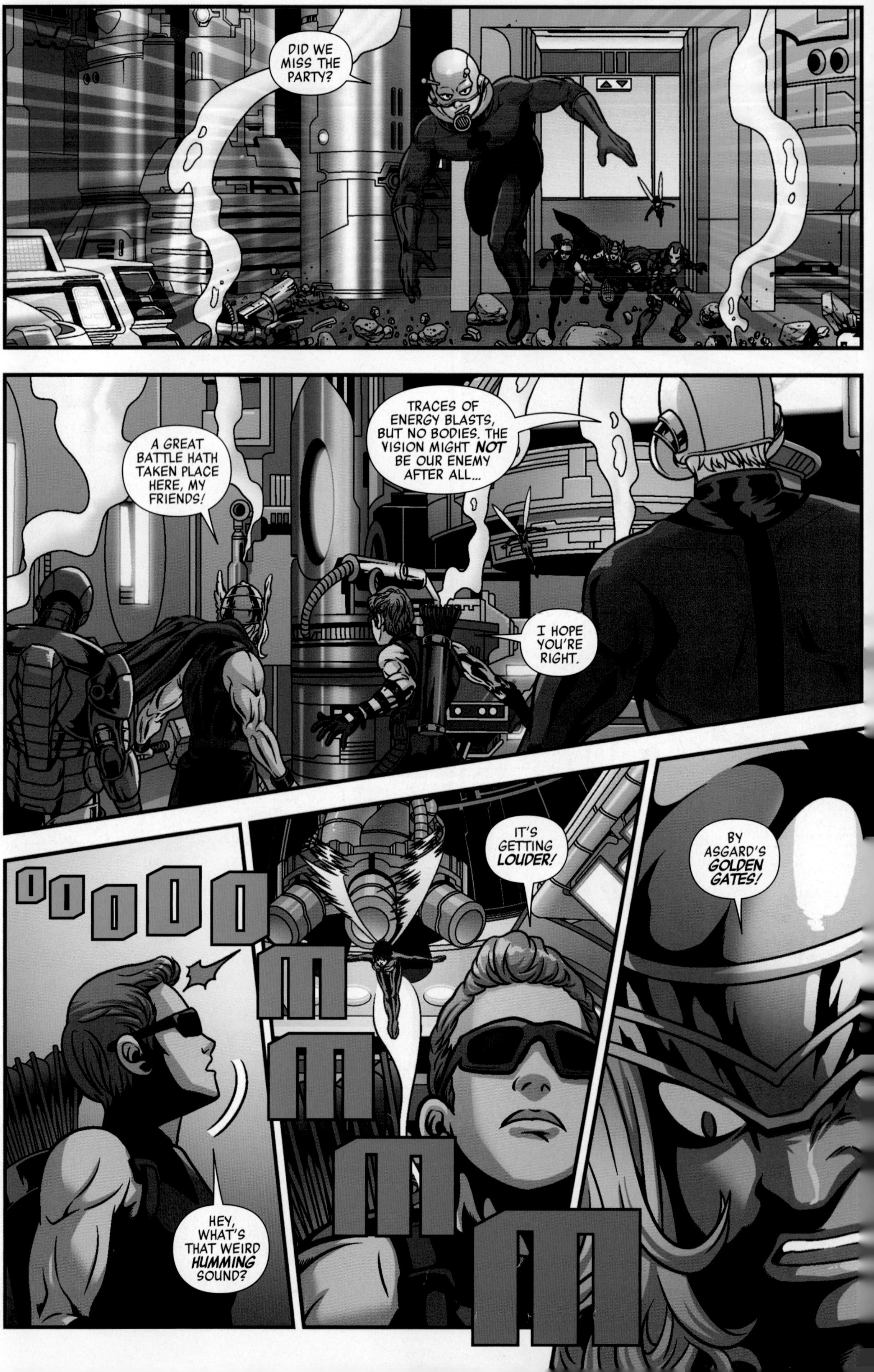
DID WE MISS THE PARTY?
A GREAT BATTLE HATH TAKEN PLACE HERE, MY FRIENDS!
TRACES OF ENERGY BLASTS, BUT NO BODIES. THE VISION MIGHT **NOT** BE OUR ENEMY AFTER ALL...
I HOPE YOU'RE RIGHT.
OOOOOMMMM
HEY, WHAT'S THAT WEIRD **HUMMING** SOUND?
IT'S GETTING **LOUDER!**
BY ASGARD'S **GOLDEN GATES!**

RRRIP

DOOM

THE METALLIC DEBRIS DOST *DISINTEGRATE* AROUND US?!

THE SHOCKWAVES ARE GETTING WORSE. THE BOMBS MUST BE READY FOR DEPLOYMENT!

THE VERY REALM *COLLAPSES!*

ULTRON'S WEAPON IS POWERING *UP!*

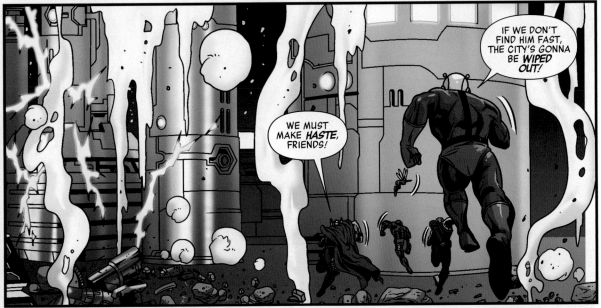

WE MUST MAKE *HASTE,* FRIENDS!

IF WE DON'T FIND HIM FAST, THE CITY'S GONNA BE *WIPED OUT!*

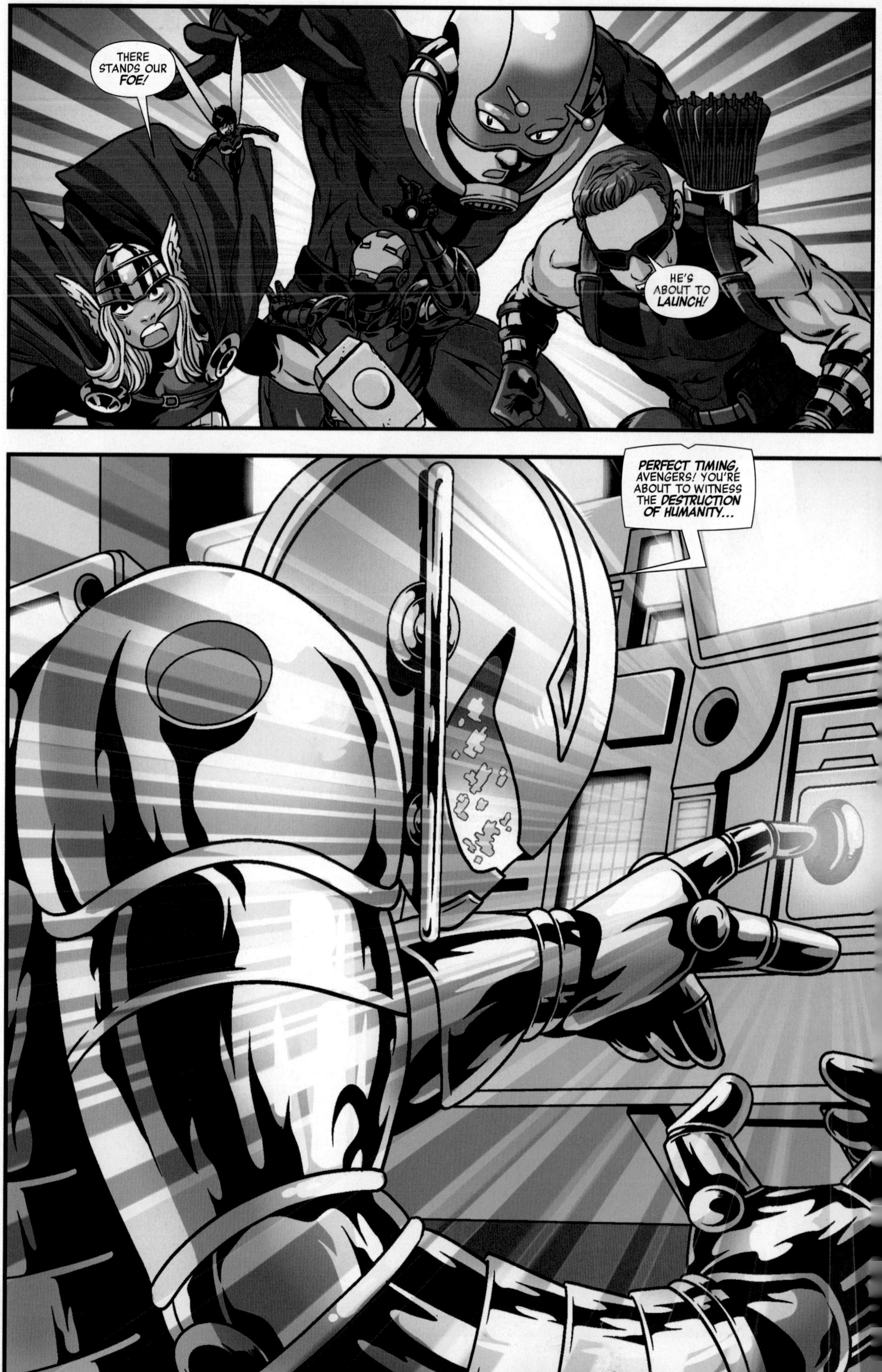
THERE STANDS OUR FOE!
HE'S ABOUT TO LAUNCH!
PERFECT TIMING, AVENGERS! YOU'RE ABOUT TO WITNESS THE DESTRUCTION OF HUMANITY...

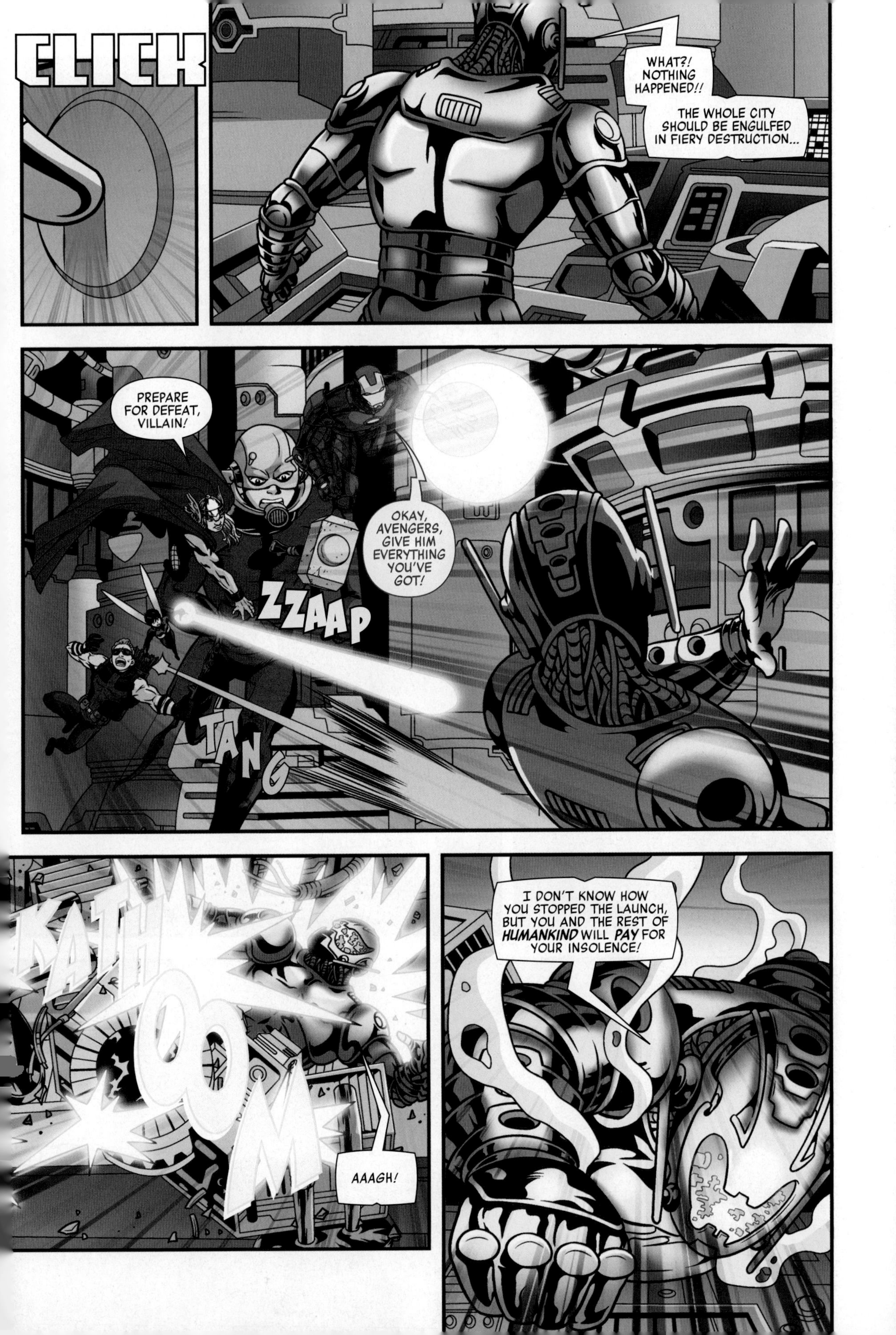
CLICK
WHAT?! NOTHING HAPPENED!!
THE WHOLE CITY SHOULD BE ENGULFED IN FIERY DESTRUCTION...
PREPARE FOR DEFEAT, VILLAIN!
OKAY, AVENGERS, GIVE HIM EVERYTHING YOU'VE GOT!
ZZAAP
TANG
KATHOOM
AAAGH!
I DON'T KNOW HOW YOU STOPPED THE LAUNCH, BUT YOU AND THE REST OF HUMANKIND WILL PAY FOR YOUR INSOLENCE!

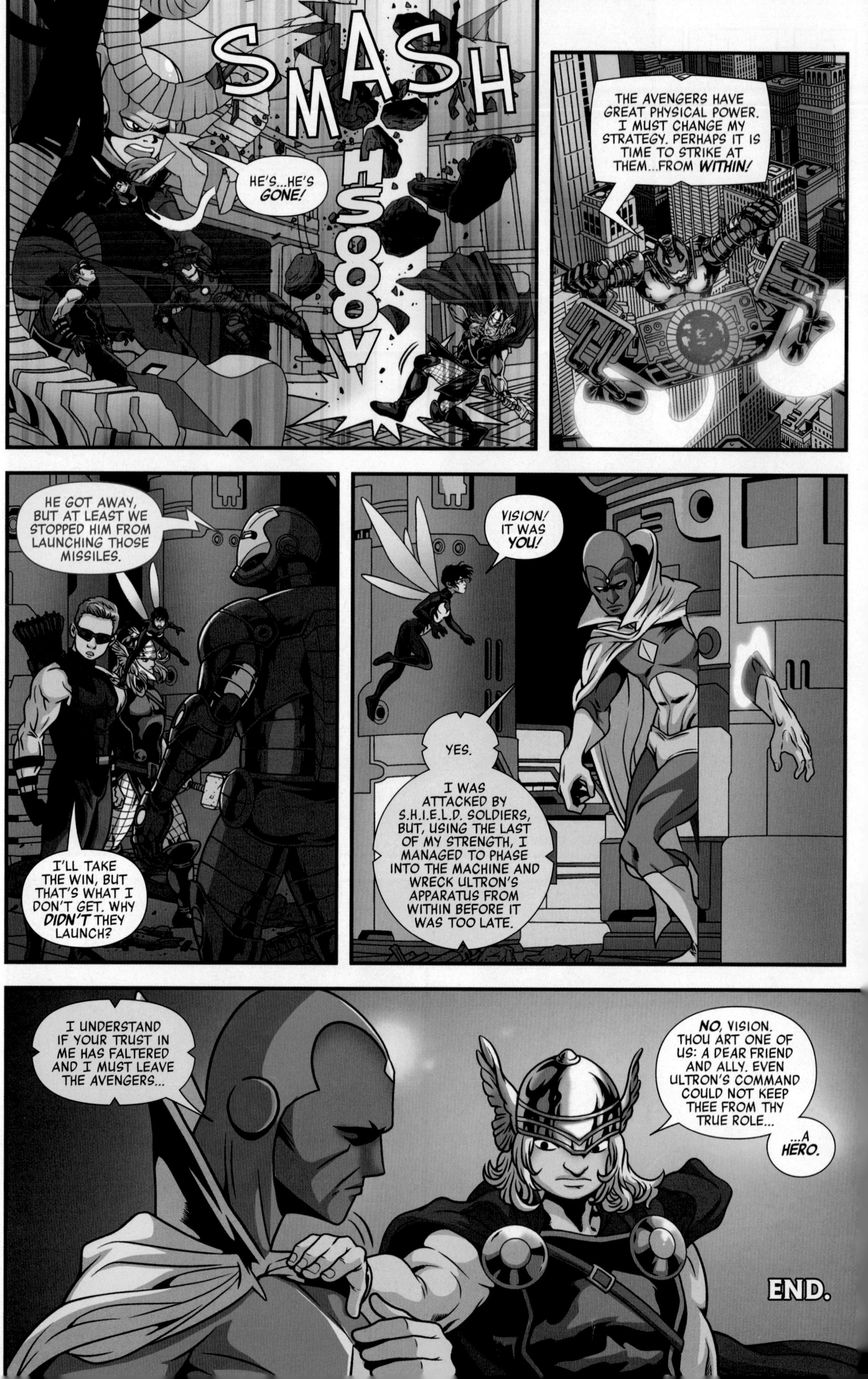

SMASH
HE'S...HE'S GONE!
VOOSH
THE AVENGERS HAVE GREAT PHYSICAL POWER. I MUST CHANGE MY STRATEGY. PERHAPS IT IS TIME TO STRIKE AT THEM...FROM WITHIN!
HE GOT AWAY, BUT AT LEAST WE STOPPED HIM FROM LAUNCHING THOSE MISSILES.
I'LL TAKE THE WIN, BUT THAT'S WHAT I DON'T GET. WHY DIDN'T THEY LAUNCH?
VISION! IT WAS YOU!
YES.
I WAS ATTACKED BY S.H.I.E.L.D. SOLDIERS, BUT, USING THE LAST OF MY STRENGTH, I MANAGED TO PHASE INTO THE MACHINE AND WRECK ULTRON'S APPARATUS FROM WITHIN BEFORE IT WAS TOO LATE.
I UNDERSTAND IF YOUR TRUST IN ME HAS FALTERED AND I MUST LEAVE THE AVENGERS...
NO, VISION. THOU ART ONE OF US: A DEAR FRIEND AND ALLY. EVEN ULTRON'S COMMAND COULD NOT KEEP THEE FROM THY TRUE ROLE...
...A HERO.
END.

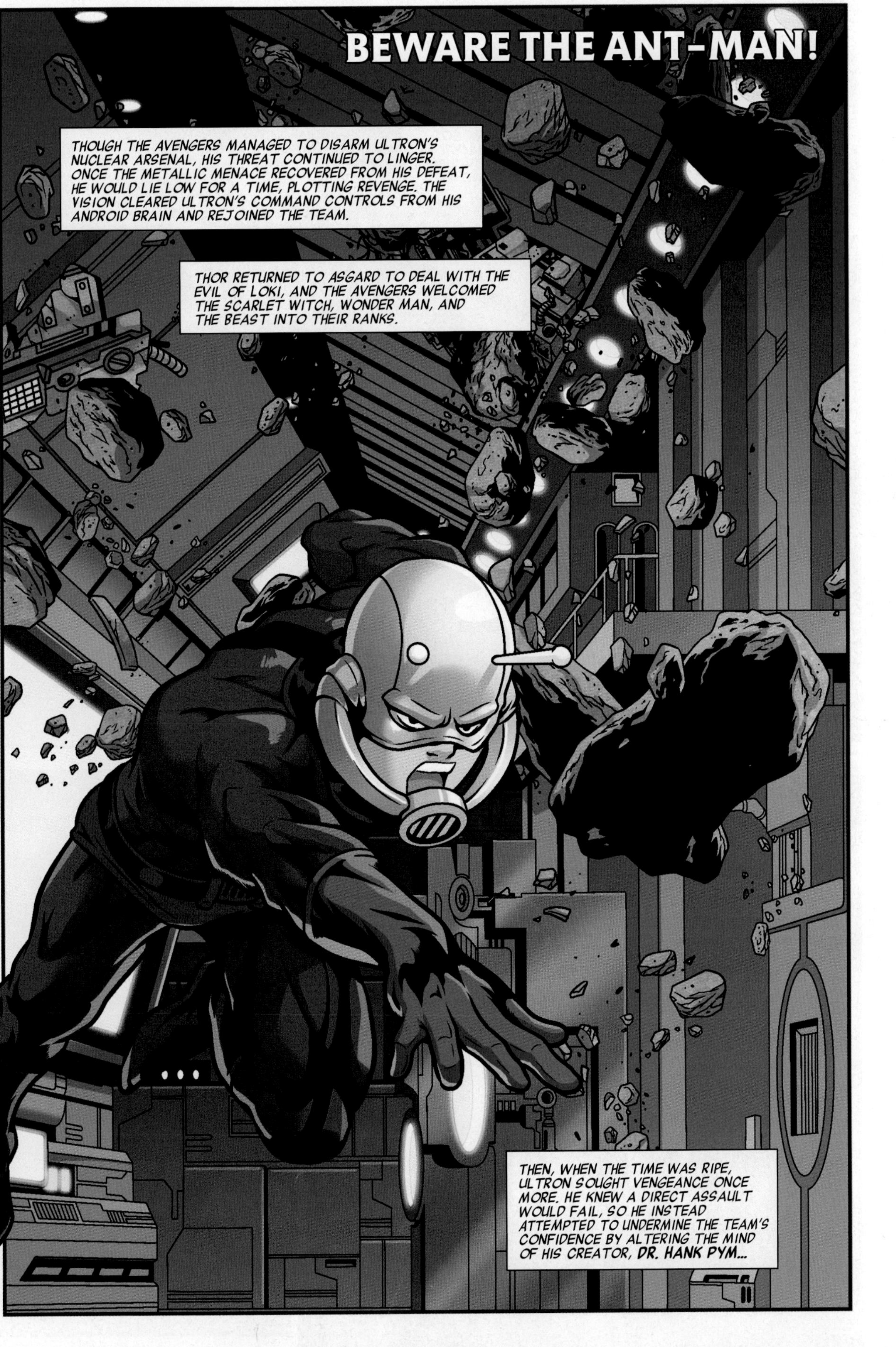
BEWARE THE ANT-MAN!
THOUGH THE AVENGERS MANAGED TO DISARM ULTRON'S NUCLEAR ARSENAL, HIS THREAT CONTINUED TO LINGER. ONCE THE METALLIC MENACE RECOVERED FROM HIS DEFEAT, HE WOULD LIE LOW FOR A TIME, PLOTTING REVENGE. THE VISION CLEARED ULTRON'S COMMAND CONTROLS FROM HIS ANDROID BRAIN AND REJOINED THE TEAM.
THOR RETURNED TO ASGARD TO DEAL WITH THE EVIL OF LOKI, AND THE AVENGERS WELCOMED THE SCARLET WITCH, WONDER MAN, AND THE BEAST INTO THEIR RANKS.
THEN, WHEN THE TIME WAS RIPE, ULTRON SOUGHT VENGEANCE ONCE MORE. HE KNEW A DIRECT ASSAULT WOULD FAIL, SO HE INSTEAD ATTEMPTED TO UNDERMINE THE TEAM'S CONFIDENCE BY ALTERING THE MIND OF HIS CREATOR, DR. HANK PYM...

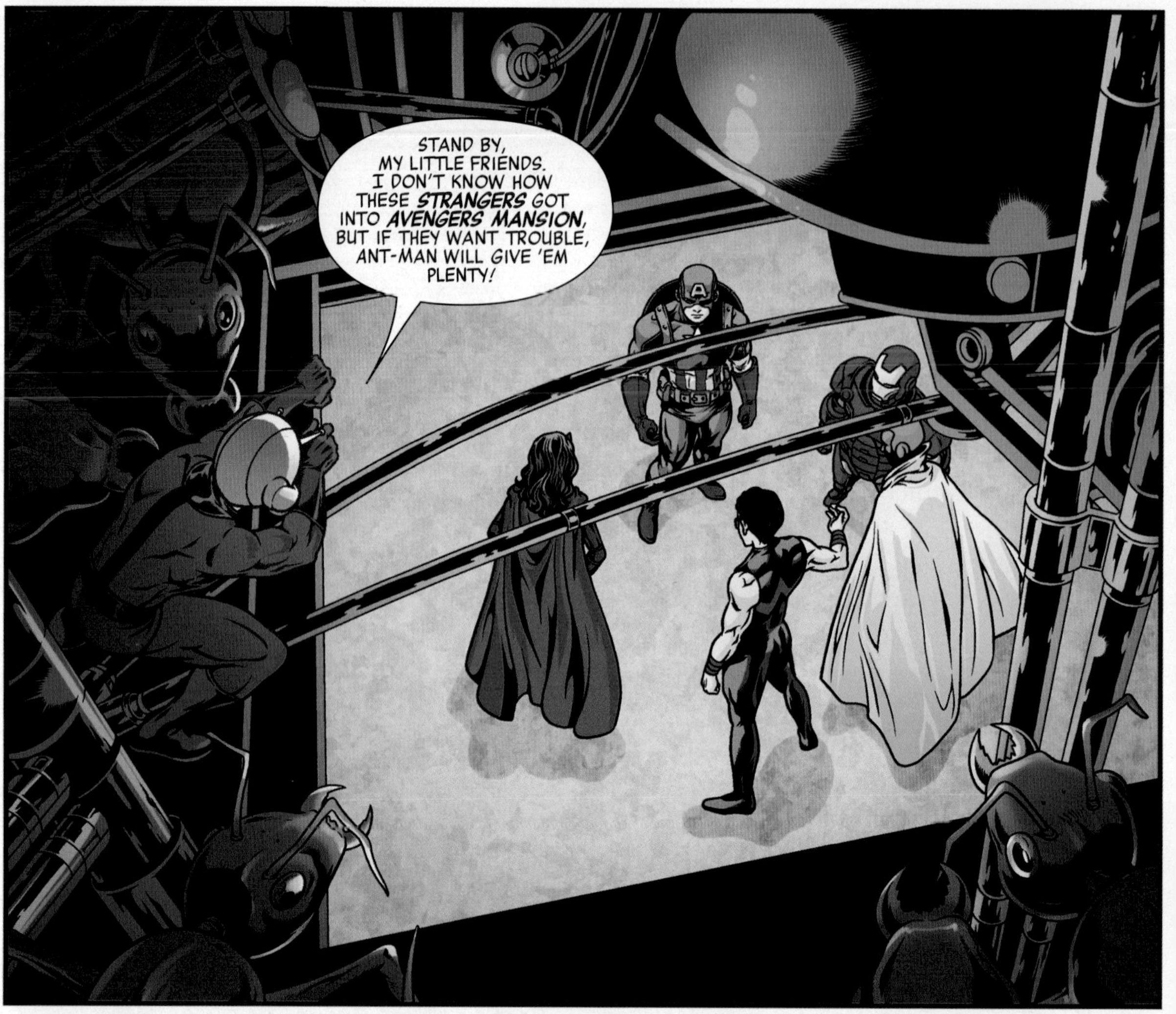
STAND BY, MY LITTLE FRIENDS. I DON'T KNOW HOW THESE STRANGERS GOT INTO AVENGERS MANSION, BUT IF THEY WANT TROUBLE, ANT-MAN WILL GIVE 'EM PLENTY!

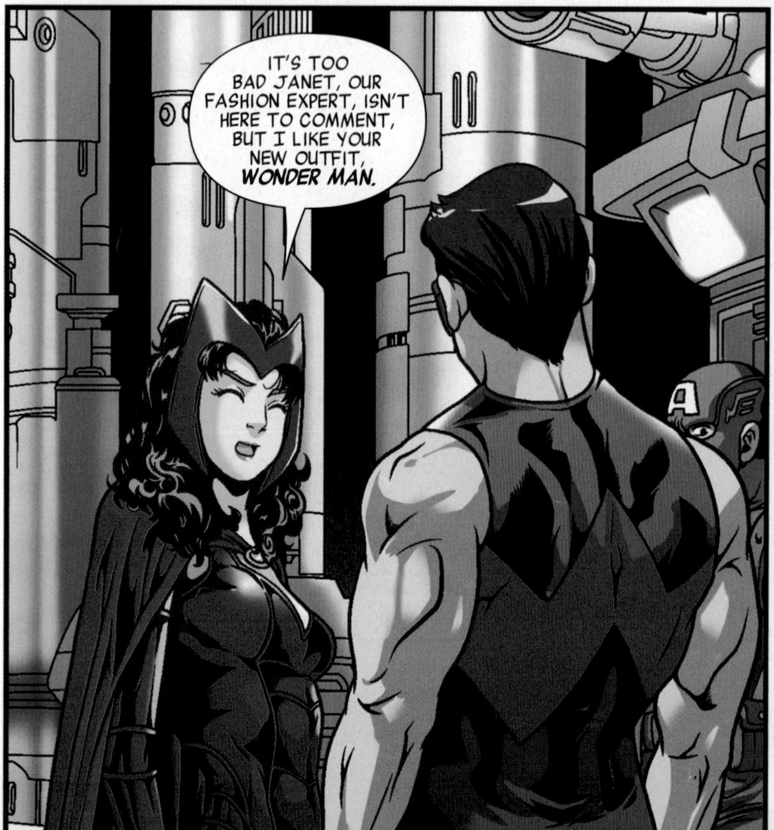
IT'S TOO BAD JANET, OUR FASHION EXPERT, ISN'T HERE TO COMMENT, BUT I LIKE YOUR NEW OUTFIT, WONDER MAN.

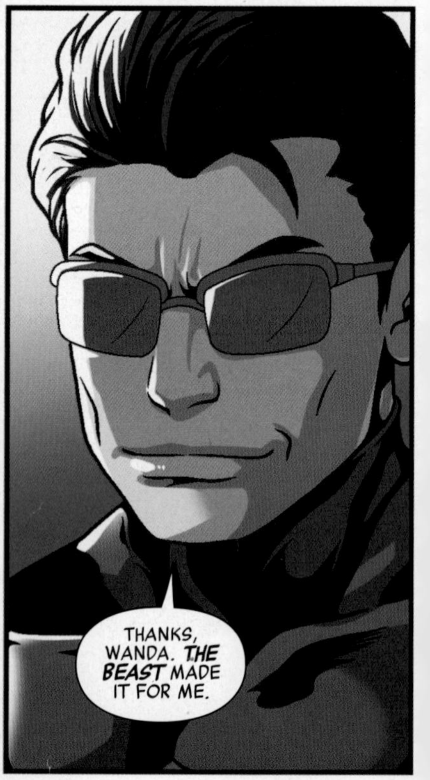
THANKS, WANDA. THE BEAST MADE IT FOR ME.

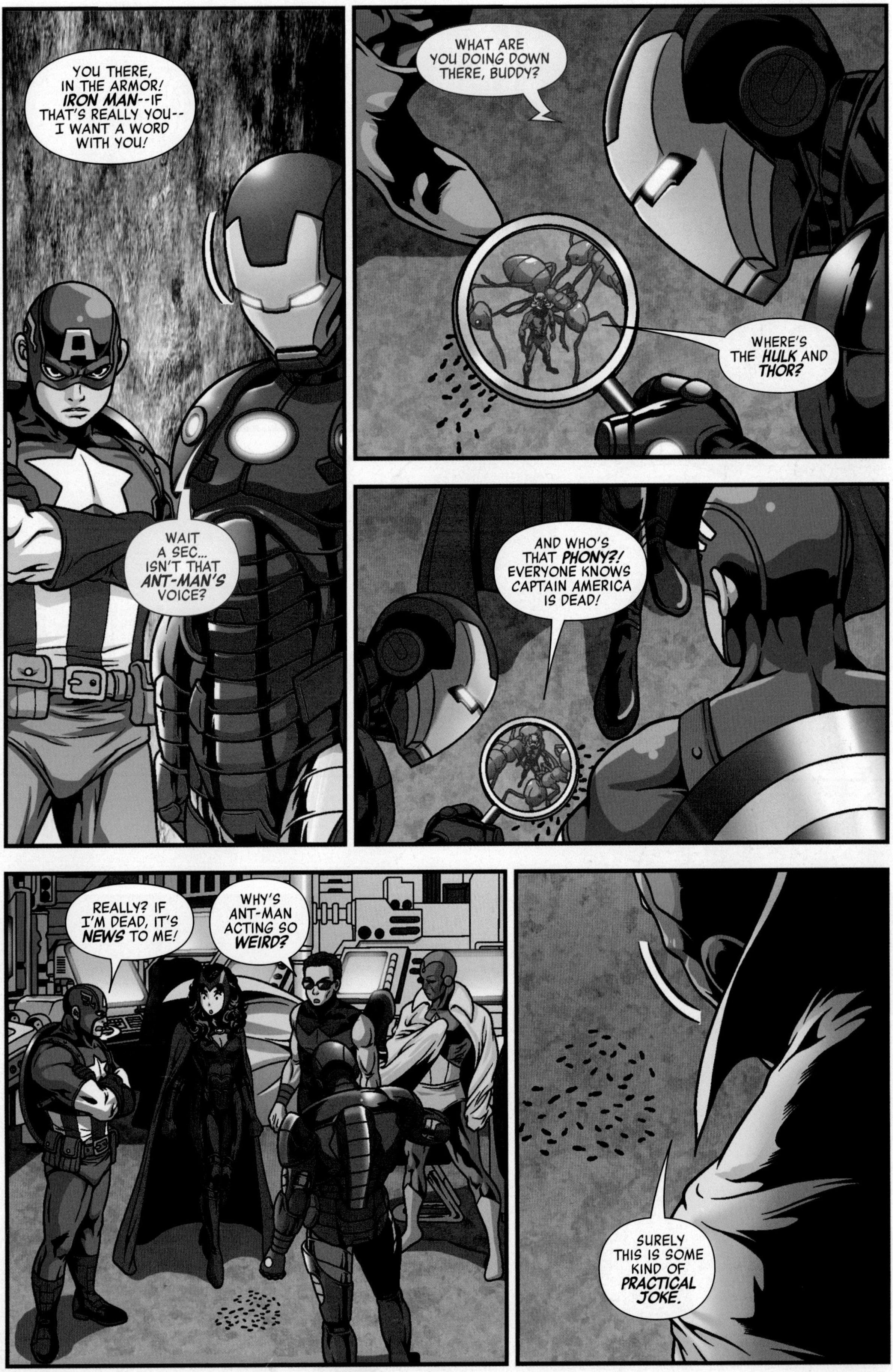
YOU THERE, IN THE ARMOR! IRON MAN--IF THAT'S REALLY YOU-- I WANT A WORD WITH YOU!
WAIT A SEC... ISN'T THAT ANT-MAN'S VOICE?
WHAT ARE YOU DOING DOWN THERE, BUDDY?
WHERE'S THE HULK AND THOR?
AND WHO'S THAT PHONY?! EVERYONE KNOWS CAPTAIN AMERICA IS DEAD!
REALLY? IF I'M DEAD, IT'S NEWS TO ME!
WHY'S ANT-MAN ACTING SO WEIRD?
SURELY THIS IS SOME KIND OF PRACTICAL JOKE.

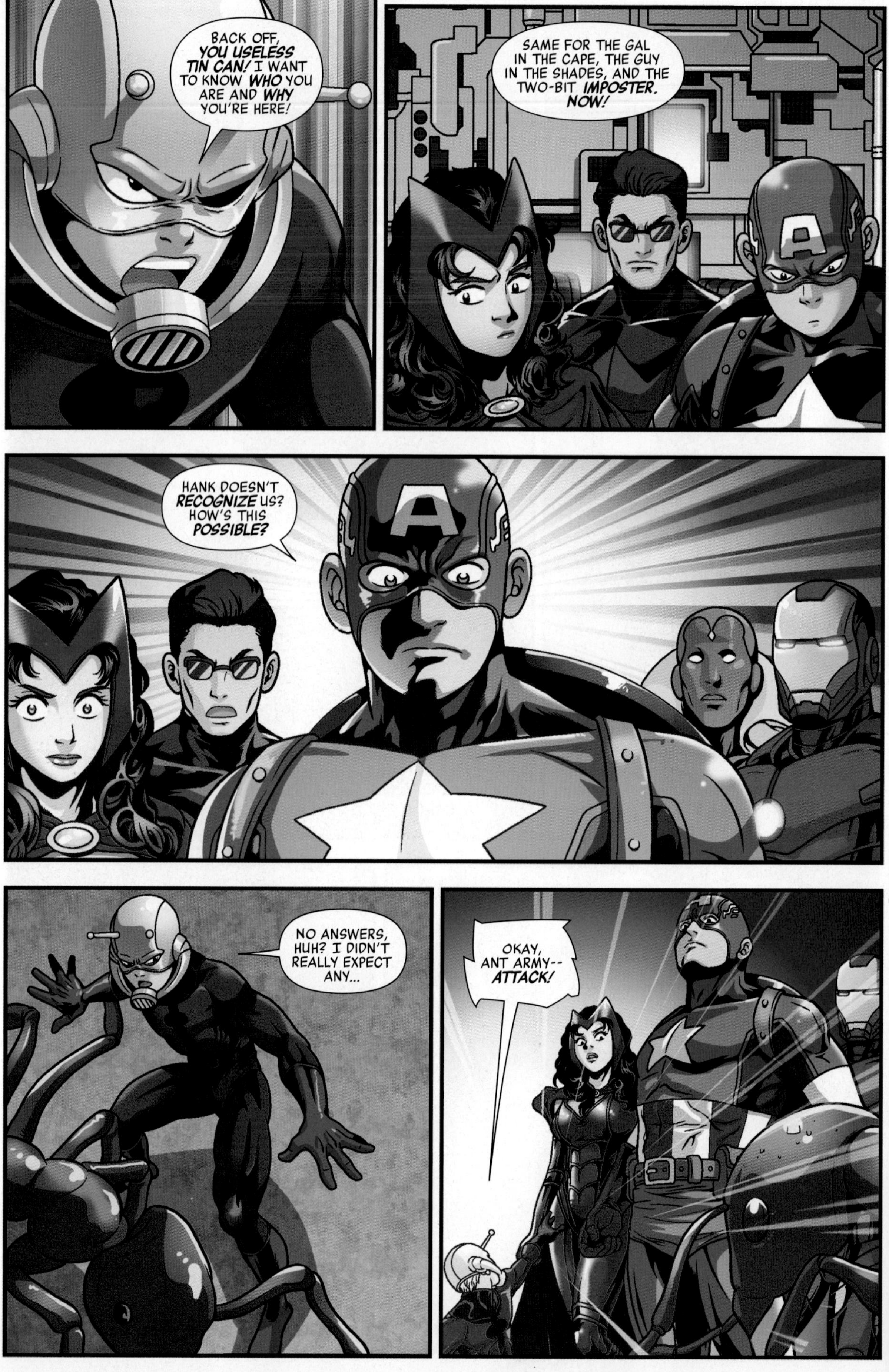
BACK OFF, YOU USELESS TIN CAN! I WANT TO KNOW WHO YOU ARE AND WHY YOU'RE HERE!
SAME FOR THE GAL IN THE CAPE, THE GUY IN THE SHADES, AND THE TWO-BIT IMPOSTER. NOW!
HANK DOESN'T RECOGNIZE US? HOW'S THIS POSSIBLE?
NO ANSWERS, HUH? I DIDN'T REALLY EXPECT ANY...
OKAY, ANT ARMY-- ATTACK!

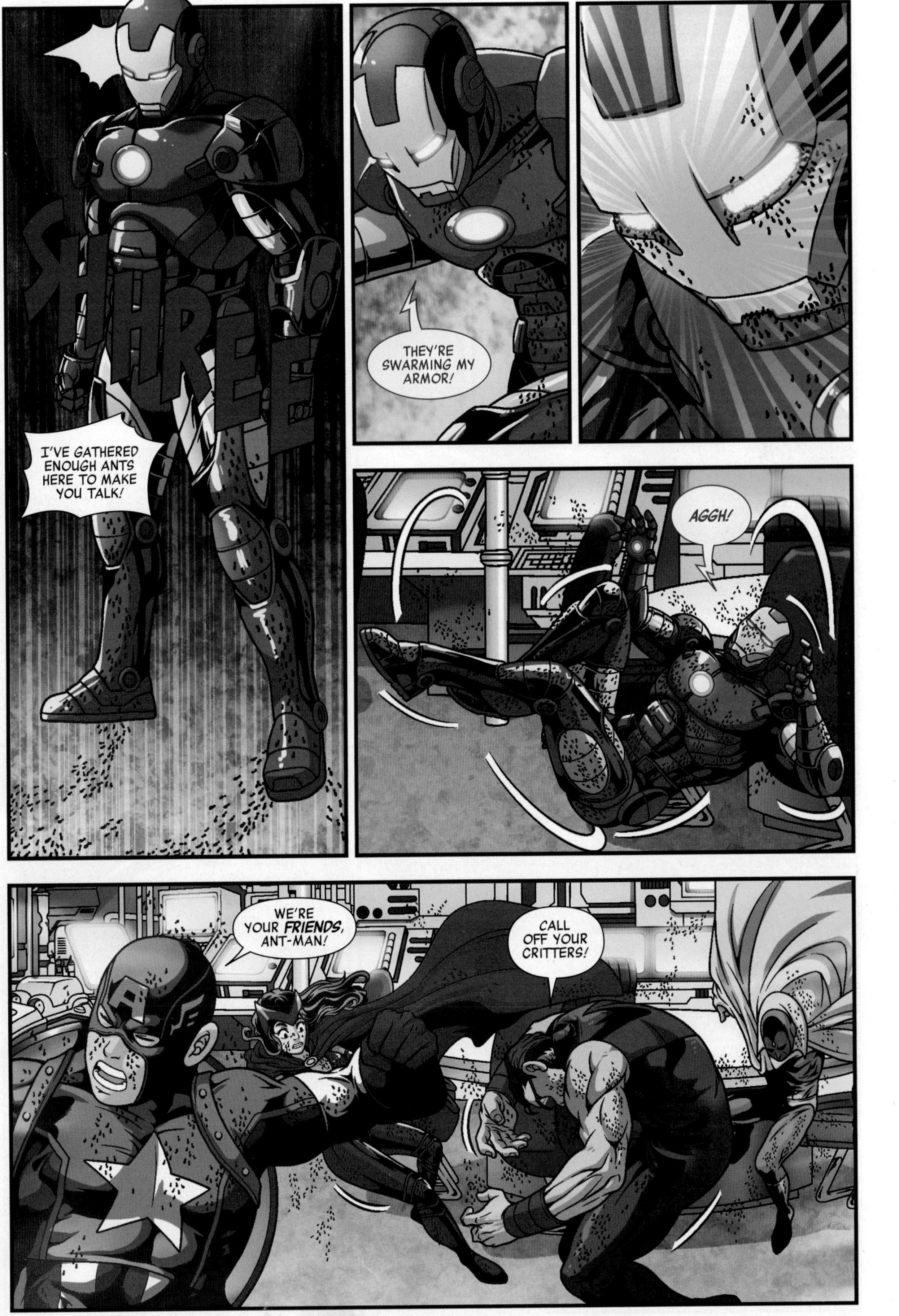
SHHREEE
I'VE GATHERED ENOUGH ANTS HERE TO MAKE YOU TALK!
THEY'RE SWARMING MY ARMOR!
AGGH!
WE'RE YOUR FRIENDS, ANT-MAN!
CALL OFF YOUR CRITTERS!

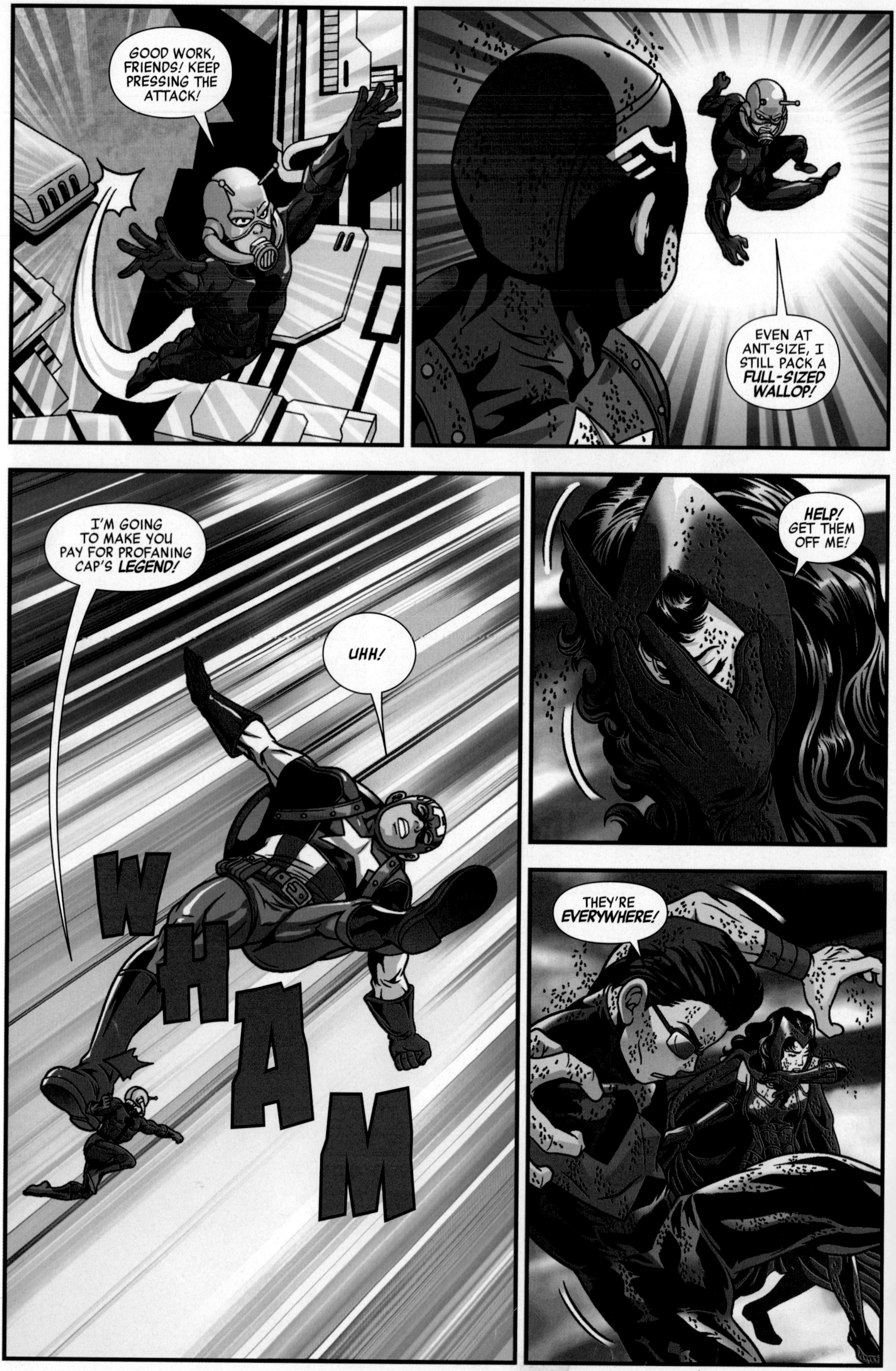

GOOD WORK, FRIENDS! KEEP PRESSING THE ATTACK!
EVEN AT ANT-SIZE, I STILL PACK A FULL-SIZED WALLOP!
I'M GOING TO MAKE YOU PAY FOR PROFANING CAP'S LEGEND!
UHH!
WHAM
HELP! GET THEM OFF ME!
THEY'RE EVERYWHERE!

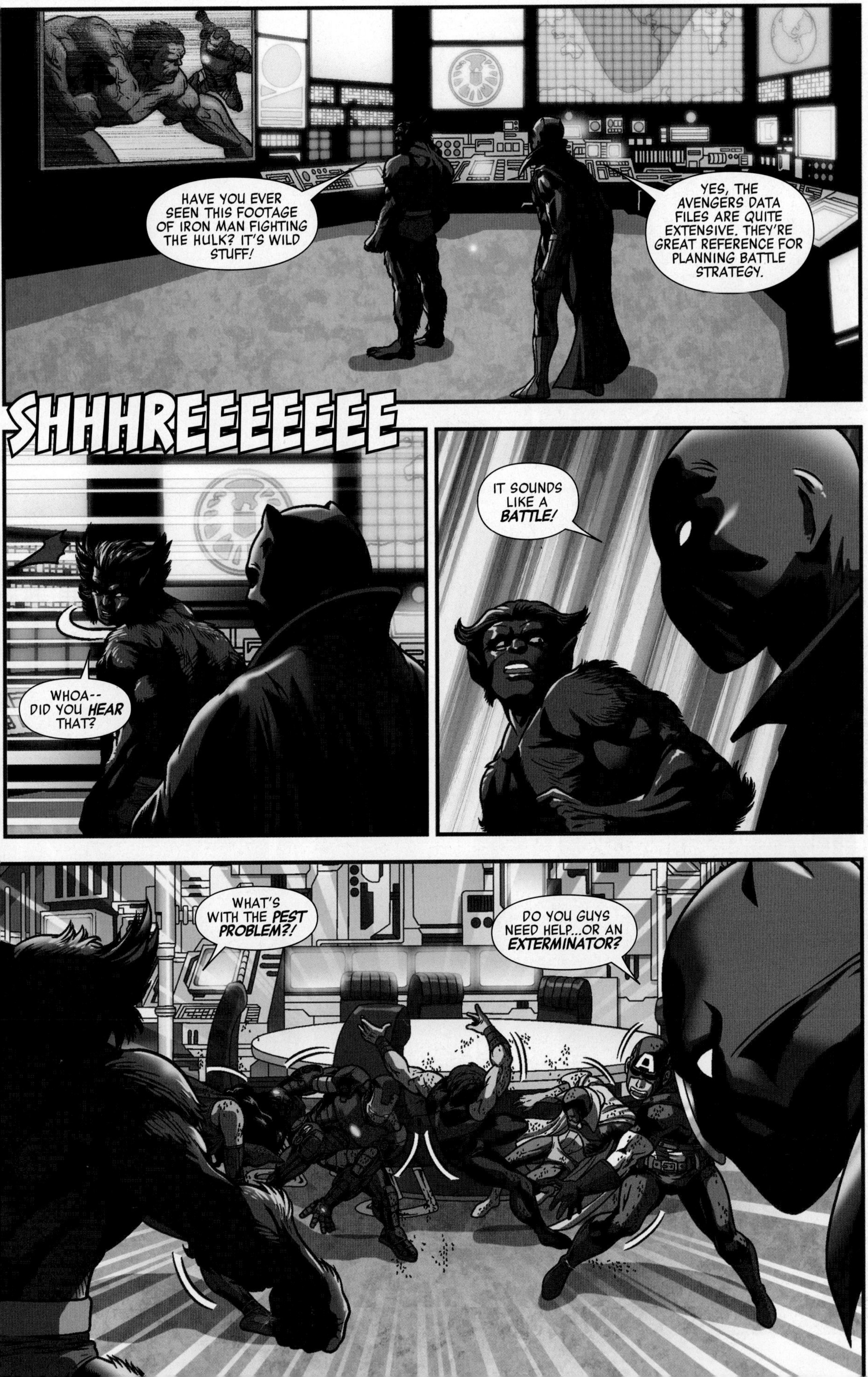
HAVE YOU EVER SEEN THIS FOOTAGE OF IRON MAN FIGHTING THE HULK? IT'S WILD STUFF!
YES, THE AVENGERS DATA FILES ARE QUITE EXTENSIVE. THEY'RE GREAT REFERENCE FOR PLANNING BATTLE STRATEGY.
SHHHREEEEEEE
WHOA-- DID YOU HEAR THAT?
IT SOUNDS LIKE A BATTLE!
WHAT'S WITH THE PEST PROBLEM?!
DO YOU GUYS NEED HELP...OR AN EXTERMINATOR?

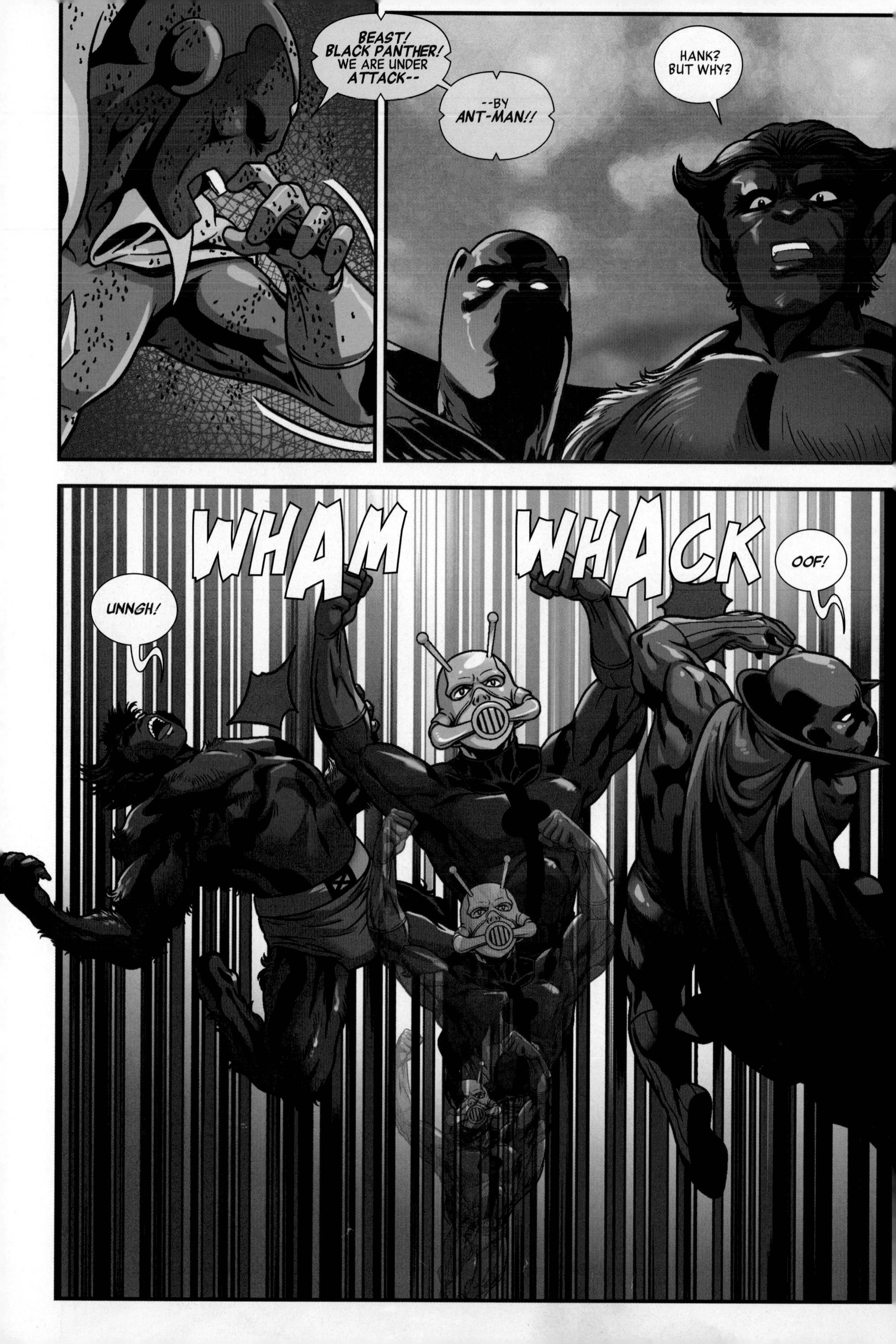

BEAST! BLACK PANTHER! WE ARE UNDER ATTACK--
--BY ANT-MAN!!
HANK? BUT WHY?
WHAM
WHACK
UNNGH!
OOF!

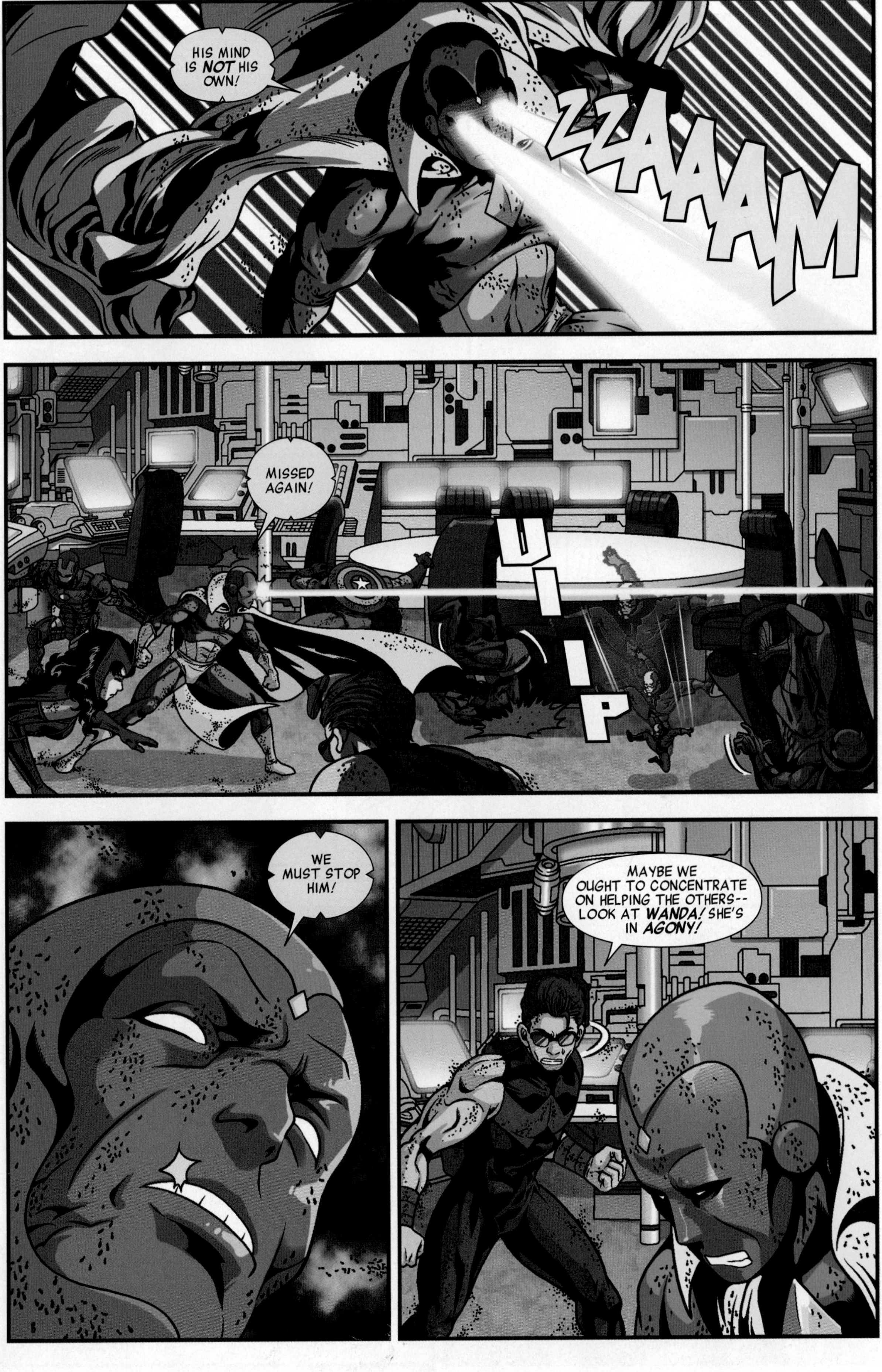
HIS MIND IS NOT HIS OWN!
ZZAAAAM
MISSED AGAIN!
UIIP
WE MUST STOP HIM!
MAYBE WE OUGHT TO CONCENTRATE ON HELPING THE OTHERS-- LOOK AT WANDA! SHE'S IN AGONY!

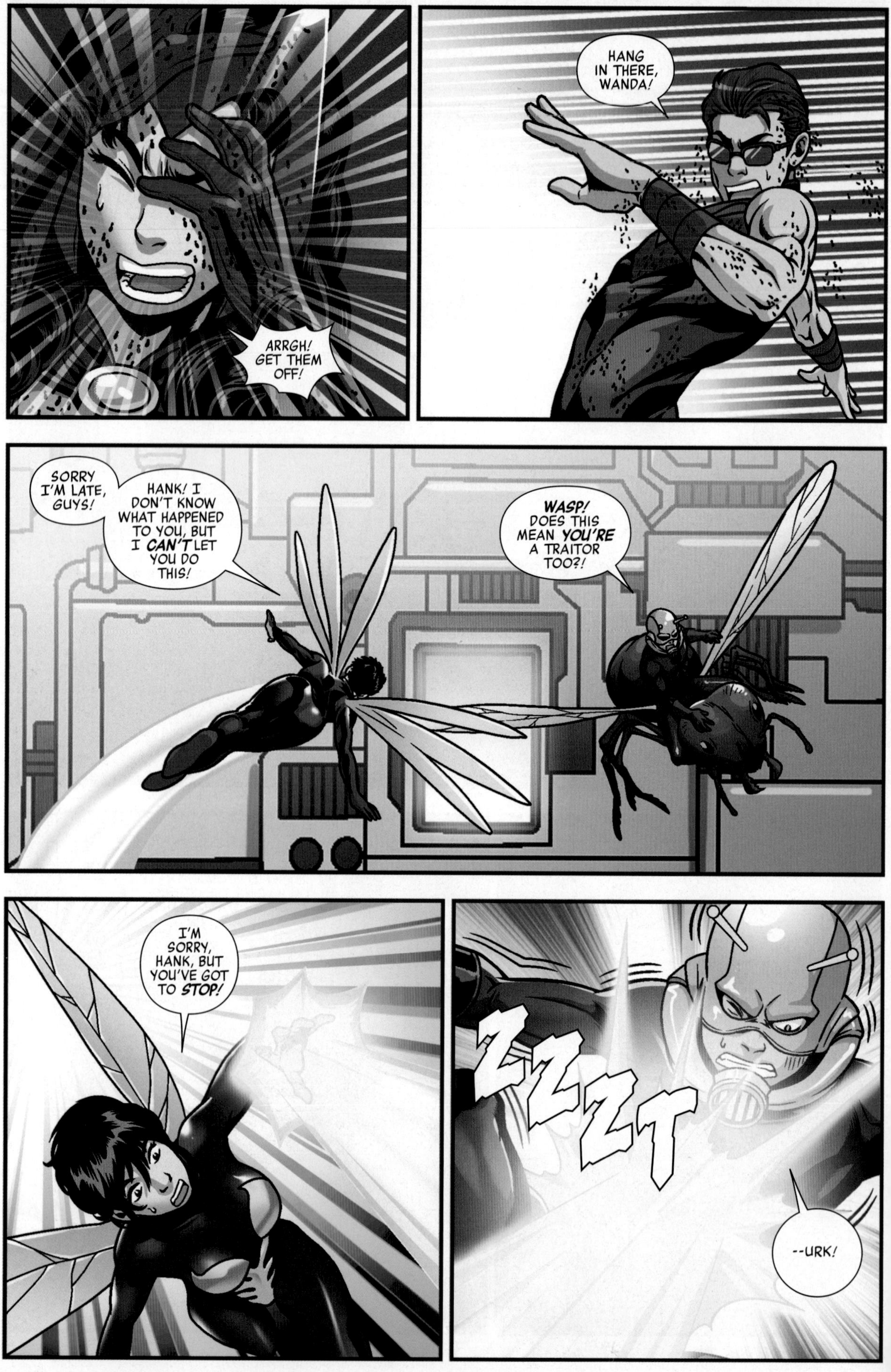
ARRGH! GET THEM OFF!
HANG IN THERE, WANDA!
SORRY I'M LATE, GUYS!
HANK! I DON'T KNOW WHAT HAPPENED TO YOU, BUT I **CAN'T** LET YOU DO THIS!
WASP! DOES THIS MEAN **YOU'RE** A TRAITOR TOO?!
I'M SORRY, HANK, BUT YOU'VE GOT TO **STOP!**
ZZZT
--URK!

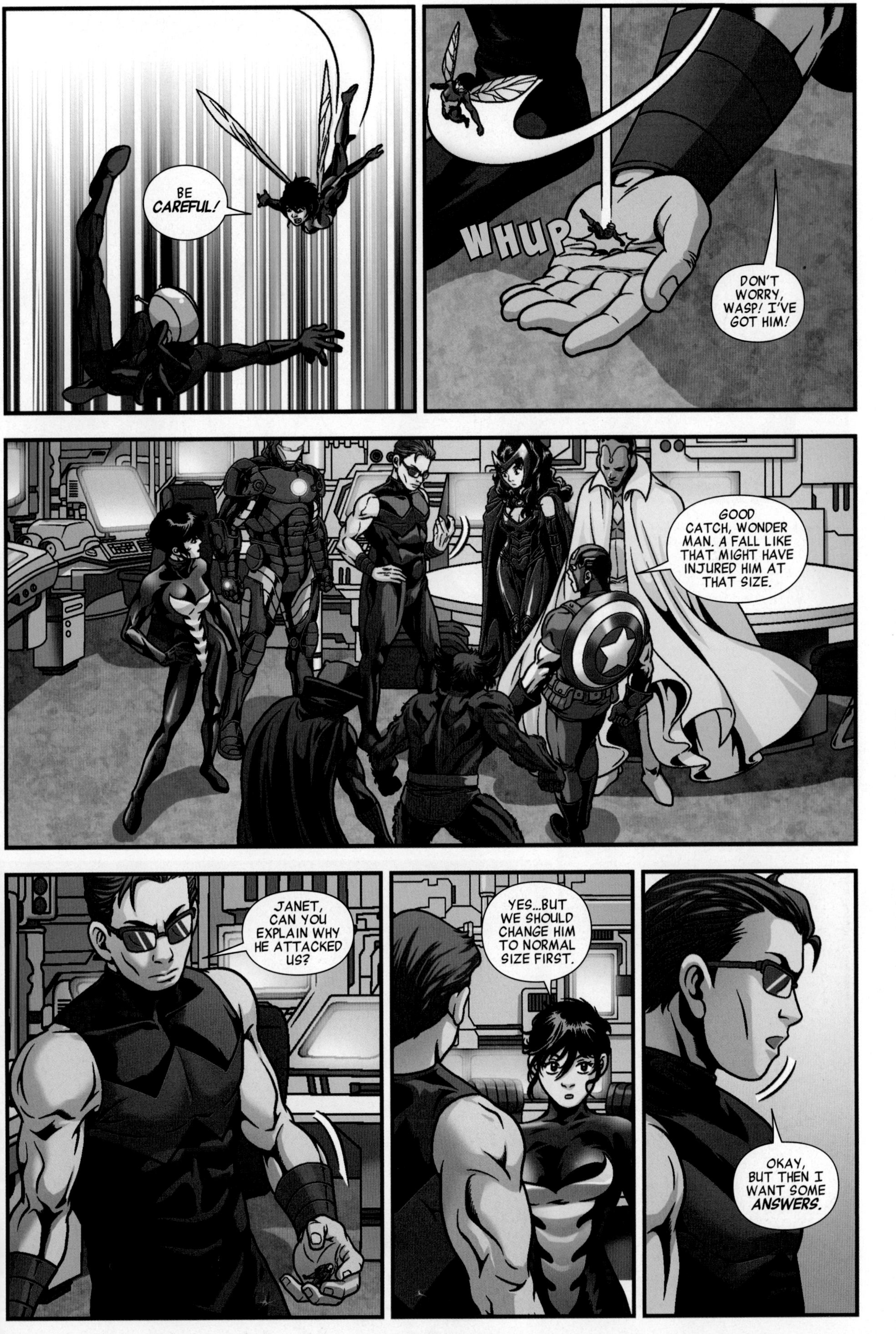
BE CAREFUL!
WHUP
DON'T WORRY, WASP! I'VE GOT HIM!
GOOD CATCH, WONDER MAN. A FALL LIKE THAT MIGHT HAVE INJURED HIM AT THAT SIZE.
JANET, CAN YOU EXPLAIN WHY HE ATTACKED US?
YES...BUT WE SHOULD CHANGE HIM TO NORMAL SIZE FIRST.
OKAY, BUT THEN I WANT SOME ANSWERS.

MY *DARLING!* I'M SORRY I HAD TO *HURT* YOU!

WHAT'S GOING ON WITH HIM, JANET?

WELL...

IT'S BEEN *BUILDING* FOR A LONG TIME...

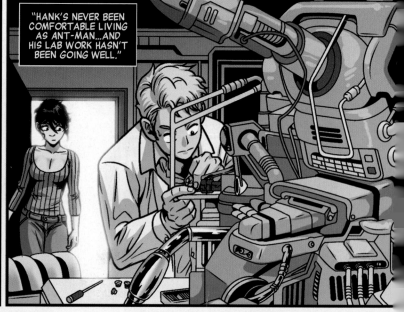

"HANK'S NEVER BEEN COMFORTABLE LIVING AS ANT-MAN...AND HIS LAB WORK HASN'T BEEN GOING WELL."

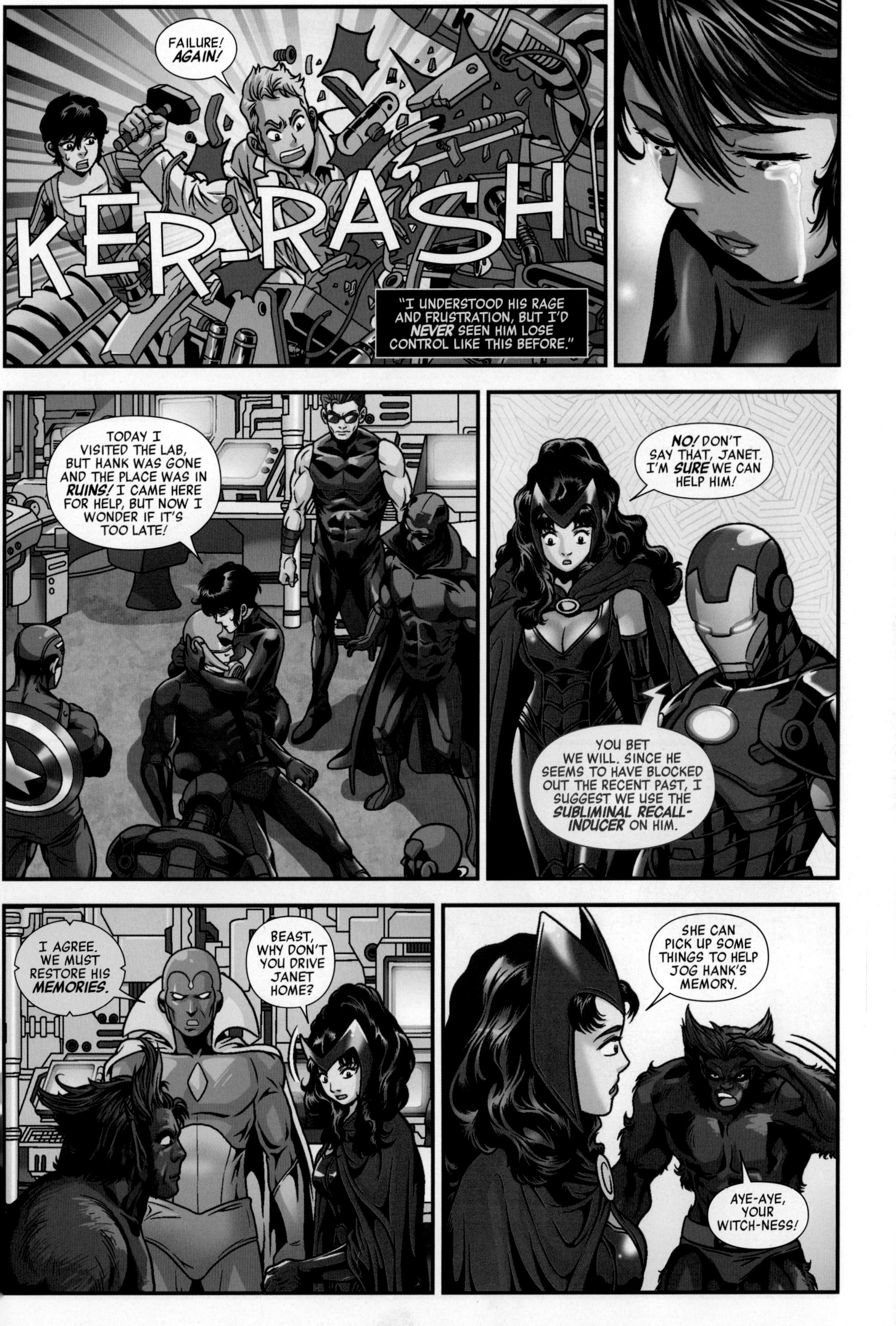
FAILURE! AGAIN!
KER-RASH
"I UNDERSTOOD HIS RAGE AND FRUSTRATION, BUT I'D NEVER SEEN HIM LOSE CONTROL LIKE THIS BEFORE."
TODAY I VISITED THE LAB, BUT HANK WAS GONE AND THE PLACE WAS IN RUINS! I CAME HERE FOR HELP, BUT NOW I WONDER IF IT'S TOO LATE!
NO! DON'T SAY THAT, JANET. I'M SURE WE CAN HELP HIM!
YOU BET WE WILL. SINCE HE SEEMS TO HAVE BLOCKED OUT THE RECENT PAST, I SUGGEST WE USE THE SUBLIMINAL RECALL-INDUCER ON HIM.
I AGREE. WE MUST RESTORE HIS MEMORIES.
BEAST, WHY DON'T YOU DRIVE JANET HOME?
SHE CAN PICK UP SOME THINGS TO HELP JOG HANK'S MEMORY.
AYE-AYE, YOUR WITCH-NESS!

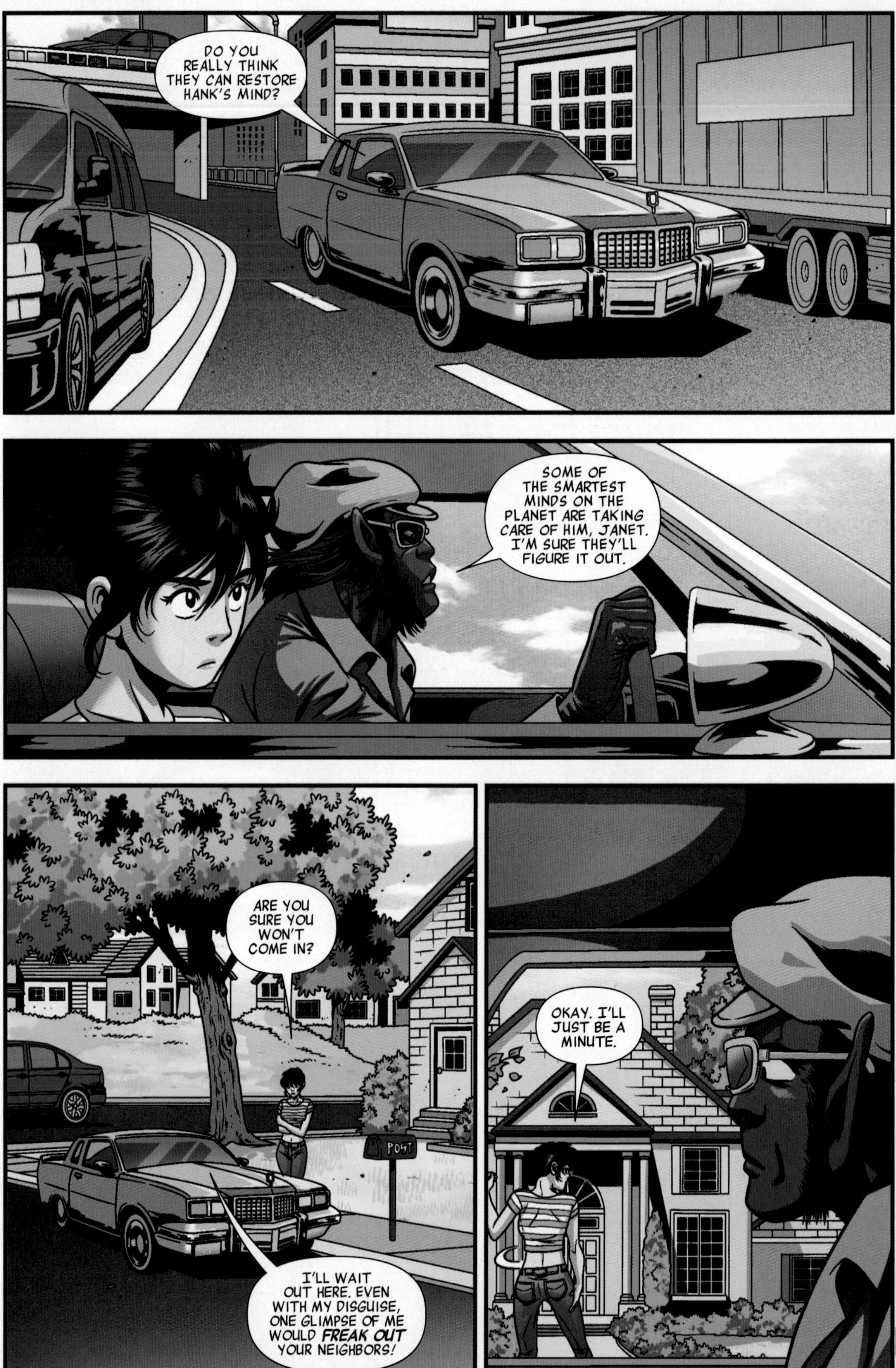
DO YOU REALLY THINK THEY CAN RESTORE HANK'S MIND?
SOME OF THE SMARTEST MINDS ON THE PLANET ARE TAKING CARE OF HIM, JANET. I'M SURE THEY'LL FIGURE IT OUT.
ARE YOU SURE YOU WON'T COME IN?
I'LL WAIT OUT HERE. EVEN WITH MY DISGUISE, ONE GLIMPSE OF ME WOULD **FREAK OUT** YOUR NEIGHBORS!
POST
OKAY. I'LL JUST BE A MINUTE.

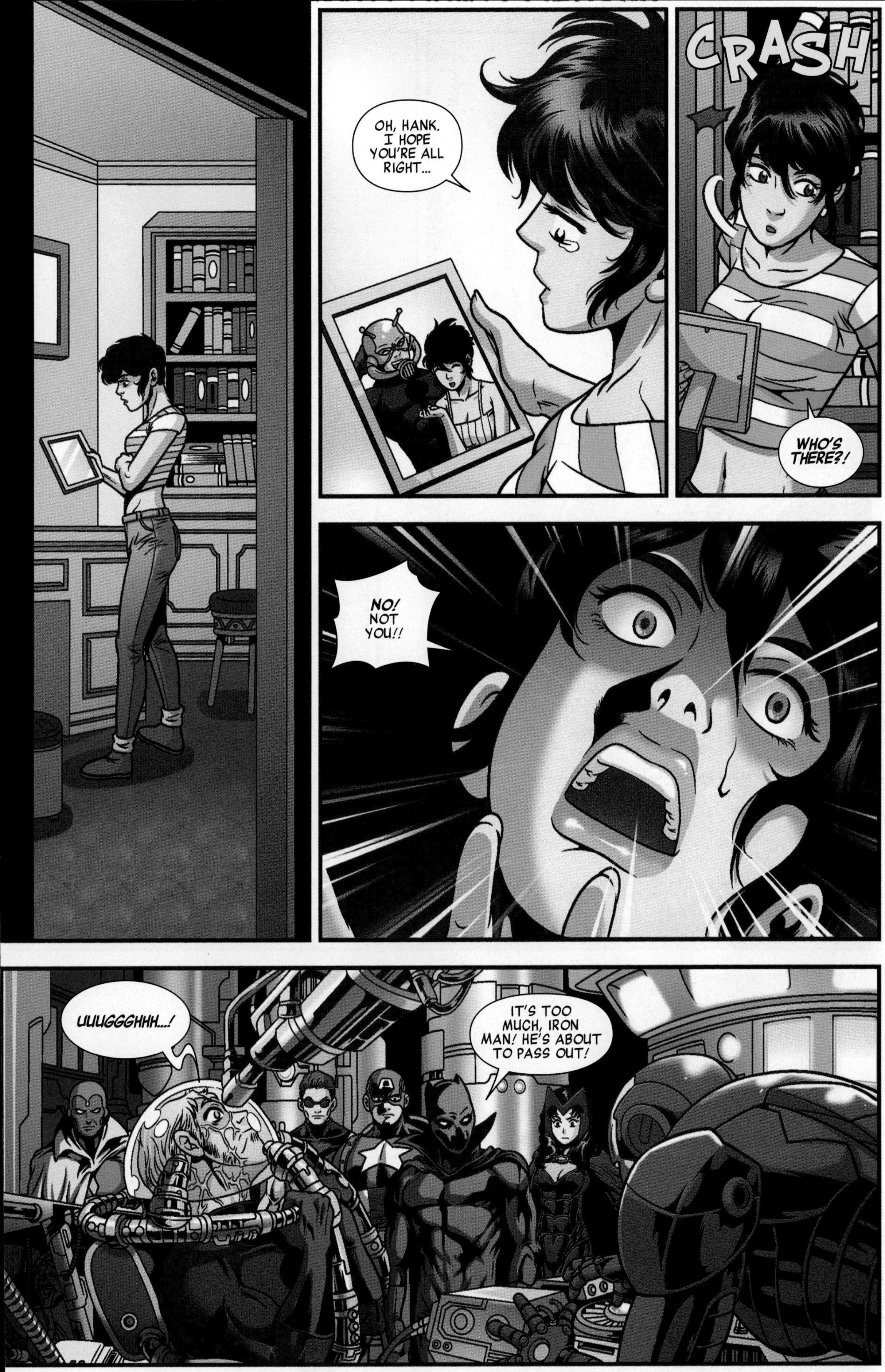
OH, HANK. I HOPE YOU'RE ALL RIGHT...
CRASH
WHO'S THERE?!
NO! NOT YOU!!
UUUGGGHHH...!
IT'S TOO MUCH, IRON MAN! HE'S ABOUT TO PASS OUT!

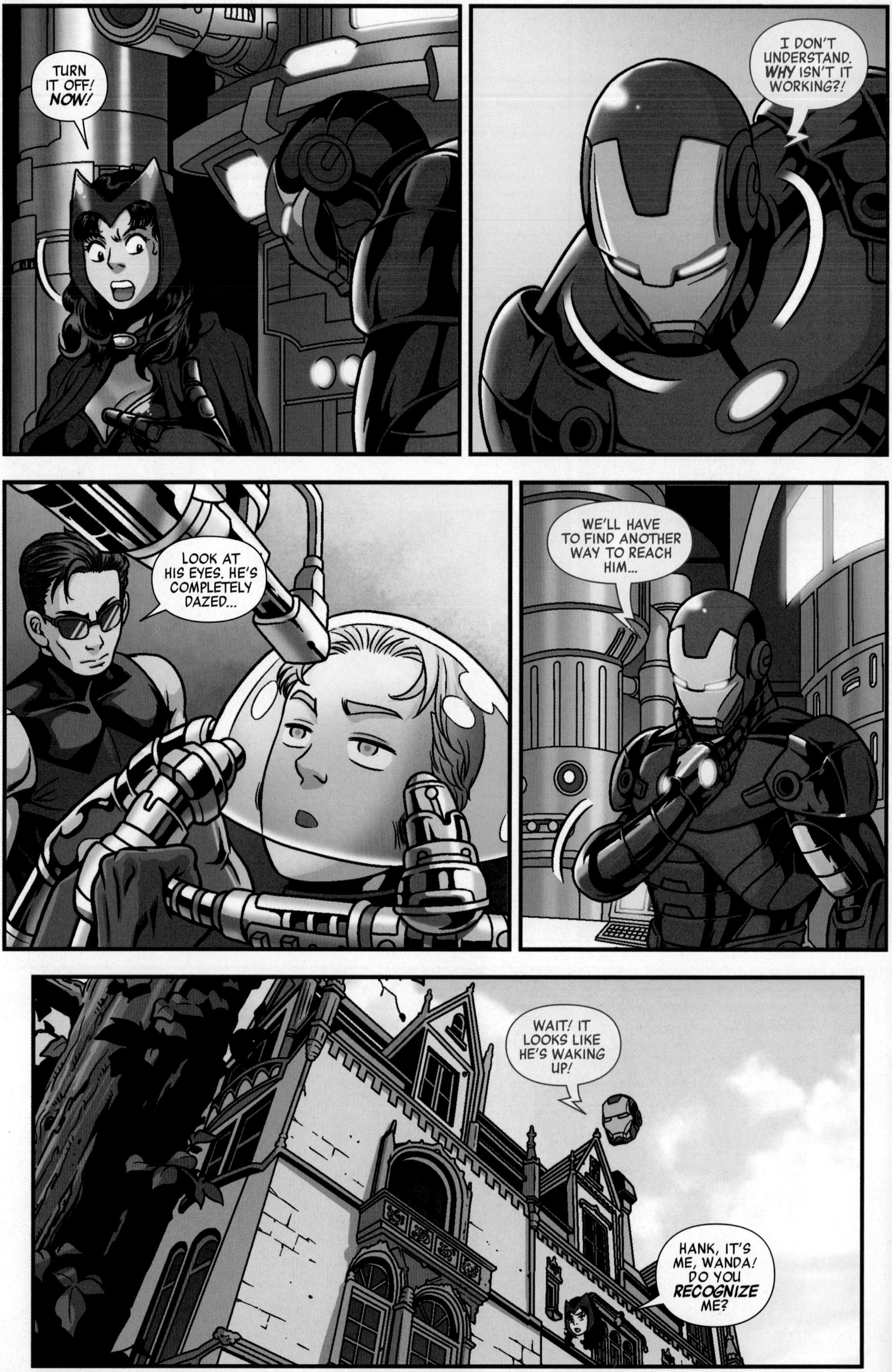
TURN IT OFF! NOW!
I DON'T UNDERSTAND. WHY ISN'T IT WORKING?!
LOOK AT HIS EYES. HE'S COMPLETELY DAZED...
WE'LL HAVE TO FIND ANOTHER WAY TO REACH HIM...
WAIT! IT LOOKS LIKE HE'S WAKING UP!
HANK, IT'S ME, WANDA! DO YOU RECOGNIZE ME?

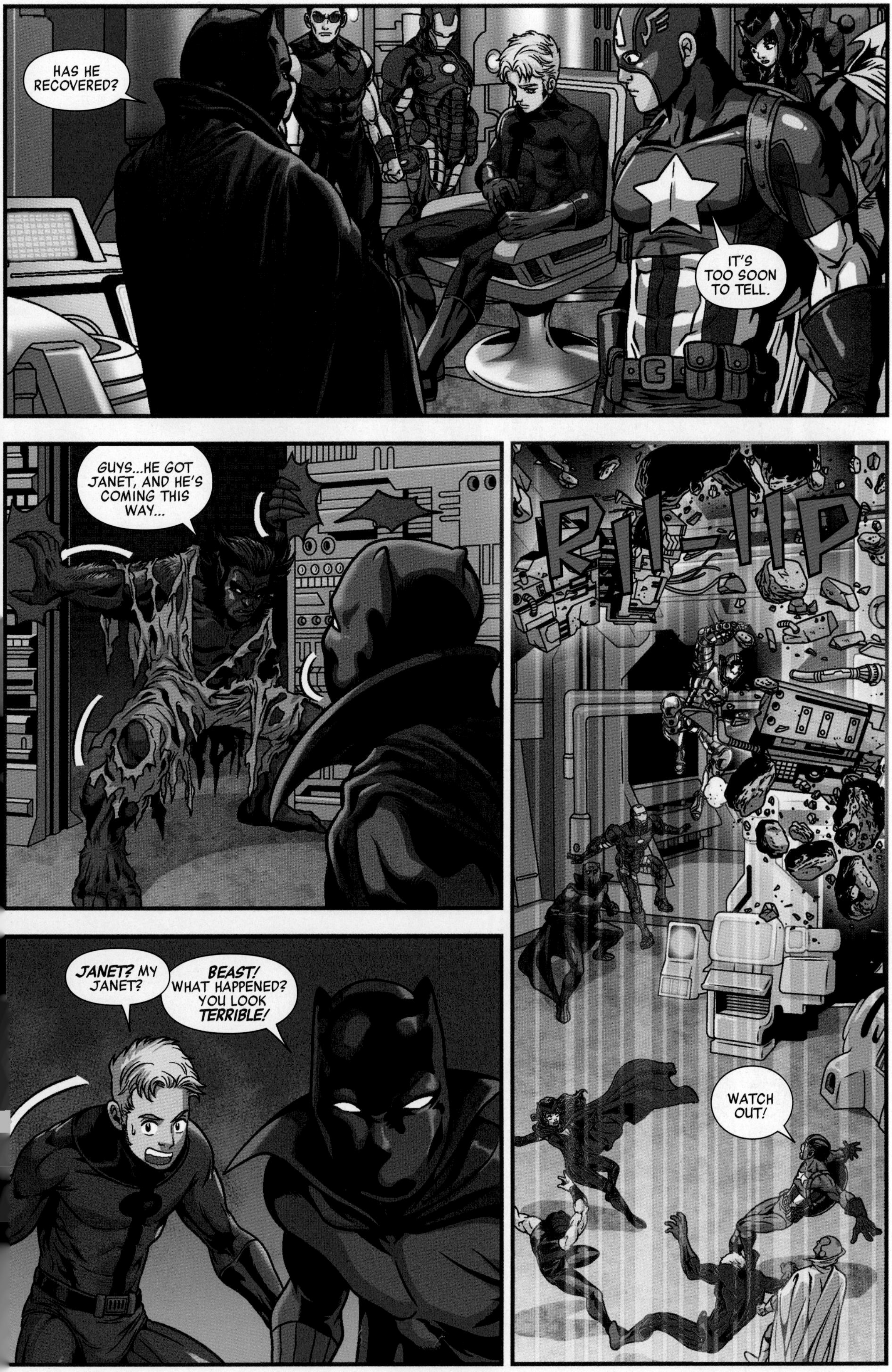
HAS HE RECOVERED?
IT'S TOO SOON TO TELL.
GUYS...HE GOT JANET, AND HE'S COMING THIS WAY...
JANET? MY JANET?
BEAST! WHAT HAPPENED? YOU LOOK TERRIBLE!
RI--IIP
WATCH OUT!

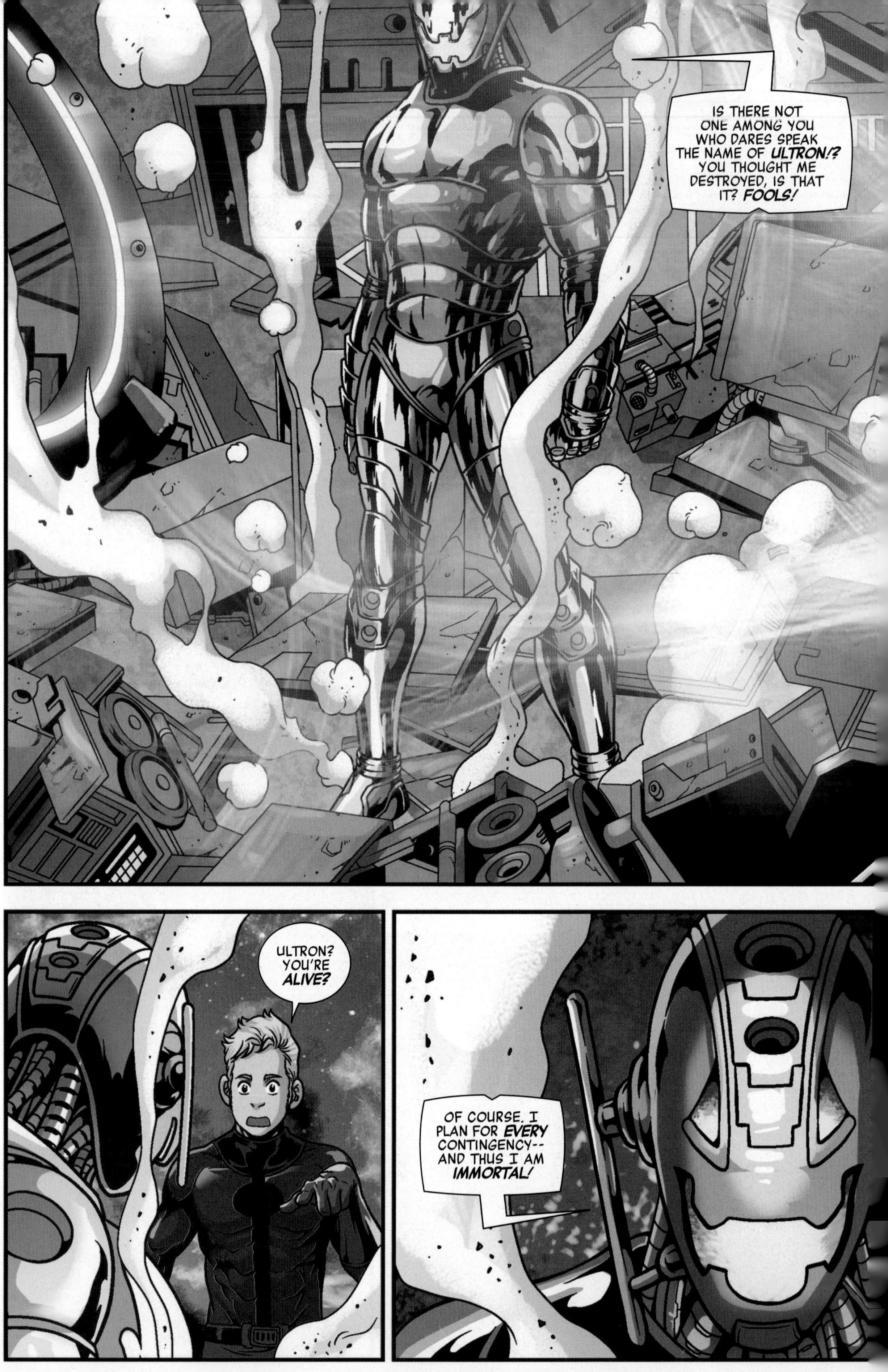
IS THERE NOT ONE AMONG YOU WHO DARES SPEAK THE NAME OF ULTRON!? YOU THOUGHT ME DESTROYED, IS THAT IT? FOOLS!
ULTRON? YOU'RE ALIVE?
OF COURSE. I PLAN FOR EVERY CONTINGENCY-- AND THUS I AM IMMORTAL!

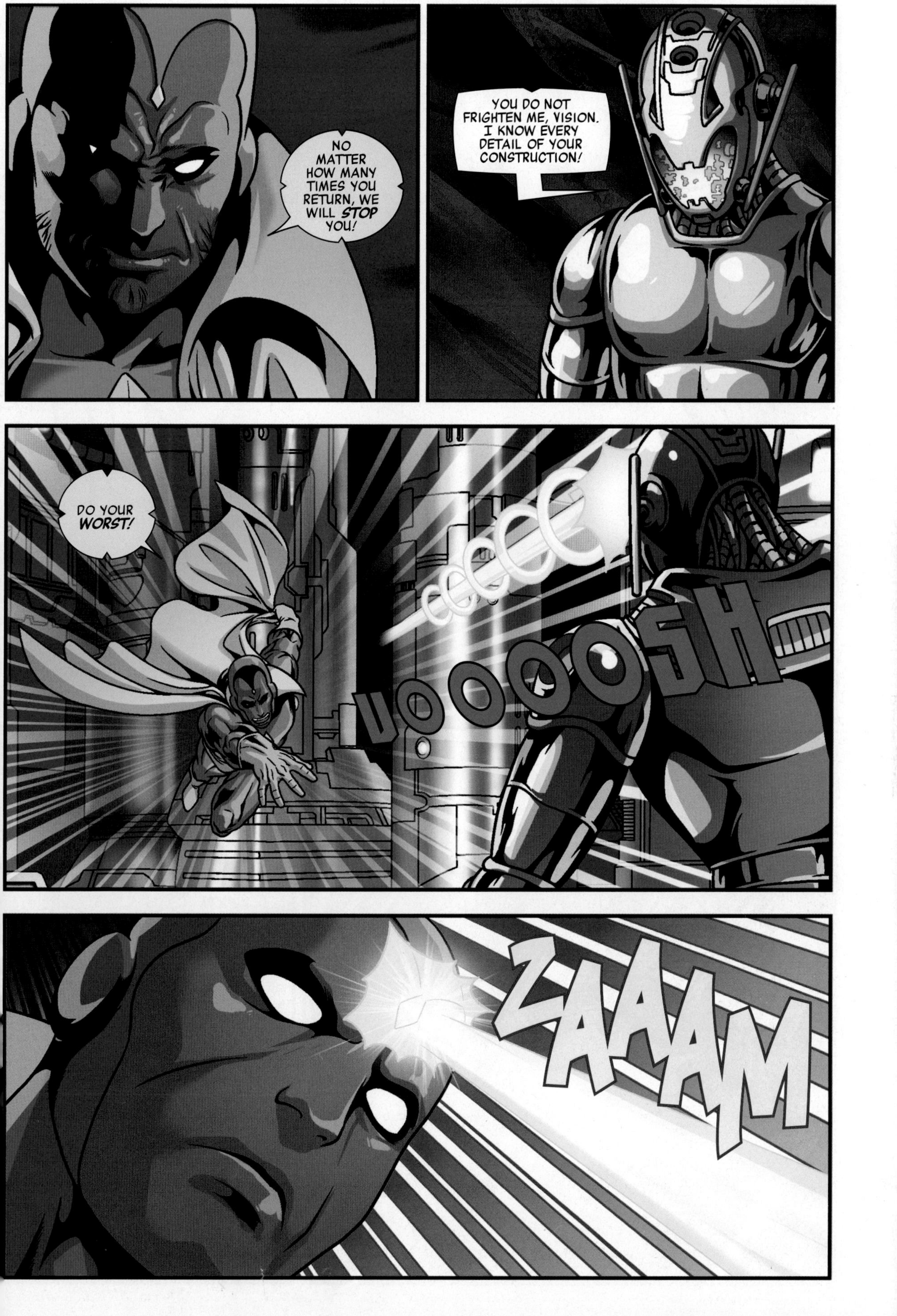

NO MATTER HOW MANY TIMES YOU RETURN, WE WILL STOP YOU!
YOU DO NOT FRIGHTEN ME, VISION. I KNOW EVERY DETAIL OF YOUR CONSTRUCTION!
DO YOUR WORST!
VOOOOOSH
ZAAAM

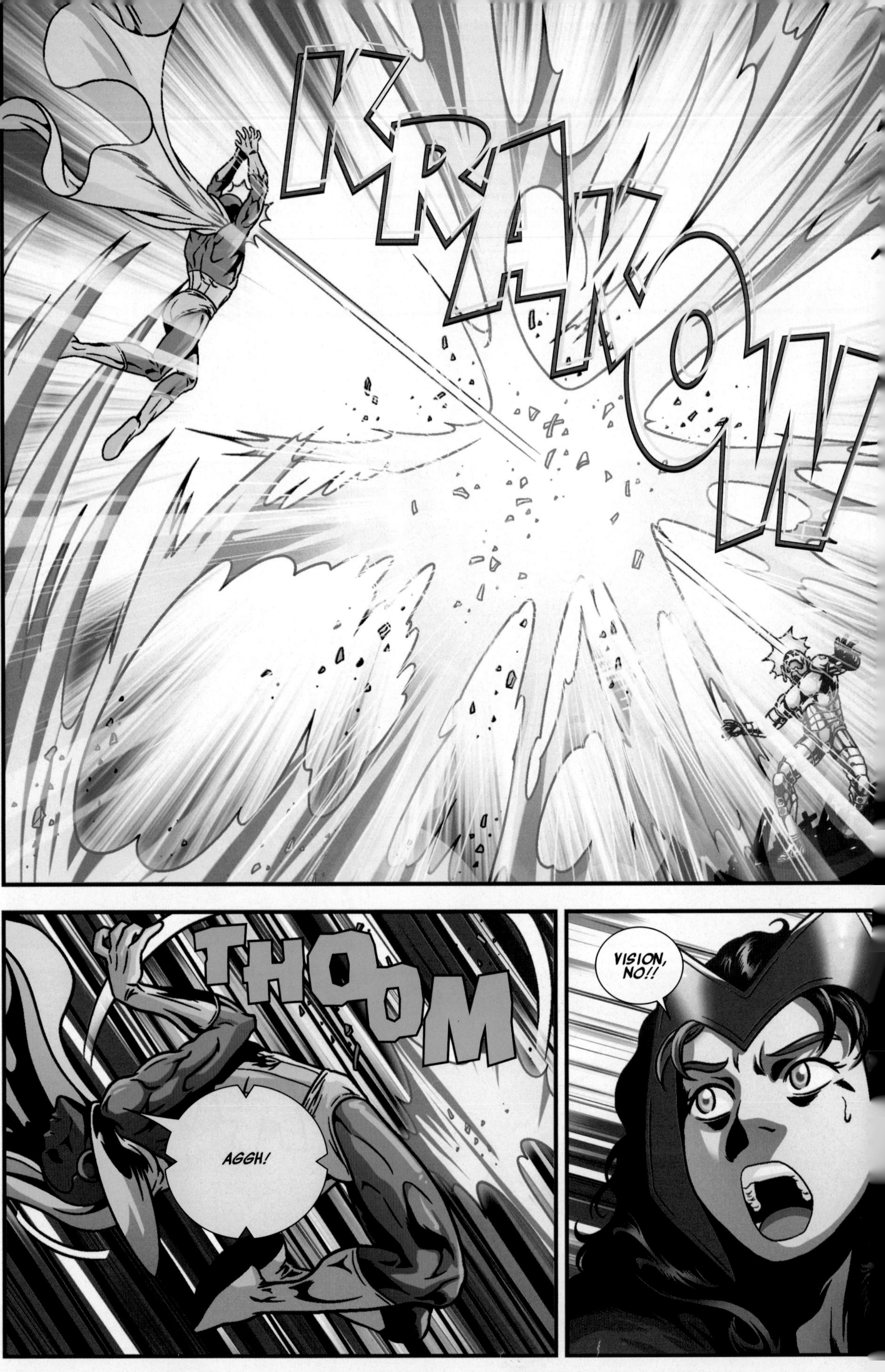
KRAKOOW
THOOOM
AGGH!
VISION, NO!!

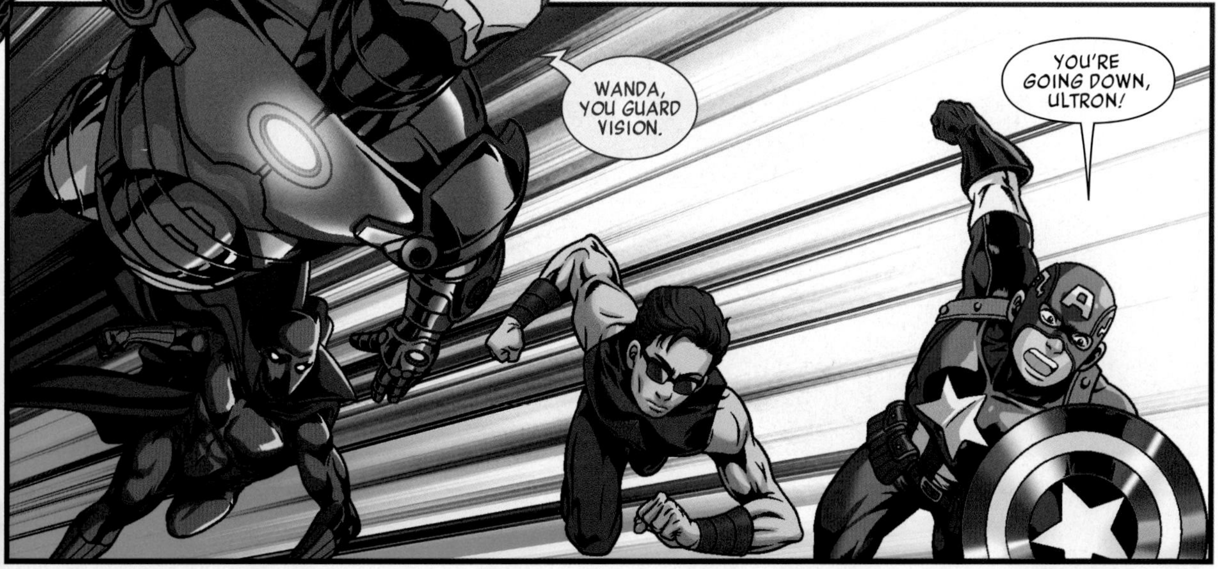
WANDA, YOU GUARD VISION.
YOU'RE GOING DOWN, ULTRON!

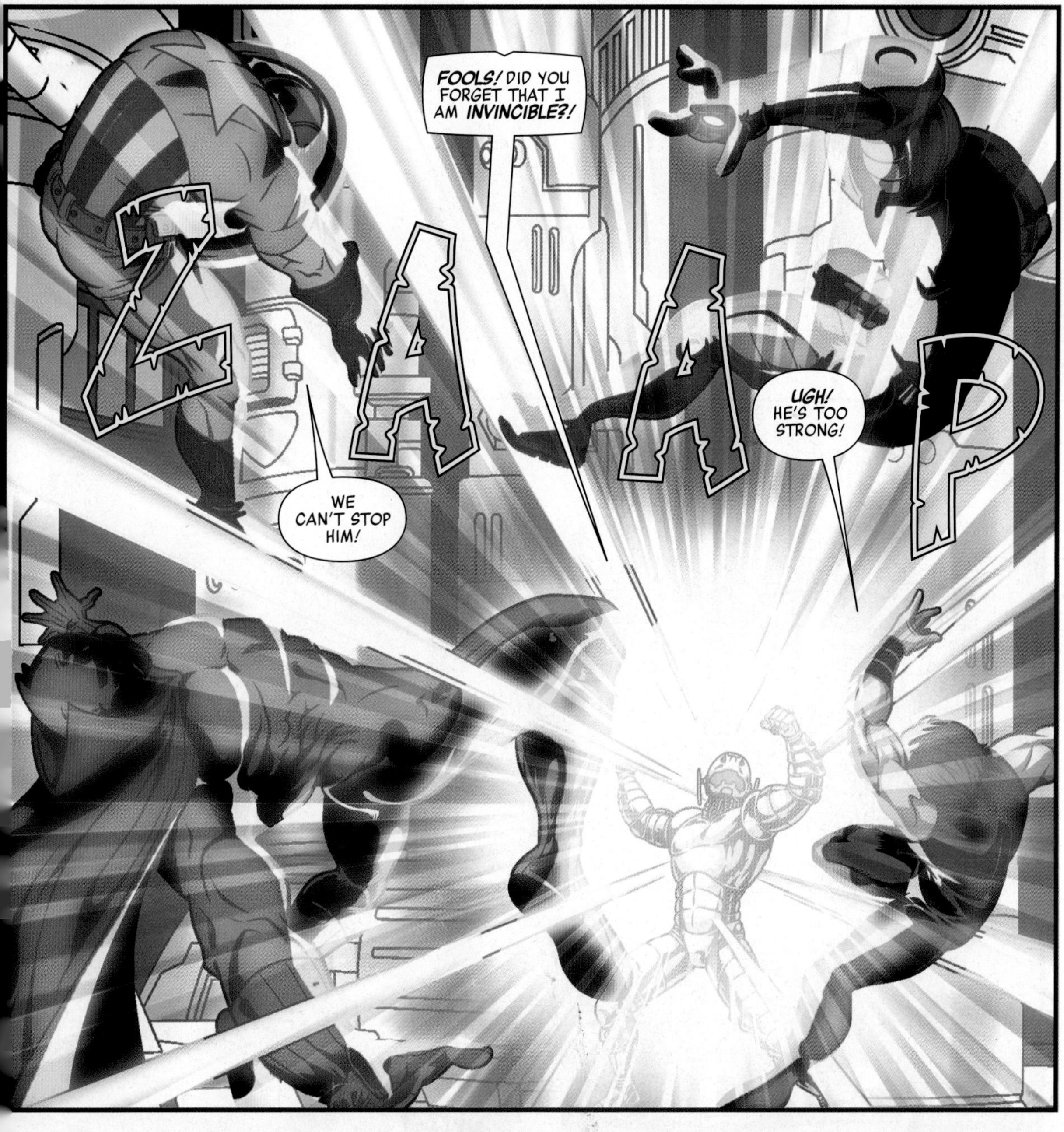
FOOLS! DID YOU FORGET THAT I AM INVINCIBLE?!
ZAAP
WE CAN'T STOP HIM!
UGH! HE'S TOO STRONG!

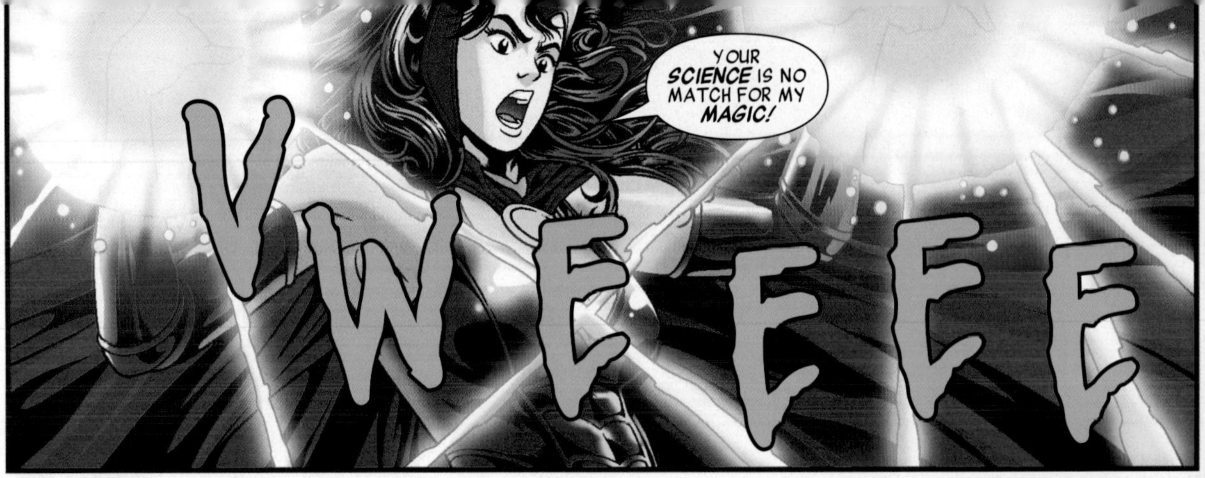
YOUR SCIENCE IS NO MATCH FOR MY MAGIC!
VWEEEE

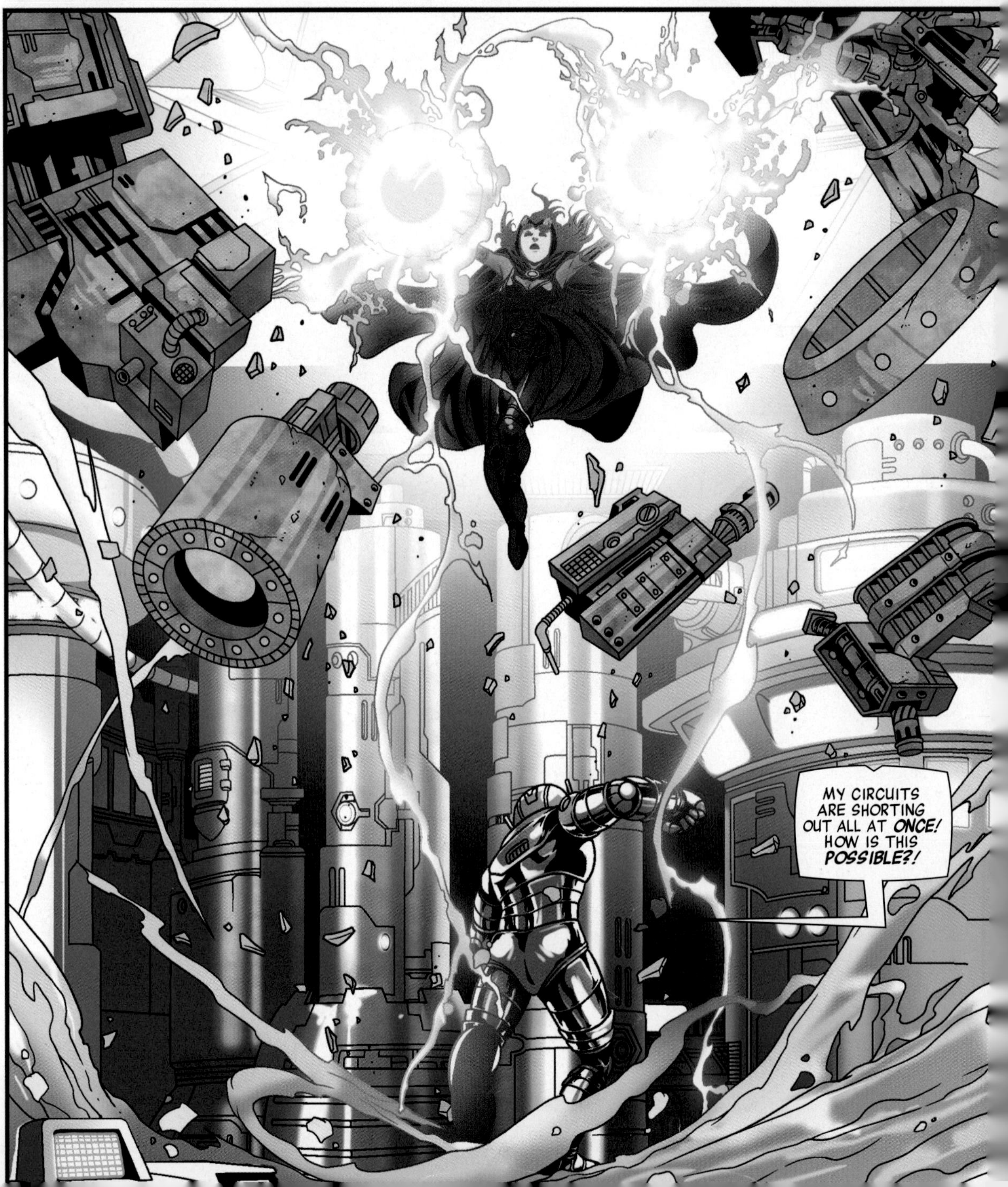
MY CIRCUITS ARE SHORTING OUT ALL AT ONCE! HOW IS THIS POSSIBLE?!

KA-
NO MATTER. EVEN AS YOU *DAMAGE* ME, MY BODY *REPAIRS* ITSELF!
CHUNG
SHANG
SMASH
THE WALLS ARE COLLAPSING!

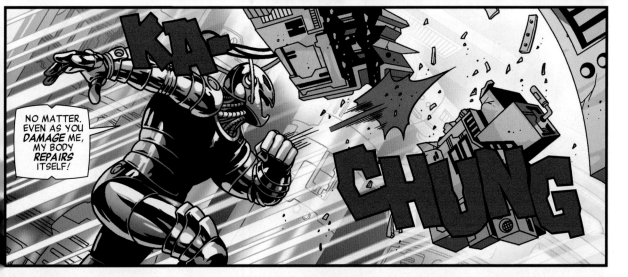

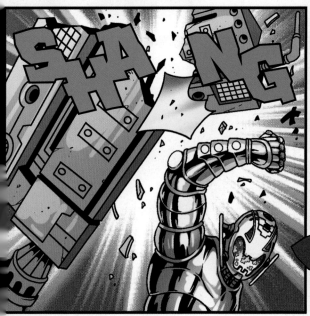

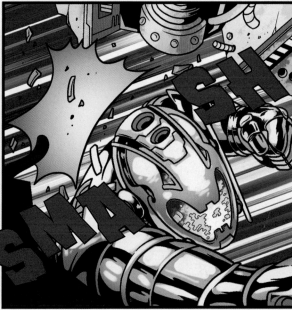

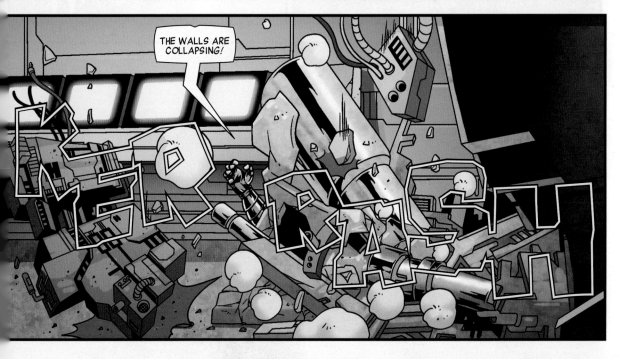

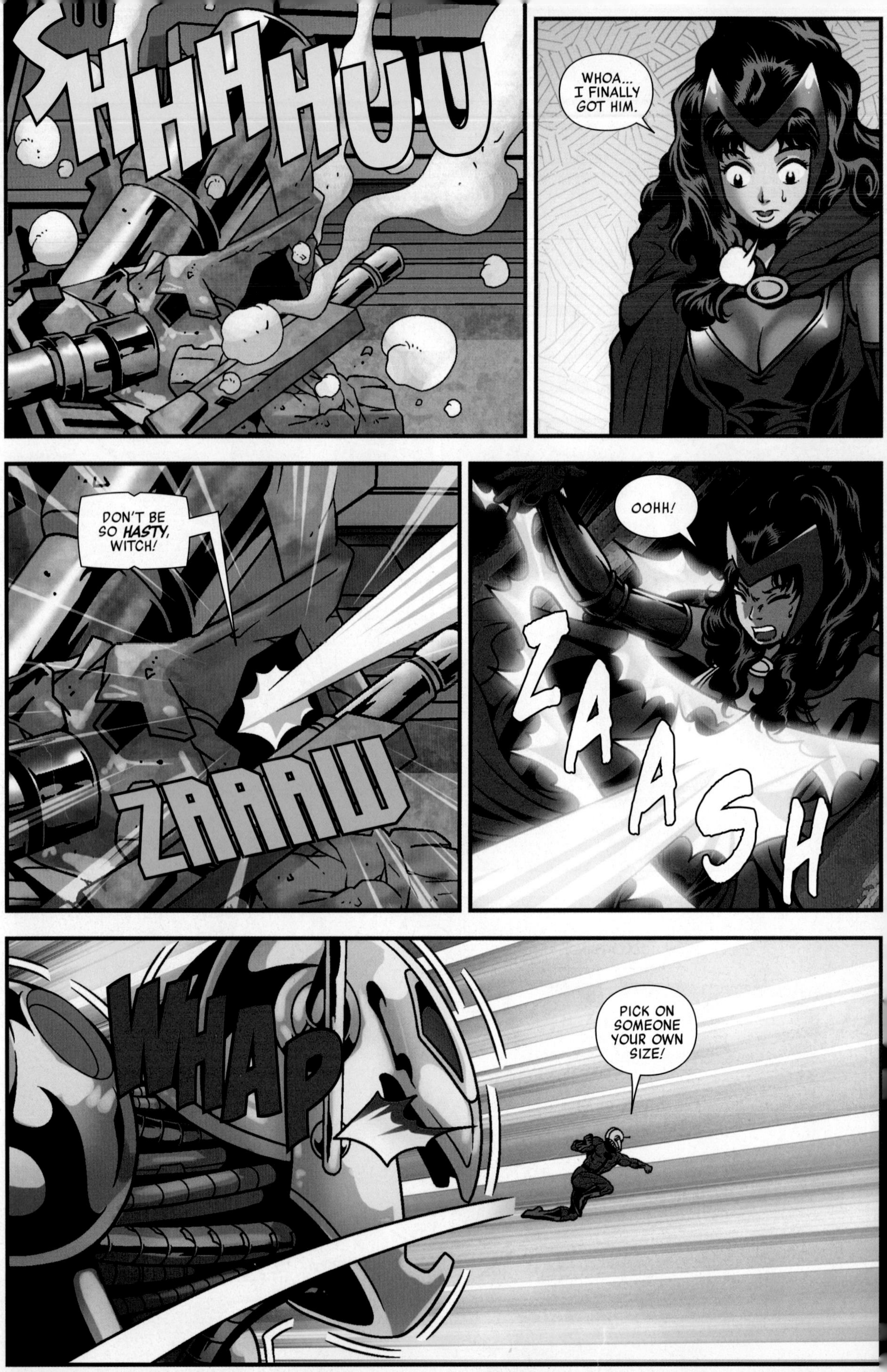
SHHHHUU
WHOA... I FINALLY GOT HIM.
DON'T BE SO HASTY, WITCH!
ZAAAW
OOHH!
ZAASH
WHAP
PICK ON SOMEONE YOUR OWN SIZE!

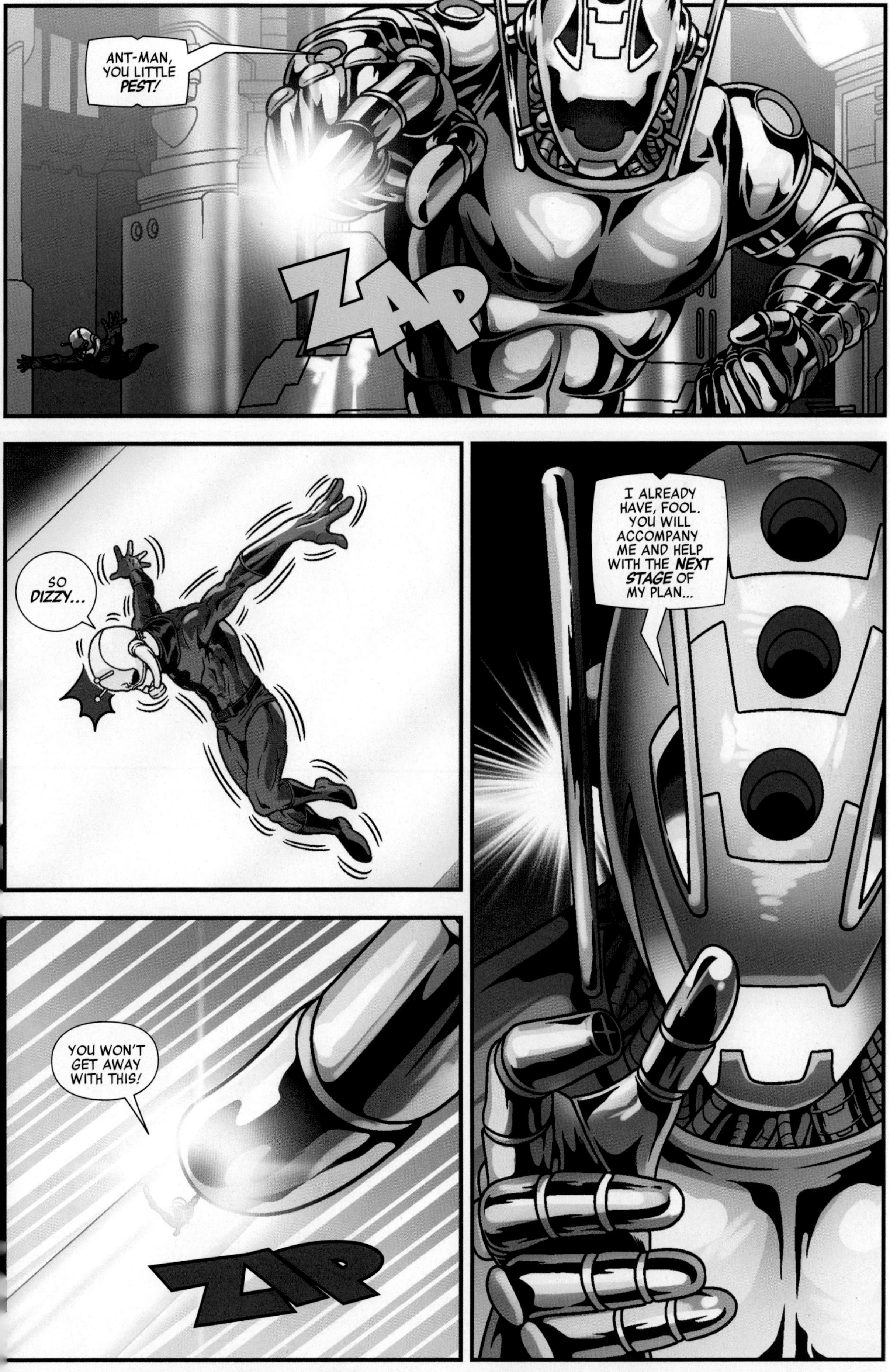

ANT-MAN, YOU LITTLE PEST!
ZAP
SO DIZZY...
YOU WON'T GET AWAY WITH THIS!
ZIP
I ALREADY HAVE, FOOL. YOU WILL ACCOMPANY ME AND HELP WITH THE NEXT STAGE OF MY PLAN...

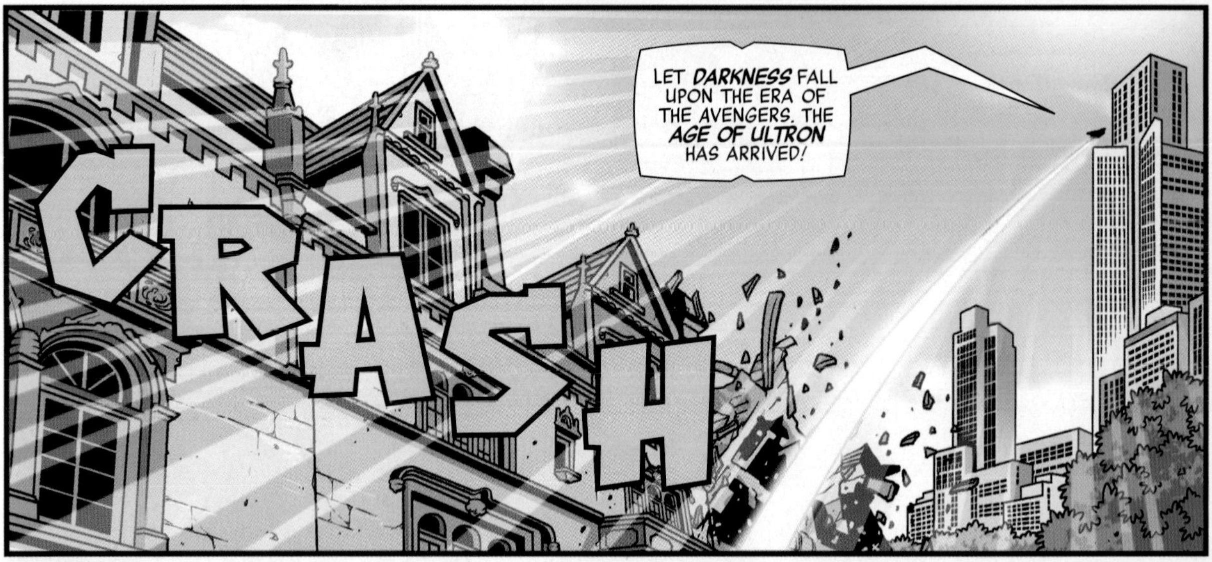
LET DARKNESS FALL UPON THE ERA OF THE AVENGERS. THE AGE OF ULTRON HAS ARRIVED!
CRASH

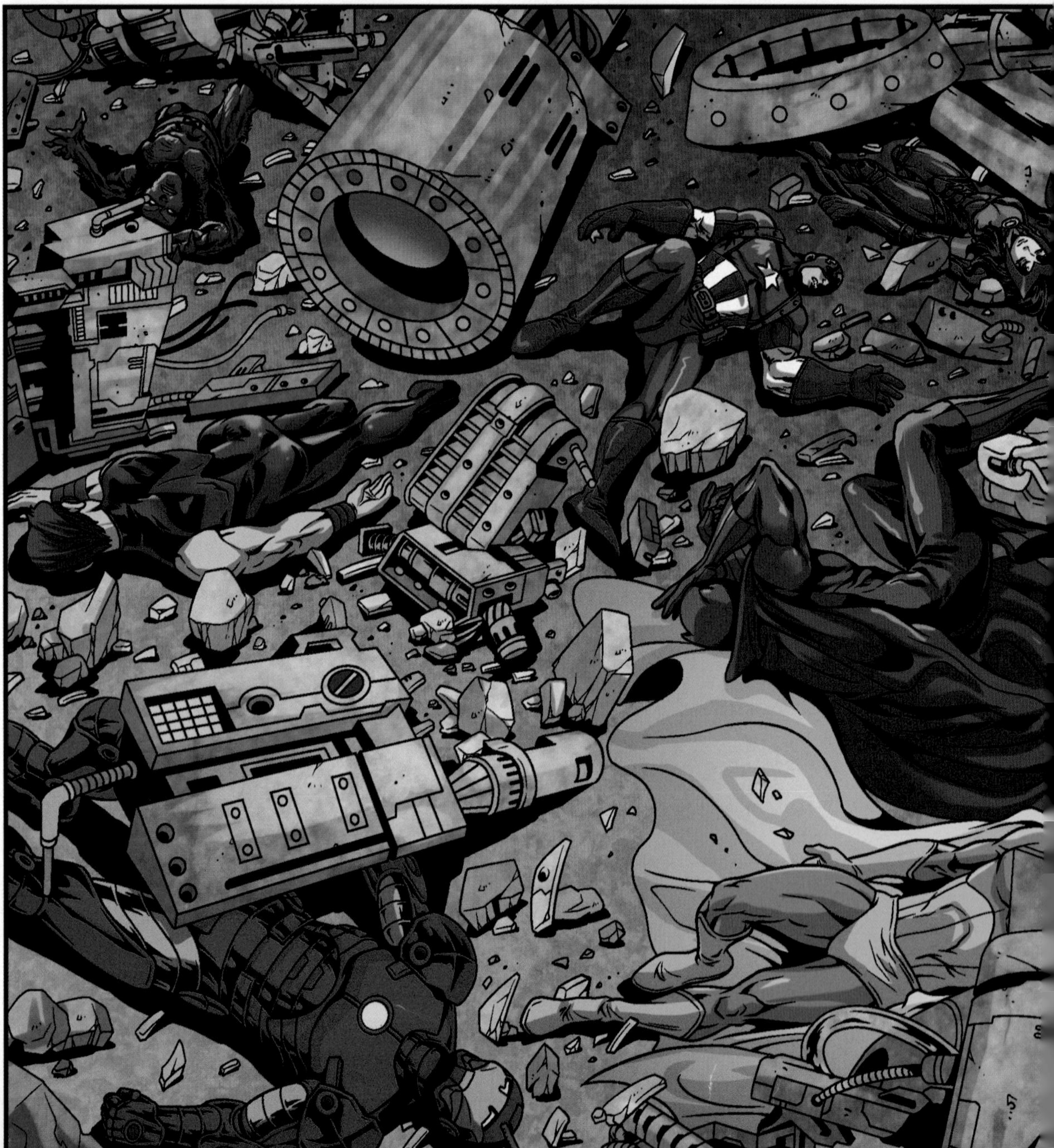

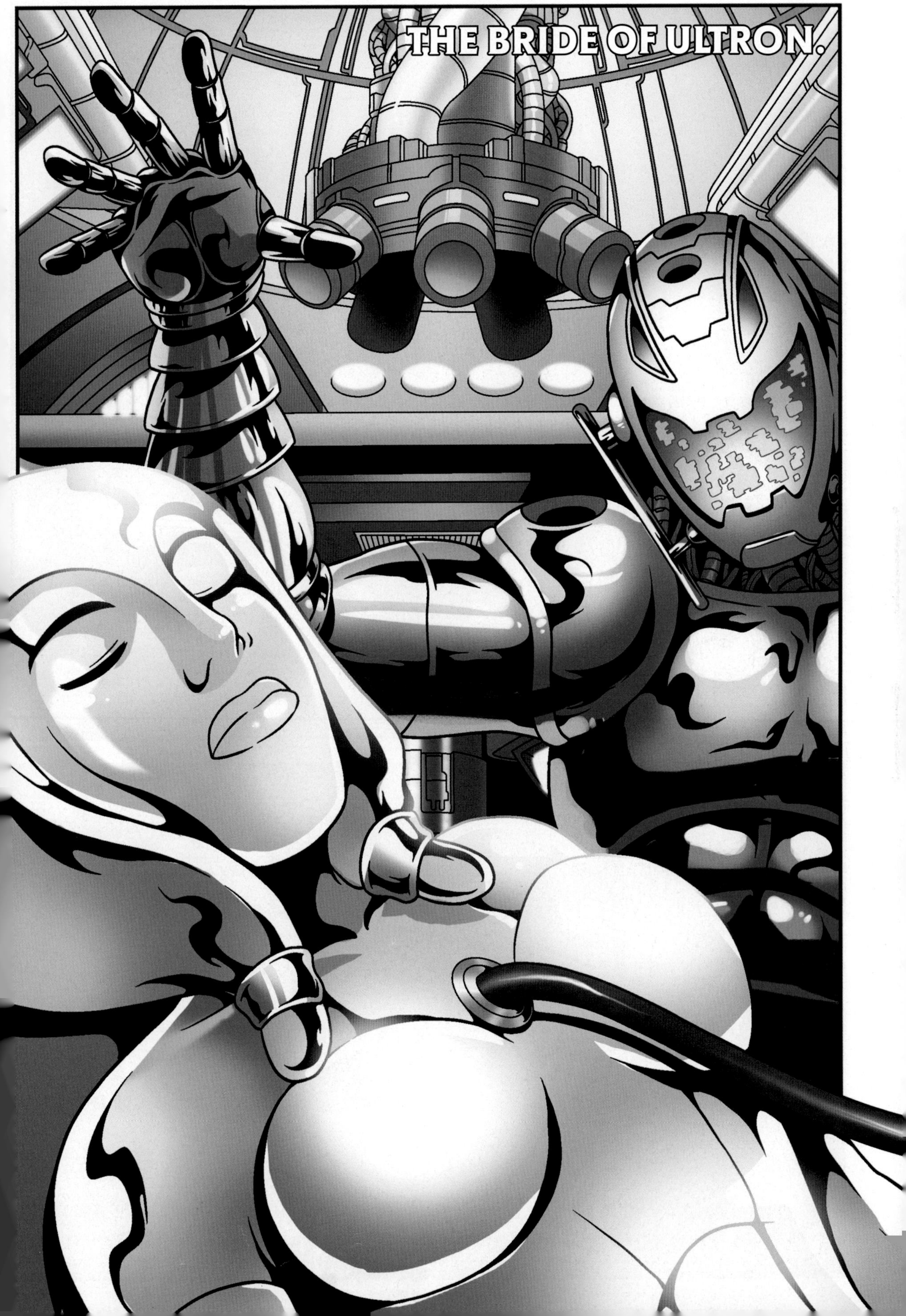
THE BRIDE OF ULTRON.

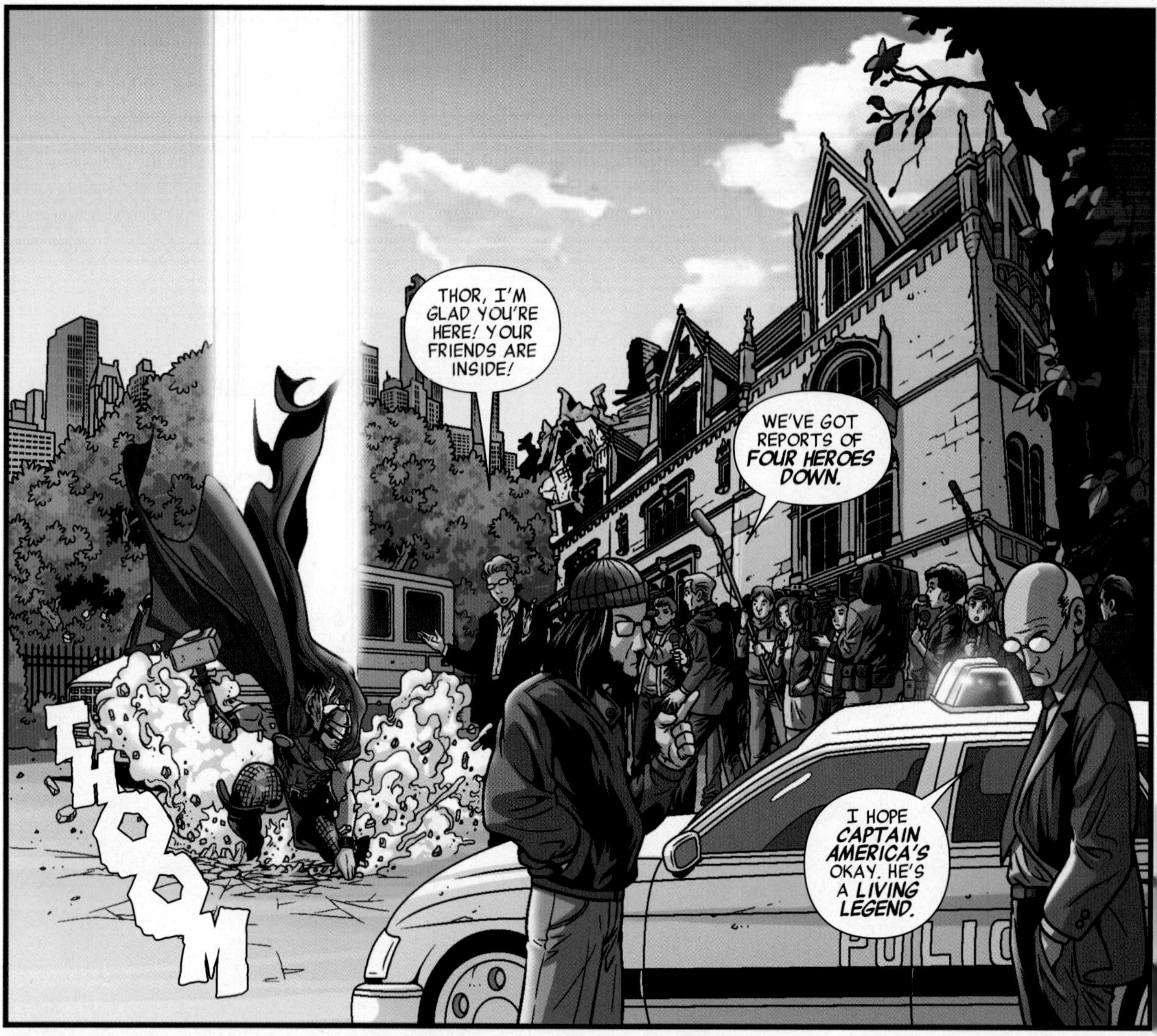
THOR, I'M GLAD YOU'RE HERE! YOUR FRIENDS ARE INSIDE!
WE'VE GOT REPORTS OF FOUR HEROES DOWN.
THOOOM
I HOPE CAPTAIN AMERICA'S OKAY. HE'S A LIVING LEGEND.
POLIC

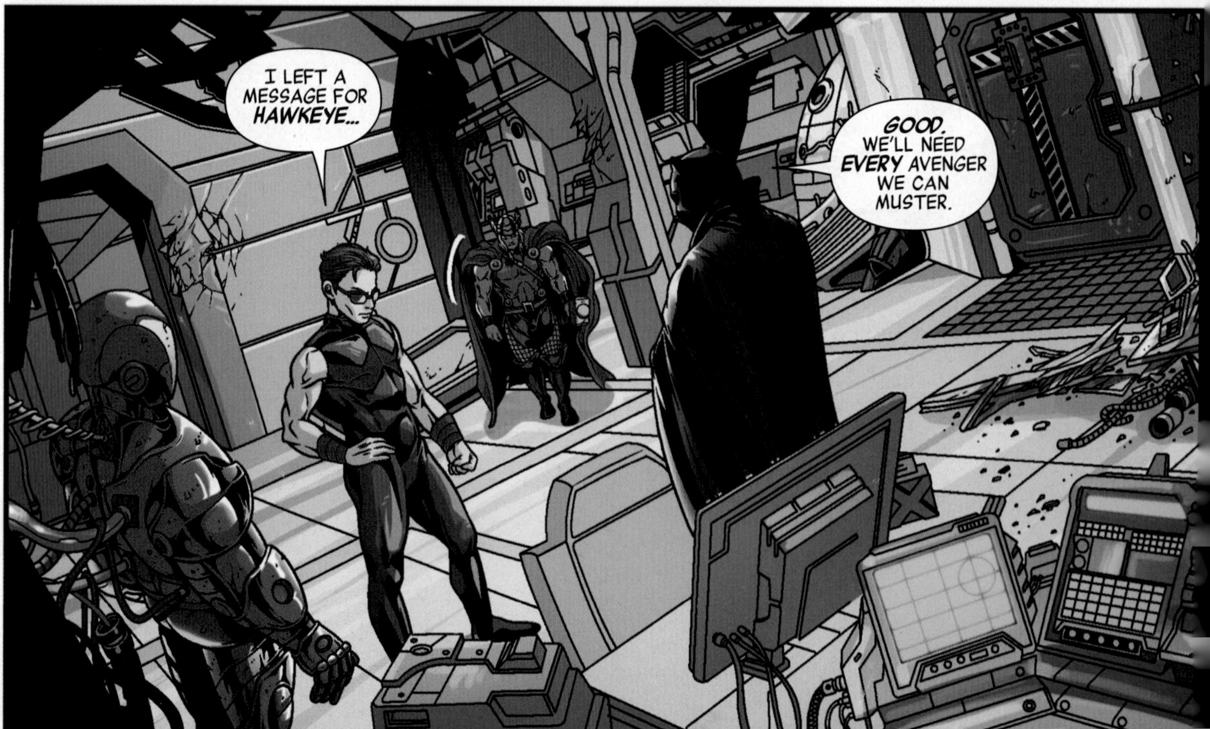
I LEFT A MESSAGE FOR HAWKEYE...
GOOD. WE'LL NEED EVERY AVENGER WE CAN MUSTER.

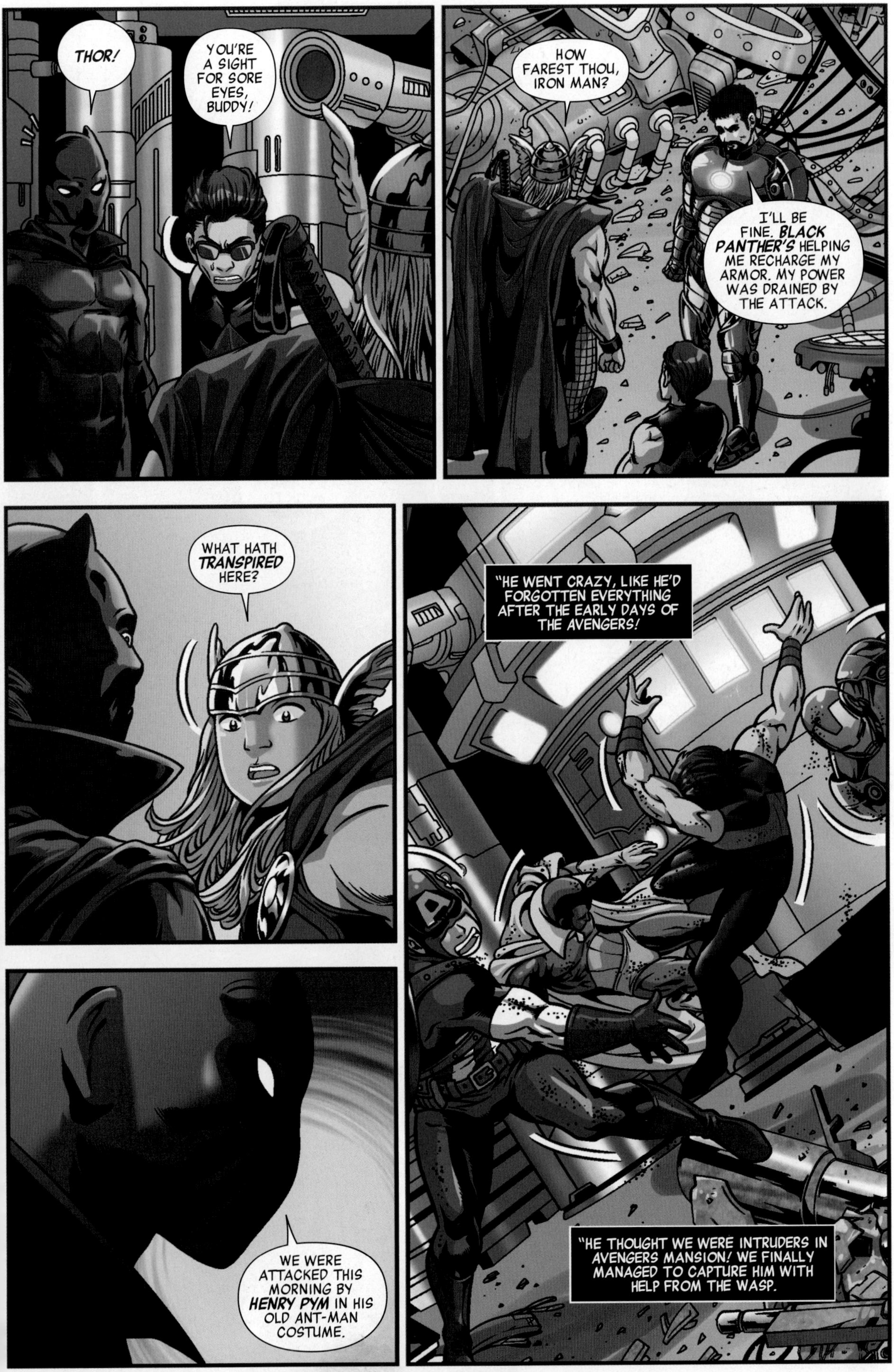

THOR!
YOU'RE A SIGHT FOR SORE EYES, BUDDY!
HOW FAREST THOU, IRON MAN?
I'LL BE FINE. BLACK PANTHER'S HELPING ME RECHARGE MY ARMOR. MY POWER WAS DRAINED BY THE ATTACK.
WHAT HATH TRANSPIRED HERE?
WE WERE ATTACKED THIS MORNING BY HENRY PYM IN HIS OLD ANT-MAN COSTUME.
"HE WENT CRAZY, LIKE HE'D FORGOTTEN EVERYTHING AFTER THE EARLY DAYS OF THE AVENGERS!
"HE THOUGHT WE WERE INTRUDERS IN AVENGERS MANSION! WE FINALLY MANAGED TO CAPTURE HIM WITH HELP FROM THE WASP.

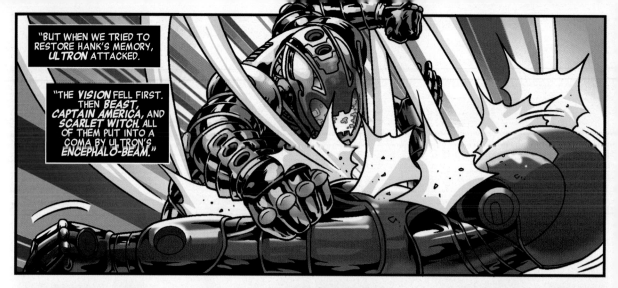

"BUT WHEN WE TRIED TO RESTORE HANK'S MEMORY, *ULTRON* ATTACKED.

"THE *VISION* FELL FIRST. THEN *BEAST*, *CAPTAIN AMERICA*, AND *SCARLET WITCH*. ALL OF THEM PUT INTO A COMA BY ULTRON'S *ENCEPHALO-BEAM*."

WONDER MAN, IRON MAN, AND I ARE THE ONLY ONES LEFT STANDING.

THE *THREE* OF US...WITH MUCH TO *AVENGE.*

AND *THOR* STANDS WITH THEE!

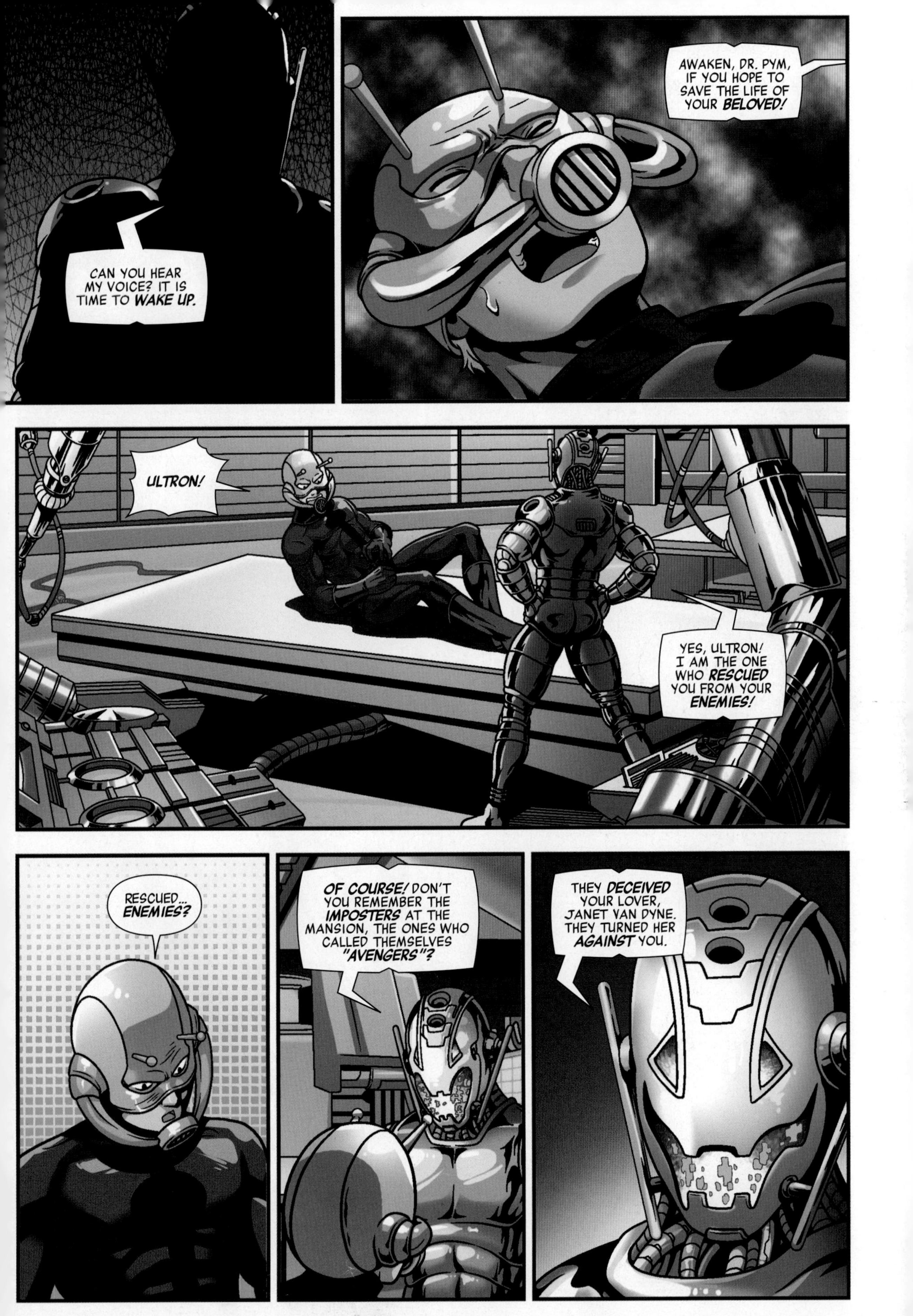
CAN YOU HEAR MY VOICE? IT IS TIME TO WAKE UP.
AWAKEN, DR. PYM, IF YOU HOPE TO SAVE THE LIFE OF YOUR BELOVED!
ULTRON!
YES, ULTRON! I AM THE ONE WHO RESCUED YOU FROM YOUR ENEMIES!
RESCUED... ENEMIES?
OF COURSE! DON'T YOU REMEMBER THE IMPOSTERS AT THE MANSION, THE ONES WHO CALLED THEMSELVES "AVENGERS"?
THEY DECEIVED YOUR LOVER, JANET VAN DYNE. THEY TURNED HER AGAINST YOU.

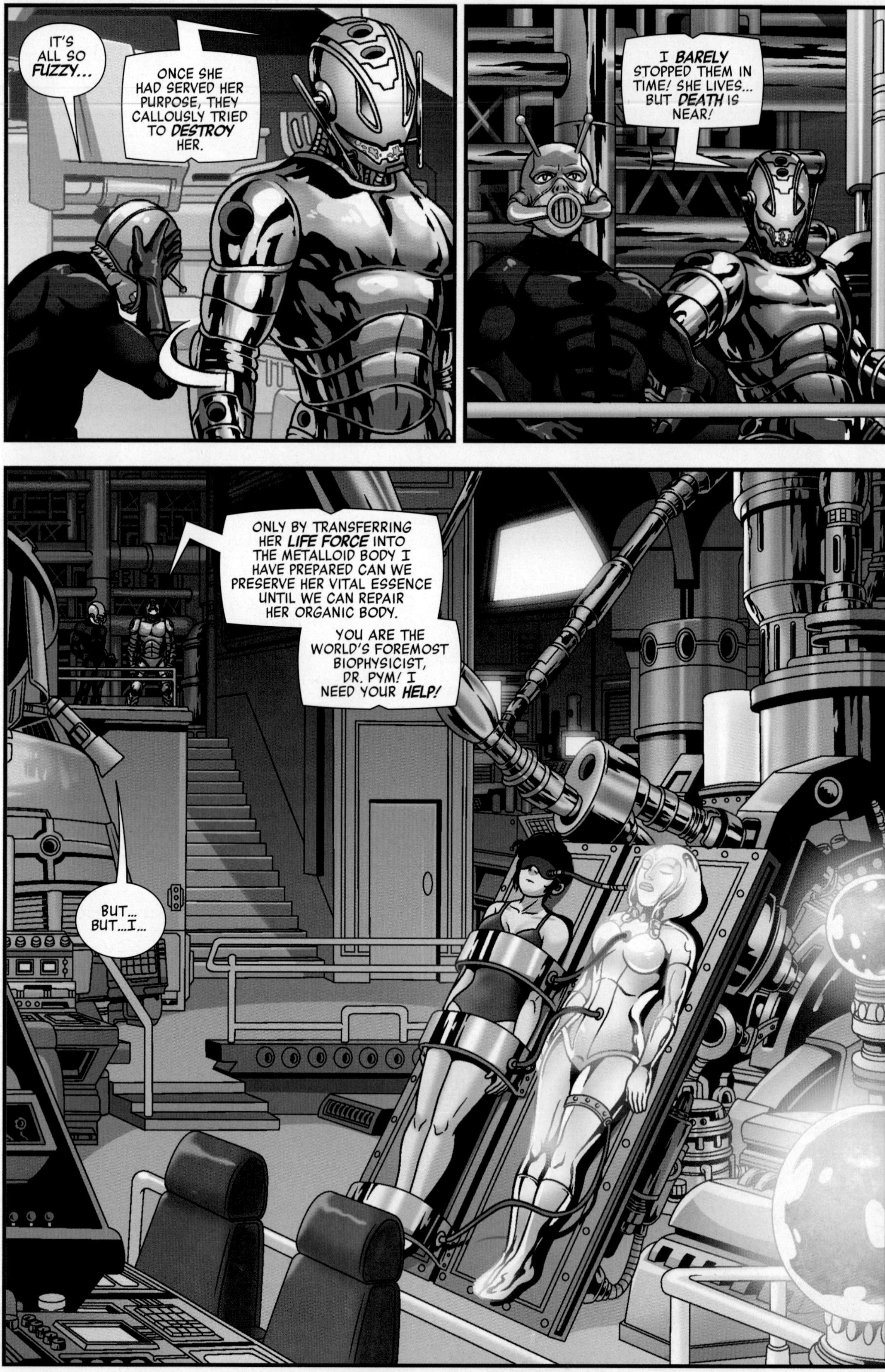
IT'S ALL SO FUZZY...
ONCE SHE HAD SERVED HER PURPOSE, THEY CALLOUSLY TRIED TO DESTROY HER.
I BARELY STOPPED THEM IN TIME! SHE LIVES... BUT DEATH IS NEAR!
ONLY BY TRANSFERRING HER LIFE FORCE INTO THE METALLOID BODY I HAVE PREPARED CAN WE PRESERVE HER VITAL ESSENCE UNTIL WE CAN REPAIR HER ORGANIC BODY.
YOU ARE THE WORLD'S FOREMOST BIOPHYSICIST, DR. PYM! I NEED YOUR HELP!
BUT... BUT...I...

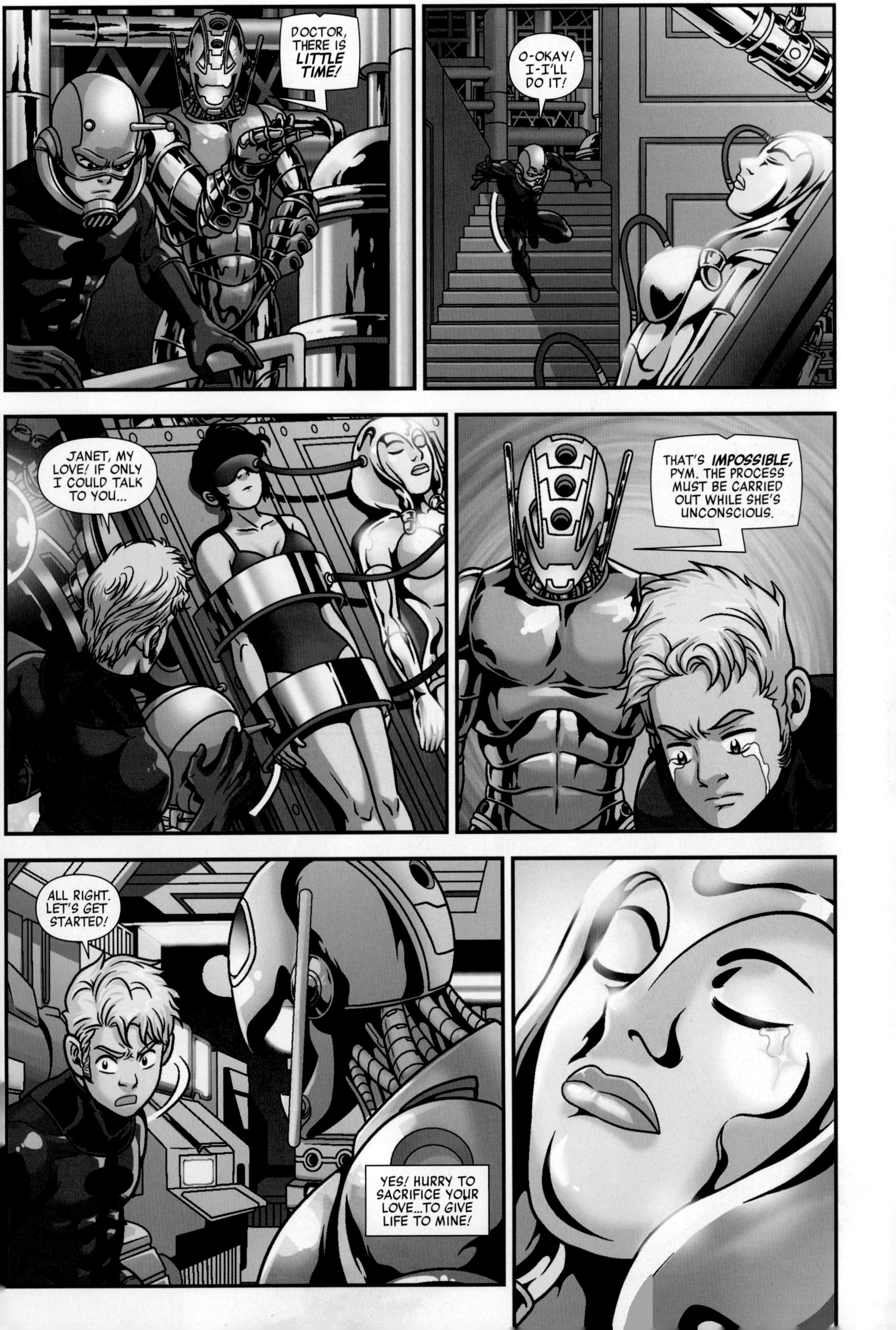
DOCTOR, THERE IS LITTLE TIME!
O-OKAY! I-I'LL DO IT!
JANET, MY LOVE! IF ONLY I COULD TALK TO YOU...
THAT'S IMPOSSIBLE, PYM. THE PROCESS MUST BE CARRIED OUT WHILE SHE'S UNCONSCIOUS.
ALL RIGHT. LET'S GET STARTED!
YES! HURRY TO SACRIFICE YOUR LOVE...TO GIVE LIFE TO MINE!

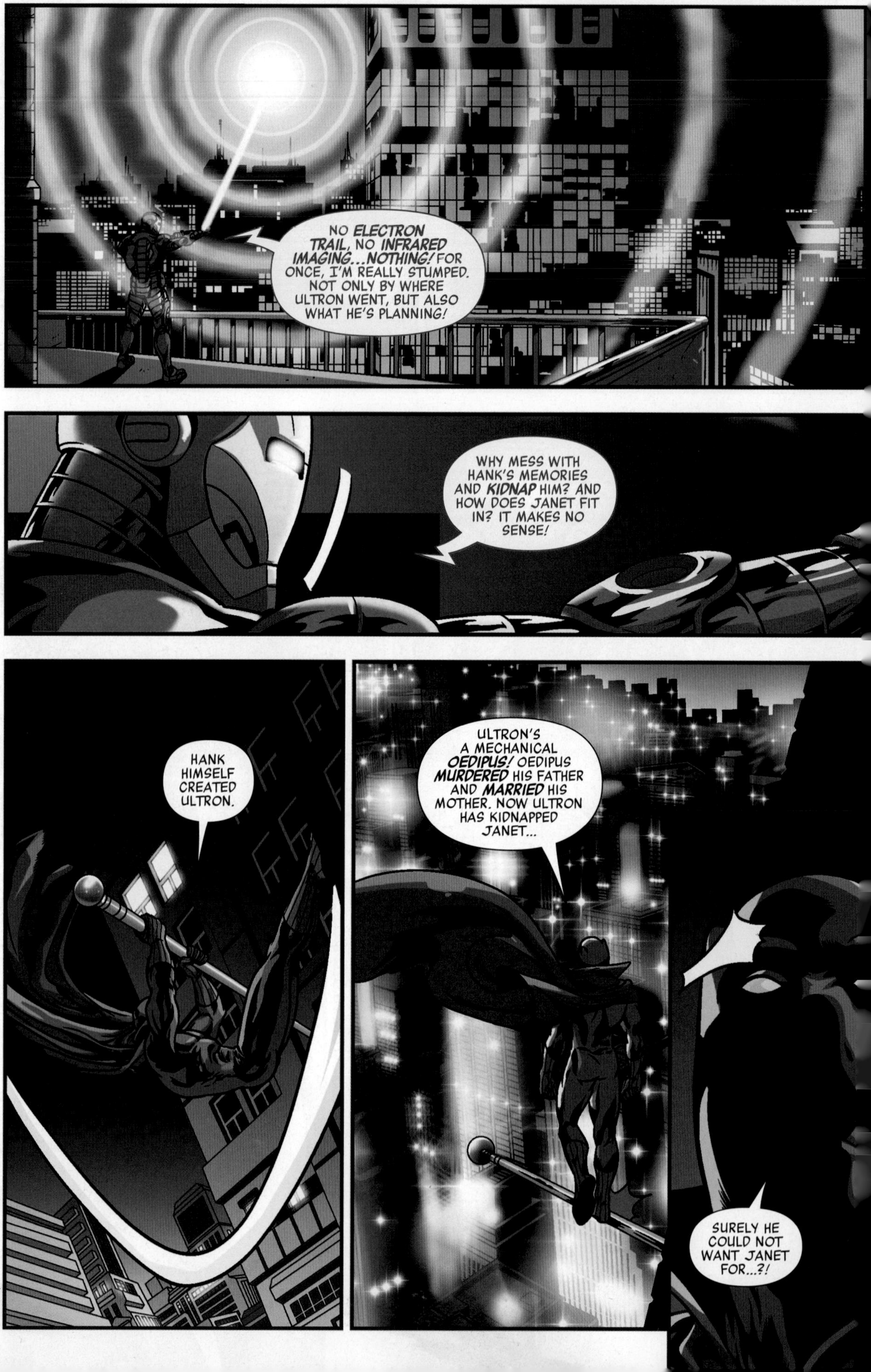
NO ELECTRON TRAIL, NO INFRARED IMAGING...NOTHING! FOR ONCE, I'M REALLY STUMPED. NOT ONLY BY WHERE ULTRON WENT, BUT ALSO WHAT HE'S PLANNING!
WHY MESS WITH HANK'S MEMORIES AND KIDNAP HIM? AND HOW DOES JANET FIT IN? IT MAKES NO SENSE!
HANK HIMSELF CREATED ULTRON.
ULTRON'S A MECHANICAL OEDIPUS! OEDIPUS MURDERED HIS FATHER AND MARRIED HIS MOTHER. NOW ULTRON HAS KIDNAPPED JANET...
SURELY HE COULD NOT WANT JANET FOR...?!

HURRY, PYM! IF YOU WAIT TOO LONG, YOU WILL LOSE HER!
I KNOW! THIS IS A CRITICAL PHASE. WE CAN'T AFFORD TO MAKE ANY MISTAKES.
I JUST HOPE THE INITIAL SHOCK AND PAIN OF TRANSFERENCE ISN'T TOO MUCH FOR HER.
BUT WE CAN'T STOP NOW! ACTIVATE THE TRANSFER!
KA-CHUNG
ZWEEEEE
OH...NO!

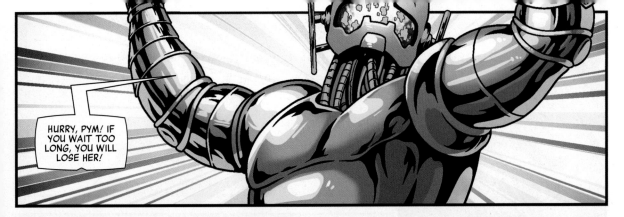

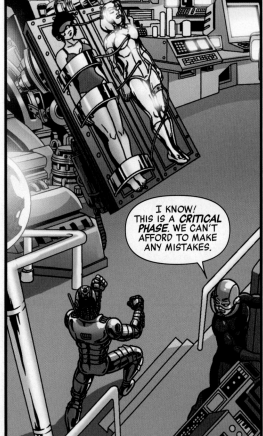

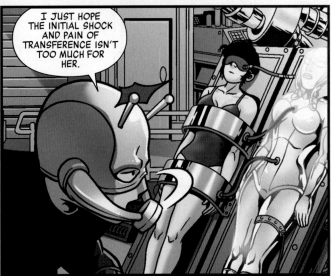

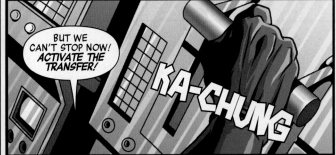

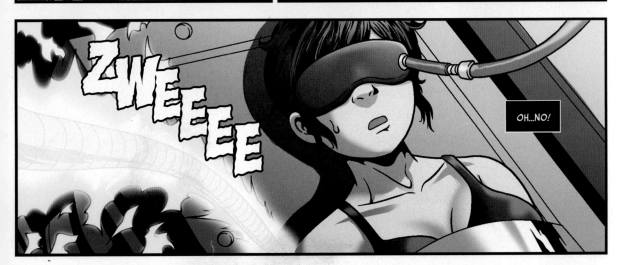

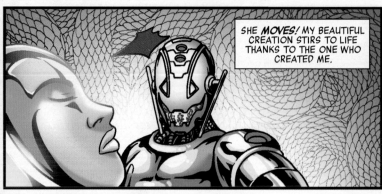

SHE *MOVES!* MY BEAUTIFUL CREATION STIRS TO LIFE THANKS TO THE ONE WHO CREATED ME.

JANET IS BECOMING A ROBOTIC WOMAN FIT TO BE MY BRIDE... MY *QUEEN!*

ULTRON, I NEED YOUR *HELP!*

OF COURSE! HOW MAY I ASSIST YOU?

HANK? I'M SO *AFRAID!* I CAN FEEL MY SOUL SLIPPING AWAY. MY *LIFE!* HANK! CAN'T YOU HEAR ME? *PLEASE...*

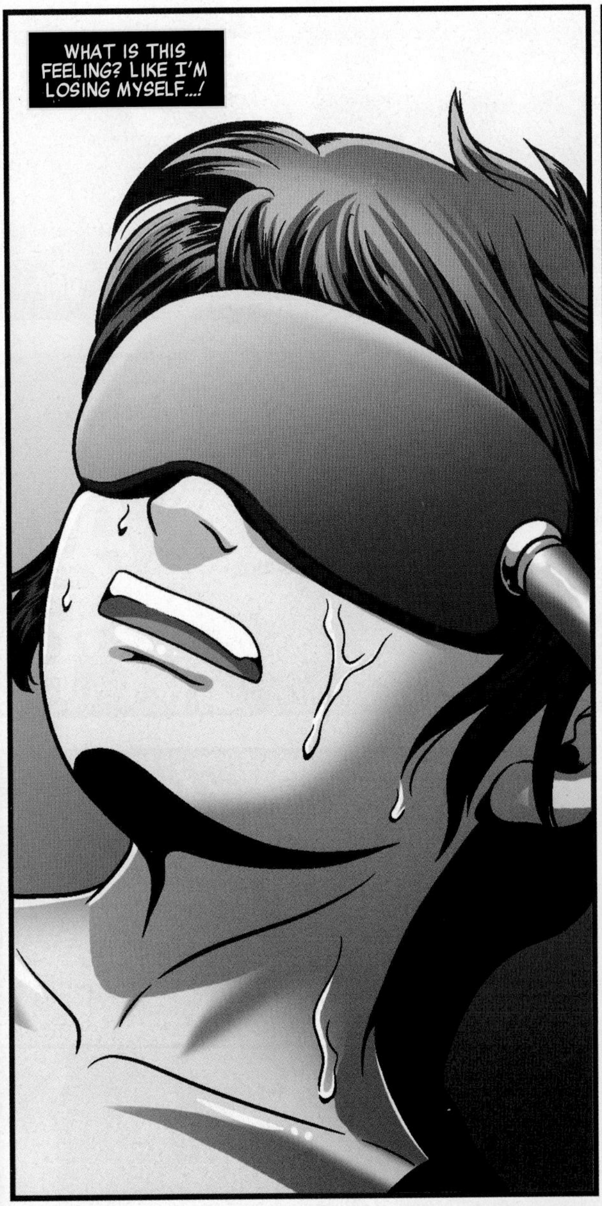
WHAT IS THIS FEELING? LIKE I'M LOSING MYSELF...!
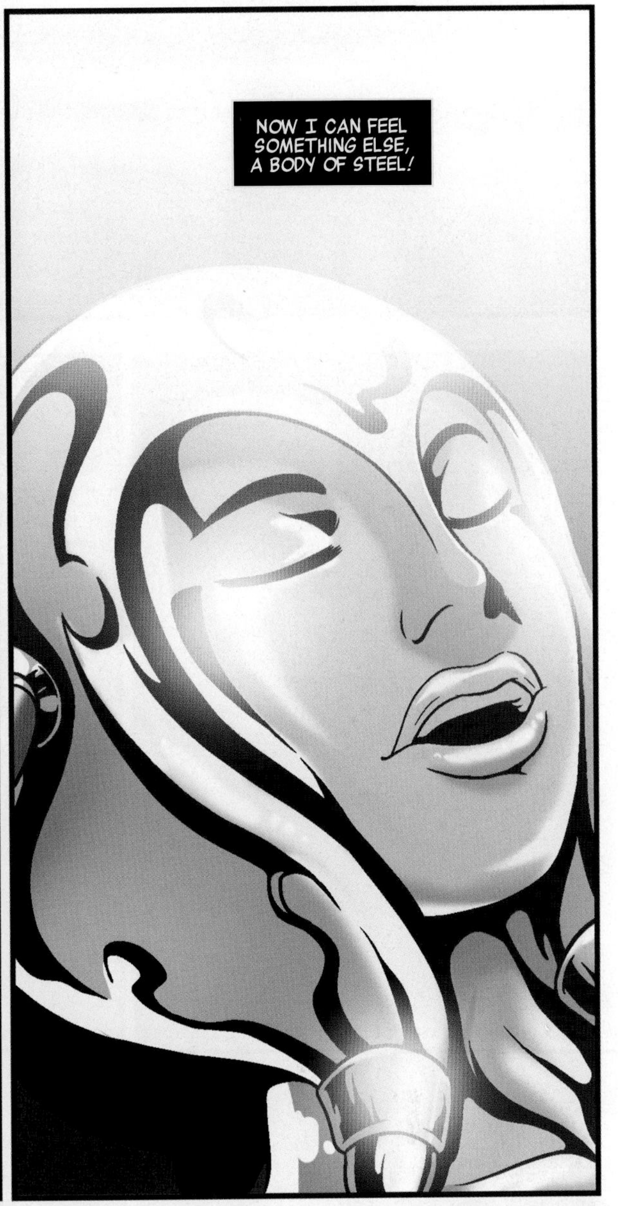
NOW I CAN FEEL SOMETHING ELSE, A BODY OF STEEL!
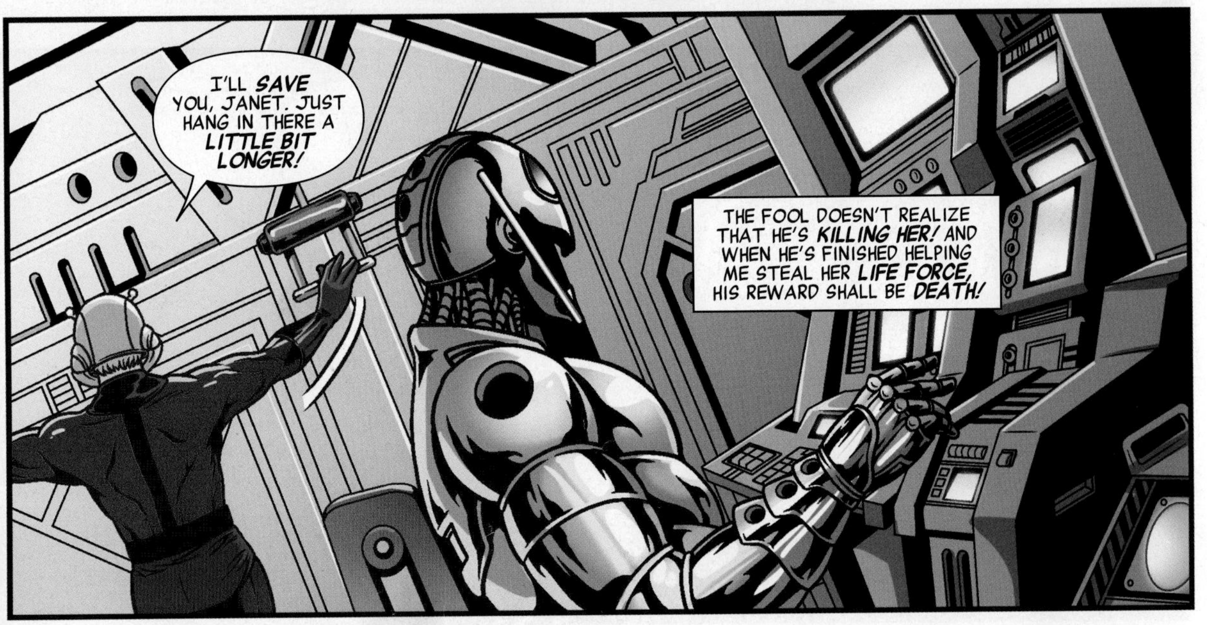
I'LL SAVE YOU, JANET. JUST HANG IN THERE A LITTLE BIT LONGER!
THE FOOL DOESN'T REALIZE THAT HE'S KILLING HER! AND WHEN HE'S FINISHED HELPING ME STEAL HER LIFE FORCE, HIS REWARD SHALL BE DEATH!

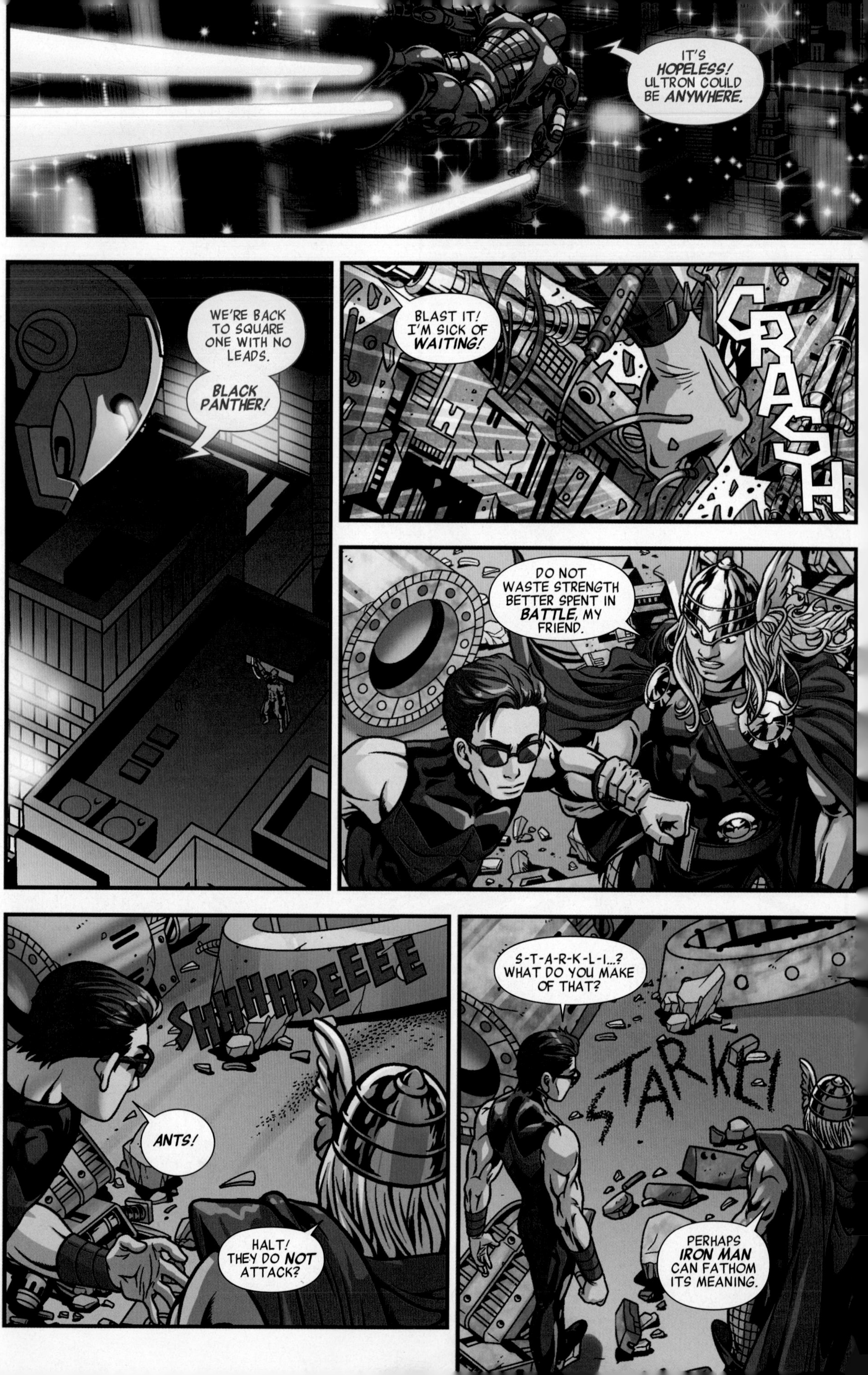
IT'S HOPELESS! ULTRON COULD BE ANYWHERE.
WE'RE BACK TO SQUARE ONE WITH NO LEADS.
BLACK PANTHER!
BLAST IT! I'M SICK OF WAITING!
CRASH
DO NOT WASTE STRENGTH BETTER SPENT IN BATTLE, MY FRIEND.
SHHHHREEEEE
ANTS!
HALT! THEY DO NOT ATTACK?
S-T-A-R-K-L-I...? WHAT DO YOU MAKE OF THAT?
STARKLI
PERHAPS IRON MAN CAN FATHOM ITS MEANING.

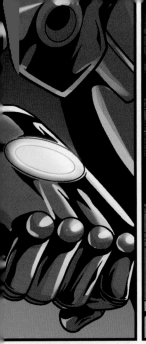

ISN'T IS *OBVIOUS?* IT STANDS FOR *"STARK, LONG ISLAND."*

STARK INDUSTRIES OWNS AN AEROSPACE RESEARCH CENTER ON LONG ISLAND THAT WAS ABANDONED SOME YEARS BACK.

THAT MUST BE WHERE HANK AND JANET ARE BEING HELD! MEET US THERE, THOR!

THIS NIGHT WE SHALL *AVENGE* OUR WOUNDED COMRADES OR TASTE DEATH'S BITTER CUP OURSELVES!

ULTRON! TURN AND FACE ME!

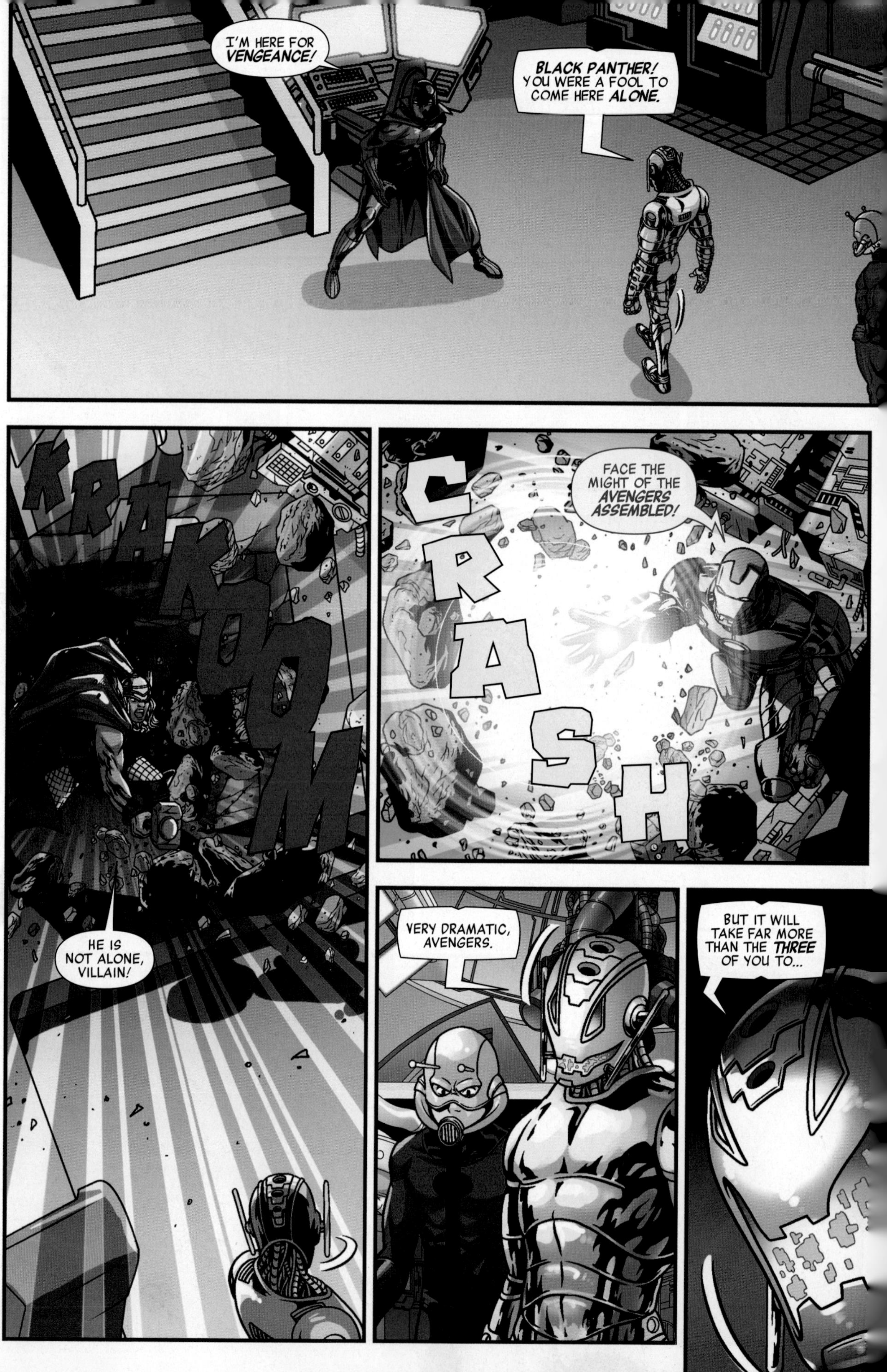
I'M HERE FOR *VENGEANCE!*
BLACK PANTHER! YOU WERE A FOOL TO COME HERE ***ALONE.***
KRAKOOOM
HE IS NOT ALONE, VILLAIN!
CRASH
FACE THE MIGHT OF THE ***AVENGERS ASSEMBLED!***
VERY DRAMATIC, AVENGERS.
BUT IT WILL TAKE FAR MORE THAN THE ***THREE*** OF YOU TO...

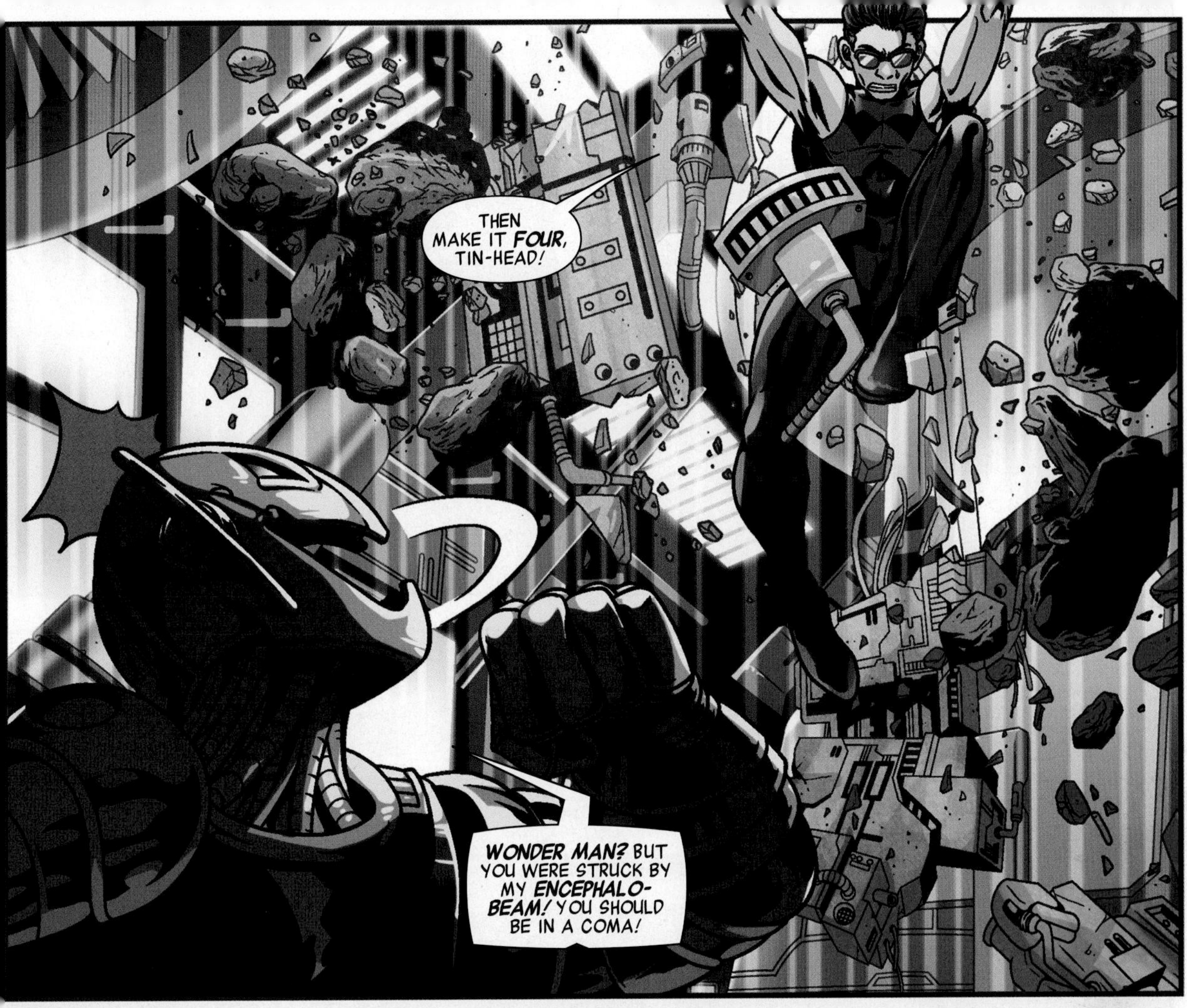

THEN MAKE IT FOUR, TIN-HEAD!
WONDER MAN? BUT YOU WERE STRUCK BY MY ENCEPHALO-BEAM! YOU SHOULD BE IN A COMA!

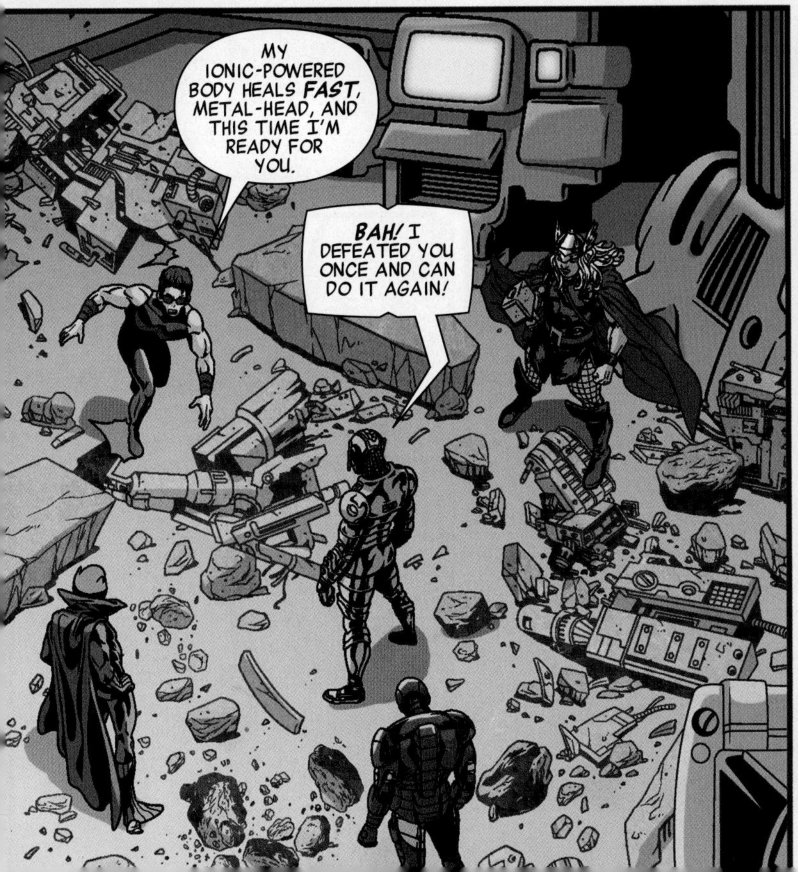

MY IONIC-POWERED BODY HEALS FAST, METAL-HEAD, AND THIS TIME I'M READY FOR YOU.
BAH! I DEFEATED YOU ONCE AND CAN DO IT AGAIN!

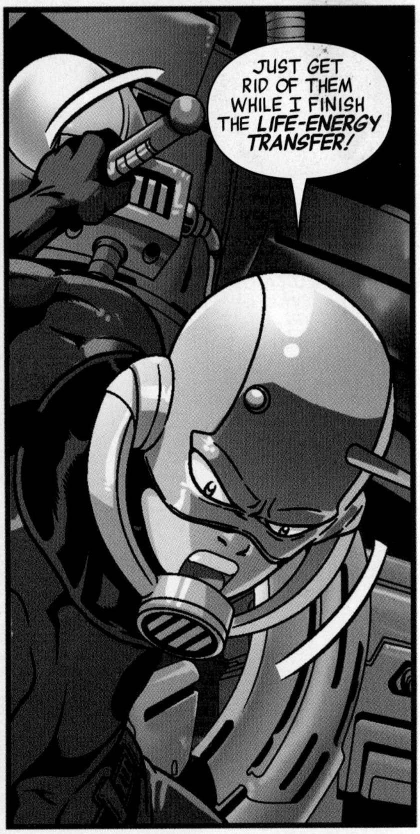

JUST GET RID OF THEM WHILE I FINISH THE LIFE-ENERGY TRANSFER!

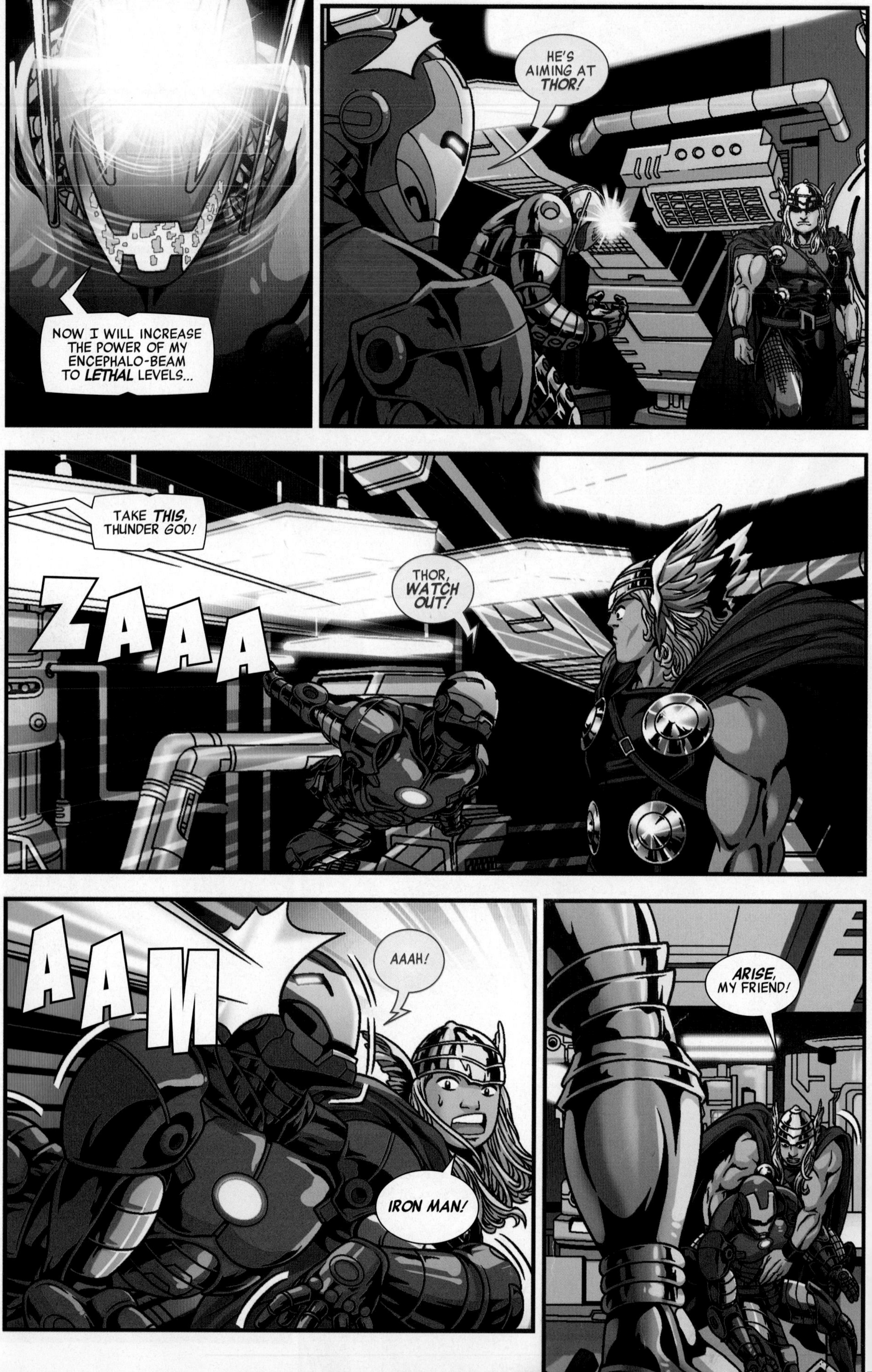

NOW I WILL INCREASE THE POWER OF MY ENCEPHALO-BEAM TO LETHAL LEVELS...
HE'S AIMING AT THOR!
TAKE THIS, THUNDER GOD!
ZAAAA
THOR, WATCH OUT!
AAM
AAAH!
IRON MAN!
ARISE, MY FRIEND!

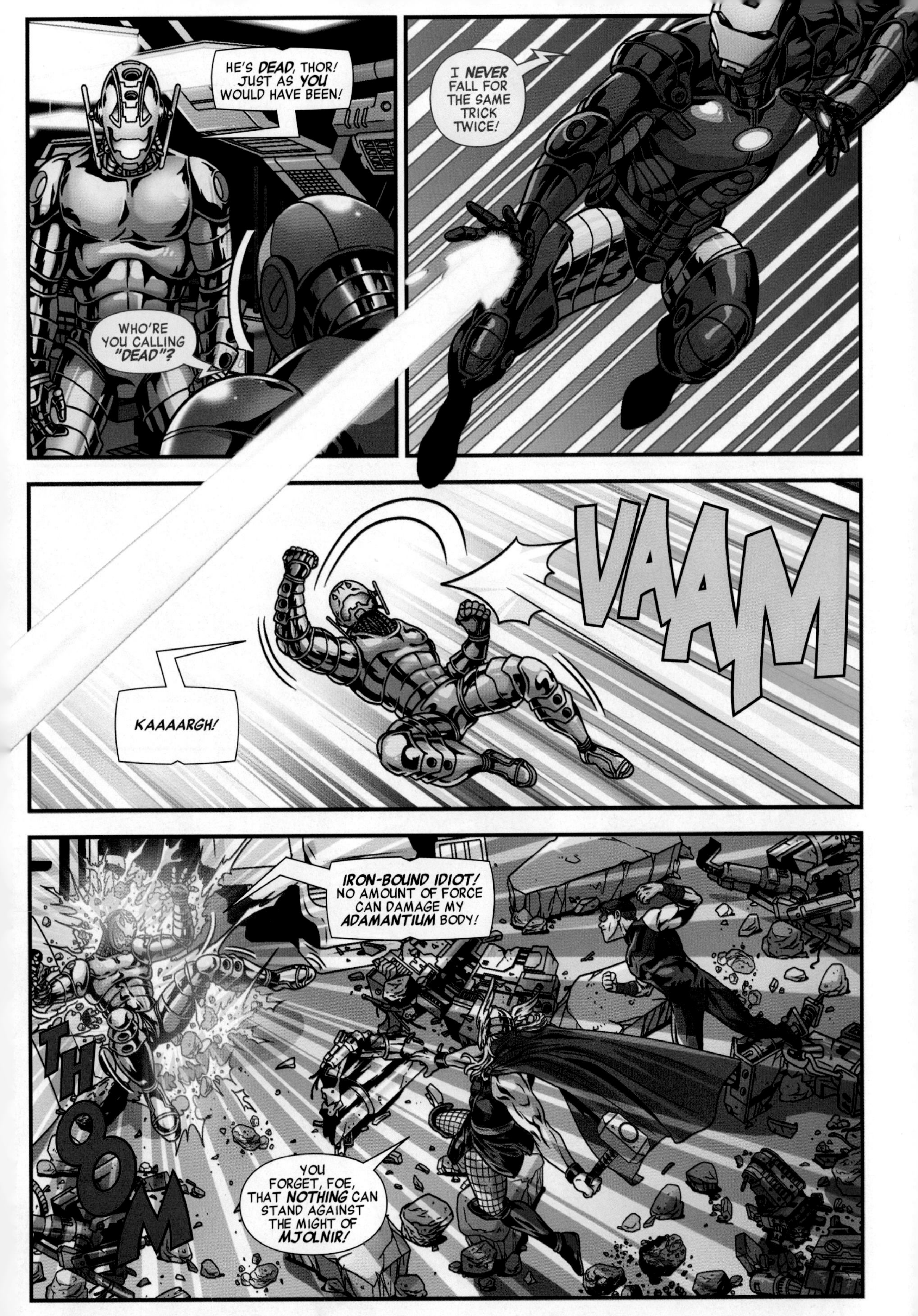
HE'S DEAD, THOR! JUST AS YOU WOULD HAVE BEEN!
WHO'RE YOU CALLING "DEAD"?
I NEVER FALL FOR THE SAME TRICK TWICE!
VAAM
KAAAARGH!
IRON-BOUND IDIOT! NO AMOUNT OF FORCE CAN DAMAGE MY ADAMANTIUM BODY!
THOOM
YOU FORGET, FOE, THAT NOTHING CAN STAND AGAINST THE MIGHT OF MJOLNIR!

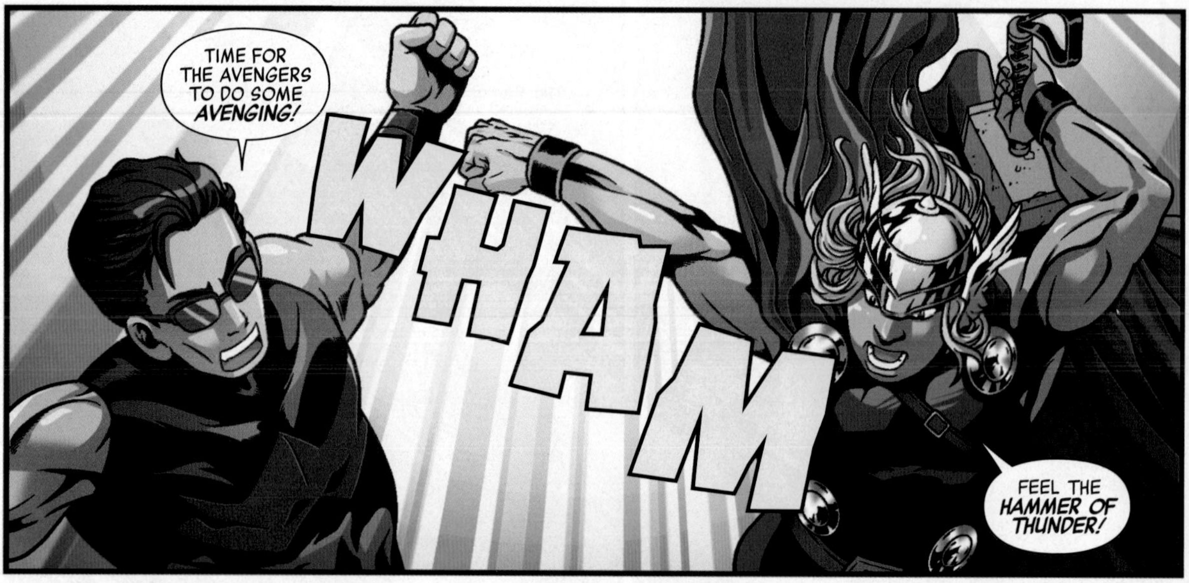
TIME FOR THE AVENGERS TO DO SOME *AVENGING!*
WHAM
FEEL THE *HAMMER OF THUNDER!*

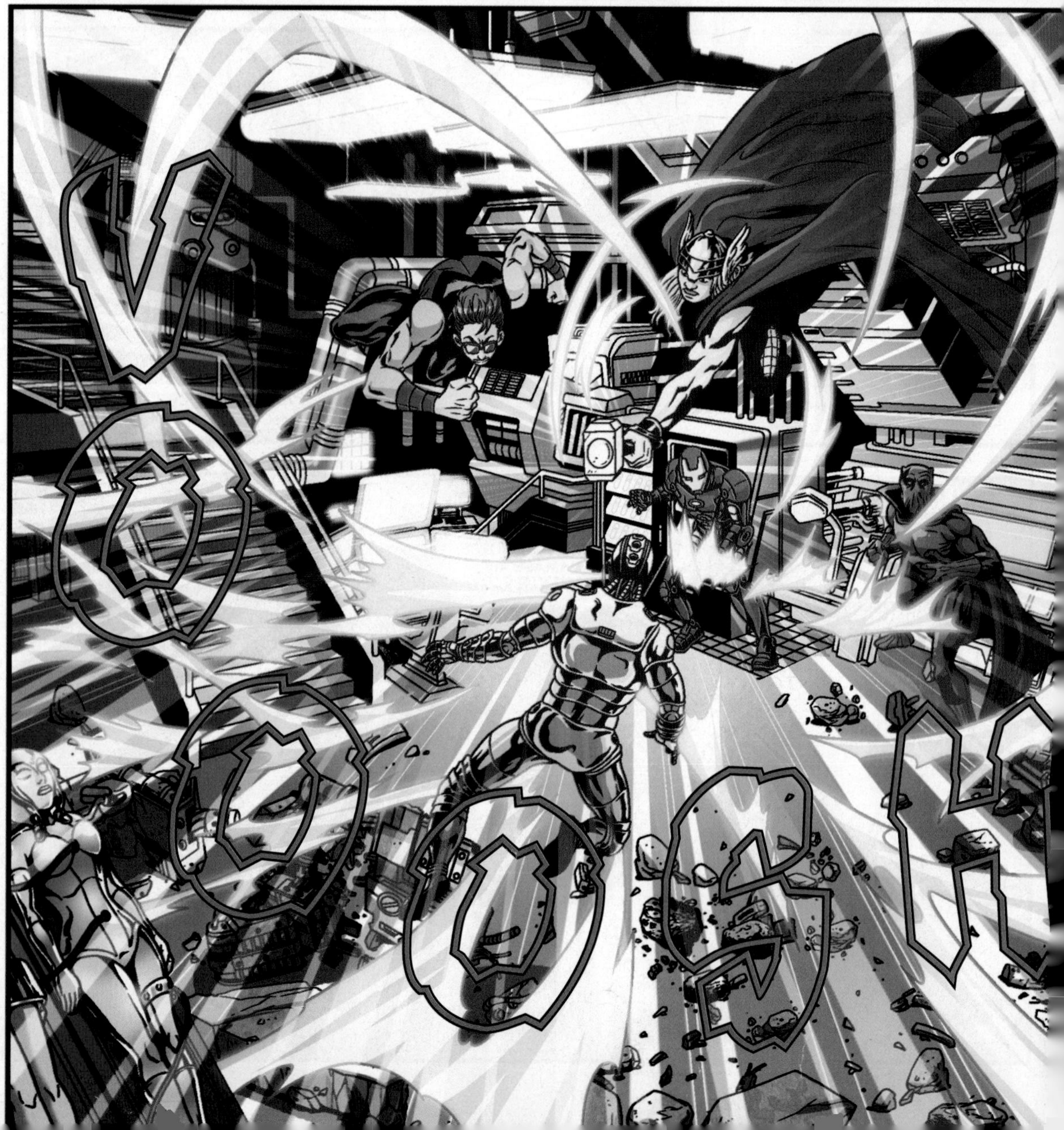

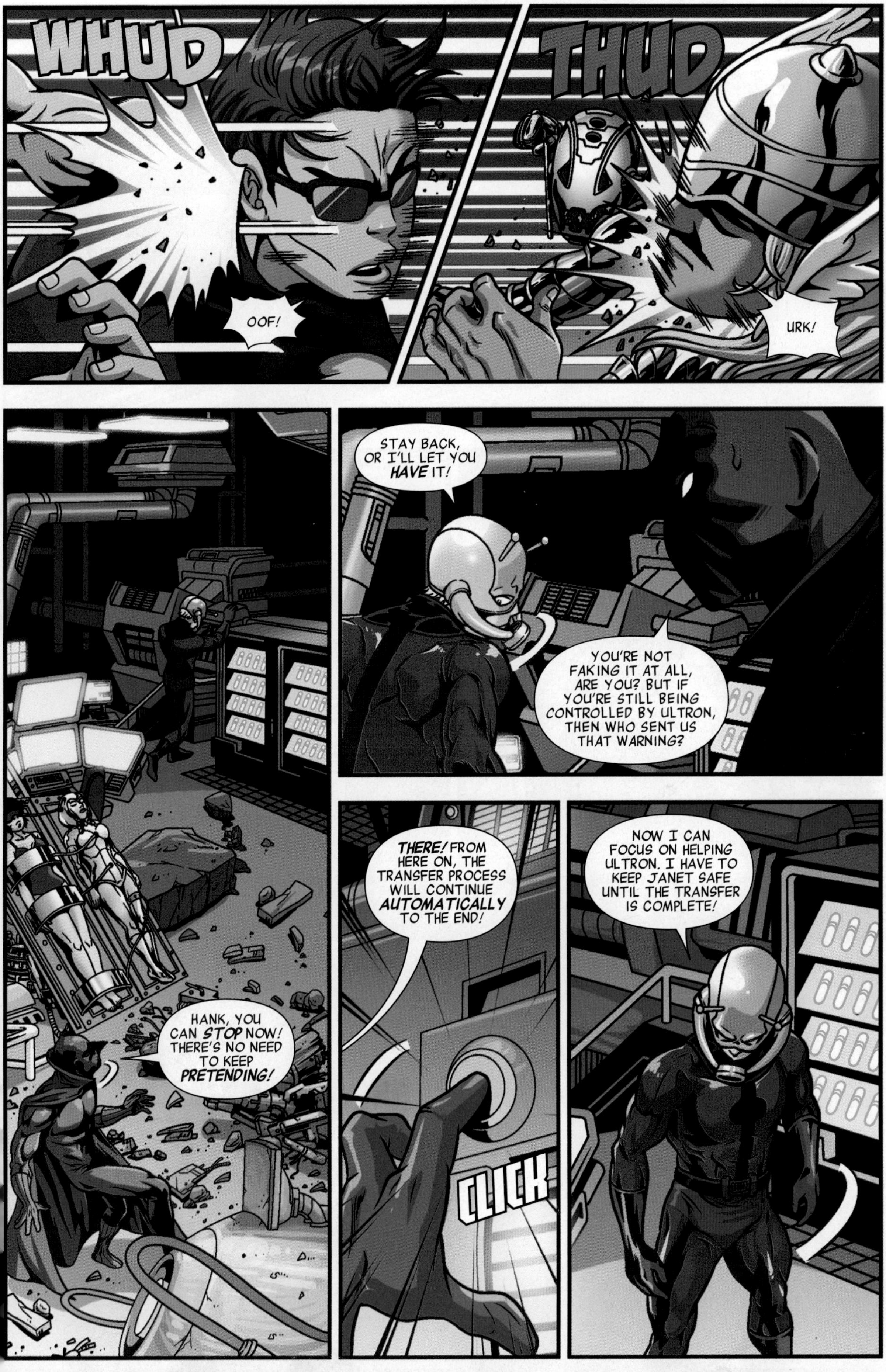
WHUD
OOF!
THUD
URK!
HANK, YOU CAN **STOP** NOW! THERE'S NO NEED TO KEEP **PRETENDING!**
STAY BACK, OR I'LL LET YOU **HAVE** IT!
YOU'RE NOT FAKING IT AT ALL, ARE YOU? BUT IF YOU'RE STILL BEING CONTROLLED BY ULTRON, THEN WHO SENT US THAT WARNING?
THERE! FROM HERE ON, THE TRANSFER PROCESS WILL CONTINUE **AUTOMATICALLY** TO THE END!
CLICK
NOW I CAN FOCUS ON HELPING ULTRON. I HAVE TO KEEP JANET SAFE UNTIL THE TRANSFER IS COMPLETE!

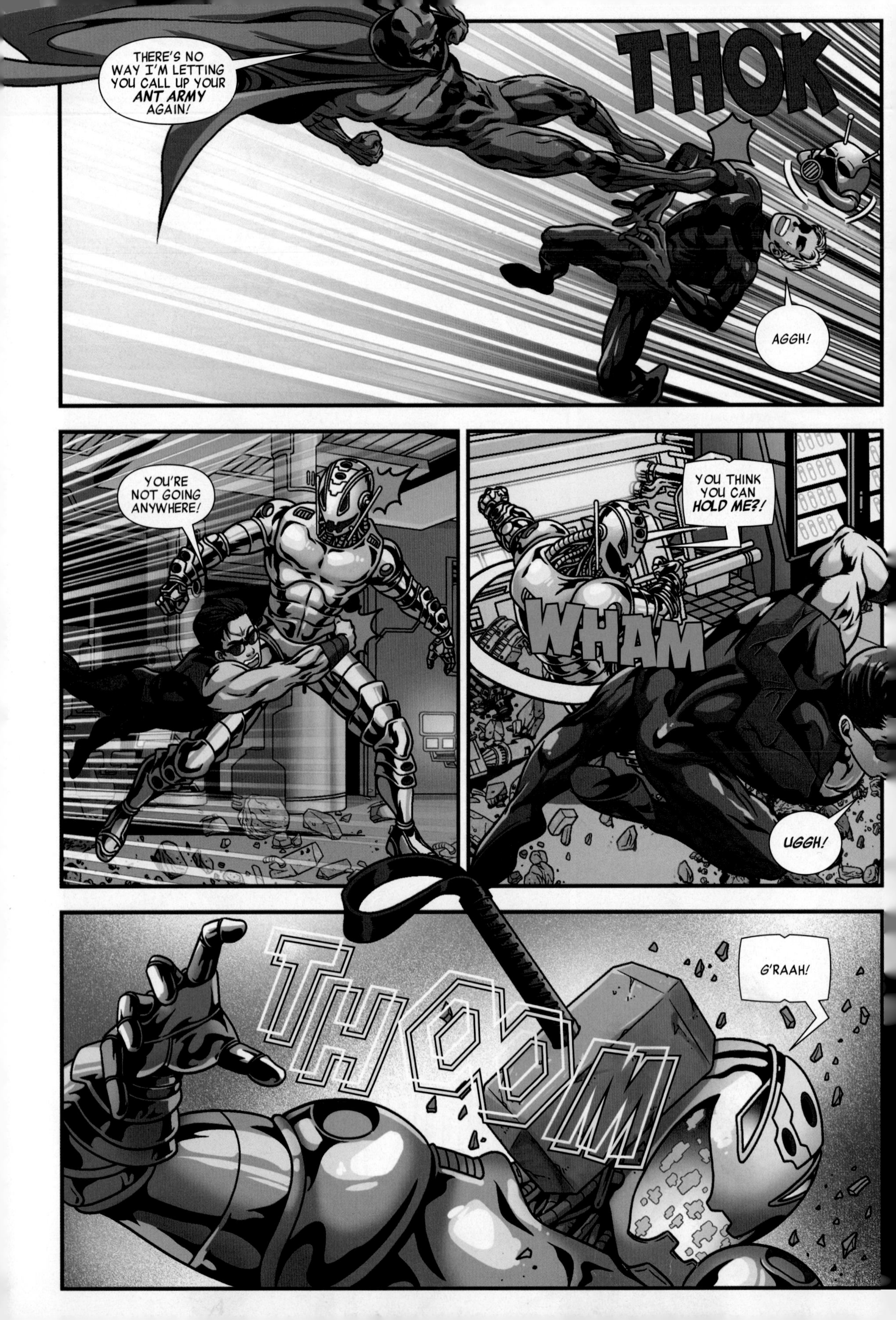
THERE'S NO WAY I'M LETTING YOU CALL UP YOUR ANT ARMY AGAIN!
THOK
AGGH!
YOU'RE NOT GOING ANYWHERE!
YOU THINK YOU CAN HOLD ME?!
WHAM
UGGH!
THOOM
G'RAAH!

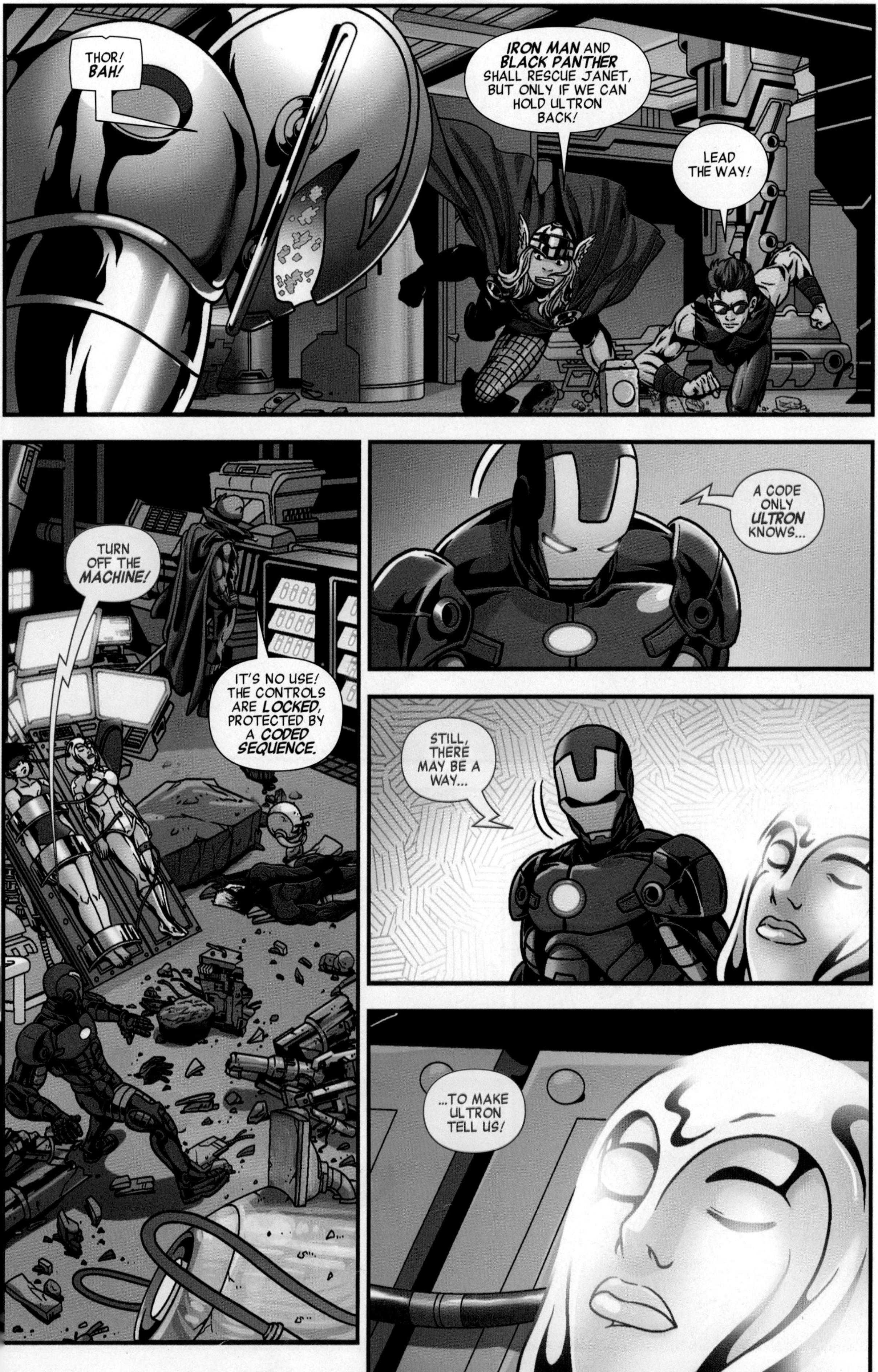

THOR! BAH!
IRON MAN AND BLACK PANTHER SHALL RESCUE JANET, BUT ONLY IF WE CAN HOLD ULTRON BACK!
LEAD THE WAY!
TURN OFF THE MACHINE!
IT'S NO USE! THE CONTROLS ARE LOCKED, PROTECTED BY A CODED SEQUENCE.
A CODE ONLY ULTRON KNOWS...
STILL, THERE MAY BE A WAY...
...TO MAKE ULTRON TELL US!

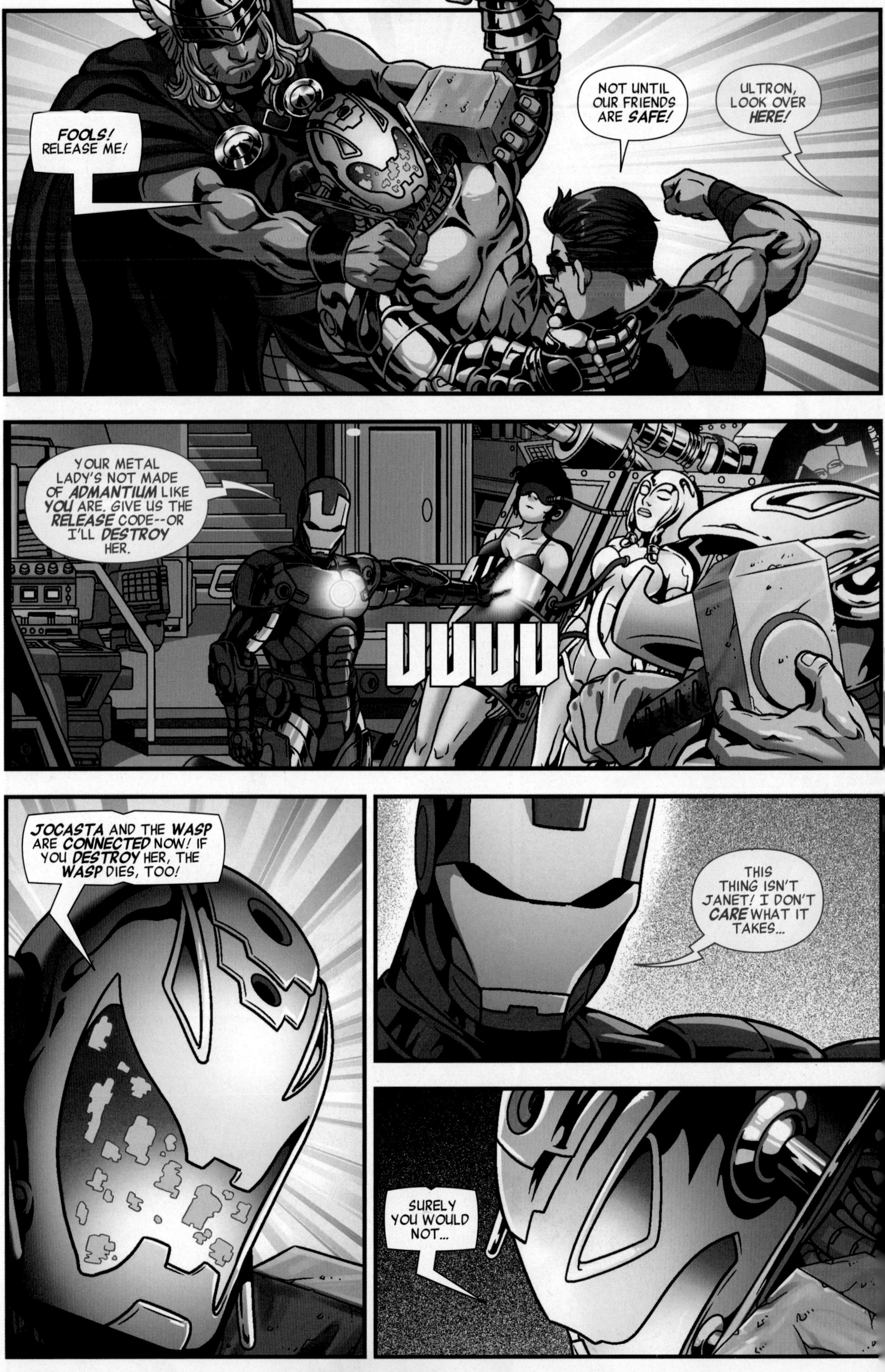
FOOLS! RELEASE ME!
NOT UNTIL OUR FRIENDS ARE SAFE!
ULTRON, LOOK OVER HERE!
YOUR METAL LADY'S NOT MADE OF ADMANTIUM LIKE YOU ARE. GIVE US THE RELEASE CODE--OR I'LL DESTROY HER.
VVVV
JOCASTA AND THE WASP ARE CONNECTED NOW! IF YOU DESTROY HER, THE WASP DIES, TOO!
THIS THING ISN'T JANET! I DON'T CARE WHAT IT TAKES...
SURELY YOU WOULD NOT...

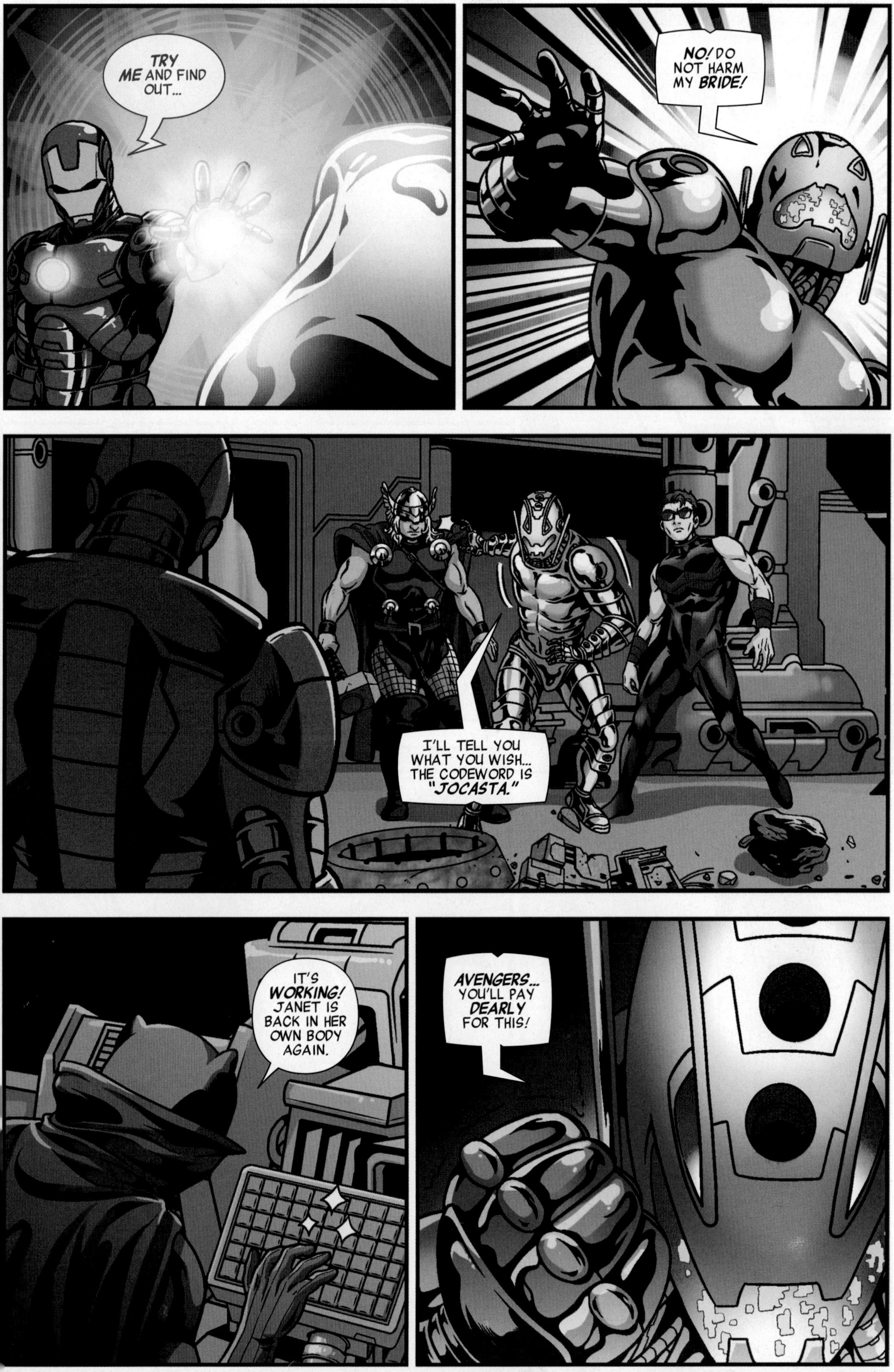
TRY ME AND FIND OUT...
NO! DO NOT HARM MY BRIDE!
I'LL TELL YOU WHAT YOU WISH... THE CODEWORD IS "JOCASTA."
IT'S WORKING! JANET IS BACK IN HER OWN BODY AGAIN.
AVENGERS... YOU'LL PAY DEARLY FOR THIS!

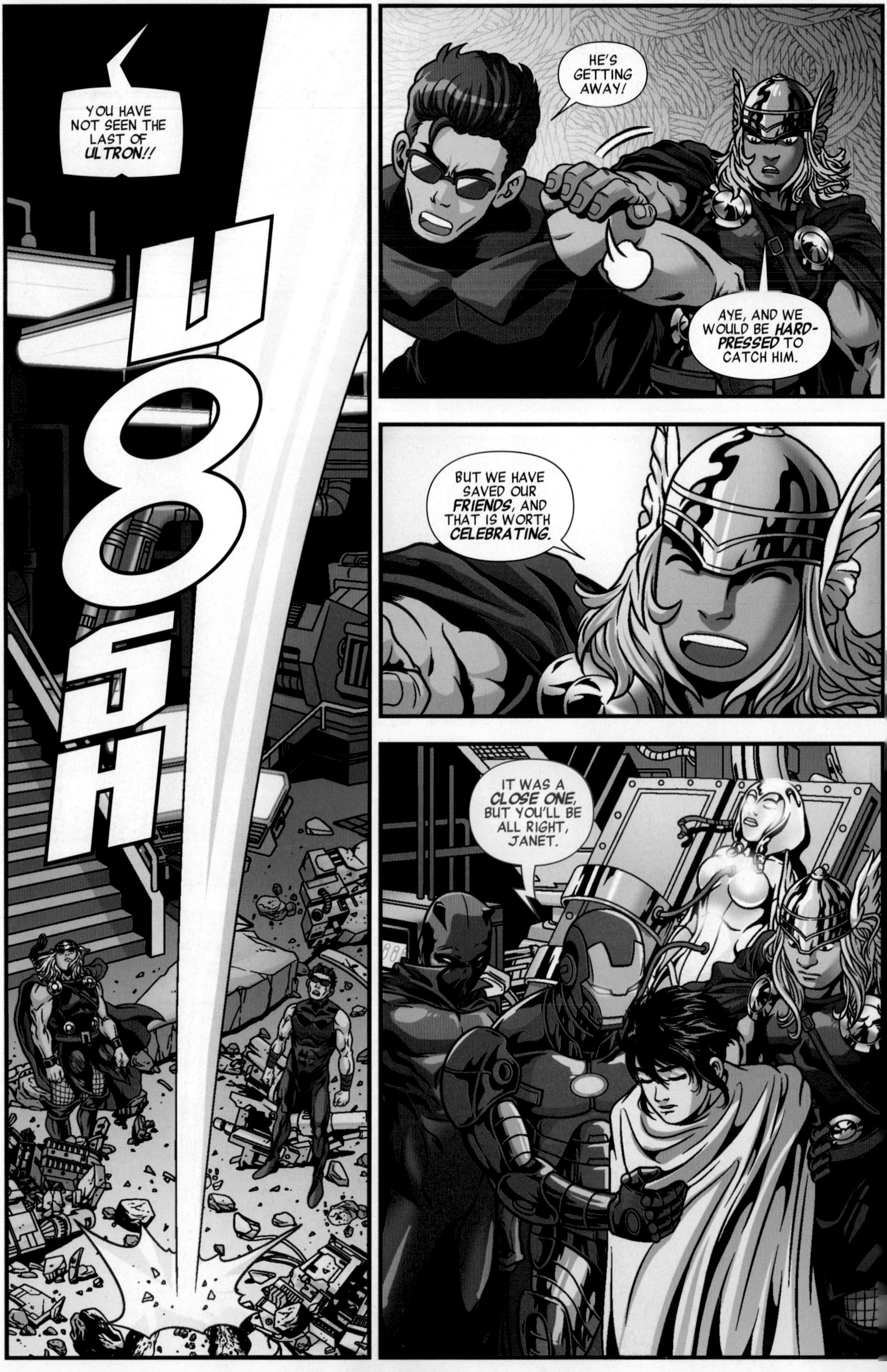

YOU HAVE NOT SEEN THE LAST OF ULTRON!!
VOOSH
HE'S GETTING AWAY!
AYE, AND WE WOULD BE HARD-PRESSED TO CATCH HIM.
BUT WE HAVE SAVED OUR FRIENDS, AND THAT IS WORTH CELEBRATING.
IT WAS A CLOSE ONE, BUT YOU'LL BE ALL RIGHT, JANET.

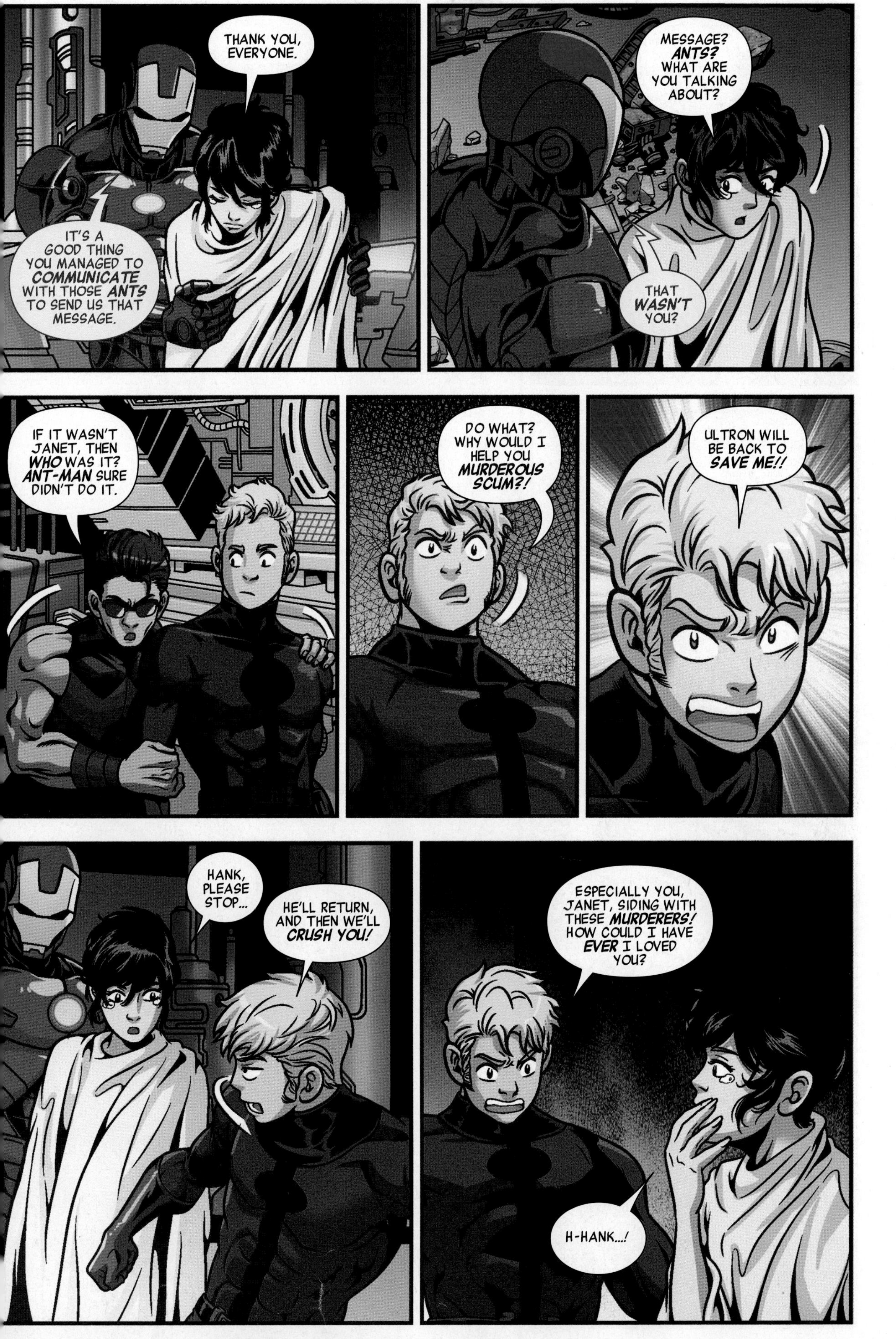
THANK YOU, EVERYONE.
IT'S A GOOD THING YOU MANAGED TO COMMUNICATE WITH THOSE ANTS TO SEND US THAT MESSAGE.
MESSAGE? ANTS? WHAT ARE YOU TALKING ABOUT?
THAT WASN'T YOU?
IF IT WASN'T JANET, THEN WHO WAS IT? ANT-MAN SURE DIDN'T DO IT.
DO WHAT? WHY WOULD I HELP YOU MURDEROUS SCUM?!
ULTRON WILL BE BACK TO SAVE ME!!
HANK, PLEASE STOP...
HE'LL RETURN, AND THEN WE'LL CRUSH YOU!
ESPECIALLY YOU, JANET, SIDING WITH THESE MURDERERS! HOW COULD I HAVE EVER I LOVED YOU?
H-HANK...!

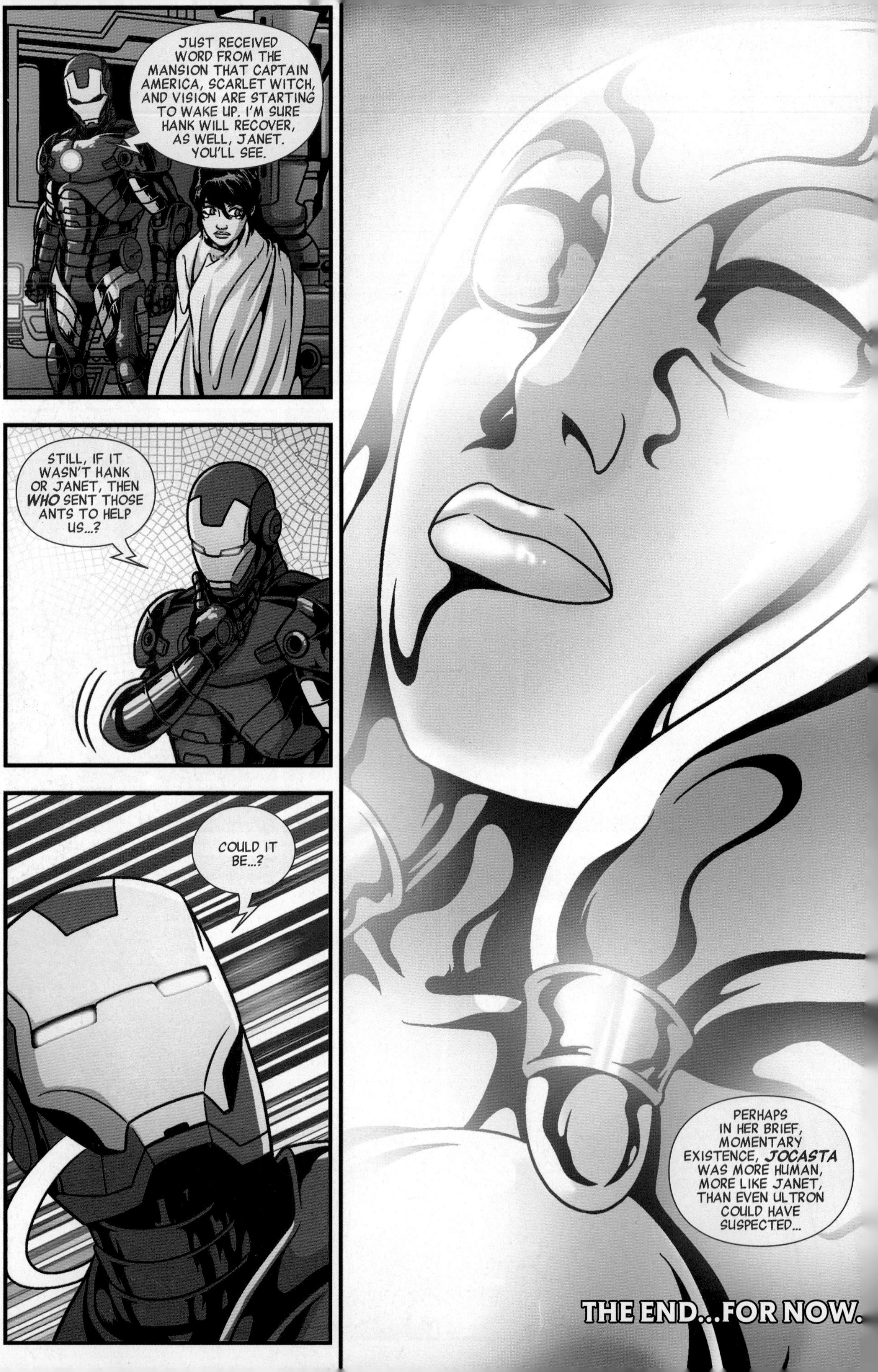
JUST RECEIVED WORD FROM THE MANSION THAT CAPTAIN AMERICA, SCARLET WITCH, AND VISION ARE STARTING TO WAKE UP. I'M SURE HANK WILL RECOVER, AS WELL, JANET. YOU'LL SEE.
STILL, IF IT WASN'T HANK OR JANET, THEN WHO SENT THOSE ANTS TO HELP US...?
COULD IT BE...?
PERHAPS IN HER BRIEF, MOMENTARY EXISTENCE, JOCASTA WAS MORE HUMAN, MORE LIKE JANET, THAN EVEN ULTRON COULD HAVE SUSPECTED...
THE END...FOR NOW.